CW00685143

To the Last Man

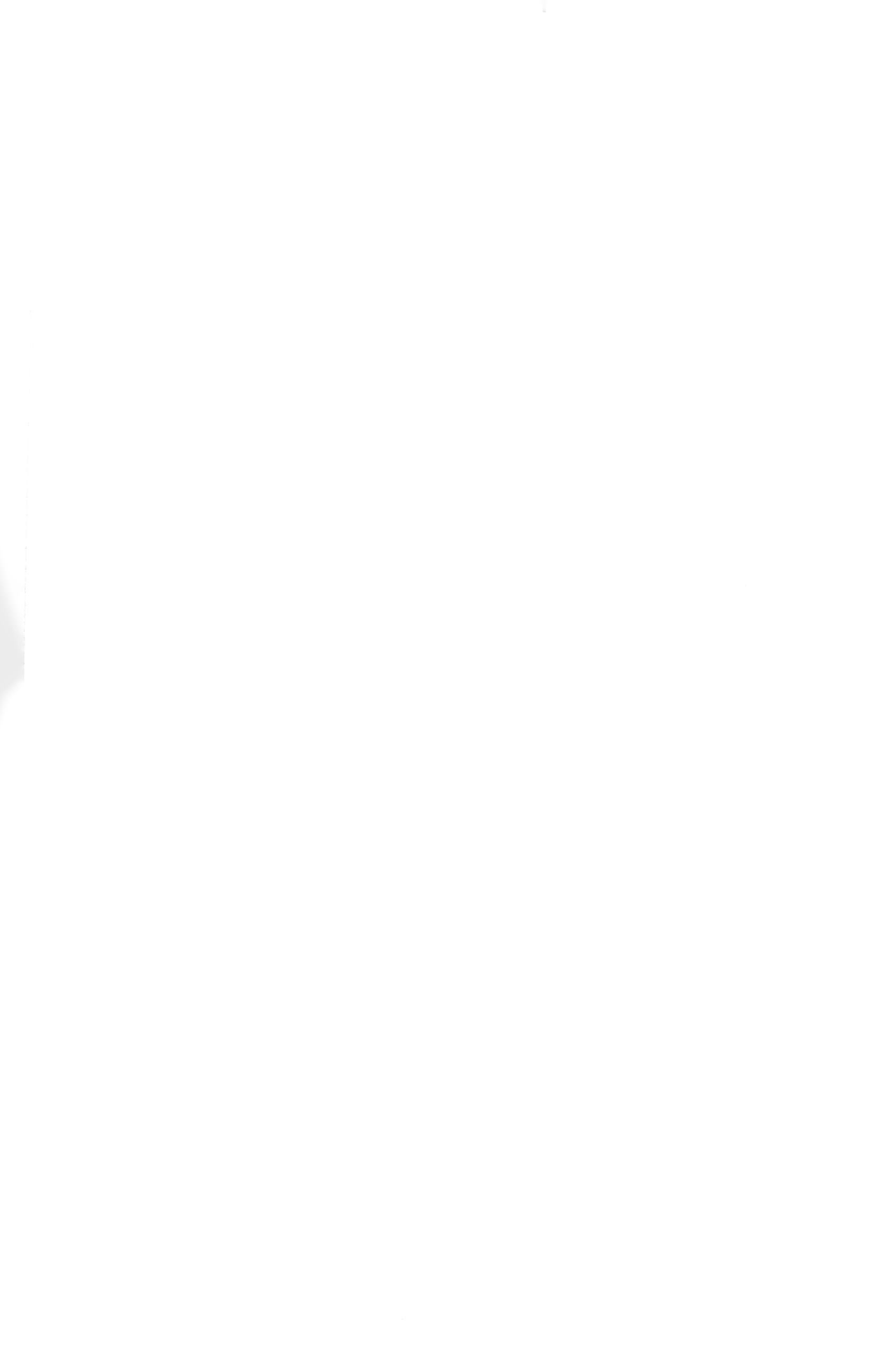

To the Last Man

The Home Guard in War and Popular Culture

Malcolm Atkin

First published in Great Britain in 2019 by
PEN & SWORD MILITARY
An imprint of Pen & Sword Books Ltd
Yorkshire – Philadelphia

ISBN 978-1-52674-593-4

A CIP catalogue record for this book is available from the British Library.

Typeset by Concept, Huddersfield, West Yorkshire, HD4 5JL.
Printed and bound in England by TJ International Ltd, Padstow, Cornwall

Pen & Sword Books Ltd incorporates the Imprints of Aviation, Atlas, Family History, Fiction, Maritime, Military, Discovery, Politics, History, Archaeology, Select, Wharncliffe Local History, Wharncliffe True Crime, Military Classics, Wharncliffe Transport, Leo Cooper, The Praetorian Press, Remember When, White Owl, Seaforth Publishing and Frontline Publishing.

For a complete list of Pen & Sword titles please contact
PEN & SWORD BOOKS LTD
47 Church Street, Barnsley, South Yorkshire, S70 2AS, England
E-mail: enquiries@pen-and-sword.co.uk
Website: www.pen-and-sword.co.uk
or
PEN & SWORD BOOKS
1950 Lawrence Rd, Havertown, PA 19083, USA
E-mail: uspen-and-sword@casematepublishers.com
Website: www.penandswordbooks.com

Contents

List of Plates

List of Figures

Abbreviations

AA	anti-aircraft
ACDBH	American Committee for Defense of British Homes, *aka* Committee for American Aid for the Defense of British Homes
ACI	Army Council Instruction
ARP	Air Raid Precautions civil defence organization
ATS	Auxiliary Territorial Service
BAR	Browning Automatic Rifle
BEF	British Expeditionary Force
CCPHB	Civilian Committee to Protect Homes in Britain, *aka* Civilian Committee for Defence and Civilian Committee for the Defense of Homes (Wickham Steed Committee)
CDAAA	Committee to Defend America by Aiding the Allies (William Allen Committee)
CIGS	Chief of the Imperial General Staff
CPGB	Communist Party of Great Britain
GHQ	General Headquarters, Home Forces
GOC	General Officer Commanding
HAA	Heavy Anti-Aircraft
HDE	Home Defence Executive
HDS	Home Defence Scheme (of Section D, SIS)
ILP	Independent Labour Party
IO	Intelligence Officer in the GHQ Auxiliary Units
IWM	Imperial War Museum
LAA	light anti-aircraft
LDV	Local Defence Volunteers (Home Guard from 22 July 1940)
M1917	United States rifle, calibre .30, Model of 1917, also known as the M1917 Enfield or the 'American Enfield', and also as the Pattern 1917 rifle or within the Home Guard as the P17
MAP	Ministry of Aircraft Production
MOI	Ministry of Information
MOS	Ministry of Supply
MTC	Mechanized Transport Corps
P14	Rifle, .303 Pattern 1914, formally designated as the Rifle, No. 3 Mk 1 in 1926, although it remained known colloquially as the P14
P17	*see* M1917
RAE	Royal Aircraft Establishment
ROF	Royal Ordnance Factory

SDB	Special Duties Branch (the intelligence wing of the GHQ Auxiliary Units)
SIS	Secret Intelligence Service
SMLE	Short Magazine Lee Enfield rifle (formally designated Rifle No. 1 Mk III in 1926)
SOE	Special Operations Executive
TAA	Territorial Army Association
UDV	Ulster Defence Volunteers
UHG	Ulster Home Guard
UXB	Unexploded bomb
VTC	Volunteer Training Corps (First World War equivalent of the Home Guard)
WHDC	Women's Home Defence Corps
WI	Women's Institute
WS17	Wireless Set No. 17 (short-range wireless set originally designed for communication between anti-aircraft and searchlight batteries)
WVR	Women's Volunteer Reserve (First World War equivalent of the WHDC)
WVS	Women's Voluntary Service

Acknowledgements

My interest in the Home Guard was spurred in the 1990s by participation in the English Heritage/CBA *Defence of Britain Project*, in which I represented the Association of Local Government Archaeology Officers. I owe a special thanks to Mick Wilks and the late Colin Jones of the local Defence of Worcestershire project, sponsored by the County Council Archaeology Service, for many happy discussions on the subject and especially to Mick for sharing his detailed local research and for reading an earlier draft of this book. I am also grateful to Tom Davis for discussions on the history of the Thompson sub-machine gun and similarly to Alan David and Martin Mace on the importation of weapons from the USA. Special thanks are owed to Helen and Ron Cadman, the family of George Fletcher, for providing details of his Home Guard service. The work would not have been possible without the assistance of Lee Richards (ARCRE) in obtaining copies of documents from the National Archives. Lee and I would like to thank the staff of the National Archives for their unfailing assistance. Thanks are also owed to the staff of the Imperial War Museum Library and Image departments for helping to access material and to Stephen Sutton for permission to quote from his unpublished undergraduate thesis of 1995. Rupert Harding and Sarah Cook of Pen & Sword eased the book through the production process with their customary skill. Thanks to my daughter Kate for the photo montage that forms part of the cover and, as ever, to my wife Susanne for her patience and support, for trying to correct my grammar, and for compiling the index.

'Watching Post' from *Collected Poems* by Cecil Day-Lewis is reprinted by permission of Peters Fraser & Dunlop (www.petersfraserdunlop.com) on behalf of the Estate of Cecil Day-Lewis. Acknowledgement is made to the other copyright owners in the image captions. All reasonable attempts have been made to ascertain the correct owner of copyright material but apologies for any errors that may have arisen. In case of any query, the author can be contacted via the publisher. The responsibility for any errors, speculation and the conclusions remains my own.

Malcolm Atkin
October 2018

Preface

> In case of attack [the role of the LDV is] to defend their post to the last man, since every minute gained may be of vital importance.
>
> *GHQ Instructions to LDV, 23 May 1940* (TNA WO 199/1885)

Scores of books on the Home Guard have been published over the last thirty years. Most are written from a local perspective and on the basis of souvenir unit histories and oral history where myths have grown up over the decades. The volunteers of the Home Guard and their champions had very clear ideas on how they should be employed and were not afraid to publicize their views, colouring the popular perception of the force. This book tries to balance such unofficial accounts with the official view of the Home Guard, based largely on original documents in the National Archives. It is often a story of frustration as the War Office tried to steer an army of volunteers who remained resolutely independent.

The popular impression of the Home Guard has become inextricably entwined with the TV comedy series *Dad's Army* and this book tries to separate fact from myth. There was humour a-plenty in the Home Guard but, especially in 1940, this was a 'gallows humour' as the men realized all too well that their role was expected to be sacrificial as the chilling 'last man, last round' order made clear. The humour was increasingly overtaken by exhaustion, with most of the Home Guard not the retired pensioners of popular myth but working men who were expected to work a full shift, often in heavy manual labour, and then turn out for Home Guard duty. The hardships created great camaraderie amongst the members but also meant that there was little enthusiasm for repeating the exercise in the 1950s. The publicity attending the new *Dad's Army* film in 2016 made it clear that the popular media was reluctant to escape the mythology of the 1970s and that the history of the Home Guard risked for ever being associated with the fictional 'Walmington-on-Sea' platoon. By all means laugh at the comic genius of Jimmy Perry and David Croft and enjoy *Dad's Army* as a 1960s/1970s television comedy – but also recognize that this was an affectionate tribute to the Home Guard where selected snippets of genuine experience were deliberately taken to the limits of absurdity for comic intent. The popularity of the series certainly inspired research but also radically distorted the perception of the Home Guard and even the memories of its veterans. The present work is not an exhaustive history of the Home Guard. Rather it is an exploration of those aspects that influenced the development of its perception in popular culture.

Above all, spare a thought for the extraordinary men, and the women who worked with them, of the real Home Guard and especially those 1,206 men who were killed whilst on duty.

Introduction

The Home Guard of the Second World War, originally intended as a small armed special constabulary, developed as a key, if suicidal, element of Britain's defence in 1940–41 and later as an important means of freeing resources for the Allied offensives. Its history has, however, been distorted by contemporary propaganda, a modern media that has often preferred fiction to fact and a tendency to view the Home Guard in isolation from the problems shared with the rest of the British military establishment. Even its name has become part of the myth. The term *Dad's Army* is entirely a creation of the late 1960s–1970s television series, whilst the term *British Resistance Organization* as applied to the Home Guard Auxiliary Units is equally a post-war fiction. The concept of a Home Guard had a basis in the Tudor and later militias whose duty it was to defend against foreign invasion or internal riot, but the direct inspiration came from its First World War predecessor – the Volunteer Training Corps (VTC). It was the scale of the Second World War iteration that has given it a unique place in British history. Only 350,000 men had volunteered for the VTC but 1.9 million volunteers were serving in the Home Guard in 1942, and probably double this number served at one time or another during the Second World War.

The importance of the Home Guard was as much political as military. For some it was a continuation of the traditional volunteer regiments and militias, defending 'hearth and home'. Some socialists saw it as the core of a 'people's army' and the vanguard of social change but others dismissed it as a Fascist organization ready to do the bidding of the capitalist state against the workers. There was an urgent need in 1940 to convince the USA government to allow the British to purchase war materials and the Home Guard offered the striking image of a nation standing united and resolute, but desperate for weapons. For Prime Minister Winston Churchill especially, it was an important morale-booster and he allowed this aspect to shape much of his thinking on the force. The volunteers, as an army of voters, equally recognized their influence over politicians and used this to shape the agenda of the Home Guard. But whatever their political opinion and objective, all parties used the Home Guard within the same romantic and entirely constructed vision of Britain that owed more to the era of Thomas Hardy and William Wordsworth than to the reality of life in 1940.

Any study of modern history risks a reliance upon undigested facts and an over-emotional connection to the period. This is particularly true of 'bottom-up' histories such as those county histories that have characterized studies of the Home Guard. Oral testimony can be a fragile entity, as participants suffer the vagaries of memory, often influenced by their reading of post-war histories. In a remarkably short time the myth of events and personalities become enshrined as the orthodox version. Such myths are difficult to shed, distorting an appreciation of history for future generations. Orwell, writing in 1940, commented of his own experiences looking back to his childhood in the First World War that 'very few of your memories come to you genuinely virgin. It is largely because of the books, films and reminiscences that have come between.' He therefore acknowledged that it was difficult to 'disentangle your real memories from their later accretions'.[1] In 1957 Peter Fleming was already warning of the problems in relying on the oral history of Second World War veterans:

> Yet legend plays a large part in their memories of that tense and strangely exhilarating summer, and their experiences, like those of early childhood, are sharply rather than accurately etched upon their minds. The stories they tell of the period have become better, but not more veracious, with the passage of time. Rumours are remembered as facts, and – particularly since anti-invasion precautions continued in force for several years after the Germans had renounced their project – the sequence of events is blurred.[2]

History written from a personal perspective, although having its own value, is not necessarily accurate or representative of official strategy. An individual Home Guard might grumble about being sent on guard with just 5 rounds of ammunition without being aware of what stocks were being held for him in case of actual invasion. As Fleming had predicted, by the time Frank and Joan Shaw published their valuable collection of Home Guard memories in 1990, dates and timescales had become muddled.[3] Submitted stories had begun to focus on those aspects in which the researcher was perceived to be most interested – heavily influenced by the comedic image presented in the television series *Dad's Army*. From the outset, there was a self-deprecating humour within the Home Guard. In part, this was a very British refusal to take the war too seriously, in the tradition of the First World War Bairnsfather cartoons. It was also 'gallows humour' in the stoic acceptance that the task of the Home Guard was essentially sacrificial in order to buy a few hours for the field army to concentrate its meagre forces. Any discussion of how 'effective' the Home Guard was must be seen in this context as few Home Guard in the invasion areas were likely to have survived the first day of invasion. These later reminiscences can be contrasted with more contemporary ones which instead emphasize uneventful routine.[4] Oral history is valuable but should be critically assessed.

The first modern history to draw extensively on official records, *The Home Guard: a military and political history* (S.P. MacKenzie's, 1995), remains an essential reference work, even though accepting some of the assumptions of the 1960s *Dad's Army* television series and Norman Longmate's *The Real Dad's Army* (1974), particularly the myth of antiquated weaponry. It is difficult from the perspective of the throw-away society of the twentieth and twenty-first centuries, in which technological change has come at breakneck speed, to appreciate that a weapon of First World War vintage was still considered 'modern' twenty-five years later and might still be in production. It is also frequently forgotten that the ad hoc weapons closely associated with the early Home Guard, including the Molotov cocktail, 'Sticky Bomb', Smith Gun and the despised 'Croft Pike', were also issued to regular forces and are a reflection of wider problems of supply for the British forces. The present study seeks to test the popular perceptions of the Home Guard against the official documentation, with the advantage of the post-1995 release of historic documents into the public domain at The National Archives.

The Home Guard was officially a male preserve until 1943. Penny Summerfield and Corinna Peniston-Bird in *Contesting Home Defence* (2007) have considered in some depth the problems of recording an accurate reminiscence of the women who served with the Home Guard or in the unofficial Women's Home Defence Corps. Unlike their male comrades, such veterans did not have the same focus or identity to curate their memories and the *Dad's Army* series ignored them, furthering the impression that they were of little value. Their place in the Home Guard was controversial but, in line with the prevailing attitude to women's services in the other armed forces, they had important roles in administration, signalling and medical duties. Ironically, it may be argued that the high-profile campaign to give women a full combat role in the Home Guard, decades ahead of its time, proved to be counter-productive in winning official acceptance of their more limited roles.

No study of the Home Guard can avoid reference to the television series *Dad's Army*. It was never intended as a documentary, but it has had a profound impact on the popular impression of the Home Guard and created a tonal background for subsequent academic research. The Home Guard was never referred to as 'Dad's Army' during its existence but the name has now become synonymous with it, confusing fact and fiction. The television series was a cosy vision of the Home Guard that was by no means representative of the organization. The industrial base of much of the Home Guard was missing and, as well as completely ignoring the role of women, the series lacks any acknowledgement of the Home Guard's anti-aircraft, coastal artillery, bomb disposal and sabotage roles. Far from being the aged pensioners of *Dad's Army* myth, most of the Home Guard were men in reserved occupations or teenagers awaiting call-up, with an average age of around 35 years. The age range is clearly shown in Plates 1–3, and in the youthful machine-gun crew in Plate 17. Even so, up to 40 per cent had served in the First World War but in 1940 'old sweats' did not necessarily equate to 'old men'.[5] It gave a solid core of men, already blooded, used to discipline and familiar with the weaponry still in use by the British army. The secret Auxiliary Units that recruited from the Home Guard have acquired their own mythology, in large part to emphasize their distinction from the *Dad's Army* image but also in a bogus nationalist attempt to claim this as a counterpart to the European resistance movements.

The Home Guard was created in response to an immediate invasion threat, but the strain of maintaining a working life and carrying out Home Guard duties over the coming months and years began to tell, and this weariness was reflected in the writing of early Home Guard historian Norman Longmate, who resented his own conscription as a teenage member of the Home Guard.[6] The Home Guard stood down on 3 December 1944 but there was an attempted revival in the 1950s during the Cold War. The proposal was met with a half-hearted response from a war-weary nation, except for Winston Churchill who perhaps saw the Home Guard as a symbol of arguably his finest hour in the crisis of 1940. The small Home Guard of the 1950s appeared to be an anachronism in the new age of nuclear warfare and was overshadowed by the conscription of thousands of young men for National Service and the Civil Defence Service.

The present book attempts not only to explain the reality of the Home Guard – its organization, equipment and changing roles – but also to understand how the myths surrounding the Home Guard came to outweigh the truth and why these misconceptions have been perpetuated, creating a false cultural consensus as to their role in history.

The Home Guard was originally formed as the Local Defence Volunteers (LDV) and officially changed its name on 22 July 1940. In this book, specific references to the LDV are named as such but otherwise the organization is referred to throughout as the Home Guard.

Chapter One

Forming the Home Guard

> The most fantastic and democratic Army ever raised in Great Britain. It was based on individual initiative and improvisation.[1]

Britain had a long history of volunteer militias ready to counter both foreign invasion and civil disorder. What distinguished the mobilization of the Local Defence Volunteers (LDV) in May 1940 was not only the scale and enthusiasm of the volunteers but also the government's lack of a clear understanding of their role. At the start of the First World War a spontaneous movement to create volunteer 'town guards' had sprung up across the country, coming together as the Volunteer Training Corps (VTC). The government initially tried to suppress the movement as a distraction from securing voluntary enlistment to the armed forces and refused to provide uniforms or weapons (which had to be provided by the volunteers themselves) but in 1916 the organization was recognized as the Volunteer Force, under the Territorial Force Association (predecessor of the Territorial Army Association). Although training explicitly for guerrilla warfare on the model of the Boer commandos, it was mainly used to guard vulnerable points, including armaments factories, then to man the new anti-aircraft batteries, and in the crisis of spring 1918 volunteers from across the country were mobilized for full-time service to help defend the east coast. With some exceptions (to guard against possible Bolshevik revolution), the VTC was formally stood down in September 1919, the notification being announced by Winston Churchill (then Secretary of State for War). Although the VTC was entirely male, it worked closely with the Women's Volunteer Reserve (WVR), frequently assisting them with weapons training. Neither organization fitted easily into the popular narrative of the conduct of the First World War that the government tried to encourage in the post-war years; both organizations have now almost completely disappeared from popular history. The debt owed by the Home Guard to the earlier VTC was clearer in 1940 than it is to a modern audience and some young volunteers served again in the Home Guard of 1940. In Herefordshire and Worcestershire the ages of such double volunteers in 1940 ranged from 39 to 63 years.[2]

At the start of the Second World War defence was in the hands of the volunteers of the small professional regular army and the territorial battalions, comprising, in all, just 892,697 men. Limited conscription had been introduced in April 1939. In addition, the National Defence Companies (a successor of the First World War Royal Defence Corps) were a small voluntary reserve to be mobilized on a full-time basis in the event of war but only intended to have a strength of 8,450. Enlistment was limited to former members of the British armed forces between the ages of 45 and 60. The National Defence Companies were mobilized in late August 1939, and in November 1939 were reorganized as Home Defence Battalions of their county regiment, helping to guard vulnerable points and prisoner-of-war camps throughout the war. They never developed into a major force but, nonetheless, in June 1940 General Ironside saw them, rather than the LDV, as a key element in his defence strategy.[3]

Two visionaries from opposite ends of the political spectrum had unsuccessfully argued in 1939 for the creation of a much larger Home Guard. Tom Wintringham, a founder member of the Communist Party of Great Britain (CPGB) and former editor of the *Daily Worker*, had been arrested in 1925 for seditious libel and incitement to mutiny. In 1936 he had been a pioneer of the concept of the International Brigades in Spain and was an instructor and then briefly commander of the British Battalion. Although expelled from the CPGB in 1938, Wintringham remained a confirmed Marxist and differed only tactically in believing it was necessary to work with the British government to defeat fascism, rather than waiting for a future workers' revolution. In April 1939 Tom Wintringham called for twelve divisions:

> formed in the same way as the International Brigades, by voluntary enlistment from among ex-servicemen and youths. The number of men required is, perhaps, 100,000, which is a smaller number than that of the volunteers who would, in fact, clamour for arms tomorrow if the bombing of our cities began today.[4]

Wintringham's proposal was ignored, not least because it was part of his wider proposals to make the army more democratic. In October 1939 the Conservative First Lord of the Admiralty, Winston Churchill, who had been closely connected with the final days of the Volunteer Training Corps, took up Wintringham's theme, sending a memo to the Home Secretary:

> Why do we not form a Home Guard of half a million men over 40 (if they like to volunteer) and put our elderly stars at the head and in the structure of these new formations? ... If uniforms are lacking a brassard would suffice, and I am assured there are plenty of rifles at any rate.[5]

Churchill's vision was for an expansion of the Home Defence Battalions, with First World War veterans taking over home duties, allowing younger soldiers to go on active service overseas. Equally rebuffed, Churchill then decided to let the matter drop. Until May 1940 there was an unreal 'phoney war' atmosphere, with the Chamberlain government dithering on how firmly to press the war effort, believing that the Nazi state was brittle and would collapse of its own accord, with Chamberlain confidently maintaining that Hitler had 'missed the bus'.[6]

As in 1914, the first practical steps were taken as a grass roots movement of raw patriotism, tinged with frustration at the government's complacency. The river-borne Upper Thames Patrol was formed in September 1939 by Sir Ralph Glyn, MP for Abingdon, in conjunction with the Thames Conservancy and War

Office to patrol the Thames and its banks from Teddington to Lechlade. At its height, the UTP had up to 6,000 members, mainly Thames water-men, and it was also the first unit to recruit women. In March 1940 the 'Essex Volunteer Army Force' was formed, based around the Romford and Hornchurch troop of the Legion of Frontiersmen and comprising around 400 men. The *Daily Mirror* described it as the 'vanguard of Britain's part-time army'.[7] At the same time Lady Helene Gleichen organized the eighty male employees and tenants on her estate near Ross on Wye into the 'Much Marcle Watchers'. She wrote to the HQ of the Shropshire Light Infantry requesting that it give her 80 rifles with ammunition, adding, 'I could do with some machine guns, too, if you have any to spare.'[8] In April Lord Kemsley offered to fund the creation of rifle clubs as the core of a new defence force and there were widespread demands in the popular press to create a new volunteer defence force; MPs began to be inundated with letters from constituents demanding action and Regional Commands with offers of help. E.R. Lansdale of Petersfinger near Salisbury offered to be part of a body of house-holders, living on the outskirts of towns and whose properties had a good field of fire, who would be issued with rifles. He cited his military experience as a private in Giggleswick School OTC from 1920 to 1924.[9] Following the invasion of the Low Countries in May, paranoia intensified over the fear of German airborne landings and the existence of a 'fifth column', bringing with it the risk of a mush-rooming of vigilante groups who would be liable to be shot as *francs-tireur* (terror-ists) under international law. One such body was formed on 11 May in Cradley, near Halesowen in the West Midlands, where a unit to watch for German para-chutists and saboteurs went on its first patrol on 13 May, the day before Eden's broadcast announcing the new Local Defence Volunteers (LDV). A government press release on Saturday, 11 May tried to dissuade civilians joining any fighting and the Ministry of Home Security was obliged to send out an urgent telegram on the night of 12 May, requesting confirmation of rumours that 'bands of civilians were forming all over the country and arming themselves with shotguns etc for the purpose of detecting and dealing with German parachutists'.[10]

Yet it would be wrong to suppose that the LDV arose purely out of popular insistence. Behind the scenes General Walter Kirke, the then Commander-in-Chief, Home Forces, had prudently begun planning a contingency plan ('Julius Caesar') in the event of a German invasion in the autumn of 1939 and was partic-ularly concerned that increasingly stretched army resources were being dissipated in having to guard a multitude of local vulnerable points. In March 1940, ignoring Chamberlain's complacency, he ordered a review of lessons from the VTC in case a similar body was needed again.[11] In conjunction with General Sir Guy Williams, GOC, Eastern Command, Kirke began to establish the broadest outline of a plan for a legal local defence force, to take action 'before civilian residents on the East Coast took the law into their own hands and formed their own private defence bands'.[12] The small scale of its First World War predecessor (350,000 men) heavily influenced the concept and was to have long-lasting consequences. The proposed volunteer body would have the same priorities as the VTC in guarding vulnerable points (a cheaper option than the full-time, paid, Home Defence

Battalions) and in providing pre-conscription training of youths. They would also help counter the risk of sabotage by a 'fifth column' or enemy agents and assist in dealing with any disruption following air raids as what was, in effect, an armed special constabulary. Such a force could also act as a reserve to be employed in the case of invasion, organized in each county by the Lords Lieutenant and operating on a decentralized basis as small groups of guerrillas 'on the principle of the Boer Commando'.[13] The upper age limit would be 55 (as in the VTC). It was also recommended that the force should be administered by the Territorial Army Associations (TAAs), as it had been in the First World War.[14]

Kirke's plan was ignored until early May, when confusion in the War Office undermined the C-in-C's efforts. As a consequence, Lewis Broad over-dramatized the situation only slightly when he claimed that the decision to form the LDV had 'passed through the stages of suggestion, approval and action within three days'.[15] The Army Council finally circulated a letter to all Army Commands on 7 May asking for views on the formation of a new volunteer force.[16] With the European situation rapidly deteriorating, hundreds of unarmed Special Constables were having to guard 'vulnerable points'. The German airborne landings in Holland on 10 May sharply focused government minds and caused paranoia over false press reports of German paratroopers landing in Allied uniforms or even nuns' clothing, with extravagant claims that the enemy could land up to 100,000 airborne troops. At the Cabinet meeting on Thursday, 9 May the Foreign Secretary (Lord Halifax) raised a suggestion made by Lord Mottistone in the House of Lords that local levies armed with rifles might be found from older men to guard isolated vulnerable points and the Chief of the Air Staff said the suggestion would be considered by the Chiefs of Staff Committee.[17] The next day Kirke became head of the new Home Defence Executive, charged as C-in-C Home Forces with coordinating anti-invasion planning. Wasting no time, on the afternoon of Saturday, 11 May he met with General Sir John Dill (the Vice Chief of the Imperial General Staff), General Sir Gordon-Finlayson (the Adjutant-General), General Sir Hugh Elles (a former Regional Commissioner now seconded to the Ministry of Home Security) and Oliver Stanley (then Secretary of State for War, on his last day before handing over the role to Anthony Eden) to consider the best ways of dealing with parachutists. Kirke believed the meeting had endorsed his plan for a new volunteer force but when Dill reported first to the Chiefs of Staff Committee and then to the Cabinet that evening he proposed merely attaching six or seven local volunteers to the scatter of searchlight units across the country, under Anti-Aircraft Command. The volunteers would not, therefore, be necessarily sited to defend towns and villages, and it is not clear what the force might have achieved. The Royal British Legion was suggested as possibly organizing the scheme, but it lacked the necessary infrastructure for such a task. Without any mention of consulting the C-in-C Home Forces, the Cabinet gave general approval and asked for a progress report on Monday, 13 May.[18] This was occurring even as General Kirke was briefing his GSO1, Brigadier W. Carden Roe, on a meeting scheduled for the following day at the War Office where, he thought, his plan was to be formally approved. Adding to the confusion, Anthony Eden took over as Secretary of State for War on 12 May and had not been party to the earlier discussions.

On the morning of Sunday, 12 May Carden Roe attended the scheduled meeting with the War Office and Anti-Aircraft Command on Kirke's behalf, believing this was a relatively low-level meeting simply to expand on Kirke's proposal, which Kirke mistakenly assumed had already been approved by the War Cabinet. Carden Roe was surprised to find himself seriously outranked, with the meeting chaired by the Adjutant-General who announced that he had been instructed to draw up a scheme and presented the plan that had been taken to the War Cabinet by Dill on the previous evening. Gordon-Finlayson tried to prevent Carden Roe from bringing Kirke's alternative plan to the attention of the meeting but General Pile from Anti-Aircraft Command, who was intended to command the force as envisaged by Gordon-Finlayson/Dill (but who had clearly not yet been consulted), declared the plan 'nonsense'. Kirke then arrived to have a blazing argument with Gordon-Finlayson and further meetings with the VCIGS. The discussions were private but it can be imagined that Kirke firmly pointed out that the War Office was usurping the authority of Home Forces and the new Home Defence Executive. Gordon-Finlayson and Dill backed down and Kirke's basic proposal was accepted. The meeting reconvened at Horse Guards the next morning (Monday, 13 May), now under the chairmanship of Carden Roe. Progress was difficult, with the Adjutant-General's representative particularly objecting to referencing the Boer commandos, which, although intended to reflect the intended elasticity of the force, to the War Office smacked of anarchy.[19] It was the beginning of a conflict of emphasis over 'guerrilla warfare' that would last for over three years. The meeting did not close until 8.00pm – but Eden had been forewarned and two hours earlier had already abandoned Dill's proposal to Cabinet and had now formally proposed the formation of the Local Defence Volunteers (LDV), under the command of the C-in-C Home Forces. Despite still having no idea on how the LDV would operate, Eden's broadcast to the nation had already been scheduled for the next evening as a means of establishing his new status in government.[20] At the close of Carden Roe's meeting, an Army Council Letter to make ready for mobilizing the LDV was produced for immediate circulation to the Regional Commands and Lords Lieutenant but was blocked by the Assistant Under-Secretary of State for War (Guy Lambert) on the grounds that the drafting committee had exceeded their authority in defining financial responsibilities without consulting the Treasury, and had not sought legal advice before classifying the volunteers as 'armed combatants'.

Further hectic meetings held throughout Tuesday, 14 May tried to resolve the outstanding issues before Eden made his broadcast, including how such a force would be armed and its exact role. The Treasury took the view that the LDV should be regarded as civilians but Eden was emphatic that they should be organized as uniformed soldiers.[21] Eden made his announcement on the BBC as scheduled at 9.10pm with still only the sketchiest idea of how the new force would operate (*see* Appendix 1.1). He spoke from notes provided by Kirke and Gordon-Finlayson, opening with words of reassurance for the country, stressing the formation of the LDV was not a matter of desperation but rather 'in order to leave nothing to chance and to supplement, from sources as yet untapped, the means of defence already arranged'. Eden did not narrow the scope of recruitment but he did say that 'reasonable fitness and a knowledge of firearms are necessary'. The initial expectation, based on the First World War experience of the VTC, was that between 150,000 and 500,000 volunteers would come forward but within just two weeks there were 400,000 and by two months over a million. There was a clearer sense of the threat and nature of the conflict with Germany but this was also the new power of radio broadcasting, for the first time instantly able to reach a mass audience.

On the following morning (Wednesday, 15 May) there were further meetings during which the senior civil servant Sir Frederick Bovenschen (Permanent Under-Secretary of State for War) complained that the whole idea of the LDV was most irregular and slap-dash, asking, 'Why all this precipitancy?' At this, Carden Roe lost his temper and snapped, 'In order to try to avoid losing the war.'[22] In Bovenschen's defence, no one was actually able to say how the LDV would contribute to this aim. It was only then that the Army Council Letter was distributed (*see* Appendix 1.2). This established a mechanism for liaison with the army Regional Commands and the civilian Regional Commissioners (who would be responsible for any devolved government made necessary by invasion), but assumed that it would be easy to limit the number of volunteers to the immediately available weapons and as determined necessary by the Area Commanders. The scheme remained principally a means to create a register of potential volunteers who could at least thereby be controlled, stemming the tide of vigilante groups. The rush made impossible Kirke's stipulation that the Lords Lieutenant (as the automatic presidents of the local TAA) should be informed well in advance, preventing them from having senior officers of the LDV in place, ready to organize the initial volunteers. The Lords Lieutenant were only informed of their role on 15 May and it was not until 17 May that legality was given to the new body with the Defence (Local Defence Volunteers) Order in Council (*see* Appendix 1.3) but by now over 250,000 volunteers had enrolled and were expecting orders.[23] By necessity, a supplementary War Office Instruction distributed on 18 May stressed (optimistically) that 'the outstanding features should be simplicity, elasticity and decentralised control, coupled with the minimum of regulations and formalities' (*see* Appendix 1.4).[24] With some good reason, General Pownall, the future Inspector-General of the LDV, complained that the organization had been set up by the War Office without thought for practicalities and was now a 'dog's dinner'.[25] The War Office would try to suppress publication of the details of the conflict between Home Forces and itself after the war (*see below*, p. 200) and the approval of the LDV without any idea of how it might operate has a striking parallel a month later in the formation of the Auxiliary Units (*see below*, p. 55), similarly reflecting the confusion of the government over home defence.

The volunteers handed in their names to local police stations for registration, but the Chief Constables had been given only a few hours' notice in which to organize a response and the instructions failed to reach many local police stations. There was much confusion as duty sergeants faced growing queues of eager volunteers.[26] Guidance on vetting only arrived the next day, expecting the local police station to check for men of 'hostile connections or origin, or whose loyalty there is reason of doubting', any men engaged in subversive activities or men with serious criminal records.[27] Any suspicious applications were to be forwarded to Police HQ and the MI5 regional liaison officer. They were then expected to send the names of unacceptable candidates back to the LDV area commander as 'services no longer required – surplus to requirements'. In practice, the process was inconsistent and haphazard (*see* Appendix 1.5 and 1.6).

But the volunteers wanted more than their names to be put on a register and in many localities, with little evident sign of central direction, they took the initiative to organize themselves. They relied on former officers for a lead and began to mount guard on key sites. Frustration over the lack of official instructions, and particularly a lack of arms, was being noted by the Ministry of Information as early as 5 June.[28] Into this uncertainty stepped Tom Wintringham with a series of newspaper and magazine articles that were confident and aggressive, exactly meeting the aspirations of the new LDV, rather than the low-key armed special constabulary envisioned by the government. Wintringham had regular columns in the *Daily Mirror*, *Tribune*, *New Statesman* and *Picture Post* and frequently broadcast on the BBC. On 17 May his article in the *Tribune* demanded 'Arm the People'. On 31 May, as the Dunkirk evacuation was under way, a supremely confident article in the *Daily Mirror* was directed at the new C-in-C Home Forces, General Ironside, and titled 'My Proposals for Him . . . and You'. He maintained that invasion would be a difficult job for the Germans and preached an aggressive policy as 'real defence always means attacking' rather than passively holding a defence line. Wintringham ended with the rousing slogan

AN AROUSED PEOPLE
AN ANGRY PEOPLE
AN ARMED PEOPLE!

Even the retired general Sir Hubert Gough (who gave a false name when signing-up to avoid revealing his real age of 70 years) might have been impressed. He recorded a sense of anti-climax following Eden's speech. 'We got no orders, no instructions whatever, for two or three weeks at least.' It was a complaint shared by the retired major general Sir Alfred Knox MP, who lost no time complaining on 21 May 'everybody is waiting for regulations, and does not know what to do'.[29] Gough was appointed to command the Chelsea Battalion of the LDV after the town clerk telephoned to say that there were a great many men who had enrolled but were now getting restless if not 'savagely angry' at the lack of a lead from government.[30] Gough was relieved when Ironside eventually told them on 5 June to 'get on with it' (*see below*, p. 28). The Ministry of Information continued to report on 15 June that there was a lack of confidence in what was seen as the amateurish and ill-organized government handling of the LDV.[31] On the same day came the first of Wintringham's influential articles in *Picture Post*, titled 'Against Invasion: the lessons of Spain'. The pioneering photo-journalism of

Picture Post gave an unparalleled impact to his words, preaching an uncompromising defence policy of public participation and aggression. In the presence of Churchill (dampening the impact of his 'finest hour' speech), Josiah Wedgwood MP launched a scathing attack on the state of the LDV:

> The main reason for the anxiety in the country to-day is that all these people have joined up in the Local Defence Force and everybody is anxious to do something, but, so far, there has been no evidence that their voluntary effort has been met to any extent. We have to look forward to a time when, as the Prime Minister says, everyone will have to bear his part. It is distressing to the ordinary man in the street, when he is so anxious to bear his part, to find that the War Office does not need his services. If we could have from any Minister opposite ... some reassurance this afternoon that the Local Defence Force is not a mere stepchild of the War Office but is genuinely intended to act in the service of this country, not as an extra policeman to guard the German soldiers when they march through London, but as an active Defence Force.[32]

As the government struggled to try to control the rush of volunteers, in the north-east an attempt was made (in the spirit of the First World War 'Derby Scheme') to syphon off young men awaiting imminent call-up into a 'Civi-Corps', to provide physical training and rudimentary drill with broomsticks (Plate 1).[33] Nationally, recruitment had to be temporarily suspended on 24 July and a waiting list established. Despite the practical reasons for so doing, Churchill was unhappy at the impact on morale, saying those refused entry would be 'bewildered and disappointed' and 'one of the primary objects of the Home Guard, which was to provide for the people as a whole an opportunity of helping to defend their homes, will be lost'.[34] Sir Edward Grigg, Joint Under-Secretary of State for War, agreed: 'It is a national asset of not only military, but moral, value.'[35]

The essence of government confusion was whether it was to be a small observation force and special constabulary or a larger combat force, and this confusion extended to the Prime Minister himself. Having suffered Wedgwood's attack in Parliament, a puzzled Winston Churchill wrote to Eden on 22 June:

> Could I have a brief statement of the LDV position, showing the progress achieved in raising and arming them, and whether they are designed for observation or for serious fighting. What is their relationship to the police, the Military command, and the Regional Commissioners? from whom do they receive their orders, and to whom do they report?[36]

Extra copies of the 29 June issue of *Picture Post* containing Wintringham's 'Arm the Citizens' article had to be printed due to popular demand. Churchill pointed out to the Cabinet on the following day that it would be 'very unfortunate if there was any failure to make the fullest practicable use of the widespread desire for combatant service', and Clement Attlee (Lord Privy Seal) and Anthony Eden (Secretary of State for War) were asked to enquire into the arrangements for the equipment and employment of the LDV.[37] On 14 July, after the recent publication of Wintringham's *New Ways of War* and the opening of the Osterley Training School (*see below*, pp. 143–7), Churchill, acutely aware of the potential of this army of voters to trigger a political disaster, tried to regain control of the situation. He championed an aggressive role for the LDV in a BBC broadcast, applauding their 'strongest desire to attack and come to close quarters with the enemy wherever he may appear'. The later Director-General of the Home Guard, Viscount Bridgeman, ruefully commented 'Never did a child take so much intelligent interest in its own growth' and acknowledged 'if ever the War Office let off trying its best to make the Home Guard efficient the Home Guard would rise up in its wrath and insist on being treated seriously'.[38] Edward Grigg was more blunt on 2 November: 'We always create the impression of being kicked into things.'[39]

With criticism mounting, Churchill believed the LDV needed rebranding. He first proposed the change of name to Home Guard on 26 June, but it was not finally confirmed until 22 July. The pithier title combined defending the local community and the wider nation, but Eden, the War Office and the Ministry of Information were not happy about the swift change of name and there were grumbles over the cost of issuing new armbands.[40] The association of Churchill with the change seemed to signify a new importance for the Home Guard but carried the risk of making Churchill ever-sensitive to its demands. Churchill's faith in the Home Guard as a morale-booster and unifying force was demonstrated in 1942 when Lieutenant General Morgan saw Yorkshire miners who had been on strike all week attend for weekend Home Guard exercises.[41]

The government was quick to establish that the Home Guard had the legal status of being part of the armed forces of the Crown, to counter the furious Nazi accusation that the LDV were *francs-tireur*: 'The British government is committing the worst crime of all. Evidently it permits open preparation for the formation of murder bands.'[42] But, as with the VTC in 1914, the War Office was wary of any suggestion that the LDV had the same status as the regular army. The supplementary instructions issued on 18 May ordered 'There will be no officers nor non-commissioned officers in the ordinary Army sense of these terms' (*see* Appendix 1.4). Rather than commissions coming from the King and the War Office, senior officers were appointed by the Lords Lieutenant and they in turn appointed more junior officers. It had its own system of rank and although section and squad commanders (NCOs) had the normal army chevrons, officers could not use the normal 'pips'. Instead there was a system of coloured braid on the epaulettes:

Zone Commander	1 broad stripe (2 inches)
Group Commander	4 stripes (0.375 inch)
Battalion Commander	3 stripes
Company Commander	2 stripes
Platoon Commander	1 stripe
Section Commander	3 chevrons
Squad Commander	2 chevrons

Much was made of the egalitarian nature of the LDV/Home Guard, exemplified by well-publicized examples of workers holding superior rank to their peace-time managers but this was not always popular. General Sir Hubert Gough fumed against what he saw as Communist tendencies at the heart of government, claiming that 'Whitehall tried to pretend that we were all equal and could do what we liked'. Falsely crediting Wintringham for this, he went on: 'These unreal and utterly anarchistic ideas emanated chiefly from various vocal gentlemen who had been fighting in Spain on the side of the Reds, even though their views do not seem to have achieved much success for the Spanish cause.'[43] There were undoubtedly some democratic tendencies at a local level when some platoons even elected their own officers, particularly in factory units. But the appointments were usually based on social hierarchy, not least because officers were expected to have access to a telephone and motor car, which created an inevitable bias towards the wealthier classes.[44] It was only from November 1940 that formal selection boards were established but this was not universally successful. NCOs and officers of one Scottish company threatened to resign in December 1941 when a rather useless private was commissioned, allegedly purely on the basis of his social status.[45]

In May 1941 Wintringham made a blistering attack in the *Picture Post* on the command structure, tabulating how this preserved the traditional social order with senior command being in the hands of elderly gentry and aristocracy – the 'blimps' of David Low's cartoon from the *London Evening Standard*. Three of the Area Commanders were titled; 22 of the 109 Zone Commanders were titled and 9 of the 134 Group Commanders; 20 of the Zone Commanders and 33 of the Group Commanders were company directors.[46] To him, such men were out of touch not just with military strategy but also with a changing modern society. George Orwell agreed, commenting 'A respectable proportion of the officers are too old to have caught up with the 1914 war, let alone anything subsequent.'[47] John Langdon-Davies also took up this theme, complaining of a battalion officer who ordered that volunteers should not drink in the same bar as officers. 'This sort of thing has been the curse of the Home Guard from the beginning – cocks determined to crow on the dunghill of discarded social and military ideas.'[48] Such opinions were even shared by the Director-General of the Home Guard, Viscount Bridgeman, who was reported in July 1941 as believing that Area and especially Sub-Area Commanders were frequently inefficient 'being retired officers who have lost their drive'.[49] Despite his enthusiasm, for General Gough the most important qualification of an officer was that he be a 'gentleman'.[50] For others, it was to be run as a social club. On 29 July the *Daily Worker* reported that the Hon. Wogan Philipps, the Labour Party candidate for South Oxford, who had driven a republican ambulance in Spain, had served diligently in his local Gloucestershire Home Guard but that some of his fellow members had asked for his expulsion. When asked for reasons they explained 'when one expels a fellow from a West End club one does not have to give reasons'. He was reinstated on 3 August.

With no management structure, the LDV had first to be administered by an already over-stretched GHQ Home Forces, but to rely on the vain hope in the instructions of 18 May of simplicity, elasticity and decentralized control would not be enough.[51] Relief came on 30 May when responsibility for the LDV was passed to a revived Territorial Army Association under the overall direction of Major General Sir John Brown of the Adjutant General's department.[52] The Territorial Army had been merged with the regular forces in September 1939 and the county TAAs reduced in size, now mainly responsible only for the administration of drill halls, rifle ranges and the Voluntary Aid Detachment. They would now become responsible for the organization and training of the LDV, under the Deputy Adjutant General (in conjunction with the Director of Military Training).[53] In mid-June organization was further strengthened by the LDV being given its own central staff, shortly followed on 20 June with the appointment of Lieutenant General Henry Pownall (formerly Chief of Staff to the BEF) as a somewhat reluctant Inspector General of the LDV.[54] The hierarchy of control was now that the War Office was responsible for the administration of the organization, the operational role was determined by the C-in-C Home Forces and the Inspector-General reported on the force's efficiency, his committee particularly monitoring the state of supply to the LDV/Home Guard.

Even tighter control was required of a force that was still growing in numbers and was increasingly well-armed but showed dangerous signs of independent thought. Despite the earlier reluctance, the answer was to bring the Home Guard within the structure of the army and in November it was given its own Directorate in the War Office. With the immediate threat of invasion lessened over the winter, the Home Guard was being prepared for a longer-term existence. As a visible change, at the end of January 1941 'customary badges of rank' were permitted, visibly integrating the Home Guard with the army. The Directorate would administer and coordinate all activities of the Home Guard but the chain of operational command was through liaison officers in the Regional Commands of the regular army. The first Director General was Lieutenant General Ralph Eastwood, who had been General Sir Alan Brooke's Chief-of-Staff in France and had earlier succeeded Pownall as Inspector General of the Home Guard. Eastwood was Churchill's personal choice, believing the force needed a young and dynamic head rather than the older, retired officers that the War Office had recommended. Eastwood began the process of reorganizing the Home Guard, assisted by his deputy Viscount Bridgeman, who succeeded him as Director General in May 1941 and remained in post until 21 June 1944 (succeeded by Major General Sir James Syme Drew).

The TV series *Dad's Army* has created a myth that the Home Guard was mainly comprised of elderly men too old for the services. These certainly were a component of the Home Guard, especially with the senior officers (as described above) and when its early anti-invasion role was simply as static cannon fodder, but a deliberate effort was made by the new Directorate to weed out older men. There were some who had fought in the Boer War and even at Omdurman who had joined for one last hurrah, and in Kent there was an effort to give priority to ex-servicemen between the ages of 38 and 55 years.[55] One of the most notable of the retired servicemen was Major General Sir Percy Hobart (1885–1957).

In 1938 Hobart was sent to the Middle East to form what became the famous 7th Armoured Division but his ideas on armoured warfare were unconventional and he was forced into retirement. Aged 55, Hobart joined the Chipping Campden LDV as a lance corporal but was soon promoted to become Deputy Area Organizer. In 1941 Winston Churchill insisted that Hobart be restored to Army command and he went on to raise the 79th Armoured Division as a unit of specialized armour which, as 'Hobart's Funnies', played a major role in the success of the D-Day landings.

The Home Guard also included those too young for call-up and, far from the stereotypical view, the average age was around 35 years.[56] Many of the volunteers had been just too young to serve in the First World War and for them there may have been a residual sense of 'missing out' or even guilt that helps to explain the enthusiasm to demonstrate their willingness to serve. Around 35 per cent of the initial volunteers had seen service in the First World War but were still active men in their 40s or 50s. The age range of the Home Guard was officially 17–65 but teenagers lied about their age to join. Frank Taylor in Essex was just 14 years and 8 months when he joined, and he served throughout the war.[57] Albert Squires was even younger at 14, and as he was too short to carry a rifle he was issued with a Sten gun![58] Harry Verlander, aged 15, joined the Essex Home Guard in 1941 and in the following year he joined the King's Royal Rifle Corps, backdating his birth date by two years. He later served with SOE. Harry had left school aged 14 and was working in an engineering factory when he joined the London Home Guard in January 1941; he worked by day in the factory and was on duty for two or three nights each week, guarding damaged property in the midst of the blitz.[59]

It was mainly an army of workers, including railwaymen, dockers, miners, farm labourers and engineers. Some 50,000 Post Office workers and 90,000 railway men joined the LDV in its first few weeks. These were physically fit men who had intimate knowledge of their localities; the countrymen were often skilled in stalking and used to firearms, often intelligent and inventive. Such men in 'reserved occupations' could be frustrated, even embarrassed, by not being allowed to join the regular forces and the Home Guard offered an opportunity to demonstrate their worth by serving in military uniform. The Home Guard also knew they were fighting directly for their own factory, village or town, giving a strong local community spirit. Ironically, this caused some concern to the War Office who tried to contain the enthusiasm for forming factory Home Guards for fear that their loyalty would be too parochial. The high percentage of men who were in reserved industries also caused headaches for guard rotas, and how they would be mobilized upon invasion. Until compulsory service was introduced in 1942, there was concern that men could not be compelled to muster, whilst teachers, Post Office workers, railwaymen, etc., could claim their work might have higher priority.

A small but culturally significant element of the Home Guard were the volunteers from the Caribbean. The total pre-war immigrant population in Britain was only around 7–8,000, concentrated around the ports of South Wales, Liverpool, South Shields and in London, and the number who came to serve in the Home Guard was correspondingly small. Despite being poorly documented, they are recorded from Liverpool, Gloucestershire, London and Worcestershire; their presence is important in reflecting the all-encompassing nature of the Home Guard (at least in so far as the male population was concerned) and their participation in the community war effort. Garage mechanic Richard Carty was born in Malvern to a West Indian father who had arrived in Malvern with the circus in 1908 and decided to settle there, marrying a local girl in 1912. Richard became a sergeant in Malvern Home Guard and was awarded a Certificate for Good Service. Sidney Wilkins was born in England to West Indian parents and served in France during the First World War. He joined the 25th Battalion, County of London Home Guard but was badly injured whilst on duty in an air raid and spent nine months in hospital. He demanded to be allowed to rejoin and in 1943 was a lance corporal.[60] The Ministry of Supply recruited around a thousand engineering technicians from the West Indies from 1940 onwards to work particularly in munitions factories on Merseyside. Angus Wood from Kingston, Jamaica, was employed at Royal Ordnance Factory Fazakerley, Liverpool, a newly opened rifle manufacturing factory. His job was to set up the machines that the women workers used to cut and grind components, and he also joined the factory Home Guard. Local families took pity on the migrant workers, and after initially staying at the YMCA Wood lived for two years with the Roberts family in Fazakerley, before meeting his future wife at the factory and setting up their own home. He continued to work at the factory until it closed in 1962. Such a welcome was not universal. As with anti-Semitism, there was some antipathy towards the small black population in Britain before the war but it tended not to be openly displayed; it was perhaps more a matter of curiosity, expressed through the casual use of racist names that in the twenty-first century would be considered unacceptable. Many of the known Home Guard of colour became NCOs, like Sidney Wilkins or Lance Corporal John Wade from Montserrat in Liverpool, and were thereby in positions of authority over other Home Guard with no reports of discrimination. A Home Guard remembered as 'Black Joe' in Lye, Worcestershire, appears to have been a warrant officer, seated in the official platoon photograph next to the CO (Plate 3). This would have been unthinkable in the US Army and the arrival of the US forces, with overt and official segregation, transformed race relations for the worse.

To protect its lucrative income from US servicemen, the Grafton Dance Hall in Liverpool (which already had a poor pre-war reputation for race relations) began to impose a colour bar. In August 1944 newspapers widely recorded the 'shameful business' of George Roberts, an Antiguan electrician aged 31, who had come to Britain in December 1942 to work in a Liverpool munitions factory and had joined the factory Home Guard, where there were twelve other West Indians in his unit. In October 1943, whilst in civilian clothes, he was refused admission to the Grafton Dance Hall because of his colour. He returned in his Home Guard uniform to demonstrate that he was 'doing his bit' but was again refused admission. Describing himself as insulted and humiliated by his treatment in a country he had come to help, he refused to carry out his Home Guard duties thereafter and was prosecuted. His appeal against his fine of £5 was heard in August 1944 when the judge denounced the colour bar and reduced the fine to a token one farthing. The judge commented:

> I am told that the position of coloured people in this country has somewhat changed since the nationals of another of our Allies joined us in this country. ... When people come here to risk their lives they are entitled to think that they are coming to conditions of decency and order fit for a country that claims the title of imperial in its best sense. If they find what I am inclined to call a noisy and intolerant minority are not prepared to give them equal rights I think they have a right to be angry.[61]

Roberts returned to Antigua in 1945. Equally, there were several occasions across the country where residents defended black American troops against the institutionalized racism of their own army. The Home Guard on duty at Stoughton airfield, Leicestershire, intervened when a black US serviceman was assaulted by four white compatriots. Ray Elgood remembered, 'I looked at Johnno and Johnno looked at me and I thought "this is not on" so I went over and belted the thug.'[62] Servicemen of colour were generally welcomed during the war, but attitudes towards them began to change afterwards. A Jamaican airman based near Gloucester recalled that 'After the war, things changed', and he was asked 'When are you going home?' Nonetheless, many former West Indian service personnel returned to Britain on *SS Empire Windrush* in 1948.[63]

Home Guard units quickly adapted to their local circumstances and interests by creating specialized units. Some, such as signalling, medical and intelligence units, replicated those of the regular army and whilst they seemed an obvious development for the volunteers, for the War Office it reinforced its general paranoia about 'private armies'. Wintringham was explicit on the subject and seemed to confirm MI5's fear that he was trying to build a 'Red Army' (*see below*, p. 159):

> Home Guard Units must organize themselves into completely self-contained armies. Sections to deal with commissariat, transport, first aid, signals, and engineering should be formed now. Be prepared to fight through to the end without help from the Regular Army. Study your territory, practise the use of your weapons, and shoot to kill.[64]

Local doctors provided medical services within the Home Guard and units appointed their own stretcher-bearers (unofficially wearing the standard SB brassard). It did, however, take until April 1941 for a formal medical section to be sanctioned, on the basis of one medical officer per battalion and stretcher-bearers trained in first aid.[65] There was official concern that an expanding Home Guard medical service might compete with that of Civil Defence services and it was agreed that any Home Guard casualties should be passed to Civil Defence services as quickly as possible. There was still reluctance to fully acknowledge the medical role, and it was not until January 1943 that Home Guard medical officers were officially allowed to wear the Red Cross brassard. Similarly, there was great resistance to allowing the Home Guard to wear the traditional trade badges of the army, such as the armourer or marksman badges.

Mounted units of up to 50 men, often based around the local hunt, were raised in twenty-four counties to patrol upland and moorland areas (Plate 4). To modern eyes this may seem to be an anachronism in the era of the Panzer, but in 1939 all the belligerent nations had cavalry units and the Germans, despite their well-publicized use of mechanized infantry, artillery and tanks, remained heavily reliant upon horse transport throughout the war. So the concept of a mounted unit to patrol open uplands against the threat of parachute landings did not seem unusual and was an effective option. The fact that the War Office was prepared to pay a substantial allowance to maintain the horses at a time when feed was otherwise in short supply was undoubtedly an incentive to local hunts and other horse owners to raise a mounted unit. From May 1942 the allowance stood at 15*s* per month for each horse, with an additional allowance of 10*s* for saddlery and other equipment that had to be supplied by the War Office.[66]

River and canal patrols also proliferated across Britain and had to be restricted by the War Office (Plate 5). It was unclear to a puzzled meeting of the Home Guard Inspectorate on 30 July if the Upper Thames Patrol (UTP), formed before the LDV, came under War Office or Admiralty authority. Patrols wore pseudo-naval uniforms and were commanded by retired naval officers but 'called themselves LDV'.[67] Whilst there was a serious point behind patrolling the waterways against the danger of illicit traffic, there was a suspicion in the War Office that the boat enthusiasts saw this primarily as a means of protecting their fuel allowance and hobby. They are frequently photographed in motor boats mounting a Lewis gun, stylishly dressed in Home Guard denim or battledress blouses paired with seamen's blue roll-neck sweaters, naval caps and sea boots or smart double-breasted jackets and trousers. The War Office and Admiralty firmly rejected the proposal from the Truro City River Patrol that they be allowed to fly the White Ensign! They and the UTP were also refused permission to fly the ensign of the War Department Fleet. Instead the Trent River Patrol (783 strong), for one, flew the Blue Ensign of the Royal Naval Reserve. By May 1942 the number of river patrols had been cut to 184 boats operating on the rivers Fal and Trent, Lake Windermere and the Upper Thames. In Northern Ireland the Belfast Harbour Patrol operated as part of the Belfast Harbour Police.

Northern Ireland

The Home Guard was organized on a different basis in Northern Ireland, where there were particular political considerations, its own threat of invasion and a 'fifth column'. Part of the overall German invasion plan in 1940 ('Operation Sealion') included 'Operation Green', which envisaged the landing of 39,000 German troops on the south-west coast of Eire, who would then form a bridgehead for the invasion of England. In 1941 there were also plans for an airborne assault on Northern Ireland, with 20,000 parachute troops capturing airfields to make way for the Luftwaffe transport planes to land more men. It was one place where the threat of a fifth column was very real – in the shape of the IRA, which had already launched a bombing campaign in England during 1939, and this greatly affected the attitude toward the recruitment of Irishmen to the Home Guard in the rest of Britain.

There was not the same system of TAAs to organize a Home Guard in Northern Ireland and it was, in any case, felt wise not to distribute arms too widely in the community. In 1940 the IRA infiltrated the Ballykinlen army camp and stole 200 rifles. Northern Ireland Minister of Public Security John MacDermott advised that:

> It is most important that the [British] Army should not become involved in political differences. At the same time it is equally important that weapons should not get into the hands of undesirable elements, and that the latter should not get a foothold in our military machine. It is difficult for the Army to differentiate. At present it is best done for them by the Constabulary on the best information.[68]

The Ulster Defence Volunteers (UDV) was therefore raised on 28 May as the Local Defence Volunteer Section of the Special Constabulary (the 'B Specials') of the Royal Ulster Constabulary. The name was formally changed to the Ulster Home Guard (UHG) in April 1941. The legal status in war of the UDV was the subject of much angst. Although entitled to bear arms as part of the RUC, the latter remained a civil power and the UDV (unlike its counterparts in the rest of the UK) therefore did not have combatant status. Government legal advice in 1940 was that military status could be given, without the need for formal attestation, at the point that they were called upon to resist invasion but they would not thereafter be able to revert to the civil role of special constables. The legal dispute as to whether this would bring the Volunteers within the bounds of the Hague Convention rumbled on until 1942, when a system of formal attestation was introduced.

The UDV had a strength of 12,500 in May 1940, doubling to 26,115 in October 1940, but recruitment slowed thereafter and at stand-down in 1944 it still had not risen above a strength of 30,000. Recruitment was hampered by the fact that, like its parent 'B Specials', the UDV retained the sectarian divide and remained overwhelmingly Protestant. Denim overalls were issued, as on the mainland, but were of a darker green colour, almost black (to match the dark green uniform of the RUC), with a black field service cap. Paired with a khaki greatcoat, the colour scheme was disturbingly close to the uniforms of the hated British paramilitary 'Black and Tans' during the War of Independence. By March 1942 they were wearing normal battledress. The Ulster Volunteers performed much the same duties as their counterparts in the rest of the UK but had the initial pressures of having to help guard a land border with the neutral Irish Republic and the continuing activities of the IRA. Consequently, they were well armed from the start, able to draw upon the plentiful supply of SMLE rifles and ammunition held in RUC police stations as well as Lancia armoured personnel carriers. To counter the risk of airborne landings, in 1942 North Derry UHG was issued with eight 25-pdr field guns to defend local airfields. Later in the same year the UHG relieved the RAF of responsibility for airfield defence, including manning their 75mm anti-tank guns.

Isle of Man

The Isle of Man also had separate legal status and formed its own Home Guard of 2,500 men (out of a total population of 50,000). The island occupied a strategically important position protecting the west coast ports and was also the site of large internment camps for enemy aliens. The Home Guard established over fifty observation posts and helped guard the camps and the growing number of RAF bases and radar stations.

Chapter Two

The Role of the Home Guard, 1940–41

As the organization struggled through the chaos and confusion of its initial formation, as a 'Frankenstein's monster' it went through several changes before becoming an integral part of strategic planning.[1] As late as mid-August even Winston Churchill was having to ask whether the functions of the Home Guard had yet been properly established.[2] In 1940 preparations against invasion could no longer be confined to defending the coastline. Parachute troops could land behind a traditional 'front line', made obsolete by the tactic of *blitzkrieg*, using armour and mobile infantry combined with aerial close support, to drive deep into enemy territory before turning in a hook movement to encircle the defenders. There was also a risk of invasion via Ireland, rumours of a plan for the invasion of Scotland via Norway, and paranoia about the presence of a 'fifth column' that would cause disruption from within and engage in sabotage. A national defence network was needed as never before.

General Kirke had been heavily influenced by the rationale of the First World War VTC and its model of the Boer commandos, able to operate independently if the command structure was disrupted by invasion. The official history of the VTC had claimed that 'the force was to take the form of bands of irregulars, and its duty in case of invasion was to carry on a form of guerrilla warfare'.[3] Its Regulations of 1916 had explained its role as 'to constantly harass, annoy, and tire out the enemy, and to impede his progress, till a sufficient force can be assembled to smash him'.[4] This tactic would have new resonance in 1940 and was to remain central to arguments over the role of the Home Guard until 1943. Ever fearful of independent action, the Boer commando concept was rejected by the War Office in favour of a centralized, controllable, body initially to act primarily as a special constabulary but the VTC model continued to influence the minds of Home Guard volunteers.

An 'Armed Special Constabulary'

General Kirke retired on 26 May 1940 and his replacement as C-in-C Home Forces, General Edmund Ironside, first accepted the LDV primarily as an 'armed special constabulary', responsible for the static guard of strategic 'vulnerable points', as an observer body to warn against any parachute drops, and as guides for regular forces moving through their locality.[5] The nickname 'Look, Duck and Vanish' was an accurate summary of their anticipated function at this time. It would also assist the police in dealing with any outburst of the supposed fifth-column threat.[6] After any invasion, the LDV would fulfil the harrying role as envisaged by Kirke, although no detailed advice on how to achieve this was given. The LDV was never intended to hold anything approaching a 'front line' but rather to do its best to hinder what were assumed might be scattered parties of paratroops before they could consolidate the landing grounds. The first official instructions to the volunteers were contained in LDV Instruction No. 2 (June 1940) and were a warning not to be too ambitious:

> The Local Defence Volunteers are neither trained, armed nor equipped to offer strong prolonged resistance to highly-trained German troops, and they will therefore best fulfil their role by observation, by the rapid transmission of information, and by confining the enemy's activities. They will also act as guards at places of tactical or industrial importance.[7]

The task of guiding regular forces continued throughout the war and from February 1941 designated Home Guard guides, who were to base themselves at local post offices or on the main approach to a village, wore a green/yellow brassard on the right arm.[8] This role was particularly important given the removal of road signs and the deployment of troops not familiar with the local area. Journalist John Langdon-Davies proposed a more ambitious scheme for their use in February 1941, with shades of the SIS Home Defence Scheme and the GHQ Auxiliary Units (*see* Chapter Four), suggesting a force of 100,000 Home Guardsmen, operating in teams of two men, lightly armed with a revolver, three grenades, a knife with an 8-inch blade, a knuckleduster and a cosh. These scouts would provide a network of hidden observers and act as guides to both direct the army towards the enemy and help the civilian population to safely evacuate an area under attack.[9] He castigated some Home Guard units for not taking this role seriously and it was one of the drivers in creating his fieldwork school at Burwash in June 1941.[10]

LDV Instruction No. 5 (July 1940) explained the need to assist the police in countering potential fifth-column activity and to establish crowd control in the aftermath of any bombing. According to General Gough, 'During the first weeks of our existence the Home Guard were first told that we were to assist the police – an idea which the police looked on as a positive nuisance.' He went on scathingly, 'Then some bright authority announced that we were to be armed with batons and march in bodies of about fifty – solemnly up and down the streets, under the absurd impression that our calm appearance would inspire confidence among our terror-stricken civilian countrymen!'[11] Lord Croft (Joint Under-Secretary of State for War) expanded on their policing role on 11 July:

> In some of the large cities a force of disciplined men organized in companies, platoons and sections would in case of serious [air] raids be of first-rate service to the State. They would be able to deal with any panic amongst the population, or any panic in perhaps some quarters of great cities where we have alien populations congregated together ... They would keep the streets clear in the case of serious fires, and arrest at once anyone showing

> any indication of sabotage or of what has wrongly perhaps been called fifth-column activities.[12]

Their most visible, and contentious, guard role was the establishment of road-blocks and checkpoints across the country. It was a duty they took seriously, at times risking the easy movement of British army vehicles, and their strict adherence to orders caused several casualties. The background atmosphere of suspicion over possible infiltration by fifth columnists or enemy agents was reflected by Wintringham in his lectures at Osterley:

> All cars and lorries working behind the enemy lines must be treated as enemy vehicles. They must be dealt with even if the Germans in them are being driven by Englishmen acting under compulsion ... it may be advisable to shoot or bomb even if the car is driven by your best friend.[13]

In some areas, the police became concerned over the LDV/Home Guard's rigorous use of the powers of stop, search and arrest, especially when, taking to heart the warnings that the Germans might use false ID papers or cause British citizens to collaborate under duress, they stopped policemen and ARP workers going about their duties.[14] In London Sir Philip Game, Commissioner of the Metropolitan Police, wrote to GOC London District complaining that his men were repeatedly being stopped and asked for identification by the LDV, wryly adding that the latter were 'becoming better shots daily'.[15] In Glasgow the Chief Constable, Sir Percy Sillitoe, was himself confronted at an armed checkpoint. In response, Sillitoe put adverts into local papers saying the police would take action where drivers were stopped and threatened for no good reason.[16] Admittedly, they did sometimes use their new-found power to settle scores; Stoughton LDV in Leicestershire, for example, repeatedly stopped one doctor simply because earlier he had verbally abused them at the roadblock.[17] But generally, the problems were due to the LDV/Home Guard following their instructions to the letter (having been warned that to have done otherwise was a military crime) and sections of the public not treating this novel situation with due seriousness. In Wallasey a bank clerk was sentenced to fourteen days' imprisonment for wilfully obstructing the LDV at a checkpoint, failing to show his ID card and giving a joke false name.[18] Such a dismissive attitude could have fatal consequences. The guards were instructed to carry loaded rifles (but no round in the breech) and fixed bayonets. Local Defence Volunteer Instruction No. 5 was clear on the objective: 'The essential is that the challenger does not challenge until he is certain he can kill the challenged person.'[19]

> If the order to halt is disobeyed, fire will be opened without hesitation ... Sentries will not 'challenge' until they are certain that those approaching are so close that the section cannot possibly miss them with fire. On very black nights it is usually better to rely on the bayonet, in which case the sentry will not challenge until the last possible moment.[20]

Southern Command did at least order that two warnings be given before opening fire![21] Civilians were unused to the idea of military checkpoints and in Saltwood during June 1940 it was an *army* checkpoint that fired upon the local police sergeant.[22] But as the Home Guard was responsible for the majority of road-blocks, it was inevitable that it was involved in the majority of confrontations. On the night of 2/3 June four people were shot dead in separate incidents.[23] On 22 June another six were killed in three incidents, including one in Romford where a noisy exhaust prevented the driver hearing the challenge, resulting in four deaths.[24] Another tragedy came in September when a 16-year-old boy on a bicycle was shot dead at a Wolverhampton checkpoint for refusing to acknowledge the challenge – the sentries were not aware that he was deaf.[25] In August 1941 a drunken serviceman in the Fleet Air Arm was bayoneted and killed at a Home Guard night-time checkpoint at Holt Heath, Worcestershire, after failing to heed the challenge after leaving the local public house. A verdict of accidental death was reached by the subsequent inquest but the jury did request the Coroner to recommend to the Home Guard authorities that greater care should be given as to the proper use of the bayonet.[26]

Some army officers, who should have known better, did not take kindly to being stopped by what they dismissed as civilians in uniform. Egbert Ganderton and Cyril Buggins of the Cookhill Home Guard in Worcestershire were manning a road-block when they stopped an army staff car with a colonel and an ATS driver. The officer asked Ganderton for directions but was refused the information until he produced an appropriate pass. The colonel protested, at which point Ganderton told Buggins to make ready to shoot if the car was driven off! At this point, the ATS driver sensibly suggested that perhaps the officer should comply, which he did reluctantly. The colonel had apparently already been stopped by Home Guard three times that night and was getting annoyed.[27]

The guarding of factories, bridges, power stations, reservoirs, airfields along with a host of other strategic installations had become an impossible strain on the resources of the regular army. Whilst waiting for the invasion that never came, the Home Guard stood guard duty across the country, night after night, month after month, year after year. The efficacy of the guard posts was tested by under-cover teams of the Field Security Section of the Intelligence Corps and later by commandos training for sabotage raids in Europe (*see below*, p. 45). The Windsor Castle Defence Company of the Home Guard had a special duty in guarding the royal princesses who lived there throughout the war, and the king and queen when they came to stay at weekends. It comprised members of the royal household and estate workers, and was commanded by Owen Morshead, the royal librarian. Supporting a company of Grenadier Guards, they patrolled the castle at night and in the case of imminent attack, if relieving forces did not arrive, their task was to safely escort the royal family to an airstrip on Smith's Lawn, where a waiting Lockheed Hudson would fly them to safety. (Details of the role of the Auxiliary Units in protecting the royal family at Balmoral in 1944 are contained in Chapter Four.)

The strains of guard duty began to tell almost immediately. In Craven Arms, Shropshire, platoon leaders of the LDV wrote a formal letter of complaint, commenting 'We the undersigned, who are keen platoon officers, find the operation of constant nightly patrols impossible at least until the enemy is expected. None of the men are not working all day, and therefore we cannot patrol all night [too].'[28] As early as 23 August 1940 official concern was raised about the strain interfering with agriculture and industrial production.[29] It was not always a passive duty. The surviving log book of the Home Guard post on Dulwich College golf course in West Sussex is a remarkable record of their nightly guard duty. The guard post was adjacent to an anti-aircraft and searchlight battery and the guardsmen assisted the latter in putting out incendiary 'breadbaskets' and parachute flares. On 11 September is the first notice of ammunition being issued for their M1917 rifles (30 rounds of ammunition each). They had seen all too clearly the rising intensity of the blitz on London and this must have been a sign to them that invasion might be imminent, especially when from 16 to 23 September the whole guard was ordered to 'stand to' for the night. Their first success came on 30 September when they exploded a descending parachute land-mine. Another flare was shot out on 11 October as it drifted over the post. Then on 14 October the guard post had to join with the AA battery and an RAF post in firing at a concentration of descending parachute flares. It was a risky duty and on 25 October they had a lucky escape when an incendiary 'breadbasket' exploded over the course, showering it with around a hundred incendiary bombs. One Home Guard was injured whilst putting out the fires.[30]

Another early role was the securing of downed Luftwaffe crews. Colin Cuthbert (aged 17) and Roy Addison (aged 16) of Margate LDV, armed with rifles, rescued and arrested the crew of a Heinkel III that crashed into the sea off the beach.[31] Again, there could be tragedies. In one case a Home Guard unit killed an RAF pilot who had baled out, by shooting through the shroud lines of his parachute canopy. In poor light the blue RAF and Luftwaffe uniforms looked very similar. Before adding this to the popular litany of Home Guard 'incompetence', it is worth pointing out that the order to fire had come from a Royal Artillery officer.[32]

Anti-Invasion Defence

Only with hindsight does the serious prospect of any invasion in 1940–1 seem debatable. Hitler ordered preparations to be made through the issue of Directive 16 on 16 July, a plan (Operation Sealion) was formulated, troops and barges were assembled. This was clearly a threat for which preparations had to be made and the British government was not to know that the German High Command was unenthusiastic about the scheme. But even in July 1940 the risk was secretly doubted by Churchill, who nonetheless recognized the political value in maintaining the invasion scare into late 1942:

> He emphasized that the great invasion scare ... is serving a most useful purpose: it is ... keeping every man and woman tuned to a high pitch of readiness. He does not wish the scare to abate therefore, and although personally he doubts whether invasion is a serious menace he intends to give that impression, and to talk about long and dangerous vigils, etc., when he broadcasts on Sunday.[33]

Even with air superiority, the practicality of taking an invasion force across the channel in 1940 without the specialized equipment that was available to the Allies on D-Day in 1944 is doubtful. There were no purpose-built landing craft and no large landing ships that could disgorge heavy equipment direct onto the beaches, no swimming or mine-sweeping tanks, no Pluto pipeline. The German Navy also recognized that they could not protect the landings over the long length of coast demanded by the German Army, giving the Royal Navy the opportunity to disperse the invasion fleet and block any reinforcements. Nonetheless, along with the U-boat blockade, the very threat of invasion (with the obvious signs of its preparation in the channel ports) and then the 'shock and awe' of the blitz were key elements in Hitler's tactic of trying to break the morale of the British government and people, and thereby encourage a negotiated peace. John Langdon-Davies explained in his lectures over the winter of 1940:

> This is a war of nerves. It will be won by the side which destroys the morale, the will to resist, of the other side, and not the morale and the will to resist of the armies opposed to it so much as the citizens who form the population as a whole.[34]

Against this backdrop, the Home Guard posed a unique threat to the German High Command in presenting a physical and psychological defence in depth unseen in previous German campaigns. It may have been rash for 'Operation Sealion' to have taken no explicit account of the Home Guard in its battle plan, and just as important for the German High Command, the Home Guard was a symbol of national resolve that cast doubt on the expectation of a collapse in British morale that might make invasion unnecessary. Journalist Norman MacKenzie, who attended the second Osterley Home Guard Training School training course, explained:

> If the Government had made peace that summer we would have rebelled; abortive, no doubt, but we would have tried. We saw ourselves as the heirs of Spain. We wanted a socialist government and we were going to fight fascism at home, if needs be, as well as the Nazis.[35]

The LDV wanted a more active role in resisting invasion than the 'special constabulary' concept allowed and Tom Wintringham captured their confident and aggressive spirit:

> Invasion is a difficult job for the Germans. If we are ready, we can make it almost impossible – and destroy the men who try it ... First, real defence always means attacking. It doesn't mean holding passively a line or a town or a home.[36]

This was an attitude that naturally appealed to Churchill and he supported the enthusiasm of the volunteers to 'attack and come to close quarters with the enemy, wherever he may appear' but it was up to the C-in-C Home Forces to define their part in countering an invasion.[37] Having been in post for just a few days, on 30 May General Ironside identified three roles for the LDV in the case of invasion: 1) static defence of villages and roadblocks; 2) information from bicycle patrols; and 3) Molotov cocktails thrown from the windows of houses to deal with tanks.[38]

Ironside outlined his ideas to leaders of the LDV on 5 June, prioritizing their input first as a static defence to block movement through every village, and then to provide information to the army on enemy movements. He urged them to be aggressive – when dealing with parachutists, he said, 'shoot them, shoot them, shoot them without any reference to taking care of their future' – but gave little clear direction otherwise and made only vague promises of future arms.[39] By then, 80,000 rifles had been issued but the large-scale importation of US rifles had not yet begun. The priority for rifles would go to rural areas (where cover from regular forces would be thinnest) but Ironside was wary of using high-velocity rifles in towns, preferring shotguns. Yet when he reported on the strength of the country's defences to the new CIGS, General Sir John Dill, just a few days later on 11 June, the LDV did not feature significantly in his core plan. At that time he had just 170,000 men in the field army, 502 tanks and 430 field guns. Vulnerable points were defended by 26,000 men of the Home Defence Battalions and 10,000 men of the Infantry Training Centres. To supplement these, Ironside looked primarily for an expansion of the Home Defence Battalions of 'old soldiers and immatures' to relieve further regular troops from guard duty, rather than the LDV.[40] He admitted to Dill that the latter were 'problematical'.[41] Unsurprisingly, Josiah Wedgwood MP accused Ironside of treating the LDV as a 'despised step-child'.[42]

At this stage, Ironside saw the LDV only as a dubious bonus to his defence plan, to guard vulnerable points of secondary importance and to act as a human sponge to distract the enemy across a broad area, obliging them to use up their limited stocks of ammunition and petrol whilst dealing with a succession of small, static defence posts. The limited regular forces could not defend all potential invasion beaches (thinly defended by a 'coastal crust' of sacrificial second-line troops) or provide a defence in depth to cover all potential air landing sites, unable to predict the *blitzkrieg* thrusts into the interior that might penetrate the inland Stop Lines and, in Ironside's words, 'rip the guts out of the country'. The LDV could well be the first body that made contact with the enemy and its observer role was critical; its volunteers were then to be sacrificed to buy valuable time for the single armoured division in the country to be deployed to where it could best mount a counter-attack with the field army. GHQ instructions for the LDV to 'defend their post to the last man, since every minute gained may be of vital importance' illustrates the urgency of the situation.[43] Wintringham explained:

> Because of its organization and its local character, the Home Guard is a force that cannot be pierced. It is not a line on the map. It fills the whole map. No attack can get beyond it to an unarmed, unprotected area – there is no 'beyond'.[44]

With little to offer beyond encouragement, Ironside gave the LDV licence to use their imagination and sell their lives dearly. 'I want you to know you have authority from us to get on with things. You will not be held responsible for anything except absolutely gross stupidity.'[45] Aldershot Command called for the LDV to be ready to engage in 'immediate offensive action'.[46] Neither the War Office nor the LDV were under any illusions as to their fate and it was with good reason that West Cornwall LDV described themselves as a 'suicide squad'.[47] A.G. Street's character old Shepherd Yates put it thus in 1942:

> But each village'll hinder he a bit. P'raps only ten minutes apiece. But six villages'll mean a full hour. Be that time 'tes to be hoped as the regular strikin'-force'll be got going, and 'it 'im fur zix.[48]

Behind the village yokel speech of the 'common man' was a chilling truth. On 25 June (three days after France surrendered), Ironside formally presented to the Chiefs of Staff the anti-invasion plan he had already implemented as Operational Instruction No. 3.[49] There was disquiet with the 'coastal crust' concept and the Vice-Chiefs of Staff on the following day described the plan as suicidal.[50] The Stop Lines (pillboxes and anti-tank ditches, etc.) were too reminiscent of the static trench lines of the First World War and the plan assumed huge casualty rates, not least among the LDV. Major Maurice Petherick MP (an SIS officer in the intelligence branch of the Auxiliary Units) explained the philosophy: 'it is surely the duty of even one man, finding himself alone against a company, to kill as many enemy as he can before being killed himself'.[51] For Churchill 'there rose that last consoling thought of unslavable man – you can always take one with you'.[52] Any delay they caused, however small, would be of value and no one was under any illusions about the human cost.

> Our lads down here in the southeast corner of England expected to be invaded: they had only twelve old .300 Ross rifles between 120 men. They expected to die and accepted that fact: they wouldn't have run away.[53]

Such stories were common across the country. Frank Bryant was a member of Cheltenham's cycle platoon, likely to be the first on the scene of a local parachute landing. They were to

> fire a few rounds to slow down the enemy for the five minutes or so that he would need to register the size and scale of the opposition, thus allowing the Regular Army an extra five minutes to organize themselves into action. We were, it goes without saying, expendable.[54]

They were resigned to their fate but in a peculiarly British way, one of the chief concerns of the LDV at the height of the invasion scare was that they should have an extra tea ration whilst standing guard. After due thought, guard posts were classed as canteens for the purposes of the Food Controller.[55]

Britain was not invaded but there were a number of invasion scares that demonstrated the LDV/Home Guard's resolve to fulfil that sacrificial policy. On the afternoon of 30 June there was a false alarm at Bewdley, Worcestershire, when low-flying aircraft sent several haycocks into the air that were then mis-taken for descending parachutists. The army and LDV were called out and young

Leonard Burrows of Kidderminster was given a clip of 5 rounds and told to 'make them all count'.[56] On 7 September 1940 the blitz of London began, which coincided with suitable tide and moon for invasion. With reports of the massing of invasion barges in the coastal ports, there was a major alert; the code-word CROMWELL was issued at 8.00pm, which was a warning of imminent invasion – but not of invasion itself. The Home Guard was mobilized and, confusing the signal with that for actual invasion (OLIVER), church bells were rung in some localities as a warning of attack. Rumours began to spread of German sea- and airborne landings and, although it was a false alarm, the Home Guard, however poorly armed, who turned out to meet the invader were not aware of this fact. Their determination was not in question and many assumed this would be their last few hours of life.

> Most of them calculated that their personal task would be sacrificial ... Every night, whether it was their turn to patrol and watch the skies or to sleep at home, they had to face the question: 'Will the Nazis come before morning?' Such awareness is not to be lightly borne, in the hours of solitude, by men who have outgrown the irresponsibility of youth.[57]

At first German radio dismissed the LDV as an illegal 'rabble' and a 'mob of amateurs armed with broomsticks and darts'. But a recognition of their potential to impede the invasion plans is suggested by the repeated radio denouncements of the LDV as *francs-tireur* (terrorists) who would not be taken prisoner:

> The British government is committing the worst crime of all. Evidently it permits open preparation for the formation of murder bands. German official quarters warn the misled British public and remind them of the fate of the Polish *francs-tireur* ... Civilians who take up arms against German soldiers are, under international law, no better than murderers, whether they are priests or bank clerks. British people, you will do well to heed our warning.[58]

On 23 June Bremen Radio broadcast a back-handed compliment to the *Picture Post* campaign:

> Mr Tom Wintringham, who commanded a battalion in the International Brigade in the Spanish Civil War, is giving lessons to British civilians in *Picture Post* on how to participate effectively in encounters between British regular forces and German forces invading Great Britain. This correspondence course in guerrilla warfare is illustrated by numerous photos, and contains admonition to civilians to use old shot-guns or cans of explosives for the purpose of killing Germans. It is irresponsible of the British censor to permit publication of such reckless appeals to the natural fighting spirit of the British citizen.[59]

Undeterred by such threats, the LDV/Home Guard abandoned all thought of the Hague Convention and filed their rifle bullets into 'dum-dums' that would expand on impact, loaded their shotguns with 'lethal shot', stripped shops of piano wire to make garrottes, experimented with means of exploding sheets of burning petrol across a road and made home-made mortars from drain pipes (Plate 12).

In early July, with substantial quantities of arms beginning to arrive from the USA (*see* Chapter Six), Ironside was able to take a more strategic view of the LDV and now intended to use them to replace regular troops manning the pillboxes and other emplacements on Stop Lines, thereby allowing the transfer of troops to strengthen the field army.[60] The publication of *LDV Instruction No. 8. Tanks and Tank Destruction* in July 1940 also put the LDV at the forefront of the crucial defence against the Panzers. The expanded instructions for the army – *Tank Hunting and Destruction, Military Training Pamphlet No. 42* – was not published until the end of August. No longer considered an unstoppable menace, thanks in great part to Wintringham's confident press articles and the teaching at Osterley, tank hunting was treated as a new and deadly sport. From September 1940 Western Command organized one or more tank hunting sections in each Home Guard battalion, comprising a minimum of a section leader and nine men. They were armed with Molotov cocktails, rifles and a Lewis gun, and equipped with an axe for tree-felling (to make road-blocks) and two crowbars. Each section would operate within a 5-mile radius, tasked with stalking and destroying enemy tanks. By March 1941 there were 171 specialist tank-hunting sections in Western Command alone, with an average strength of 39 and comprising in all 7,141 men.[61] The optimistic assumption that tanks would operate singly and without infantry support reflected the experience during the French campaign when the Panzers had outrun their infantry support.

General Alan Brooke replaced Ironside as C-in-C Home Forces on 19 July, shortly before the name of the LDV was changed to the Home Guard, both marking a new stage in the organization. Brooke had the advantage of recent experience in France and, with increasing resources pouring into the country from across the Empire, as well as arms from the USA, he already had greater flexibility in planning a defence. The Home Guard was now given a more structured part in the plan.[62] The beaches would still be thinly defended, although Brooke and Churchill intended to use poison gas on the enemy as they landed.[63] A stronger mobile field army was better able to mount a counter-attack before the landings became well established, and instead of Ironside's static Stop Lines there would be a greater reliance on defence in depth focused on a network of 'defended localities' in towns and villages, largely defended by the Home Guard, with a particular role to protect communications hubs ('nodal points'). It had been pointed out in June 1940 that the German armour in France had largely kept to the roads and that in Britain there were few roads that ran parallel but instead they tended to converge on 'nodal points', which might be towns, village crossroads or river crossings. By securing these nodal points and using road-blocks, the enemy blitzkrieg could be significantly disrupted.[64] A 'defended locality' was defined in 1943 as 'Squad and platoon posts each capable of all-round defence and mutually supporting. The whole to be strong, independent and self-supporting.'[65] One or more 'defended localities' might be required to defend a town, which was then classed as a 'defended area'. In 1943 the key role of the Home Guard was simply stated: 'The fighting task of the Home Guard is to deny rail and road communication to the enemy.'[66] In the light of the independently minded spirit of the Home Guard, the ACI No. 924 of August 1940 stressed that its value lay not in an insular attitude but in proper coordination with the rest of the army and under the latter's control.[67] The defences included more elaborate anti-tank obstacles using concrete cylinders and bent steel rails ('hairpins') ready to be set into prepared, covered sockets in the road surfaces, and an increasing number of anti-tank mines. What was lacking was sufficient quantities of effective anti-tank artillery, as the priority for new 2-pdr guns was the field army. Instead both army and Home Guard relied heavily on Molotov cocktails and the SIP grenade (Plate 18). The Northover Projector was issued from January 1941 but the Smith gun arrived even later in Home Guard service from June 1942 (*see* p. 104).

As far as many in the Home Guard were concerned, this was a passive concept of defence but was not entirely static. Throughout the war the War Office struggled to balance the principle of holding fixed positions at all costs whilst accepting the need for the Home Guard to have some mobility to harass an advancing enemy in the immediate surrounds of their defences – but controlling their enthusiasm to break out completely into offensive warfare. Home Guard General Instruction No. 10 (1 August 1940) identified the role of delaying the enemy 'by any means in their power'. It would include 'dispute, with desultory fire, every fence, ditch, wall, etc., covering the approaches to their village, and, if driven in, harass the enemy from house to house as he attempts to advance through the village'.[68] Flexibility was thereby allowed in a fighting withdrawal from outlying defences, but at the heart of each 'defended locality' would be a 'keep' that was to be defended to the last. Central to the concept was a need for new specialist skills in street fighting that were well articulated by a number of Home Guard publications, initially using a First World War manual as a model but with practical instruction coming first from the innovative Osterley Home Guard Training School and then from a number of official Town Fighting Schools (*see below*, Chapter Seven).[69] The men were taught how to safely move through a built-up area, how to 'mousehole' from house to house by breaking through walls, how to take up concealed firing positions and use upper windows to launch Molotov bomb attacks, the correct way to man barricades and how to organize assault squads. The tactics were consolidated in *Home Guard Instruction No. 51: Battlecraft and Battle Drill for the Home Guard Part IV, the Organization of Home Guard Defence* (1943), which continued to appeal to the imagination of the Home Guard by including details of simple booby traps to set in houses.

In the summer of 1940 the Osterley Home Guard Training School provided unique training in these tactics but to the concern of the War Office, it elevated them to a strategy of 'guerrilla warfare'. Students were told to pick off stragglers on the flanks of an advance, including tanks, transports, dispatch riders and sentries. 'It is our job, when the enemy is on the march, or his foraging or scouting parties are out, to harass his flanks, to snipe every straggler. Hit and run. Hit and hold them up. Hit and scatter them.' They were also prepared for working behind enemy lines: 'Since offence is the best form of defence, operations against such units must be carried into areas which may be overrun by the enemy.'[70] There were no illusions about what was to befall them or how they should respond: 'Above all remember the enemy is ruthless, and similar medicine must be handed to him.'[71] Osterley students were no doubt proud of the description given to them by William Joyce (Lord Haw Haw) as the 'Osterley cut-throats'.[72]

The War Office's issue with Osterley (in contrast to that of MI5) was one of control rather than the 'Communistic tendencies' of some of its instructors and it wanted harrying tactics clearly tied to the overriding strategy of defending the 'nodal points', rather than the Home Guard pursuing an unsanctioned guerrilla war across the countryside. By then, official Home Guard guerrilla units had already been established, first in the XII Corps Observation Unit and then in the GHQ Auxiliary Units (*see* Chapter Four). Whilst Wintringham diplomatically stressed that Osterley students would operate in conjunction with military forces, he also explained that 'as communications are so uncertain in modern wars, small bodies of the defenders must be trained to work entirely alone and under the initiative of their own leader'. 'Guerrilla warfare', a traditional Spanish term for a 'small war' fought by small, possibly isolated, units of troops, became a fashionable term over the summer of 1940. It had not been mentioned in Wintringham's *New Ways of War* but he seized upon the term at Osterley and it was used to subsume the existing harassing tactics to protect 'defended localities'. For many in the Home Guard it was an exciting strategy that gave them an enhanced status as guerrilla fighters, reinforcing their sense of masculinity whilst trapped on the home front. The War Office had been unhappy from the start with the idea of linking the LDV to any concept of Boer Commandos or guerrilla warfare but in 1940 the shortage of equipment meant that the War Office had little choice but to accept local interpretations on how best to slow down an enemy advance. This was best expressed by Ironside's exhortations on 5 June to use their imagination without fear of censure. For Major Gray, a company commander in Edinburgh Home Guard, the choice lay in training 'second-class regular soldiers' or 'first-class guerrillas'. The company trained a sniper scout section under a veteran of the Lovat Scouts and nicknamed it 'Rutherford's hired assassins'.[73] The War Office belatedly tried to restrict the term 'guerrilla warfare' when they realized it played into the Home Guard's predilection for independence but by then the term had become established in the Home Guard for any mobile force, from individual sniping to the battalion-strength mobile column of Cambridgeshire's 'Grace's Guerrillas' (*see below*, p. 35). The terminology was validated in *Home Guard Instruction No. 14: Winter Training* for 1940:

> Time must not be wasted in attempting to train for roles for which the Home Guard is neither organized nor intended; this, however, should not debar elementary training in guerrilla warfare which, indeed, may be an important part of the tactics of the defence of a locality.[74]

A memo of 1941 then stated 'Home Guards may be allocated a guerrilla and mobile role or a static defence of an area, factory, road-block, etc.' and in August

1941 the Director General of the Home Guard, Bridgeman, commented in *The Times* 'The Russians have laid stress on the importance of sabotage and similar activities behind the enemy lines. This is a task for which, if invasion comes, the Home Guard will be particularly suitable.'[75]

The aura around guerrilla fighting received a boost after the entry of the Soviet Union into the war and stories of partisans there and in Yugoslavia operating behind enemy lines. It became a media selling point and Alfred Kerr's *The Art of Guerrilla Fighting and Patrol* (1941) simply attached the name 'Guerrilla' to normal Home Guard training. This is seen not least in the assertion that the patrol's supplies would be carried in packs, transported in a lorry from one rendezvous to the next.[76] Not helping matters, the official War Office definition of a guerrilla in 1942 was loose enough to encompass any small-scale action in the midst of a blitzkrieg, where the concept of a front line was at best elastic:

> a guerrilla is one who is fighting in an area of his own country, or of a country favourable to him, which is at the moment in the grip of a superior enemy. He may be a regular soldier cut off from his main armies, he may belong to a para-military organization, or he may be a civilian with arms in his hand ... The main objects of guerrilla operations are to inflict the maximum damage on the enemy, to force him to tie up regular troops who might otherwise be engaged in the main effort, and to form a basis upon which regular forces can ultimately reconquer the country, or, alternatively, to persuade the enemy that it is simply not worth his while attempting to garrison the country any longer.[77]

Langdon-Davies exaggerated the improvements in equipment and organization during 1941, when he claimed the Home Guard was 'as up-to-date as General Wavell's army or the fighter command' but the improvements were such that the War Office could now emphasize the need for orthodox military operations to defend fixed positions.[78] George Taylor, Chief of Staff in SOE, had given a pessimistic analysis of the potential of guerrilla warfare to resist any further Nazi invasion in Europe, believing that 70 per cent of the schemes for guerrilla warfare during the German invasion of Yugoslavia had proved ineffective due to the speed of the German advance and the inability of lightly armed guerrilla troops to counter the enemy's mechanized force.[79] This opinion was reflected in a draft instruction leaflet for the Home Guard by Lieutenant Colonel Short of the Directorate of Military Training later in August 1941. Although it acknowledged that if Home Guard were able to slip away from an indefensible position they should stay in action for as long as possible, to 'harass the enemy, cut off single men, small parties, cut field telephones, destroy transport, destroy every man and everything German within striking distance', the core strategy of defending nodal points from fixed positions was still considered more effective than guerrilla operations by small independent bands, stressing: 'Blind imitation of Russian guerrilla tactics by local Home Guard Units without the authority of the local commander will hinder, not help, our defence plans' (underlining in original).[80]

The War Office waged a constant battle to rein in the tendency of the Home Guard towards what the latter saw as mobile, modern warfare but Langdon-Davies maintained the Home Guard was no longer a stop gap defence but 'the essential machinery of mobile defences in depth'. To him, the Home Guard were no longer 'Village Maginot Line minded'.[81] The argument would continue for the next two years. Wintringham's *Deadlock War* of March 1940 had challenged the convention of rigidly holding a position at all costs in favour of the principle of an 'elastic web of defence' whereby a unit would pull back or move to a flank in order to avoid annihilation and preserve the ability for counter-attack, a network of defended points preventing any overwhelming breakthrough from a single collapse of defences.[82] Fellow Spanish Civil War veterans Ferdinand Miksche and Hugh Slater expanded on this in 1941, describing a web of defended localities, each able to provide mutual support through aggressive action and where the loss of one would not enable an enemy breakout.[83] Such a strategy depended on a high degree of mobility and from the start the Home Guard had created its own mobile columns, some of which were remarkably well equipped. Cambridgeshire Home Guard had two mobile columns at battalion strength, formed as early as July 1940. The 7th Battalion column was formed in July 1940 from evacuated students of the University of London and local men and was known as 'Grace's Guerrillas' after its CO, Lieutenant Colonel John Grace (Director of French Studies at Magdalene College, Cambridge).[84] In 1941 it had 815 men with 492 rifles, 104 Thompson SMG, 24 Lewis guns, 7 Northover Projectors, 3,500 assorted grenades, plus a truck, 2 cars and 2 motorcycles, having further ear-marked for requisition 15 lorries, 46 cars, 30 motorcycles and 400 bicycles. It acted as a mobile reserve for the defence of Cambridge. Even more impressive, the 8th Battalion column was formed from the Cambridge University Senior Training Corps and operated as a mobile reserve for the county as a whole, with the advantage of having a number of regular army officers and NCOs and not having to be armed from Home Guard sources. In May 1942 it comprised 1,529 men and even had a light tank, four armoured cars, four Beaverettes, four 18-pdr guns and four 75mm guns. It was organized as five infantry companies with armoured, engineer and signals sections.[85] In February 1941 the 12th (Motor Reconnaissance) Battalion, Leicestershire Home Guard, had a strength of 400, operating with 100 private cars. In Glasgow two motorized companies comprised 360 men and were equipped with twenty-four Browning machine guns.[86] Impressive as such units were, the War Office tried to restrict their spread. Their potential for unsanctioned independent action was exacerbated by a lack of portable wireless sets (which only began to be distributed from 1942) to exercise a measure of control and they also conflicted with a financial imperative in May 1941 to reduce Home Guard petrol consumption by 10 per cent.[87]

The invasion of Crete on 20 May 1941 renewed the panic over possible airborne assault, either establishing bridgeheads on airfields or mounting small 'land and burn' raids, and it caused a fresh evaluation of the Home Guard's role.[88] On 25 May Langdon-Davies's immediate assessment of the invasion in *Sunday Pictorial* concluded that the Germans did not drop their main force immediately but used smaller units to encourage British forces to scatter and deal with them. Langdon-Davies suggested that in the event of a similar invasion in Britain, the mopping-up of these initial forces should be left to the Home Guard in order to preserve the integrity of the British field army, thereby putting the Home Guard again in the forefront of defence and giving further weight to the need for their mobility.[89] On 8 June fellow journalist John Brophy went further and seized the opportunity to call for 'armoured mobility'.[90] The War Office did not have the resources to go so far but on 30 June GHQ gave a more aggressive structure to the long-established harrying role by ordering the Home Guard to form small permanent 'fighting patrols' or 'battle platoons' of up to twenty-five men, using bicycles or motor transport, which would operate 2–3 miles beyond the bounds of a defended locality and be ready to engage for the 'complete destruction of the enemy wherever and whenever he may land'.[91] In 1943 their mission was summarized as being to 'observe, plan, strike, withdraw', with each patrol organized as an HQ section, three rifle squads and a Browning Automatic Rifle (BAR) squad.[92] Such fighting patrols proved popular with the Home Guard but there was an inevitable concern in the War Office that they would proliferate unchecked and expand into independent strike forces. Ever-sensitive to the ambitions of the Home Guard, Churchill, with characteristic over-enthusiasm, suggested in October 1941 expanding the small number of existing Home Guard mobile columns to formations at brigade strength. The War Office despaired! It would draw away a considerable number of men from defending their fixed points and it was doubtful if the Home Guard had the organizational strength to operate in this way, not least because of the time it would take to assemble such a force of part-time soldiers and the lack of transport. There were also fears that the Home Guard would abuse the role and use it to pursue the enemy on a 'wild goose chase'.[93] Churchill, unwilling to drop the idea completely in the face of polite War Office objections, suggested battalion-strength columns, with four in each Corps area (on the model of Cambridgeshire). The Secretary of State for War David Margesson successfully argued that the idea was impractical due to the impossibility of releasing men in reserved occupations for additional training and the increasing pressures on the Home Guard to take over anti-aircraft duties.[94] The argument over the mobility of the Home Guard would continue well into 1942.

Factory and Communications Defence

The defence of factories and infrastructure was largely in the hands of the Home Guard but there were issues with parochialism. Lord Beaverbrook, Minister for Aircraft Production, set the tone by regarding his factory Home Guard as his own private army (*see below*, p. 109). At first, a secret report to Parliament appeared to give official approval for this independence, stating 'Where factories etc. have raised LDV units for their own defence, the volunteers will be used only for the defence of those premises.'[95] But on 16 July 1940 concern was expressed in the LDV Inspectorate over the raising of 'private armies' by factory managers, fearing that these units would not cooperate with wider LDV strategy.[96] The issue was raised at a meeting with the Prime Minister on 10 August when the Adjutant

General, General Gordon-Finlayson, said that in many cases factory units refused to cooperate with surrounding Home Guard units.[97] There was also a fear of infiltration by the Communist Party, with officers appointed to factory Home Guards having to be acceptable to both employer and employee.[98] Factory Home Guards were only fully integrated into the Home Guard system in July 1941, when it was suggested that the term 'defence of the factory' should be interpreted 'liberally' as meaning the defence of the factory in the best way possible, which might include defending it as part of a wider plan of area defence.[99] Charles Graves later emphasized the importance of mobile detachments from factory units that were ready to deploy for the general defence of an area, leaving older men for the static defence of the factory.[100] Nonetheless, the Ministry of Aircraft Production jealously guarded its independence in supplying its factories into 1942.[101]

Across the country thousands of railway workers joined the LDV and Home Guard (Plate 2). Within a month of the formation of the LDV, 16,000 men of the Southern Railway Company had enrolled and the company seconded eighty of its officials to act as full-time officers for what became the Southern Railway Group of the Home Guard. By December 1944 they numbered 35,510 men organized in six battalions and eight anti-aircraft troops. Their task was to keep the railways running for as long as possible after invasion whilst defending key assets so that they did not fall into enemy hands. They were also responsible for creating rail-blocks to prevent enemy armour from using railway lines as convenient trackways to bypass nodal points. This focus meant that there was concern over the winter of 1940 that the Railway Home Guard was also developing into a private army. On 7 February 1941 the GOC Western Command saw an 'impertinent' circular from LMS to its employees in the Home Guard which said they could ignore mobilization orders from military commanders but should instead report for work as normal. The GOC angrily wrote to GHQ warning that there was a risk that Battalion and Area Commanders would refuse to arm or even dismiss railway workers from the Home Guard if they did not accept their orders.[102] The answer was to regard the Railway Home Guard as reserve troops to general service battalions, with Home Guard Circular No. 2 of June 1941 acknowledging that railway workers might have defence duties more important than mobilizing with the rest of the local Home Guard until the enemy was in the immediate vicinity. This was a problem shared with many other classes of workers and GHQ urged commanders to take such difficulties into account when calculating available resources for rapid mobilization. Some 50,000 Post Office workers joined the LDV in the first few days, organized in zones that matched the Post Office structure, and identified from April 1941 by a diamond blue/white sleeve badge to indicate that they could not be taken from other duties for general Home Guard service. Their role was to defend Post Office buildings and form fighting patrols to defend working parties maintaining and repairing civil and military telecommunications systems and to act as messengers.[103] Unfortunately in March 1941 they still had only 17,000 rifles and shotguns.[104]

Bomb Disposal

The first Home Guards to find themselves on 'active service' had volunteered for bomb disposal work and several gallantry medals were awarded to Home Guards for this task, which demanded great coolness under pressure and extraordinary bravery. Many of their stories have been gathered together by Chris Ransted.[105] Some Home Guardsmen had become involved unofficially in bomb disposal work from the start. In September 1940 Thomas Williams, a platoon commander in the London Home Guard, organized rescue work after Buckingham Palace was hit during an air raid and organized the construction of a 6ft-high sandbag wall around an unexploded bomb to protect the palace. In a subsequent air raid he removed another unexploded bomb from the palace and took it to a place of safety in the grounds.[106] The highest civilian medal, the George Cross, was awarded to two Home Guardsmen in Croydon. Captain Roy Thomas Harris, aged 37, of Croydon Home Guard and a member of Croydon ARP Engineers' Service was awarded the George Cross for helping to disarm more than eighty unexploded bombs and parachute mines, including on 18 September 1940 dismantling a 50kg unexploded bomb at Langdale Road School in Thornton Heath, Surrey. One of Harris's assistants was another Home Guard, Robert Cocksedge, a fitter for Croydon Corporation. He was also awarded the George Cross as leader of Croydon's Heavy Rescue Squad and for his work in excavating and removing unexploded bombs. Albert Tilyard-Burrows, aged 36, was a Home Guard section leader at the Vickers Aircraft Factory at Weybridge, Surrey. On 21 September 1940 he was awarded the George Cross for dealing with a 500lb unexploded bomb at the factory. He led a party that heaved it on to a corrugated iron sheet, lashed it down and then towed it behind a truck 200 yards to safety. On 2 October 1940 a bomb fell – but failed to explode – beside one of the gun posts defending the Hurlingham Home Guard Training School, putting it out of action. The bombing instructor, Thomas Gray, took charge of the students who dug out the bomb and he then fixed a charge to it, allowing its safe demolition. Gray was awarded the George Medal for this and a subsequent incident.[107]

After such ad hoc efforts, in October 1940 the Ministry of Aircraft Production established volunteer Auxiliary Bomb Disposal Squads (ABDS), joined by some members of the factory Home Guard, to detect and report the sites of unexploded bombs, clear and excavate the sites of unexploded bombs around factories, erect sandbag blast protection and, if necessary, to move the bomb to a safe place – all in advance of the arrival of an Army Bomb Disposal Section. Some men went further and Platoon Officer Reginald Cooke of the Cooke's Auxiliary Bomb Disposal Unit in Birmingham was awarded the George Medal for dealing with a 250kg bomb which fell on his factory on 28 October 1940. When the bomb was reached it was found to be ticking, and had already been there for forty-eight hours. Cooke made two attempts to remove the fuse and it was then decided to flood the shaft in the hope that the water would stop the fuse; this proved successful and the bomb was later safely removed.[108]

In December the scheme was extended to all factories undertaking government work. The ABDS were formally part of Civil Defence and for the Home Guard

Directorate this was another distraction for its volunteers. In April 1941 Harry Dunn was a tool-setter at Webley & Scott in Birmingham and a corporal in the local Home Guard. He was on duty during an air raid and saw a bomb strike the building but without exploding. Having organized the evacuation of the factory air raid shelters, he returned to the scene with a police constable and a Home Guard lance corporal. Dunn then removed the fuse and put it in a bucket of water. The factory opened as normal and the RE Bomb Disposal team arrived at lunchtime to finally make the bomb safe.[109] On 14 April 1941 the A.V. Roe factory at Chadderton, Lancashire, was hit in an air raid and the ARP and factory Home Guard undertook a search for any unexploded bombs. One was found and dragged from the factory behind a lorry on a 12yd-long rope, although at one point the rope broke and had to be reattached. Another bomb was discovered and, after a 'jerk test' on the rope, was likewise towed out of the building, with Platoon Commander Shepley sitting on the trolley with the bomb to make sure it did not fall off. The men were all awarded the King's Commendation for Bravery.[110] It was not until June 1941 that Home Guard factory units were given permission to form their own ABDS units, affiliated to the bomb disposal companies of the Royal Engineers for training.[111] In September 1942 formal responsibility for all ABDS passed to the Home Guard, the units forming part of the local Home Guard battalions (Plate 6). Their primary responsibility was to protect the factory, but they could volunteer for bomb disposal work in the surrounding area to support the hard-pressed Royal Engineers. Their work went beyond ground clearance in advance of the arrival of Royal Engineers bomb disposal teams: Category A ABDS were authorized to carry out actual bomb disposal work, including the removal of fuses, without the supervision of Royal Engineers personnel.[112] Clifford Lord was an apprentice in the Maintenance and Engineering Department of the Royal Ordnance Factory at Blackpole, Worcester. He enrolled in the factory Home Guard in 1942 and was invited to join the Bomb Disposal Unit. He recalled Captain Phillips of the Royal Engineers welcoming him to the unit with the words: 'Welcome to the Suicide Squad!' By the time he joined there were about thirty people in the factory's Bomb Disposal Unit. Their training included study of the various bomb types, the effect of blast on buildings, techniques of shoring up excavations, removal of fuses, and slinging and lifting bombs from the excavations. There was also the delicate technique of gently placing bombs, some with their fuses still intact, on sandbags in the back of a lorry to be driven very carefully to the destruction site. In 2012 Clifford still vividly remembered the phenomenon of hairs standing up on the back of his neck when handling live bombs![113]

From August 1943 Home Guard ABDS units were issued with a special badge, comprising two crossed bombs in yellow on a red circle, to be worn above the left cuff of the battledress. Bomb disposal was vital and highly dangerous work, but the contribution of the Home Guard has been all but forgotten. In all, 7,000 men of the Home Guard were trained in bomb disposal.

Chapter Three

Integration with the Army, 1942–44

> We see on the chessboard of war the Home Guard as the Castle guarding the King, while the Knights of the Regular Army went overseas in search of the King's enemies.
>
> *Viscount Bridgeman*[1]

From late 1941 the Home Guard became ever more absorbed into the structure of the British army. In November 1941 the HQ of the Cambridgeshire District of Eastern Command had to acknowledge, somewhat ruefully,

> The time has come when we must all take a deeper interest in the administration of the Home Guard . . . the new Operational Administrative Instructions to be published shortly take full account of the Home Guard as part of our military defence, and assign the Home Guard Commands many responsibilities on equal terms with regular commands.[2]

From October 1941 each battalion of over 1,000 men was given a seconded army adjutant (to improve War Office monitoring), and a paid clerk and storeman.[3] Officers, who were after all volunteers and most with full-time jobs, were now at increasing risk of being overwhelmed by a barrage of forms, instructional leaflets and handbooks as per the long-established British army tradition of documenting every eventuality. The Home Guard was also becoming significantly younger and now looked more like regular soldiers with standard rankings, woollen battle-dress and uniform equipment (Plate 17); only their BAR pouches, leather gaiters and their M1917 rifles now distinguished them (Plates 9 and 18). In addition to Home Guard shoulder titles and battalion flashes, some wore the formation sign of their army Command, District or, in the case of artillery units, their parent Royal Artillery formation, as a symbol of their integration. A defining act was the large-scale distribution of the new Sten sub-machine gun from March 1942, which came to arm 40 per cent of the Home Guard and put them on a par with the regular army. Mobile columns, now issued with army trucks, began to be equipped with army backpack wireless sets to communicate with HQ. The Home Guard was described in 1943 as 'the biggest, toughest, civilian army in history' but, nonetheless, in the modern public mind the Home Guard remains the poorly equipped and chaotic organization of mid-1940.[4] The disparity was clear in the 2016 film *Dad's Army* which, although set in 1944, showed scant appreciation of the changes that had occurred in the organization.

It is ironic that even though the Home Guard was better armed and equipped, a problem for the government was maintaining morale in the face of increasing workload and a lack of the direct focus that the threat of imminent death in an invasion had provided. For many members the Home Guard had seemed most useful in the era in which it was least able to undertake its task. Radnor commented, 'If ... the Home Guard as a whole had lost some of the old original urgency and splendid desperation, it had gained in nearly every other respect as part of the fighting forces.'[5]

The chances of invasion decreased during 1942 but with more British forces having to be drawn away from the UK for the global conflict and the battles of El Alamein and Stalingrad yet to be won, to have rejected the possibility of invasion completely would have been complacent. Without the Home Guard, thousands of troops would have had to be left in Britain to guard against the possibility of invasion. Instead, the Home Guard took on an expanding range of duties that freed regular troops for service overseas and this, arguably, had more practical consequences in winning the war than defending against invasion that never came. As Lord Croft explained: 'We could not have sent our great reinforcements to the Middle East and Singapore but for the fact that the Home Guard stands behind the regular army.'[6] A continuing but exaggerated fear of invasion also helped secure national unity amidst the grinding hardship of war and motivate the exhausted Home Guard.

A major change in the character of the Home Guard came in February 1942 when conscription for eligible males was introduced as part of the National Service Act, requiring everyone aged between 18 and 60 to undertake some form of war work. At first conscription was implemented in the Home Guard only where volunteer levels were low (particularly in the east and south-east).[7] Service was placed on a compulsory basis for those aged 18 to 50, although volunteers of 'reasonable physical fitness' were still accepted between 17 and 65. The increasing demands of Home Guard service meant that many older men took the changes as an opportunity to resign. Compulsion gave more reliability of service, necessary as the Home Guard increasingly took over roles previously undertaken by the regular army on a full-time basis and they would no longer be able to resign by giving fourteen days' notice. Any member who absented himself from duty or parade without reasonable excuse would be subject to a fine of £10 and/or one month's imprisonment. After mustering had been ordered, absence without leave and desertion would be dealt with under the Army Act. Members had to perform a minimum of 48 hours' training and operational duty per month but many were already undertaking over 60 hours' service per month at a time when those in reserved occupations were under pressure to increase war production.[8]

As when the VTC underwent similar revisions in 1916, the change to compulsory service was met with protests of being 'un-British' and many men resigned from the force before the new policy took effect.[9] Colonel R. Painter, a Sector Commander in Worcestershire, commented that he thought the introduction of compulsory service was 'the biggest mistake ever made'. Approximately 1,600 Worcestershire Home Guardsmen resigned between October 1941 and

March 1942.[10] There could be tension between the original volunteers and the later 'directed' men. The history of the 46th Battalion, Lancashire Home Guard recounted how those recruited by compulsion often had no heart for the task, while William Bently Capper blamed the decision to abruptly end compulsory duty in September 1944 on the unwillingness of the conscripted Home Guards to turn out for drill and training, claiming the decision had been made 'as an easement for those who did not share the spirit of the Home Guard, but merely wore the uniform under compulsion as "directed" men'.[11]

The War Office was still wrestling with the need to persuade the Home Guard to focus on defending fixed strategic positions, whilst accepting the need for an increased local mobile capability to deal with a perceived increasing threat of German airborne raids. In April 1942 ACI No. 872 omitted the word 'static' from the definition of Home Guard roles so that it was responsible for an undefined 'local defence'.[12] In early July 1942 GHQ also removed the restrictions on mobile columns, providing that they did not exceed 1,000 men and did not require additional resources.[13] In explanation, a conference at GHQ in July 1942 put forward the opinion that

> The Home Guard will not just engage in static defence but will also take mobile and aggressive action. Strong points are to be held with no withdrawal, but reserves are necessary to counterattack and harass if the opportunity arises, or to reinforce threatened localities ... Even if villages are bypassed by enemy armour, the actions of the Home Guard in holding localities will cut off enemy troops from their ammunition supplies.[14]

Even as the War Office still struggled to contain the mystique of 'guerrilla warfare', a new fashion was the creation of 'commando units' within the Home Guard (Plate 7). The new army commandos had become famous, labelled by *Pathé News* as the 'Big Men' of the people in 1942, and association with such elite forces was another means of reinforcing the Home Guard's sense of self-worth whilst confined to serving on the home front.[15] Sharing their cachet had a particular appeal to the younger men of the Home Guard. Major Scott, the commanding officer of the Alvechurch Home Guard in Worcestershire, decided to form a small commando unit and after a series of tests – including a 3-mile run from Alvechurch to Rowney Green firing range, where live firing was conducted – eight men were chosen from the three platoons of the Alvechurch Company. All were excellent shots and carried out extra physical training for their new role including runs and learning to swim in the deep end of Major Scott's swimming pool, all in full kit. More seriously, they also spent time training with army Commandos.[16] After attending the official Denbies training course in January 1942, A.G. Street was in no doubt that the task of the school was not to mould the students into regulation soldiers but 'to develop any flair for improvisation, to encourage individualism, and to produce first-class irregulars or even rural bandits'.[17]

Although later denied, official instructions continued to refer to a guerrilla role for the Home Guard. Eastern Command in January 1942 ordered, 'When defended localities and central Keep are overrun, the remaining men must RV at a pre-arranged spot and carry on guerrilla tactics.'[18] Lord Croft, in February 1942, advised that where the Home Guard lacked a full complement of rifles, 'they should endeavour to train their men in other essential forms of fighting which I have indicated, so that they can learn from the Russian guerrillas'.[19] The continuing validation of the Home Guard's role as guerrilla fighters even seemed to undermine the *raison d'être* of the Auxiliary Units (*see* Chapter Four). In early 1942 the then commanding officer of the Auxiliary Units, Colonel 'Bill' Major, wrote to General Gregson-Ellis, the Deputy Chief of Staff, Home Forces, complaining that the Home Guard, especially in Eastern Command (where he had previously served), had established a policy of guerrilla warfare, saying openly that they were going to 'take to the woods'. He concluded rather meanly: 'I cannot believe that they will be of the slightest use in this role, and will not function at all in the face of some Bosche attack pressed home. In my humble opinion they will run like stink without firing a shot.'[20] Colonel Major was ignoring the fact that his own operational patrols were drawn from those same Home Guard.

By April the War Office had decided that the use of the term 'guerrilla warfare' had to be reined in but by now it was deeply entrenched at the highest level. A lecture to the Home Guard in Western Command on 21 April by Lieutenant General James Marshall-Cornwall, GOC Western Command, maintained that for the rural Home Guard 'training should be in guerrilla warfare and nothing else'.[21] The very next day Marshall-Cornwall received a letter from GHQ which restricted the use of mobile patrols, requiring the express permission of GHQ.[22] A furious Marshall-Cornwall saw it as unduly restrictive to local initiative and counter to encouraging a generally aggressive attitude in the Home Guard. He complained to the Chief of Staff at GHQ, Lieutenant General Swayne:

> I feel very strongly on the subject. If we are only going to allow offensive patrols 'in certain districts', and if the formation of mobile units is a matter in which authority is centralized solely in GHQ, and then only in special circumstances, we seem to be striking at the whole principle of local mobility, local counter-attack, and tank-hunting activities which are essential if we are to defeat a ruthless and vigorous invader, and we shall be making our Home Guards pill box-bound and impotent for war.[23]

In response, GHQ accepted that the Home Guard needed to have the necessary mobility to patrol the immediate surrounds of their defended localities, but equally insisted the Home Guard were not to be used as striking forces beyond their own districts.[24]

The conflict with Western Command occurred at the same time as Major George Walker of GHQ Home Forces was writing a report to better define the harassing role of the Home Guard and finally outlaw the term 'guerrilla warfare'. Walker decried the 'unavoidable lack of discipline and training' of the Home Guard which meant that, in his opinion, they were not, and could not be, trained for a guerrilla role, and that their presence on the battlefield as irregulars outside the normal chain of command would only confuse regular troops in the area. He even tried to claim that the Home Guard considered guerrilla warfare as being part of their function only because no one had ever said it was not, which, as illustrated above, was demonstrably untrue. A Cambridge Area Operational Instruction in December 1941 instructed survivors of a captured nodal point to rendezvous and 'take up guerrilla warfare', advising that they establish hidden caches of food and ammunition in advance.[25] The problem had arisen because the Home Guard Directorate and the War Office had been equally caught up in the fashion of 1940–41 for labelling almost any small-scale action as 'guerrilla warfare' and had revelled in the international media attention that it had aroused. Walker insisted that the concept of guerrilla warfare proper damaged the primary role of the Home Guard in defending fixed locations. He tried to untangle the role of fighting patrols and tank hunting sections that were to hinder access to a defended locality from the broader assumption of guerrilla bands living off the land and mounting an independent campaign in enemy-held territory.[26] The Progress Report on the Home Guard for April 1942 confidently asserted 'the old imaginary antagonism between "static" and "guerrilla" roles is no longer a serious difficulty' and Walker's report was formally accepted by General Paget, now C-in-C Home Forces, in June. Paget ordered that the term 'guerrilla warfare' must no longer be allowed in connection with the Home Guard, although the need for frequent repetition over the coming months suggested a lack of success.[27] In early November GHQ issued a further clarification, warning 'The use of the term "guerrilla" will be strongly discouraged, as if guerrilla activity is generally regarded as a possible role for Home Guard there is grave risk that the obligation to fight to the last in defended localities will not be met.'[28] Following this, the Operational Orders for Eastern Command in December 1942 again tried to clarify the terminology:

> The role of these [fighting patrols] will be to observe, report and harass the enemy's movements, denying him the free use of the roads and destroying small parties wherever the opportunity offers. They will NOT in future be referred to as 'Guerillas'.[29]

Home Guard Instruction No. 51 Part IV in November 1943 made the policy clear and was also a warning for the Auxiliary Units, whose purpose was now under threat:

> There is no room in modern war for uncontrolled bodies of men wandering about the country imagining they are doing guerrilla fighting, demolishing communications essential to the counter-attack, and being as much danger to our own fighting patrols as to the enemy's.[30]

But in 1943, with the Allies taking the offensive, the arguments over the definition of guerrilla warfare in the Home Guard had finally become academic. The main threat to Britain was now seen as sabotage raids and although this proved illusory, and was perhaps never a serious danger, the stakes were too high for it to be ignored, especially as Allied invasion planning for D-Day included the same tactic of dropping the SAS behind enemy lines to disrupt supply lines. After the

Allied occupation of North Africa, German parachute and glider-borne units of ten to twelve men, usually in uniform, were inserted by night using a single Ju-52 or glider on sabotage missions. One team successfully carried out its mission and then evaded capture for 150 miles across the desert in its attempt to reach German lines. Fears were also stoked by the successful rescue of Mussolini in September 1943 by twelve gliders packed with paratroopers and SS commandos. By January 1944 Southern Command was warning of the possibility of raids by up to 800 men, within 10 miles of the coast.[31] It was assumed that the raiding parties would then attempt to escape back to the sea for extraction by E-boat or submarine. This fear increased in the lead-up to D-Day, as any interruption to the supply chain or kidnap of key figures could have proved disastrous. The initial responsibility for containing such raids lay with the Home Guard in order not to divert the attention of regular troops preparing for D-Day and an anti-raiding role was similarly included as the main operational duty for the Auxiliary Units in August 1943.[32]

For some, the raiding threat was paranoia and the Auxiliary Units Training Officer Nigel Oxenden viewed the preparations as another means of maintaining useful tension in the country.[33] Yet in 1944 there were repeated requests from German intelligence to their supposed agents in Britain (fortunately under MI5 control) to provide the location of Eisenhower's SHAEF headquarters. On 19 May 1944 Guy Liddell of MI5 noted that the Germans had asked double-agent 'Garbo' for information on the street addresses of other HQ which would be sent, as a priority, to the special forces Brandenburg Regiment.[34] In response, British Intelligence placed a priority on any information concerning the movement of *Fallschirmjäger* airborne units in France. In his anniversary broadcast to the Home Guard from the USA in May 1943 Churchill encouraged the Home Guard, saying that any German raiders who landed would find themselves not in the poultry-run or sheep-fold but 'in the lion's den at the Zoo'.[35] He ended by confirming that the Home Guard had to take on the greater part of the burden for home defence whilst the Allies planned to go on the offensive.

As part of the Home Guard response, the number of guards was increased at vulnerable points (key factories, airfields, dockyards, communications, sources of petrol, stores and dumps, etc.), code named 'VITGUARD'. The Home Guard units were required to provide a permanent night guard, and factory Home Guard units, in particular, found that production during the day was being affected by exhaustion. The numbers of men on guard had to be decreased, but they were backed up by 'Red Warning' troops on stand-by. The code word BOUNCER was the advance warning signal, with BUGBEAR issued when air-borne raids were expected. The Auxiliary Units would also abandon their hidden operational bases and act as reconnaissance patrols to other Home Guard units hunting down any raiders.

A secret reason for some of the Home Guard anti-raider exercises was that they were designed to train Allied special forces for the D-Day campaign, including the joint SOE/OSS Jedburgh teams. Exercises 'Curb' and 'Curb II', involving companies of three battalions of the Home Guard in Leicestershire in early and mid-May 1944, were officially designed to test the defences of vulnerable points against surprise night attacks by demolition teams but the enemy was a force of sixty officers and NCOs of an 'Allied Commando establishment' and the exercise would be preceded by two nights of supply drops from a single aircraft to the 'enemy'. It was stressed that no information on the opposition formation or their 'method of employment' was to be discussed outside the exercise and that if captured 'the refusal to discuss their work on the part of the German forces, will be due to their being security-minded and not to bad manners'.[36] They were actually members of the Jedburgh teams (small three-man SOE/OSS teams who were to parachute into occupied France after D-Day and liaise with the Resistance and advancing Allied armies) who were based at Milton Hall, near Peterborough. It was followed on a much larger scale by 'Exercise Lash' in the Charnwood Forest, which took place immediately before the D-Day landings and continued to 8 June. From the perspective of the Home Guard, this was claimed as necessary to test the mobile battle platoons in their support of vulnerable point guards and involved units of six battalions of the Home Guard against 300 Jedburgh trainees whose mission was to contact 'resistance groups' in the Charnwood Forest and direct attacks on railway communications and vulnerable points. It was their largest, and final, training exercise before dropping into France.[37]

Compulsory service meant that the Home Guard could reliably take on tasks that allowed regular troops to be relieved for service elsewhere, with large numbers of units in Home Forces transferred abroad or later into the 21st Army Group training for D-Day. Seemingly endless months of guarding vulnerable points and other duties were to follow. The major threat that many of the Home Guard now faced was one of boredom and exhaustion. Attempts to maintain interest led to increasingly complex training programmes and battle exercises. At the same time the strain of maintaining the war effort was telling on the wider labour force and there were demands for better coordination with the reorganized Civil Defence Service (which included the Air Raid Precautions and the Auxiliary Fire Service) to avoid dispute over priorities in allocating resources. This would have consequences for the integration of women in the Home Guard (*see* Chapter Nine). Civil Defence workers were encouraged to enrol in the Home Guard (their Civil Defence duties still having priority), whilst the Home Guard were ordered to assist in Civil Defence, including fire-watching – although it was on the strict understanding that their orders would come from Home Guard officers.[38] C Company of Edinburgh Home Guard, for one, thought that cooperation was a one-way affair and that the Home Guard had become a 'maid-of-all-work'.[39] The Earl of Elgin also complained about demarcation of Civil Defence jobs and as a solution suggested that the Home Guard might take the lead in the local Invasion Committees which had begun to be formed in October 1941 to improve local planning and coordination.[40] There was resistance to the military taking control prematurely and the role of the military representative was stressed as being advisory, to ensure that other services were kept informed as to the military plans against invasion. Whilst the military could request assistance, they had no power of compulsion until an area passed under martial law during an actual invasion.[41]

In December 1942 Viscount Bridgeman, Director-General of the Home Guard, warned of the difficulties in keeping up to 1.8 million men under a continuing obligation of 48 hours' drill per month and sentry duty on top of their everyday work, which was especially hard on those living on poor rations but whose everyday work was physically demanding, such as agricultural labourers, railwaymen, miners, dockers and those in heavy engineering. The health of the older officers also began to suffer through stress and long hours of completing administrative paperwork; many resigned due to ill-health. Leslie Owen worked in Crewe railway yard and on duty days he would work a full shift until 5.30pm, and then go on duty with the Home Guard from 10.00pm until 6.00am, then go straight to work until 2.00pm.[42] D-Day brought an additional strain for the twenty-six Home Guard transport columns that had been formed in 1942 to supplement the RASC in case of invasion, each with an RASC training officer and adjutant. Some 12,000 civilian vehicles had been reserved and 17,000 men enrolled for this contingency; they were partially mobilized after D-Day when the Home Guard took over some of the burden of the RASC in transporting troops and supplies across the country (the RASC transport columns having moved into Europe).[43] It is not surprising that a recurring theme in the 1942 compilation *Laugh with the Home Guard* was the Home Guard who passed in and out of his house, a stranger to his children.

> 'Who is that man in the photo on the piano, Mummy?'
> 'Why, dear, don't you know? That's Daddy before he joined the Home Guard.'
> 'Oh! I didn't know him in those clothes.'[44]

and

> **The H.G. Father**
> Small son: 'Mummy, who is that strange man in a soldier's uniform who rushes in and out and seems to know us?'[45]

As a measure of relief, in March 1943 Winston Churchill asked that commanders not impose any additional demands of exhausting exercises and that once men had reached a level of proficiency, to release them, especially if they were engaged in agriculture or industry, on the basis they could be easily recalled.[46]

Anti-Aircraft Duties

On 17 August 1940 one Home Guard platoon shot down a low-flying Dornier Do 17 bomber with 180 rounds of sustained P14 rifle fire.[47] It may have been a happy accident but by the end of 1940 many Home Guard were manning light AA guns mounted on the roofs of local factories; they were mainly Lewis guns but later included Marlin machine guns and 20mm Hispano cannon. Anti-Aircraft Command was under increasing pressure to deploy its troops overseas and began to consider extending the use of the Home Guard to assist in the anti-aircraft defences as early as January 1941. In September 1941 they began a trial in Liverpool to crew the new, secret, Z rocket batteries (Plate 23). These were batteries of sixty-four twin projectors, each firing a 3-inch unguided rocket, 6ft 4in long and carrying a 22lb warhead, which created a box barrage to a height of 19,000ft, through which the enemy aircraft would have to fly. However impressive to watch, they were inaccurate and expensive to operate; Anti-Aircraft Command was not impressed. Z batteries were, however, one of Churchill's pet projects and were deployed across the country, operated by the Home Guard with a small core of Royal Artillery personnel. A single battery demanded a huge amount of manpower: working in shifts, each battery required eight reliefs of 178 men per night, giving a total required commitment of 1,430 part-time Home Guard.[48] Not surprisingly, when the scheme was expanded in December 1941, the number of volunteers for this arduous, dangerous duty soon tailed off and the War Office resorted to an unpopular compulsory transfer from general service Home Guard battalions, or by direct recruitment from new members. From March 1942 units were reorganized as AA battalions and wore the formation badge of the parent AA division. In all, ninety-seven Z batteries were formed and in June 1942 they were integrated into the Royal Artillery structure and were given new county battalion numbers, commencing with 101. AA Command now had priority recruitment for all new members of the Home Guard with some officers trained as Plotting officers and even as Tactical Control officers. With resources under severe strain, on 28 November 1942 the War Cabinet approved a report of the Lord President of the Council recommending reducing the age of enrolment in the Home Guard to 16 so that boys of 16 to 19 could help man searchlight and anti-aircraft batteries on a part-time basis. There were already 180,000 boys under the age of 18, not in full-time education, in the Home Guard.[49] One reason for the problem was the existing shortfall in the recruitment of women ATS to full-time duties with AA Command where they performed all roles short of 'pulling the trigger', under the same restraints that prevented women in the Home Guard from taking up a full combat role. Logically, one answer to the labour crisis would have been to open up the Home Guard to women who could have performed similar duties on a part-time basis, but this was made impossible because of the government's on-going battle of trust with Edith Summerskill over giving women an official role in the Home Guard (*see* Chapter Nine).

The Z batteries were dirty weapons to operate. The gunners needed to be physically fit and have good eyesight, able to lift the heavy projectiles and set the sensitive fuses accurately. In July 1945 Brigadier B. Chichester Cooke, commander of 57 Anti-Aircraft Brigade, noted of the 12th Anti-Aircraft Home Guard Regiment who manned the Z batteries and guns defending Sheffield and South Yorkshire that they were 'operational troops of high quality'. In the spring and summer of 1944 men of the Sheffield rocket batteries were sent to London at weekends, to give much-needed relief to the local Home Guard AA battalions. Fifty-three officers and men earned decorations for their work, but the effectiveness of the Z batteries was open to question. A salvo from the rockets was an awe-inspiring sight and sound and they were, at the least, a morale booster for the general population, but local residents – who had to suffer a rain of rocket casings and shrapnel after a barrage – had more mixed feelings. At stand-down of the Shooters Hill Z battery in November 1944, the Mayor of Bexley Heath sent a message 'thank God you are standing down because you have caused more damage to property in Bexley Heath than the enemy has'.[50] From October 1942 the Home Guard also began manning 3.7-inch AA guns (each requiring a crew of eleven men), organized in twenty-seven Heavy Anti-Aircraft (HAA) batteries, but from 1943 the main threat from the Luftwaffe became the daylight 'tip and run' raids of fast, low-flying fighter-bombers. In response, Home Guard Light Anti-Aircraft Units began manning light, quick-firing guns, mainly 40mm Bofors guns, protecting factories and other key sites (Plate 24). The urgency of their work was such that they were authorized to attend for duty in civilian clothes with the old 1940 armband.

In January 1943 the divisional AA badges were replaced with the bow and arrow badge of the new Anti-Aircraft Command. The point of reference to the Home Guard could still be the early weeks of the 'broomstick army' and Edward Smith of the East London Home Guard, who became an anti-aircraft gunner whilst aged only 15, recalled how they were referred to as the 'bow and arrow squad of the pikestaff army'.[51] In April 1944 the Home Guard in AA Command, comprising ninety-three rocket batteries and twenty-seven HAA batteries, were organized into twenty-eight Home Guard AA regiments. There were also 274 Light Anti-Aircraft (LAA) troops. By stand-down in 1944 there were 141,198 Home Guard serving in Anti-Aircraft Command, making up around 50 per cent of the total strength of all AA batteries.[52] This alone freed the equivalent of almost eight infantry divisions for potential front-line service and General Pile openly admitted how much AA Command had come to rely on the Home Guard.[53] Not surprisingly, some Home Guard AA units, quite unofficially, took to wearing the Royal Artillery cap badge.

Coastal Artillery

The number of coastal artillery batteries doubled during 1940 to protect possible landing sites and harbours, engage German surface craft and provide covering fire for offshore naval inspection parties. Once the immediate invasion threat was over, General Alan Brooke sought to replace gun crews with Home Guard as part of his policy of transferring as many regular troops as possible from static defence positions into the field army. He particularly wanted to use the Royal Artillery troops to form additional armoured units.[54] From December 1941 the Home Guard began training to take over coastal defence duties.[55] At first they served as ammunition handlers but their parent Home Guard units had the first priority for the issue of field guns and by August 1944 some batteries on the east and south coasts were entirely manned by the Home Guard, typically working on a rota of one night's duty per week.[56] It was another area of demanding and arduous work, employed on a variety of 4-inch and 6-inch guns, French 138mm and 75mm guns, and 6-pdr guns. Apart from gunnery, they required training in range-finding, telephony, searchlight operation and the battery observation post. The men were also responsible for the area defence of the batteries against the threat of enemy raids. The training was not without its cost. On 11 August 1944 at Corbyn Head, Torbay, during a live fire exercise on a 4.7-inch gun, a 50lb shell exploded before the breech mechanism was properly locked and five Home Guardsmen and a Royal Artillery RSM were killed. It was the result of a known fault with the Japanese-made First World War vintage gun, and naval staff at the inquiry appeared pleased that it had happened on land as previous incidents with this weapon on merchant ships at sea meant that the fragments had been lost.[57] One of the few Home Guard memorials now stands on the site of the accident.

During the run-up to D-Day, German sea and air raids intensified to try to gain intelligence and disrupt the Allied preparations for D-Day. In May 1944 radar picked up a German E-boat force off the coast of Cornwall at Falmouth. Home Guard gunners on the 6-inch batteries at Pendennis Castle engaged the enemy and drove off the E-boats. A new challenge came with the efforts to try to shoot down the V1 rockets over the coast, but with only limited success until the introduction of radar-assisted gun-laying in August as part of the 'Diver' network of anti-aircraft guns. By November 1944 some 7,000 Home Guard were serving in coastal artillery, representing almost 50 per cent of its strength.[58] They were entitled to wear the formation badge of the regular RA unit with which they served and, unlike the AA units, were officially permitted to wear the Royal Artillery cap badge.

Morale-boosting

As the country became increasingly war weary, the Home Guard was used to bolster the morale of the general population (even as its own morale was suffering) by parades and demonstrations as part of the various fund-raising and 'Holiday at Home' entertainments. ('Holiday at Home' was an initiative in 1943 to try to persuade the population not to clog up the roads and public transport needed by the army.) Events were held in most towns and whilst it was politically useful, many in the Home Guard became frustrated by such community work, especially those who had been conscripted into the organization or otherwise resented yet more intrusions into their limited free time. The format for the performances was fairly standard. One example featured the Birmingham battalions of the Home Guard as part of a 'Wings for Victory' event at King's Heath in 1943. The show opened with a display of signalling techniques followed by a motorcycle display by the Dispatch Riders, then a demonstration of unarmed combat. A comic interlude showed the 'trials and troubles' of the LDV, contrasted with a display of current, slickly performed, ceremonial drill, designed to emphasize the professionalism of the contemporary Home Guard. There was then a demonstration of battle drill (a platoon flanking attack) with the finale being the blowing up of a minefield.[59] Other popular entertainments included demonstrations of the 2-pdr anti-tank guns (Plate 21) or the Blacker Bombard on a mobile mount. The comic comparison of the poorly equipped LDV of 1940 with the current Home Guard was *de rigueur* at such events and has contributed to the collective memory of the early period Home Guard.

Figure 1. Total strength of the Home Guard in September 1944.

General Service	1,567,219
Anti-Aircraft Artillery	141,676
Coastal Artillery	7,000
Bomb Disposal	7,000
Auxiliary Units	4,200
Women's Home Guard Auxiliaries	30,696
TOTAL	1,757,791

The end of over four years' hard slog came with a sudden radio announcement on 6 September 1944 by Sir James Grigg that compulsory duty in the Home Guard would cease, taking almost immediate effect, on 11 September.[60] At the time, the total strength of the Home Guard stood at 1,757,791, including over 30,000 Women's Home Guard Auxiliaries (Fig. 1). The manning of AA batteries on a voluntary basis did, however, continue. Stand-down was on 3 December 1944 and was marked by parades across the country, although the Home Guard remained as an inactive reserve until 31 December 1945.

Chapter Four

The Secret Home Guard

At the same time as the force of 1.8 million Home Guard were being mobilized in a very public show of determination to resist invasion, smaller Home Guard units were being recruited in secret for more specialized roles.

Industrial Sabotage Teams

In 1940 MI5 and the Secret Intelligence Service (SIS *aka* MI6) surveyed key industrial assets for the risk of sabotage and all factories were obliged to submit a plan for how they would deal with an imminent threat of takeover by the enemy. Home Guard battalion commanders were also given a secret list of key factories. The intention was not to destroy the assets but to disable them by removing vital pieces of equipment and hiding them until the territory could be recovered. As part of this planning, individual 'key holders'/'key personnel' and special teams of Home Guard were created to conduct industrial sabotage in factories and petrol stations about to fall into enemy hands. Such work was especially important regarding fuel supplies. In France German tanks had filled up at local petrol pumps because no one had given the order to destroy them. But equally, if there were to be a successful counter-attack, British vehicles would need continued access to fuel, so simply destroying fuel stocks was a poor option. General instructions were issued to garage owners to remove pump handles each night and be ready to spoil their petrol supplies if absolutely unavoidable.[1] Home Guard 'Pump Destruction Squads' were also ready to dismantle and hide key parts of machinery at the point when the Nazis were about to overrun an area. Only the members of the team would know the location of the hiding places, and they would then be responsible for refitting the vital parts if enemy occupation was thwarted. At the motor servicing company Harold Goodwin & Company Ltd in Warley, Worcestershire, which was then working for the Ministry of Aircraft Production, there was a sabotage team of three Home Guard workers responsible for immobilizing the vehicles and battery charging equipment, hiding vital parts and denying access to vital spares and tyres.[2] At the Air Defence Research and Development Establishment in Christchurch careful plans were made to carry out sabotage at the last possible moment, leaving no material or plant in operation at the establishment which could be used by the enemy. The plans included destruction or removal of essential mechanisms to a hiding place; removal or destruction of war materials that the enemy might use; concealment of valuable records or destruction of them if copies were available elsewhere; cutting off gas and electricity supplies; immobilizing transport; ensuring that any stocks of fuel did not fall into enemy hands; and removing or concealing any currency.[3]

The identity of the saboteurs was a closely guarded secret and the lengths that the Gestapo would go to in order to identify the members of such sabotage teams and their families can only be imagined. Even today, very little is known of this vitally important secret role of the Home Guard.

XII Corps Observation Unit[4]

Just eleven days after the foundation of the LDV, with the government still floundering over its purpose, Colonel Joe Holland, head of MI(R), a small research unit of the War Office developing a para-military methodology of irregular warfare, was already exploring ways of using some LDV as official guerrillas to fight behind enemy lines. To develop this, on 25 May MI(R) officer Captain Peter Fleming, a well-known author and adventurer, was attached to Home Forces 'for the purpose of training LDVs etc in fighting behind the German lines in case of invasion of this country'.[5] Fleming did not, however, have a mechanism with which to implement his ideas. That came with the independent initiative of General Thorne, commander of XII Corps (responsible for the defence of Kent and Sussex). His XII Corps Observation Unit became the blueprint for the later GHQ Auxiliary Units. Thorne needed to find ways of strengthening his command and created army 'Battle Patrols' of twelve men in each battalion (twenty in all) ready to fight as small units of guerrillas behind enemy lines and slow down the enemy advance, cutting off German supply lines to the sea and giving more time for a counter-attack. It was not a purely defensive strategy as the Battle Patrols were also to disrupt any retreat to the sea and so ensure the enemy's complete annihilation. The XII Corps Observation Unit was operational from early June with Peter Fleming soon appointed to command and develop it. In the MI(R) diary for 17 June is the entry:

> Colonel Gubbins to be in charge of 'Auxiliary Units' for Home Defence, with Major Wilkinson as a G2. Much the same methods as Captain Fleming is using in Kent with his little headquarters.[6]

Upon his arrival, Fleming supplemented the army Battle Patrols with LDV patrols and brought down a detachment of Lovat Scouts as the core of a training unit. Fleming was armed with a letter of authority from the general commanding Tunbridge Wells Home Guard to choose whatever men he needed 'which may necessitate their going with Captain Fleming or his subordinates in the event of an emergency'.[7] He also introduced the use of underground hides to protect the patrols whilst the enemy swept across their area, and thereby try to extend the life of the guerrillas for as long as possible. General Thorne visited a hide and was delighted: descending a rope ladder he found some Lovat Scouts and half a dozen Home Guard sitting on barrels of explosives.[8] The most spectacular hide was dug into the bottom of the 'Airship Hole' in King's Wood above The Garth, Bilting, in Kent. It became a command centre and redoubt, with food, water and sleeping accommodation for up to 120 people. The hides were linked to observation posts by field telephone and some were also linked by wireless to Corps HQ, meaning they could act as an integral part of the battle strategy of XII Corps, the patrols being capable of receiving intelligence and being retasked. Fleming described the respective roles of the army Battle Patrols and LDV patrols but was not hopeful about their survival:

> This [the Battle Patrols] was a nucleus to which in time we precariously linked a network of picked sub-units of the Home Guard, who would in theory – after fighting like lions in their normal role – withdraw to well-stocked hide-outs in the woods when their localities were overrun by the Germans. The whole scheme in its early stages was typical of the happy-go-lucky improvisation of those dangerous days, and though we gradually built it up into something fairly solid I doubt if we should have been more than a minor and probably short-lived nuisance to the invaders.[9]

The suicidal character of the concept imbues much of the thinking of the use of the Home Guard in 1940. It is curious that the LDV patrols were only expected to go to ground *after* having defended their allotted posts with their battalion. How many would have survived to join the Observation Unit is debatable and Fleming warned that their life expectancy would then be just 48 hours.[10] Although the XII Corps Observation Unit was absorbed into the Auxiliary Units in late 1940, it still retained its original title until its stand-down in 1944.

GHQ Auxiliary Units

At the same time as the LDV was being recruited into the XII Corps Observation Unit, some in the War Office became aware that Section D of SIS was creating a nationwide organization of civilian guerrilla cells and intelligence gatherers, known as the Home Defence Scheme (HDS) and commanded by Viscount Bearsted. It would operate during any invasion at a level above the existing top secret deep-cover resistance organization known as Section VII, which would only begin to operate after enemy occupation.[11] The War Office was horror-struck at the idea of an SIS private army of *francs-tireur* fighting on the same ground as the army but outside its control, and made the most of the embarrassment caused by a small number of security breaches in the distribution of HDS arms dumps. However, the War Office had little idea of how any military alternative would operate. The initial proposal for what became the GHQ Auxiliary Units, with the LDV/ Home Guard at their core, came from Joe Holland, who had been monitoring Fleming's efforts in the XII Corps Observation Unit, and briefed the Chief of the Imperial General Staff (General Sir John Dill), and C-in-C Home Forces (General Ironside). They in turn took the broad idea to Churchill and the War Cabinet for approval on 17 June. It was an agreement in principle for the development of LDV commando teams:

> Steps were also being taken to organize sections of Storm Troopers on a full-time basis, as part of the LDVs. Tough and determined characters would be selected. Some of these would be armed with 'Tommy' guns.[12]

The secrecy surrounding the Home Defence Scheme was tight enough that it was not until 22 June that a dismayed Major General Macdougall (Deputy Chief of the Imperial General Staff) discovered its existence and raised his concerns with Major General 'Pug' Ismay, Secretary to the Chiefs of Staff Committee. He wanted the HDS to be taken under military control but this did not stop him suggesting that SIS should fund the new Auxiliary Units!

> My Dear Pug,
> Regarding the question of para-military activities in this country in the event of the enemy gaining a footing, the CIGS has decided that an organization is to be set up under Brigadier Gubbins to undertake this task. The organization will be directly under the Commander-in-Chief, Home Forces.
>
> I now find that Lord Bearsted works under 'D' Section, and has also been charged with a similar role.
>
> There is thus obviously great danger not only of over-lapping but more important, of considerable confusion arising as both organizations will be working in the same areas and also seeking recruits among the same personnel ... I hope you will agree that only one organization is, not only required, but advisable and that this must be under military authority and accountable for their progress and actions to a military Commander ... A small amount of money will be required to start with, say £1,000 a month. I believe Lord Bearsted draws his funds from SIS and it would appear to be the easiest way if Gubbins could be authorized to do the same.[13]

The absence of a defined plan for the Auxiliary Units follows the pattern of indecision and confusion surrounding the formation of the LDV. Typically entranced by the romance of irregular warfare, Churchill took a personal interest in the development of the Auxiliary Units in their first few months but, following his doubts as to the likelihood of invasion, then lost interest and said that he no longer needed to see monthly progress reports. Two days after the Cabinet meeting, Colonel Colin Gubbins, who had only returned on 10 June from commanding the Independent Companies (prototypes of the Commando units) in Norway, was in place as commanding officer of the Auxiliary Units but was wracking his brain as to how to implement his vague orders, going through three concepts before mid-August. First there was a matter of basic principle. Peter Wilkinson, Gubbins' deputy, recalled the 'slight muddle' in thinking 'because nobody could quite make up their minds whether we were trying to set up something for immediate action against the Germans in the event of an invasion. Or, whether we were trying also to set up a nucleus of an English secret ... a British Secret Army'. Wilkinson, formerly attached to Section D from MI(R), favoured the development of a long-term, civilian resistance organization but he believed that Gubbins wavered half-way between the two opposing views. It was beyond the remit of the War Office to prepare for resistance following an enemy occupation (this being the task of SIS) and so Gubbins was obliged to follow their desire for a short-term, uniformed body.[14] From the outset, therefore, there was a rejection of the idea that the Auxiliary Units would become a resistance organization.[15]

At first, influenced by the essentially advisory role of MI(R) and the general brief of the LDV, Gubbins envisaged the Auxiliary Units' Intelligence Officers (IOs) as acting only as advisers to local commanders of the LDV, with the latter then forming their own small covert units which could extend the harrying function of the LDV. Despite Macdougall's views, both Gubbins and General Beaumont-Nesbitt, the Director of Military Intelligence, believed the remit of the new Auxiliary Units was sufficiently distinct as a military force that it could still work alongside the saboteurs of the civilian HDS.[16] The Auxiliary Units began to recruit on behalf of the LDV in early July, and on 5 July Gubbins sent out a letter to LDV Area Commanders to advise them of the intention for the new teams:

> Their role will be to take action against the flanks and rear of such forces as may obtain a temporary footing in this country ... The personnel will consist of existing LDV volunteers and others who will be enrolled therein for the purpose.[17]

Gubbins was clearly intending to hand over responsibility for the teams to local LDV commanders and concluded that 'The raising of these special sub-units will be decided between the local military commander and the LDV commander.' The responsibility of the Auxiliary Units' Intelligence Officer was merely to act as an adviser 'in the closest touch with the military commander and the LDV commander so as to assist in every possible way the selection, training and organization of these sub-units, and the provision and storage of equipment'.[18] Gubbins also warned LDV commanders that 'The present situation obviously necessitates speed at the expense of security, but at the same time it is important that, whatever else be known generally, the names of the operatives, the existence of dumps of stores, their location, etc., should be kept as secret as possible.'[19] Gubbins' letter was subsequently used as licence by some Home Guard commanders to claim that the later Auxiliary Units' operational patrols should come directly under their command.[20] The War Office stressed that a prerequisite of membership of the new Auxiliary Units was enrolment in the LDV/Home Guard to maintain the legality of the organization and Lieutenant General Bernard Paget, at the time Chief of Staff, Home Forces argued:

> These men, being members of the Home Guard, will of course fight in uniform ... being a uniformed and properly organized body, its members are in no way violating 'international law' even if fighting behind the advanced elements of the invading forces, where units of regular troops will also be fighting ...[21]

The purely advisory model lasted not much more than a week after Gubbins' letter to the LDV commanders. More in keeping with Gubbins' ambitious nature, the next iteration was for the Auxiliary Units to form their own 'village cells' from the LDV which would, in an extension of the LDV's guiding role, secretly guide army commandos through their territory and also undertake their own limited sabotage missions. Local organization would be undertaken directly by the Intelligence Officers, each responsible for an operational area, the first eight appointees meeting in Whitehall on 13 July. By the end of 1940 there were at least fifteen Intelligence Officers, spread over England and Wales. Gubbins produced a briefing note for the Intelligence Officers on 17 July summarizing the new strategy which relied heavily on the methodology of the HDS, and one of his first points was that because of the imminent risk of invasion 'decentralisation therefore is initially forced upon us. If time allows, organization, and hence control of these cells, can be more and more centralized; eventually larger units can be formed'. These 'larger units' were Gubbins' concept of Home Guard commando units and were to morph into the later Auxiliary Units group system.[22] The Intelligence Officers were to recruit 'key men', who would recruit the remaining members of their cells, and then train and supply them. Explosives would be supplied for small acts of sabotage – attacks on vehicles, dumps, sentry posts, HQs, signal communication, etc. The cells would act during the period when the invading forces were advancing through any bridgeheads and it was therefore stressed that as many cells as possible needed to be formed in the shortest possible time. Some Intelligence Officers went on to form fifteen cells in a week.[23] After recruiting the village cells, the next priority of the Intelligence Officers was to lay down large weapons dumps ready for army commando units to use behind enemy lines and to ensure coordination between the commandos and the village cells. Gubbins' plan was an attempt to fuse the community-based secret sabotage cells of the HDS with the Independent Company commandos that Gubbins had recently led in Norway but it was quickly realized that there were not the resources to create such units for home defence.

As Gubbins struggled to find a clear direction and methodology, there remained a necessary overlap with the HDS whose operational and intelligence wings continued to operate alongside, and to support, the new Auxiliary Units. Only in late July was it formally agreed that the Auxiliary Units should absorb the sabotage teams of the HDS into their military structure because 'the risk of reprisals incurred by allowing civilians to engage in sabotage activities was too great'.[24] The intelligence wing of the HDS would retain more of an independent character, with continuing SIS influence, as the Special Duties Branch of the Auxiliary Units but this had no link to the Operational Patrols or to the Home Guard (and is consequently beyond the scope of the present book). Colonel Laurence Grand, Head of Section D, recognized the fundamental change in policy:

> as far as civilian obstruction was concerned, the organization on which D officers had been forming was no longer necessary, and its place could now be taken by Auxiliary Units working openly and using as recruits uniformed LDVs.[25]

Although ready to sacrifice the HDS as a short-term guerrilla force in favour of the Auxiliary Units, in deepest secrecy SIS continued to maintain its civilian resistance organization (Section VII).[26] The early Auxiliary Units' sabotage teams continued to rely heavily on Section D for supplies and by 25 August the latter's Technical Section at Aston House had supplied 7,200lb of plastic explosives, 7,470lb of gelignite, 4,000 SIP grenades, 36,020 detonators and 67,400 time pencils to the Auxiliary Units. It also supplied 200 copies of its *Brown Book* manual on the use of explosives in what became the first training manual for the Auxiliary Units.[27] Section D organized some of the first training for the Auxiliary Units' Intelligence Officers at Aston House, and some of the HDS personnel, already trained in making home-made explosives, joined the Home Guard and became local commanders of the Auxiliary Units – although none ever subsequently spoke of their service with SIS.[28] Nigel Oxenden, Intelligence Officer for Norfolk during 1940 and later the Training Officer and official historian of the Auxiliary Units, acknowledged:

> most IOs were assisted by introductions to one or two men who had already been chosen by MI5 [*sic* – Section D] and equipped with bottles of sulphuric acid and little capsules of potassium chlorate and sugar, with which to make a crude and unreliable delay incendiary out of a bottle of petrol. These were generally outstanding individuals, who eventually became group commanders. Meanwhile their local knowledge made them invaluable in finding the right recruits.[29]

It was not until 15 August that the methodology of the Operational Branch of the Auxiliary Units was again changed to create what might be regarded as their classic form. Borrowing from the model of Fleming's XII Corps Observation Unit, patrols of six to eight men under a sergeant were formed from the Home Guard with their base of operations being a secret underground 'hide-out' (as Gubbins first called them), later known as 'Operational Bases' (Fig. 2 and Plate 9). Usually built by teams of Royal Engineers, they were designed to extend the operating lifespan of the patrols beyond that expected of the general Home Guard.[30] The hides were essentially buried 'elephant shelters' made from corrugated iron hoops, with entry down a shaft protected by a carefully camouflaged trapdoor. They contained bunk beds for the patrol and supplies for up to a month, together with stores of weapons and explosives, and were usually connected to a hidden observation post up to half a mile away, linked by a field telephone which allowed warning of any approaching enemy. There was also an escape tunnel for emergencies. They did not, however, have wireless communication, leaving them isolated once they had 'gone to ground'. The patrols were managed and equipped through the Intelligence Officers from a new administrative HQ and training base in the stable block of Coleshill House, Highworth, Wiltshire (Plate 8). In Scotland Melville House in Fife was used as the main training base.

The Auxiliary Units had a more pronounced Home Guard character than the XII Corps Observation Unit because it proved more difficult to establish an equivalent of the XII Corps army Battle Patrols to work alongside the Home Guard operational patrols. Gubbins was not in the position of General Thorne,

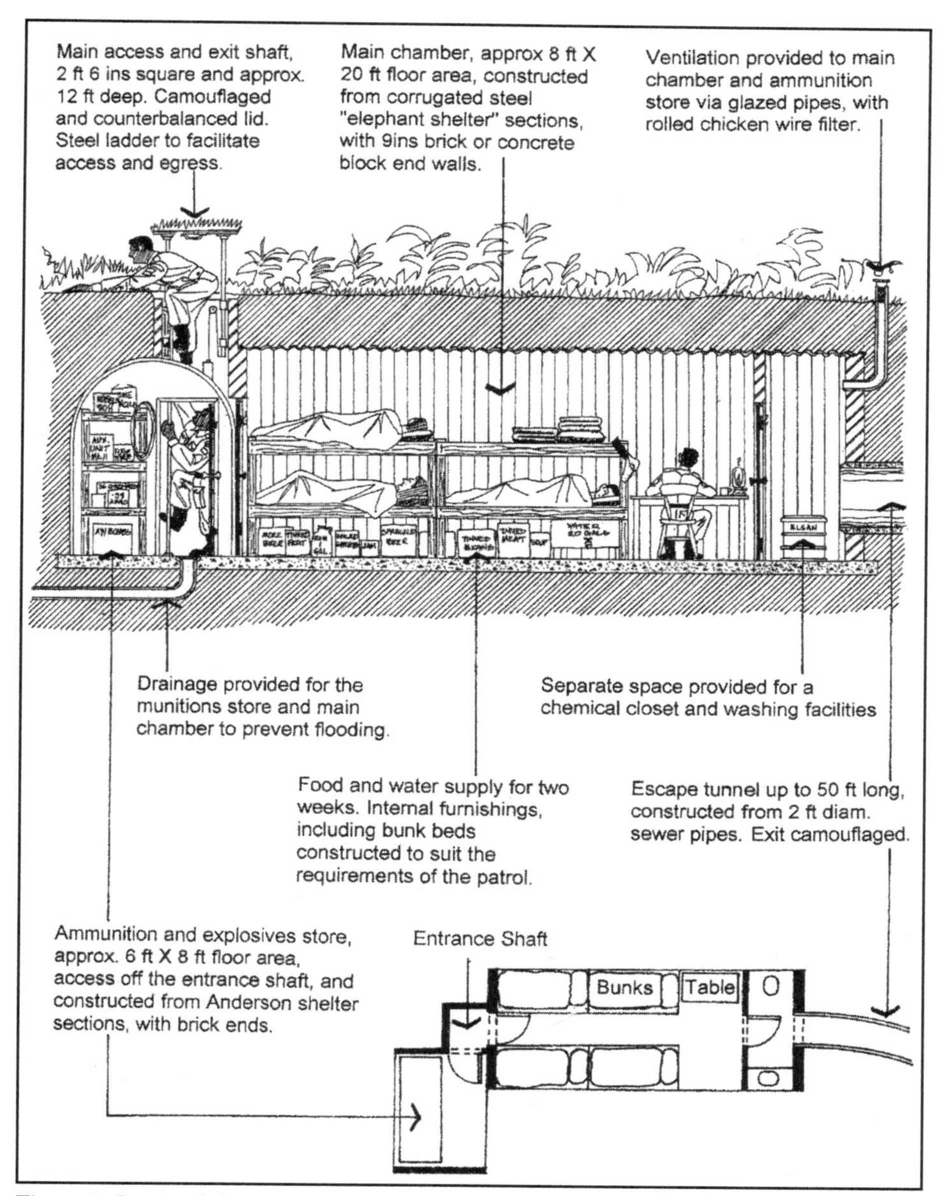
Main access and exit shaft, 2 ft 6 ins square and approx. 12 ft deep. Camouflaged and counterbalanced lid. Steel ladder to facilitate access and egress.
Main chamber, approx 8 ft X 20 ft floor area, constructed from corrugated steel "elephant shelter" sections, with 9ins brick or concrete block end walls.
Ventilation provided to main chamber and ammunition store via glazed pipes, with rolled chicken wire filter.
Drainage provided for the munitions store and main chamber to prevent flooding.
Separate space provided for a chemical closet and washing facilities
Food and water supply for two weeks. Internal furnishings, including bunk beds constructed to suit the requirements of the patrol.
Escape tunnel up to 50 ft long, constructed from 2 ft diam. sewer pipes. Exit camouflaged.
Ammunition and explosives store, approx. 6 ft X 8 ft floor area, access off the entrance shaft, and constructed from Anderson shelter sections, with brick ends.
Entrance Shaft
Bunks
Table

Figure 2. Sectional drawing of a reconstructed Auxiliary Units Operational Base. (*Mick Wilks*)

who had been able to order the regiments under his command to cooperate, and the Auxiliary Units Scout Sections were not introduced until November, and then only by taking soldiers from reserve units and depots rather than from front-line service.[31] Two Scout Sections were then allocated to each Intelligence Officer, each one consisting of twelve soldiers including an officer and often a

Royal Engineers sapper.[32] They did not have any specialist training in irregular warfare, and their own training therefore was initially just one step ahead of the Home Guard Patrols that they were expected to train. They were more heavily armed than the Home Guard Patrols, and did have wireless communication, allowing them to be more-easily retasked after having 'gone to ground'. At the height of the organization, there may have been up to fifty Scout Sections but by September 1942 reductions were already being considered as demands on front-line troops increased across the war fronts.[33] This marks the point at which the Auxiliary Units were effectively deemed to have fulfilled their purpose. By January 1943 there were just eight Scout Sections and the last were withdrawn in late 1943.

By September 1940 there were 371 Home Guard patrols in the Operational Branch of the Auxiliary Units (Fig. 3). It was not a national organization but was first established in the coastal counties of the south-west and along the south and east coasts of England and South Wales (the likely invasion areas), plus the two anomalous inland counties of Herefordshire and Worcestershire where the Auxiliary Units were part of the strategy for protecting the Midlands from attack up the Severn Valley or from Ireland (Fig. 4). The Auxiliary Units' Intelligence Officers in Herefordshire and Worcestershire are believed to have been those deputed by Section D of SIS and still linked to the known SIS resistance organization in the Midlands and north-west. In August 1941 there was a considerable expansion of the Auxiliary Units in northern England and around the coast of Scotland (Fig. 3). General Thorne had been appointed GOC Scotland in May 1941 and saw the Auxiliary Units as a natural means of improving the defences of the country, with its long coastline, at minimal cost, reflecting concerns of a possible invasion via Norway.

The Operational Branch was to act as part of the military campaign following any invasion. Rather than the 'last ditch' defence of modern myth, it was part of a multi-faceted strategy to delay the enemy advance and cut enemy supply lines ready for the field army to counter-attack. As such, it was a covert extension of the Home Guard's wider role to protect nodal points, attacking pre-determined targets on the flanks and rear of an advancing enemy and focusing on communication assets such as railways and airfields. Unfortunately, the absence of wireless communication with higher command meant that it was impossible to maintain

Figure 3. Total of Auxiliary Units Operational Patrols, September 1940.

County	Patrols	County	Patrols
Caithness and Sutherland	20	Sussex	11
East Highlands and Aberdeen	35	Isle of Wight	13
East Riding	37	East Hampshire	13
Lincolnshire	23	Dorset and West Hampshire	40
Norfolk	23	Somerset	40
Suffolk and Essex	42	Devon and Cornwall	34
Kent	25	South Wales	15

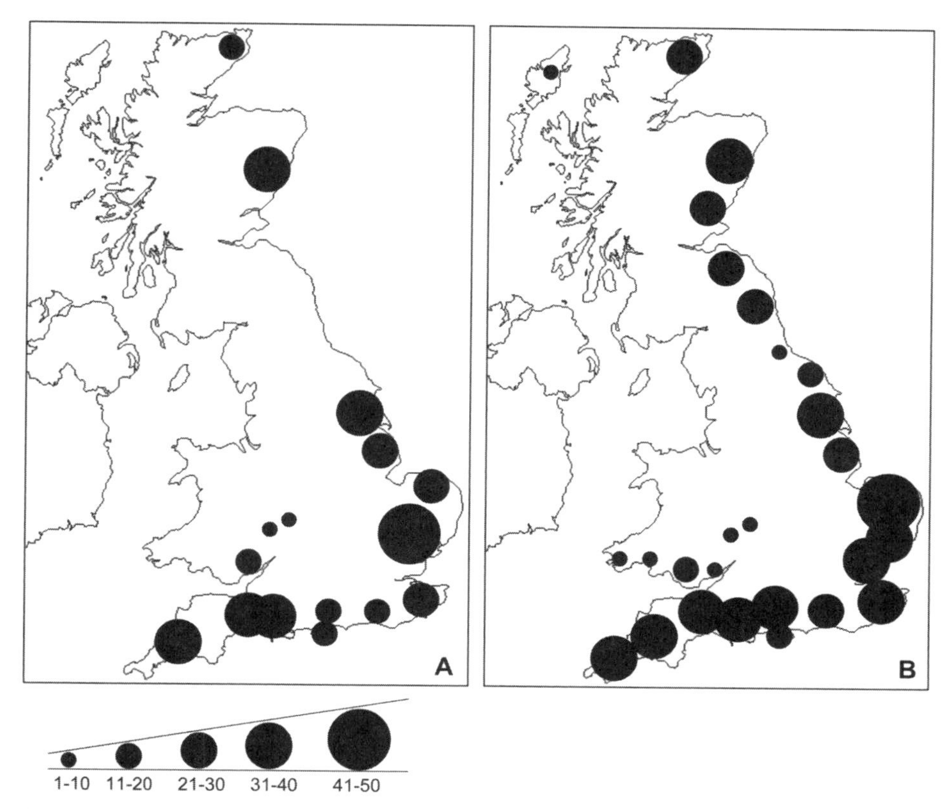

Figure 4. Distribution of Auxiliary Units Operational Patrols by counties in September 1940 (a) and June 1944 (b). *(TNA CAB 120/241; after Atkin 2015, fig. 8)*

operational control once the patrols had 'gone to ground', relying instead on personal initiative to attack opportunist targets such as new enemy fuel dumps and, in the words of Geoffrey Morgan-Jones of Adam Patrol in Herefordshire, to be a 'bloody nuisance' to the Germans.[34] By 1943 this would bring the Auxiliary Units into conflict with wider War Office instructions over uncontrolled guerrilla warfare (*see above*, p. 44). Training Officer Nigel Oxenden was brutally honest in his assessment of their strategic effectiveness, describing the patrol members as 'guided by a flow of directives that often proved impractical . . . It was somehow assumed that observers would obtain priceless information on targets which no other service had been able to find.'[35] In fact, Oxenden believed that it took two years to arrive at a suitable methodology for using observers to scout out targets.[36] By this time, the likelihood of having to use these skills had passed.

The principal tool of the Auxiliary Units were packs of explosives, primed with the new plastic explosive and fitted with a variety of time delays to allow time to escape. Oxenden complained that they were supplied with an increasing range of booby trap devices and weapons which, in his opinion, only encumbered the patrols and produced a 'mental fog'.[37] Peter Fleming was scathing about what he later saw as the romanticism of Gubbins and his staff 'for whom an enemy is hardly worth killing unless he can be killed with a tarantula fired from an airgun by a Bessarabian undertaker on Walpurgis night'.[38] The aim was to complete their mission without using any firepower which would draw enemy attention. The legend of their special status as regards armament rests largely on the 100 per cent allocation of pistols (typically a .38 calibre US revolver or a .32 automatic) which had been completed by September 1940, although Oxenden maintains that the ammunition followed much later.[39] They also had a sheath knife, later replaced by the Fairbairn Sykes fighting knife, for silent attack and studded, lead-weighted wooden truncheons or rubber coshes. Each patrol had a support weapon, initially the cumbersome BAR automatic rifle and later the Thompson sub-machine gun or Sten gun. Contrary to popular myth, they were not the first British troops to receive the Thompson and not even necessarily the first in the Home Guard, which began to receive it from March 1941.[40] The training notes for March 1941 only mention the BAR, suggesting the Thompson had not yet been issued to the Auxiliary Units in any number. It is, however, included in the August 1941 training timetable.[41] The patrols also retained two standard Home Guard M1917 rifles but 'nobody knew quite why' as, although extremely accurate, they were heavy and awkward to carry on patrol.[42] SIP Grenades (*aka* AW Bomb, *see* p. 98) were supplied from 10 September 1940, although they had been supplied to the rest of the Home Guard from mid-July.[43]

Each patrol was later issued with a silenced .22 rifle, some fitted with telescopic sights. This was not included in the 1941 list of weapons to be carried as standard on operations and, although there were some early issues of .22 rifles, the contract with Parker Hale for 660 silencers for the Home Guard (assumed to be the Auxiliary Units) is only from March 1942.[44] This matches the diary entry of Patrol Leader Bill Webber from Firle Patrol, Sussex, as receiving his silenced .22 rifle on 30 April 1942.[45] Oxenden identifies them as 'at first for the sniping of enemy sentries, and to fill the larder'.[46] They do appear in the SOE weapons inventory as a possible sniping weapon but they were of limited effectiveness, and for the Auxiliary Units they were only generally introduced after the main threat of action had passed. The possession of a silenced weapon did, however, provide a cachet to the organization at a time when morale was beginning to slip. The .22 rifles were too underpowered to guarantee a silent kill, especially as most operations were at night. They had an accurate range of only 100m but, being of such small calibre, they required not only a head shot but a careful aim to the eye socket to ensure a quiet kill. Lampe's extravagant claim that they were capable of killing a man a mile away is a misinterpretation of the standard warning on packs of .22 ammunition as being 'dangerous to 1 mile' as representing its maximum flight distance.[47] The Auxiliary Units' armourers also complained that the telescopic sights frequently drifted out of alignment and needed professional realignment. They would have been most useful operationally against guard dogs but were mainly used throughout the war in shooting 'for the pot'. The need for a silenced weapon would eventually be met by a proposal to issue .32 Welrod silenced pistols to the Auxiliary Units as their only firearm.[48]

The silenced .22 rifles have become part of the mystique of the Auxiliary Units as assassination weapons to kill suspected collaborators or those who knew the location of their operational bases, even though the rifles were not generally introduced until the main threat of invasion was effectively over. Oxenden makes no mention of an assassination role in his 1944 draft history of the Auxiliary Units but some patrol members reported being given sealed lists of suspected collaborators or security risks to eradicate upon invasion, which may have arisen out of a local assumption of what they should do to protect their security, or was stimulated by a fit of pique in the War Office when MI5 refused to detain many suspected collaborators, preferring to keep them under surveillance.[49] The role has been greatly exaggerated for dramatic effect, with some Auxiliary Units personnel maintaining that they were ready to execute men such as the local Chief Constable simply because he knew their identities. At the time, the head of any city police force was ranked as a Chief Constable and police checks on prospective Auxiliers were carried out via requests from Home Guard battalion COs – who therefore also knew the names of the recruits. Any such programme of assassination would have severely disrupted the local civil and military establishment and was likely to have created widespread panic over presumed fifth column activities. More significant a risk would have been anyone who knew the location of the Operational Bases; when a patrol member asked to resign from Jehu (Alfrick) Patrol in Worcestershire because of stress, the Intelligence Officer politely shook his hand and wished him well – but then told the patrol sergeant that he would have to be killed if the invasion occurred.[50] Fortunately, when Scottish Auxiliary Units received a mistaken warning of invasion and went to ground, there was no murder of the local population. In fact, the Auxiliers would have been shocked to discover just how far their secret had been spread.

If the assassination role became part of the bravado of the Auxiliary Units, there was an official incitement to commit acts of terrorism which would have had profound consequences. Jim Caws, an Auxilier from the Isle of Wight, explained how they were taught to deal with fifth columnists: 'We could either sort of tear them to bits to start with or shoot them first and then tear them to bits ... The purpose of that, I presume, was that if someone was helping the Germans and you could catch up with them we would make a mess of them and leave them on the side of the road to deter other people from doing it.'[51] In Worcestershire the men were taught the techniques of evisceration by a local butcher (who became an instructor at Coleshill), to be used against German sentries in order to unsettle their comrades.[52] In Herefordshire John Thornton similarly remembers 'After killing the enemy we were told by Todd to cut their "knackers" off to demoralize the rest.'[53] A local bloodbath would surely have ensued, not least because the Auxiliers wore Home Guard uniform and the SS were not likely to have been too concerned to discriminate in apportioning the blame. Such tactics had been recommended abroad by Section D of SIS from as early as March 1939 but Mike Calvert (XII Corps Observation Unit, later a commander of the Chindits and the

SAS Brigade) believed this was also a deliberate part of the British government's anti-invasion strategy as widespread reprisals on the civilian population would have hardened the British resolve and might have shocked the Americans into joining the battle.[54] His view is supported by Churchill's comments of 12 July 1940 on the morality of allowing civilians to attack German soldiers 'with scythes and brickbats'. Colville reported that 'W[inston] is sufficiently ruthless to point out that in war quarter is given, not on grounds of compassion but in order to discourage the enemy from fighting to the bitter end. But here we want every citizen to fight desperately and they will do so the more if they know the alternative is massacre.'[55]

Training was an urgent priority but initially there was no structure for its delivery. Wilkinson recounts how he was in the first London office at 7 Whitehall Place from 8.30am to 5.00pm and was then driven out to meet a patrol; he would give a lecture or instruct on a night exercise, finishing around midnight, and he would sleep in the car and then be back in the office again at 8.30am.[56] In early August Gubbins managed to beg a small temporary training staff from Southern Command. Brigadier Richie of HQ Southern Command duly asked for help for this from 3rd Division:

> There exists an organization, in reality a part of the H.G.s, [Home Guard] which works under one Brigadier GUBBINS and whose role is highly secret ... The Chief is most anxious to help GUBBINS' show by getting hold of five good young officers, one for each of our areas, to train this personnel in intensive scouting and battle patrol training.[57]

The 3rd Division consequently provided five training officers, mainly from the Guards Brigade. Further support was provided from 20 August by the tank hunting platoons of the 1st and 2nd Battalions, Grenadier Guards, but these were all regular army troops with no experience in irregular warfare.[58] It is, therefore, no surprise to find Scottish Intelligence Officer Eustace Maxwell believing the training provided at the Osterley Home Guard Training School (where the Guards tank hunting platoons may have received instruction) as being better than that provided for the Auxiliary Units.[59] From 22 August the new HQ in the stables of Coleshill House, Highworth, Wiltshire, began to build up its own training establishment of instructors in patrolling, explosives and unarmed combat, providing weekend courses for patrol leaders (Plate 8). The debt owed to Osterley is clear. When the army Scout Patrols were introduced from November, part of their role was to provide local training (so avoiding the trips to Coleshill); first, however, they themselves had to be trained in the techniques of irregular warfare, drawn as they were from ordinary regimental depots, and this caused additional delays. The progress report to 1 September 1940 gives a summary of the standard of training achieved during the period when they were most likely to have had to go into action against an invasion:

> By the 1st September all members of the Home Guard enrolled have had preliminary instruction in the use of the special weapons. At least 50%, in

> some areas 90%, of them have had practical experience in using High Explosive, in pistol firing and dummy Mills Bomb throwing. 70% of the patrols have had training in field stalking and at least 50% have carried out two or more night schemes.[60]

The level of training for the 2,300 Auxiliers was therefore by no means complete or in any depth. During the same period 4,000 members of the Home Guard attended an intensive weekend course in explosives handling and manufacture, stalking, tank hunting and camouflage at Osterley Home Guard Training School and, crucially, then disseminated their new-found knowledge in local training courses. In 1940 the Osterley students were, arguably, as well prepared for an ambush and harassing role as the Auxiliary Units and, trained in how to make home-made explosives and instructed to blend back into the community, better prepared to continue the fight in a resistance role. Fortunately, the most likely invasion areas were those covered by the former XII Corps Observation Unit which was the best organized of the Auxiliary Units and had the clearest strategic direction. Training greatly improved – but ironically only after the main threat of invasion had diminished.

Once Gubbins and Wilkinson left the Auxiliary Units for SOE in November the organization drifted away from its original plans for irregular warfare. Indeed, as early as August 1940 Wilkinson, never happy with the original War Office concept, was expressing further concern as to the direction of the organization and especially its relationship to the Home Guard: 'By the middle of August security was finally thrown to the winds ... With its increased numbers the character of the organization changed and it became virtually a guerrilla branch of the Home Guard.'[61] The introduction of the larger teams and hidden operational bases (Fig. 2 and Plate 9) symbolized this shift in emphasis. By disappearing from the local community they ironically made their secret role more obvious. By contrast, the SIS resistance cells were instructed to remain at home during the invasion period and to do nothing that would attract attention, so protecting their cover for later operations.

Even before Gubbins left there were rumours that the Auxiliary Units had served their emergency purpose and would be disbanded. Gubbins is reputed to have saved the organization through a timely lunch with War Office staff at the Cavalry Club.[62] Although the threat of immediate invasion had dissipated, and overall resources available to Home Forces had improved, it would have been rash to disband the Auxiliary Units and the men had been assured they would not be returned to general Home Guard duties. A more structured organization was introduced to manage a longer-term existence but none of the later COs had any experience in irregular warfare and the early dynamic senior officers were steadily replaced by ageing officers waiting out their retirement in the comfort of Coleshill House. Under Gubbins' replacement, Colonel 'Bill' Major, a long-time staff officer in the Directorate of Military Intelligence and latterly GSO1 in Eastern Command, patrols were grouped together under a Home Guard Group Commander to provide tighter local management and theoretically to allow larger-scale group action. The new hierarchical system weakened the security of the individual patrols but may have been an attempted step in the direction of Gubbins' earlier dream of creating Independent Company-type units from the Home Guard, capable of attacking larger targets.[63] Colonel Lord Glanusk, aged 51 and in poor health, became CO in February 1942. He was a former Welsh Guards officer who had retired from service in 1924 and was concerned about the social status of his command. The quality of the Coleshill wine cellar was said to have improved considerably as the officers' mess became more of a social club, dominated by Guards officers, and less a hub of clandestine warfare. The first question Glanusk asked the Intelligence Officer for the Scottish Borders, Peter Forbes, was 'Do you have any Gentlemen, Forbes?'[64] Former music-hall performer and actor Anthony Quayle (Intelligence Officer in Northumberland) clearly did not fit the mould and the dislike was mutual. Quayle believed the superior and patronizing manner of his new commanding officer interfered with the smooth running of his patrols.[65] Unable to shake off traditional military values, Glanusk introduced parade ground drill and drill competitions (under Captain Lord Delamere of the Welsh Guards) to the weekend guerrilla training courses.[66] The camp commandant, yet another fellow Welsh Guards officer (Captain Wickham-Boynton), insisted that the kit of the participating Auxiliers had to be laid out in Guards Brigade fashion.

Glanusk's most positive contribution was his review of operational procedure as it had evolved since 1940, and the conclusions hardly fit the modern legend of superhuman prowess:

> Tests of cross-sections of the unit here and there showed that, after two years' training, less was known about the use of explosives than in 1940, that many of the 'toys' since issued would never, and could never successfully be used, and that liaison between patrols was little more than wishful thinking, and of questionable use at that.[67]

Glanusk abandoned the system of group action to re-establish individual patrol security, and the Group Commanders now only had an administrative role – but one which increased as the number of regular army Intelligence Officers was reduced. Training Officer Nigel Oxenden was coldly analytical in his appreciation of these changes: 'From now on the patrol was self-contained and would fight alone; from now on the rank and file would not be asked to think.'[68] Oxenden wanted sabotage options to be simplified by removing the proliferation of timing and ignition devices and for the patrols to carry a minimum of weapons, proposing only the new .32 Welrod silenced pistol and a No. 77 phosphorous grenade.[69] Glanusk also clarified the lines of responsibility for operational patrols once they prepared to go into action. From May 1942 formal responsibility was handed over to regional corps commanders, giving them the strategic control over the patrols that had been lacking except in the original XII Corps area.[70] A cynic might suggest that the changes meant that the small Coleshill staff could now spend less time on tiresome operational matters, about which they increasingly knew very little, their main responsibilities being confined to administration and training. In 1944 the HQ comprised just ten officers and eighty-seven other ranks.[71] The county Intelligence Officers each had a small HQ staff comprising a clerk, a Royal Engineers corporal, two drivers and two or three NCO instructors who could together act, if necessary, as an additional operational patrol, but remarkably it was not until May 1942, with realistic prospects of invasion decreasing, that Major Beyts (Operations and Training Officer) finally asked for underground operational bases to protect these local HQ sections. He also asked for them to be equipped with standard WS17 sets so that they could communicate with Corps and Divisional HQs and with the Scout Sections. Authorization was given for the construction of nineteen operational bases for Intelligence Officer HQs on 1 June but by now the WS17 was out of production and Auxiliary Units were told that they would have to source them locally.[72] The WS17 sets were ill-suited to clandestine warfare: they had a short range and were notoriously 'noisy', which made for easy detection. But it was not automatic that the Intelligence Officers would be able to continue to work, as best they could, with the hidden patrols. The role of Intelligence Officers after invasion was to be at the discretion of the Corps Commander and whilst in the majority of cases the Intelligence Officers were given permission to go to ground with the rest of the patrols, some were ordered to remain with Corps HQ and, as a measure of how seriously, or otherwise, the Auxiliary Units were being taken, one Intelligence Officer had been tasked with acting as Police Liaison Officer after invasion! [73] The final abdication of strategic direction by Auxiliary Units HQ to the army Corps was a return to the original principle of the XII Corps Observation Unit, but had been made inevitable by the lack of communications and suitable infrastructure at Coleshill.

As the threat of invasion decreased, the Auxiliary Units had to find a new role that better fitted the current needs of home defence. For two years the secrecy surrounding the Auxiliary Units had prevented scrutiny but this protection began to crumble. Oxenden summarized the changes of fortunes in the organization as being in 1940 'a blaze of wild priority' when, under the threat of imminent invasion, they could get whatever they wanted. The Auxiliary Units were able to continue to capitalize on that threat in 1941–42 in a phase of 'organized power, guarded by a security that nobody could get past, however much they might resent it', but in 1943–44, as questioning of their importance mounted, there came 'a realization that the soundest attitude was unobtrusiveness' in the hope that senior officers might forget their existence.[74] The operational patrols, like the wider Home Guard, shifted their focus towards an anti-raiding role, although there was difficulty in claiming it was part of their secret role and it made their hidden operational bases redundant. The Auxiliary Units from 1942 to 1944 are often photographed more heavily armed for a reconnaissance role, with an increased allocation of Sten guns. Oxenden was cynical about the retasking, describing the rumours of raids as 'a wonderful tonic for fading enthusiasm in the ranks'. He went on: 'Sceptics wondered whether it was ever intended as anything more. The effects, with careful nursing, lasted for the next two years.'[75] But the mobile patrols and covert guiding teams of the Home Guard were in many respects better equipped and trained for the task than were the Auxiliary Units, still essentially focused on sabotage missions. Local Home Guard battalions had formed their own commando units, had received specialist training in street fighting and had undergone battle inoculation under live firing. The Auxiliary Units had relied on their secret status for the survival of the organization, but it also meant they had been left behind in the changing course of the war. In coming out of the shadows to work as reconnaissance units with the Home Guard on exercises, the Auxiliary Units now risked their special status.

Gubbins had not been overly concerned with the secrecy of the Auxiliary Units, other than the location of their operational bases and supplies. After all, in the threat of immediate invasion in 1940 they were not expected to survive long enough to become security risks.[76] It was explained:

> in order to ensure the necessary degree of secrecy, the sites of the dumps of special stores for these units are not disclosed except to the local leader, and the units are given the general title of 'Observation Units' to mask their real role. Secrecy beyond this degree would merely handicap efficiency.[77]

Wilkinson also explained that in the early days 'security was not a paramount consideration'.[78]

This relaxed attitude changed when it was realized that the organization would continue for a number of years but in many respects the Auxiliary Units were hiding 'in plain sight', relying on the wartime habit of not asking too many questions when gossip could be a criminal offence. The volunteers were ordered to be modest, to pretend that their job was dull and uninteresting, and they were never to be mysterious. If asked what they were doing they were never to say 'something secret' but to give a matter-of-fact response – fighting patrol, scout patrol, observer, runner, etc.[79] Drinking in the same pubs as the general Home Guard cannot have helped security. In Worcestershire, John Boaz from Samson Patrol remembered them going to the Plough Inn at Broadheath on a Sunday lunchtime after one night-time exercise. Plastered in mud, with blackened buttons and rubber boots, they met in the same pub as the neat and tidy local Home Guard who had just returned from Church Parade. The Auxiliers had to rebuff questions as to what they were doing. It was not unusual for David Patrol (north of Pershore) and the local Home Guard to march past each other to and from their respective exercises! The Malvern Home Guard later tried to track their local patrol to its operational base and a friendly game of hide and seek ensued.[80] Samson Patrol was once 'captured' by the local Home Guard whilst on exercise trying to breach the guard on the bridge over the Laugherne Brook. It would have been hard in such circumstances to deny their existence and purpose.[81] Despite instructions, sometimes it was hard to resist showing off. One patrol from Stobswood near Morpeth was remembered after the war as the 'Death or Glory Boys':

> One recalled how eyes popped in a public house when a 'Glory Boy' walked in with hand grenades dangling from his belt, .45 Colt revolvers strapped on each leg and a sub-machine gun over his shoulder.[82]

It was not standard for privates in the Home Guard to be issued with revolvers, which inevitably drew attention to the special status of their owners and the Auxiliers had to be instructed not to wear them on the train journey to the Coleshill training courses. Most patrols came from small rural communities and locals must have had suspicions even if they were never voiced. Many Auxiliers claimed, perhaps naively, that not even their wives knew of their secret activities – despite their nocturnal activities, their blackened faces, muddy uniforms, unusual revolvers or disappearing for weekend courses at Coleshill.

When the full story of the Auxiliary Units began to emerge in the 1990s, the volunteers took pride in their secrecy and distinction from the rest of the Home Guard as a symbol of special status. They would have been shocked to discover that security at an official level was not as absolute as they had assumed. The link between the Auxiliary Units and the Home Guard was repeatedly stressed in official documents, and the progress report provided to Churchill on 8 August described the 'Auxiliary Units of the Home Guard' which were organized 'within the framework of the Home Guard organization'.[83] Until late May 1941 local Territorial Army Associations held the supplies of clothing, arms, ammunition and equipment for Auxiliary Units, before this responsibility was transferred to the local HQs of the Auxiliary Units.[84] Historian John Warwicker confidently asserted in 2008 that no name of an Auxiliary Unit officer was recorded on any army or Home Guard list.[85] As more documents have become publicly available, this secrecy has proved to be a fallacy. A letter of 20 January 1941 from the Director-General of the Home Guard to the TAAs stated that the men were to be formally enrolled into the Home Guard, with their enrolment form 'endorsed to show membership of Auxiliary Units'. Bridgeman was obliged to remind county TAAs that 'It is important that the existence of these units should be mentioned as seldom as possible', already suggesting that secrecy was not absolute. It is ironic that this instruction was to be securely kept in a locked safe whilst the names, patrol structure and details of transfers in and out of the Auxiliary Units, including the officers, could be found posted, for all to see, in Part II Orders until late 1942 (Plate 10 and Appendix 1.11 and 1.12).[86] Although managed operationally by the Auxiliary Units' Intelligence Officers, the men were originally recorded on the battalion strength of the local Home Guard as a mechanism to establish capitation funding and the processing of claims for allowances.[87] The names of officers recommended by the Auxiliary Units' Intelligence Officer went to the normal selection boards and NCOs were appointed by the battalion CO on the recommendation of the Auxiliary Units Group Commander. Not surprisingly, sometimes battalions were reluctant to lose some of their best men and in November 1943 the CO of the 2nd Banffshire Home Guard tried to block the transfer of one of his lance corporals to the Auxiliary Units.[88]

In September 1942, as a belated attempt to increase security at a local level, the patrols were removed from the local Home Guard battalion structure and were grouped together as GHQ reserve battalions of the Home Guard. Record-keeping passed from the local TAAs to three regional TAA HQs: Inverness TAA managed 201 Battalion covering Scotland and Northumberland; York TAA managed 202 Battalion from Yorkshire to the Severn–Thames line; and Reading TAA managed 203 Battalion for the Southern and South-East Commands.[89] It was only then that details of the patrols stopped being posted locally on Part II Orders. From October 1942 the civilian identity cards of Auxiliers were even stamped with 201, 202 or 203 (GHQ Reserve) Battalion Home Guard.[90] From the time of this reorganization the Home Guard enrolment forms of Auxiliers in Herefordshire and Worcestershire were both signed and countersigned by the Auxiliary Unit's Intelligence Officer, usually carrying the official stamp of 'Intelligence Officer, Auxiliary Units'. They were then forwarded directly to regional TAA in York without contact with the local Home Guard organization.[91] This more secure procedure occasionally caused problems when new recruits were called up for compulsory enrolment in the Home Guard and the Intelligence Officer had to explain that they had already been enrolled through the regional TAA. The three regional TAAs then compiled detailed registers of members of Auxiliary Units' operational patrols, including their postal addresses and ID card numbers.[92] SIS would have been shocked by such a consolidation of supposedly secret information and in relation to its resistance organization in Britain, it told MI5 that 'I do not think it necessary under present circumstances to place on record in your section or in any other MI5 section a list of agents whom we [SIS] are employing in this country. The keeping of such records is always a danger even though the most stringent rules are made for their safe custody.'[93]

On their uniforms the Auxiliers wore the normal Home Guard shoulder titles but there was a delay until April 1942 before the county letter code/battalion number flashes were permitted to prevent them standing out as an anomaly. Soon afterwards, the reorganization into GHQ Reserve battalions caused a new complication and an instruction of 2 October 1942 removed the county battalion numbers. The problem was finally resolved in 1943 when the battalion numerals 201, 202 or 203 were worn beneath the county letter code, which was a clear visible identifier of their special status.[94] Despite the transfer to regional TAA control, by May 1943 the scope and purpose of the Units was known within the Home Guard in some areas down to the level of the local Company Commander.[95] For later historian John Warwicker, 'Auxiliers became less and less like a band of secret saboteurs and, although still under the control of their Intelligence Officer, more like just another arm of the Home Guard.'[96]

In January 1943 a War Office analysis of the potential future use of the Auxiliary Units concluded that they were unlikely to be used in the future, other than to protect the flanks of a zone from Norfolk down to Hampshire, and that the fit army officers and men in their ranks were better employed elsewhere.[97] This was immediately followed in February by a cancellation of the exemption from call-up given to the Home Guard Auxiliers (already disregarded by some Auxiliers eager for more active service). It was not, however, until November 1943 that all 'A' medical grade army officers and other ranks serving with the Auxiliary Units had to be listed as ready for redeployment. These were important signals as to the declining status of the operational patrols and were unsurprisingly accompanied by a fall in morale. Auxiliary Units Intelligence Officers now wisely avoided contact with division or corps HQs in order to avoid hostile questioning on their activities and purpose.[98] The Auxiliary Units took on an unreal atmosphere and they began to overplay their tactic of presenting themselves as so important and secret that no one should question their function. In February 1944 they had to be firmly told that they did not have priority for ammunition over other army units.[99] Pressure for their disbandment intensified from April 1944, ironically as they made ready for active service on the Isle of Wight: 'There is a very strong feeling in high places in the War Office that the time must be approaching (if it has not already arrived) when Auxiliary Units will have ceased to justify their continued existence.'[100]

The final edition of the Auxiliary Units' explosives manual was published in 1944 under the disguise of the *Countryman's Diary 1939* but it was almost a souvenir edition. The cover contains a jokey reference to their HQ at Coleshill House, Highworth – 'produced by Highworth Fertilisers', with the rider that 'You will find the name Highworth whenever quick results are required.' Security was clearly no longer a high priority. On 17 May the War Office recommended the withdrawal of all regular army personnel from the Auxiliary Units. Some Intelligence Officers had already been recruited from the Home Guard and it was decided that, if it survived, the organization would be reorganized on a purely Home Guard basis.[101] However, on 5 June the final decision was made to disband the Auxiliary Units. The civilian Special Duties Branch (the intelligence wing of the Auxiliary Units) was disbanded in July 1944 but the Operational Branch would stagger on until November, when it was stood-down with the rest of the Home Guard (*see* Appendix 1.13 and 1.14). By then many of the operational bases, long redundant, were in poor repair and some of the explosives were in a dangerous condition.

Ironically, even as the decision was being made to disband the Auxiliary Units, there finally came an opportunity to demonstrate their practical worth. Some men who answered a vague appeal for volunteers to serve 'overseas' were sent to assist army guards on the Isle of Wight during May and June, at a time when all spare military capacity was dedicated to reinforcing the D-Day campaign. The first inkling of the operational deployment came when on 22 April 1944 the War Office circulated a memo to the TAAs, advising them that they might receive some travel and subsistence claims from 'certain Home Guard units'![102] The risks of enemy commando raids on the Isle of Wight had been recognized from the start of the war and by 1944 there was a garrison of over 17,000 men plus two Home Guard Battalions and fourteen Auxiliary Units patrols. They protected a number of key installations needed for the success of D-Day, including pumping stations for the PLUTO pipeline, a secret communications centre, a radar station, an airfield and munitions supply dumps, as well as the defences on the Needles and Spithead approaches. Concern had been raised in March over the risks of small parachute assaults on the island and in late April a squadron of Royal Gloucestershire Hussars with nineteen tanks was moved to reinforce the island defences.[103] Without knowing their destination, volunteer Auxiliers from Scotland, Northumberland, Durham, Yorkshire, Norfolk, Suffolk, Herefordshire and Worcestershire, with several of their Group Commanders, found themselves loaded onto trains and army lorries to serve for periods of ten days to a month in relays during May to the end of June 1944. The Auxiliers were to supplement the existing garrison over the invasion period, scattered across the island providing night-time patrols along the pipeline, on roads around the various installations and on parts of the coastal path. It is a romance to imply that the small numbers of 'imported' Auxiliary Units in a rolling deployment (less than a hundred men at a time), who had no knowledge of the local landscape, were sent to plan a defence or were even a major element of the defence – but they were useful in providing relief for the overstretched regular garrison. Some Norfolk Auxiliers were armed only with pick-axe handles as they guarded the Pluto pipeline![104] Geoffrey Morgan-Jones of Adam Patrol in Herefordshire recalled spending ten days on the Isle of Wight, guarding an AA battery. John Boaz of Samson Patrol in Worcestershire remembered night-time patrols outside the defences of a munition store and being accommodated in a bell-tented camp. Jehu Patrol also went down for ten days and was quartered in the Warden's house next to Albany barracks, Newport (then No. 1 Infantry Training Centre). Overbury Patrol operated near Cowes.[105] Typically the patrols were used to relieve regular troops on night-time duty but at Freshwater the considerable Auxiliary Units' presence from Herefordshire, Norfolk, Durham and Yorkshire patrolled a stretch of the coastal path day and night. Patrols from Norfolk arrived at Sandown approximately three weeks before the D-Day invasion to relieve troops guarding the Pluto pipeline pumping stations at Sandown and Shanklin, the 620,000-gallon fuel tank at Shanklin and a nearby airfield.[106] They were accommodated in the Sandringham Hotel and, in a holiday atmosphere, whilst off duty enjoyed walks along the cliffs and visits to the cinema to see *Nancy Drew Detective*, *Northern Pursuit* and the newly released *Angels Sing*.[107] It was probably a disappointment to be relieved by Northumberland patrols who arrived just before D-Day and remained for a week following. Another building guarded by the Auxiliers was ostensibly a hospital, identified by Red Cross symbols, but was, in fact, a secret communication centre relaying vital information from Normandy. A Suffolk patrol was also tasked with guarding the radar station at Bembridge. Their deployment to the Isle of Wight may have been intended as a final attempt to prove the worth of the Auxiliary Units in the face of threats of disbandment. It certainly provided a 'battle honour' for men who, frustratingly, had been obliged to maintain their secret role but increasingly seemed to be on the sidelines of the war.

A postscript to the Isle of Wight deployment came when the northern Auxiliary Units provided a last-minute supplement to the guard of Balmoral Castle during a royal visit, to help thwart any possible German kidnap attempt. Almost inevitably, this has spawned the myth that the Auxiliary Units provided the royal bodyguard and the duty was not unique. (*See* p. 25 for the role of the Home Guard in protecting the royal family at Windsor.) The threat of an airborne raid on Balmoral was taken very seriously throughout the war and the usual guard during a royal visit consisted of a close protection team from Special Branch, an armoured unit of the Household Cavalry (earlier in the war the 'Morris

Detachment'), an infantry battalion and a light anti-aircraft troop. The Morris Detachment/Household Cavalry and one infantry company were quartered in the Balmoral stables, with the rest of the battalion at Abergeldie Castle and Braemar. Until 1944 a further infantry battalion was held in reserve at Aberdeen. Air cover was provided by a fighter squadron deployed to the area. Further Special Branch officers in the neighbouring village also kept a discreet watch for strangers in the area.[108] This was clearly no mean logistical exercise. The royal family was due to visit Balmoral from 11 August to late September 1944 (in the event the Queen extended her stay until 16 October) but the requirements of the Normandy campaign led to a shortage of available troops for the normal guard. It was only on 18 July that it was agreed that the 5th Manchester Regiment would provide the infantry component but the battalion was only at three-quarters strength. C-in-C Home Forces therefore wrote to General Thorne, GOC Scottish Command, suggesting that the Auxiliary Units could take some part in the defence of Balmoral. Thorne met Colonel Douglas, the current CO of the Auxiliary Units, at the estate on 27 July and agreed the deployment with only days before the arrival of the advance party on 6 August.[109] At extremely short notice volunteers from several Auxiliary Units patrols from Scotland and Northumberland served in shifts to supplement the Manchester Regiment's guard of the castle grounds. Lambert Carmichael was Group Commander of the North Northumberland Auxiliary Units and served on two occasions with Scremerston Patrol. As a farmer he did not have to justify his absence but it must have been more difficult for the miners in the contingent, without revealing their role in the Auxiliary Units. Robert Hall, a 42-year-old First World War veteran and now a bank manager, recalled taking a twelve-man contingent from Bedlington. Their role was to maintain a covert guard in the grounds to spot any intruders, but they were ordered to stay out of the way of the royal family and 'flitted from tree to tree with faces blackened or maintained watch in hideouts strung along the hill slopes above the castle'.[110] To describe them as 'the Royal Family's personal bodyguard' was a journalistic exaggeration, but for the officers there was occasionally an opportunity to socialize with members of the royal family who had a reputation for making their guards feel at ease.[111] Major Hall even played 'Statues' with the princesses. Soon after the completion of their hasty deployment, in October 1944 the Auxiliary Units members who had taken part in guard duties at Balmoral received a message of appreciation from the King in the form of a printed letter from Colonel Douglas:

> The King has commanded me to convey an expression of his appreciation of the manner in which Auxiliary Units detachments carried out their duties whilst His Majesty was in residence at Balmoral Castle.
>
> This has afforded the King much gratification and He would be grateful if you would inform all concerned.[112]

The popular view of the Auxiliary Units has been greatly distorted by romantic awe and their place in history greatly inflated, in large part because researchers have been carried away by the mystery of their hidden operational bases, which provide a tangible link to secret operations that excite the imagination, but, as Dale Clarke has argued, the Auxiliary Units 'have attracted interest out of proportion to their size or military significance'.[113] The founders of the Auxiliary Units, Colin Gubbins and Peter Wilkinson, coldly assessed that the organization was only intended as a short-term expedient to hinder the movement of an invasion army in the coastal counties within what was anticipated to be a month-long campaign. They were not the 'last ditch' of Britain's defence by the simple fact that they were designed to support a still-active British field army and, in the view of General Thorne, to also cover the flanks of a British counter-attack. Gubbins concluded, 'We were expendable. We were a bonus, that's all.'[114] He believed they would have justified their existence 'based heavily on the fact that they were costing the country nothing either in man-power or in weapons ... their usefulness would have been short-lived, at the longest until their stocks were exhausted, at the shortest when they were caught or wiped out'.[115] The report on the progress of the organization up to 1 September 1940 concluded 'it was, in fact doubtful whether many of them would have survived the first few days of invasion'.[116] The Auxiliary Units were to fight in uniform to keep them within the protection of the Hague Convention and there is no evidence of any training to operate on a longer-term basis as a civilian resistance organization. The location of their bases in the coastal counties, with no presence in the major cities, made the Auxiliary Units singularly unsuitable as the basis of a national organization following occupation (Fig. 4). There are therefore many reasons to reject the established myth that the Auxiliers were a 'resistance' organization.[117] This is not to denigrate the bravery of the Auxiliers but rather to suggest that their role should be re-evaluated within the context of the broader sacrificial role of the Home Guard in anti-invasion preparations.

At Stand-Down the men of the Operational Branch received a simple typed letter of thanks from the last commanding officer, Colonel Douglas. In 1946 a souvenir lapel badge was also produced for the men to purchase but wearing it only increased the mystery (*see* Appendix 1.14). Bill Ricalton, a youngster at the time, remembered men of his village in Northumberland wearing such a badge but enquiries as to its significance were met with 'I'll tell you when you are a big lad.'[118] Unlike the civilian members of the Special Duties Branch, they were also entitled to the Defence Medal on the same terms as the rest of the Home Guard (i.e. they had to have completed three years of service).[119] But many had been called up before this length of service was achieved, or had joined too late to qualify. The medals had to be applied for by the individual (or the patrol sergeant on their behalf) to the regional TAA and this process may not always have been made clear. Home Guard enrolment forms for Herefordshire and Worcestershire note a number of Auxiliers that simply did not apply for their medals. A trope therefore developed that the Auxiliary Units were not rewarded by any medal.

The Mythology of the Auxiliary Units

Immediately after the end of the war there was a brief flurry of publicity that revealed the existence of the Auxiliary Units. Stories of the European resistance had already become current in the press and, not to be left out, and with SIS remaining tight-lipped over its activities, this terminology was seized upon by British newspapers to describe the British organization. A brief account of the Auxiliary Units was even published in the service newspaper *Sunday SEAC* on 15 April 1945, describing 'an elaborately organized maquis'. *The Times* obtained a copy of the stand-down letter to the Special Duties Branch and an account was published on 12 April 1945 under the heading 'Britain's Secret "Underground" – Invasion Spy Force Stood Down'. Two months later, on 14 June, the *Western Morning News* also ran a story on the 'British Maquis'. Even an EPAC report of 1949 used the terminology to refer to the possibility of a revival of the Auxiliary Units (*see below*, p. 181). The Auxiliary Units resurfaced in a 1952 article on the XII Corps Observation Unit in the *Spectator* by Peter Fleming. He published a broader discussion of the Auxiliary Units in *Invasion 1940* (1957) in which he describes the 'stay-behind' parties of XII Corps 'or, as it would have later been called, a maquis or resistance movement'.[120] The nomenclature was taking hold. Interestingly Fleming went on to describe the Auxiliary Units as 'secret, at any rate in intention', an early clue that they were not necessarily in practice the top secret organization of legend. A brief summary of their role was also included in the volume of the official History of the Second World War dealing with Home Defence (1957).[121] It was David Lampe's pioneering publication of *The Last Ditch* in 1968 that first brought their existence to wider popular attention but also created many of the enduring myths: he repeatedly described the Auxiliary Units as the 'British resistance organization' and set the tone for the focus on drama and secrecy that has been followed thereafter. Lampe elevated the assassination role of the Auxiliary Units and their specialized equipment, falsely claiming their .22 rifles could 'kill a man a mile away'.[122] Lampe also mistakenly claimed that the Auxiliary Units were the first Britons to receive plastic explosive and the Thompson sub-machine gun – claims subsequently repeated without question and adding to the false mystique.[123]

The links of the Auxiliary Units to SIS, either through the HDS or the continuing influence of SIS in the Special Duties Branch, and the fact that in the Cold War the SAS were planning to use some of the methodology of the Auxiliary Units to go to ground in North Germany, meant that there was a reluctance to release official documentation on the history of the Auxiliary Units. The next wave of publications would, by necessity, rely heavily on the memories of veterans – a generation that took seriously their instructions to never reveal their secrets! It was only in 1992 that John Warwicker managed to secure written permission from the Cabinet Office for former members of the Auxiliary Units to tell their story, leading to a flood of county histories recounting their experiences. As early as 1957 Peter Fleming warned about the risks of distorting the history of the Second World War by over-reliance on the oral history of veterans (*see above*, p. 2). If that were true in 1957, it could be more problematic forty years later when veterans of the Auxiliary Units finally began to tell their story, exacerbated by the fact that by then many had read *The Last Ditch* and other published accounts of the Auxiliary Units, which coloured their own memories. The now famous exploits of the French resistance and SOE also formed clear supposed cultural reference points for the stories. Here was a chance to show that Britain also had a resistance organization and some accounts, with nationalist pride, even gave the Auxiliary Units false credit for having been the only resistance movement created before Nazi occupation.[124] This insular vision of history ignored the Polish, Czech, Hungarian and Belgian resistance movements, amongst others. The volunteers' vision of the Auxiliary Units had also been shaped by the *Dad's Army* television series, which seemed to turn membership of the Home Guard into a joke. They were understandably keen to emphasize their distinct nature and the history of the Auxiliary Units began to be rewritten. Former Intelligence Officer Stuart Edmundson claimed: 'There was no uniform in 1940. They were given denims to protect their clothes ... I never trained a man in uniform and we never intended them to fight in Home Guard uniform.'[125] Yet when the Auxiliary Units were founded, the only uniform for most LDV was an armband. Home Guard uniform for much of the rest of 1940 was the army-issue plain denim overalls about which Edmundson was so dismissive; the Auxiliary Units were uniformed in step with the general service battalions of the Home Guard. Indeed, the whole rationale of the Auxiliary Units was that they were a uniformed military body. The vicissitude of memory or challenges of ego are not to deny the value of oral history, and the perceptions of those who took part in conflict have their own value, but such accounts need to be tested against the official documentation – difficult if it is destroyed or suppressed.

As documents concerning the Auxiliary Units were selectively released to researchers by the Foreign Office SOE Adviser, and more have now come into the public domain, many of the assumptions made by Lampe could be shown to be incorrect. The aura of the Auxiliary Units as a 'resistance' organization nonetheless seemed unstoppable. Research focused on the local experience of county patrols and received wisdom on the wider context of the organization was passed from one publication to another without being critically challenged. To enhance their status, but without any supporting evidence, Churchill was frequently given personal credit for founding the Auxiliary Units and they became 'Churchill's Secret Army'.[126] The draft official history of the Auxiliary Units by Nigel Oxenden, written in October 1944 but not discovered until 1998, gives a very different tone to the Auxiliary Units from someone who was involved throughout, first as Intelligence Officer for Norfolk and then as its Training Officer but the critical, even cynical, analysis in this contemporary account was largely ignored. The pioneering national historian in this field, John Warwicker, fought against the tide but his fundamental assessment of the nature of the organization in 2008 could not compete against the more appealing 'resistance' media sound-bite:

> It was never intended that the Auxiliers were to compare with the men and women of the European resistance movements ... [they] were seen only as a short-term, expendable, harassing force intended – with the blessing of the British High Command – to be of some useful influence in local battles.[127]

If the War Office and the original organizers of the Auxiliary Units were all clear that it was not a resistance organization, the question must be asked why the phraseology has been perpetuated. One clue was given in the Preface to the second edition (2013) of Arthur Ward's *Resisting the Nazi Invader* (1997), republished as *Churchill's Secret Defence Army: Resisting the Nazi Invader*. In explaining why it was difficult for researchers to trace official records, Ward commented: 'John [Warwicker] later discovered that because initially the erroneous title "BRO" (British Resistance Organization) was used, as opposed to the correct designation, GHQ Auxiliary Units, records about this clandestine organization could not be found in Whitehall.' An artificial sense of mystery had been created because modern researchers were trying to find a modern mythical title that had never existed! Ward went on: 'The term BRO [British Resistance Organization] is frequently used today, I think principally because it conjures up a 007 stereotype beloved of so many "secret war" enthusiasts.'[128]

The failure of modern historians to properly recognize the character of the Auxiliary Units exasperated the original second-in-command, Peter Wilkinson, who wrote in 1997 'any suggestion that Auxiliary Units could have provided a framework for long term underground resistance is, in my opinion, absurd'.[129] Historian Arthur Ward later reported: 'Sir Peter told it like it was, obviously irritated by the myth of a secret society of ninja-like assassins that was becoming an accepted part of Aux Unit folklore.'[130] As an illustration of how difficult it can be to dislodge old terminology, the text of Ward's book is still that of the 1997 edition and, despite the above discussion in the Preface, continues to use the term 'British Resistance Organization'! The constant repetition of this misconception as a marketing tool and its fossilization in the published accounts perpetuates the same level of distorted image as the term *Dad's Army* does for the wider Home Guard. Doubts as to how the label tallied with a two-week life expectancy as uniformed units of Home Guard have been glossed over in favour of a romantic vision of the organization that allowed Britain to claim its place in resistance mythology.

Home Guard in the British Resistance

If the Auxiliary Units were not a resistance organization, other members of the Home Guard planned their own unofficial local resistance or became members of the official organization created by the Secret Intelligence Service (SIS *aka* MI6). The distinction is not always clear and such vagueness, in itself, is the mark of a well-organized intelligence operation. In briefing notes to the Home Defence Scheme in 1940, Laurence Grand suggested that officers should hint at possible courses of action without identifying themselves as SIS:

> 'D' officers should select a suitable region-wide organization, take the chief officers of it into their confidence, and allow them to plant the idea in the heads of their subordinates without betraying the fact that there is any official organization behind the scheme ... Suggest that no doubt the bloody Government, which is always years behind the times, has never thought of

> anything of the kind but we, the citizens of ... shire, will bloody well show them![131]

In *The Home Guard Can Fight* (1941), Tom Wintringham wrote: 'Part of the Home Guard's job is to carry on the struggle, if necessary, in areas temporarily overrun by the enemy. This last duty it can only carry out if it learns some of the tactics of guerrilla war.'[132] Several Home Guard units took Wintringham's teaching to heart and, as well as the proliferation of commando units, some made plans to 'go to ground' after invasion. In May 1941 Wintringham asked the Home Guard:

> 7. Are you prepared to be cut off behind the enemy's advance, and to keep on harassing him when there is no one to give you orders?
> 8. Could you lie low, if necessary, for several days, and then seize the chance for sabotage or raiding?[133]

This was exactly the role for which the Auxiliary Units were designed but Wintringham went further to preach a concept of the Home Guard, as a last resort, abandoning their uniforms and fighting on in utmost secrecy as civilians in small sabotage teams hidden within the community. It moved the teaching from the strategy of the War Office to that of the SIS. One of the students at an Osterley course noted:

> Should the area be overrun by the enemy the Home Guardsman should bury his rifle and uniform and mix with civilians ... Best results are obtained from groups of two or at most three, who should be equipped with knives and revolvers, grenades and explosives and iron rations ... The most profound secrecy should cover the actions and plans of each group. On no account should others be taken into confidence for fear of accidental betrayal.[134]

Home Guard who took this course of action would go beyond the protection of international law and be classed as *francs-tireur*. In furtherance of this role, the Osterley students were taught how to make improvised explosives and crude but effective incendiary devices. The course included advice on how to destroy ammunition dumps and vehicle parks, how to prepare ambushes, and how to poison the water supply in occupied areas by throwing dead dogs into wells. In 1941 Wintringham and Levy elaborated on the methodology to be employed by suggesting that large boxes should be hidden ready to act as caches for supplies and civilian clothes.[135] The methodology was identical in concept to that of the SIS Home Defence Scheme and there is a suspicion that SIS, which had good contacts with Edward Hulton (financier of the Osterley Training School who was involved with a Section D propaganda scheme), may have looked upon Osterley as a convenient 'arm's length' training ground for prospective recruits to their own networks, discreetly passing-on elements of their requirements.

In late 1941 the commander of the Home Guard platoon of the Beaumanor Hall Y-Intercept Station in Woodhouse, Leicestershire, formed a number of secret 'shock sections' in the surrounding district. Lieutenant Whitford, known as 'Two Gun Whitford' due to his habit of wearing his service revolver and a Luger on his hips, was a former policeman in Palestine who had joined the Wireless Intercept Service in 1936. He would therefore have had plenty of opportunities for contact with SIS, although his plan to recruit teams of young men aged 17–20 who would operate in civilian clothes after invasion and carry out 'dirty tricks' on any occupying Germans seems to have been a private initiative. In the meantime they wore normal Home Guard uniform but carried large knives on their belts. They were trained in unarmed combat and demolition, and how to use such weapons as knitting needle knives, knuckledusters and garrottes, as well as the normal range of official Home Guard weapons. Caches of supplies were supposedly hidden around the villages and there was at least one secret hide, but there is no evidence of any extraordinary supplies or external training that might suggest they were part of a larger, more official, undertaking.[136]

Unknown to but a handful of people, SIS had been planning an official secret civilian resistance organization in Britain since spring 1940, to operate from within the community, primarily in intelligence-gathering but also to include sabotage cells. It survived to at least 1943 and was known only as Section VII. Rather than risk exposure of the network to the enemy, members were instructed to maintain a low profile during any invasion to protect their chance of survival.[137] The organization naturally included some members of the Home Guard. Albert Toon, from Birmingham, was recruited by an unnamed lieutenant from a mysterious organization he knew only as 'X Branch'. He was told not to draw attention to himself within his Home Guard unit, although the various training courses that he was sent on as a cover for his secret duties qualified him as a weapons instructor. One such course was supposedly on Lewis guns at the isolated Western Command Altcar Training Area on Merseyside; in fact, he was taught there how to make home-made explosives and was trained in Morse code.[138] Although as much as possible of his equipment was to appear to be home-made, Toon was also given instruction in the use of the clockwork timing mechanisms developed by Section D from French prototypes.[139] The expectation was that he would be working alone but his instruction upon invasion was to report to a local school where he would be given further orders and told where his explosives dumps were hidden. One such arms store was discovered in the 1990s at the bottom of a garden in the south-east suburb of Birmingham, including a copy of the Auxiliary Units' *Countryman's Diary*, dating the dump's continued maintenance to 1944 (but there is no evidence that the Auxiliary Units operated in the area).[140] In 1943 at Mellor, Stockport, a corporal in the local Home Guard who was involved in 'extra-curricular' activities, presumably for SIS, and others hid a secret arms cache including a Thompson M1A1 sub-machine gun in a well at the isolated Old Vicarage. The corporal had approached Eric Nussen, then a teenage resident of the house and an underage member of his Home Guard platoon, to ask if he knew of a hiding place for some material on the property. Remembering that the garden well had a suitable ledge halfway down, Eric led a party of men there in the early hours of one morning, then was told to make himself scarce and the incident was never mentioned again. The material was placed on the ledge and, never used, was discreetly recovered at the end of the war but the Thompson had slipped off the ledge and subsequent excavation revealed it and 300 rounds of its ammunition, as well as ammunition for a .455 revolver.[141] Although the Auxiliary Units and Home Guard were both issued with M1928A1 Thompsons, they were withdrawn in favour of the new Sten gun before the Thompson M1A1 was introduced to British service in 1943. Again, the Auxiliary Units did not operate in that area, but the site is only about 30 miles from the known SIS resistance cell at Matlock, Derbyshire. There, the wireless operator knew that there were arms caches for the use of the network, but did not know their location.[142] The extent of the SIS resistance organization remains shrouded in mystery as its volunteers diligently kept their secrets to the grave, but other cells are known from Derbyshire, Manchester, Nottingham, Birmingham, Norfolk, Suffolk, Sussex, Somerset, Cornwall and Devon.[143] One secret unit in Leicestershire, in the Charnwood Forest, may have been part of this network. Samuel Hall of Ellistown was asked to form a resistance group based in the local caves, but with a large operating area. The group was trained in demolition and the charges they placed under the footbridge beside Trent Bridge in Nottingham were discovered in 1947.[144]

Chapter Five

Arming and Equipping the Home Guard

The overwhelming response to Eden's broadcast on the evening of 14 May 1940 forced a rapid reassessment of how the volunteers might best be used and consequently how they needed to be equipped. On the expectation of a maximum of 500,000 volunteers, the War Office had promised that 'you will receive uniform and will be armed'.[1] Yet within 24 hours of Eden's broadcast, 250,000 men had already volunteered for the LDV across England, Scotland and Wales (the Home Guard was not formed in Ulster until 28 May). Within six weeks there were 1.5 million volunteers. The shock of Dunkirk and the consequent overriding priority to re-equip the army as quickly as possible made the government's original promise even more unrealistic. Whilst waiting for the government's now impossible promise to be fulfilled, frustrated local units armed themselves with whatever was available and the 'broomstick army' legend was born. Farmers' shotguns, museum exhibits, First World War souvenirs and even kitchen knives tied to broom handles were all employed. On parade, they practised arms drill with broom handles (as did the regular army) in anticipation of the eventual arrival of proper rifles. The term 'broomstick army' was used by Anthony Eden at the Cabinet meeting of 17 June and quickly became current, even being used as a term of pride at recruiting stations.[2] Margery Allingham's *The Oaken Heart*, written during the winter of 1940 to encourage support from the USA, described how 'Ordinary people were thinking extraordinary thoughts just then and were preparing for extraordinary deeds.'[3] She accurately described the rationale of the Home Guard:

> Doubtless any well-armed parachutist would have killed all these dear gallant people, but it was clear that he would not be able to do much else with them, and it occurred to me that while he was killing old Miss Jane, for instance, there might be a very good chance for, say Miss Ethel with her rook rifle or a basin of lighted kerosene from the top of the stairs.[4]

Such popular belligerency was at odds with the initial concept of the LDV as a body of observers and Sir Edward Grigg (Under-Secretary of State for War) went so far as to state in Parliament on 22 May:

> As to the supply of rifles, there are plenty of rifles in the country, but it is not desirable for more reasons than one to issue rifles promiscuously to all members of the Volunteers unless special reasons exist.[5]

It was thought that weapons were only needed by men on selected guard duty. Meeting the LDV on 5 June Ironside stressed 'every man does not want a rifle'.[6] The LDV, manning static observation points and road-blocks against enemy parachute troops, were to be armed with rifles and those guarding vulnerable points and factories would have shotguns and a supply of the new 'lethal shot'. However, the 'Broadcast Warning' detachments which would keep watch from church towers, ready to ring the church bells if the enemy were sighted, would not be armed. Yet as demands to arm the LDV became more insistent, there was also concern in the populace that arms distributed indiscriminately might end up in the hands of the fifth column and even in the midst of war there was a very British concern over the application of proper procedure.[7] The Home Guard was entitled to possess arms without the usual licence 'for the performance of his official duties'.[8] Nonetheless, in June 1941 an officer of Scunthorpe Home Guard was fined 5*s* and had his revolver confiscated for being in possession of a firearm without a certificate. At Caistor, Lincolnshire, a dispatch rider had a similar case dismissed when his officer produced a regulation, of which the police were unaware, exempting the Home Guard from such restrictions.[9] In 1944 Tom Wintringham had his licence for a Colt .45 that he had acquired through the ACDBH revoked 'now that the arms situation has changed for the better'.[10] He was no longer a member of the Home Guard and was therefore not exempt from the firearms regulations.

An already hard-pressed Supply Department at the War Office had to equip a new army from scratch and without notice – a force equivalent to the size of the whole existing British army. Most of the histories of the Home Guard have relied on the reminiscences of local volunteers for whom a lack of arms in 1940 was naturally a source of frustration but later symbolized a pride in their determination to resist the enemy. Richard Brown wrote in his diary on 1 June about his friend Green who was in the Ipswich LDV: 'He has a beat round Stone Lodge Lane and shares a shotgun with another fellow, their total ammunition being <u>two</u> cartridges. When the siren goes they rush to their post and do their best to ambush any paratroops.'[11] A different perspective comes from the minutes of the Home Guard Inspectorate, which had the responsibility of sorting out mundane matters of insurance, loss of wages, provision of rations and eating utensils, etc., as well as the supply of uniforms and weapons, all the time in direct competition with the needs of the regular army who needed to re-equip after Dunkirk.

On 5 June Eden had to report that around 300,000 men had already enrolled in the LDV but only 94,000 rifles had been issued and ammunition was in short supply.[12] School Junior Training Corps provided one immediate means of supplementing the official distribution: Exeter LDV borrowed sixty .303 rifles from Exeter School, otherwise patrolling with 'shotguns, many and weird varieties of revolvers, usually without ammunition, and last, but not least, a good hefty stick'.[13] American M1917 rifles began to be issued to Exeter in July and the borrowed .303 weapons could be finally withdrawn in November 1940.[14] Lord Croft was still being optimistic on 3 July 1940, claiming in the House of Lords 'I am glad to be able to say ... that very soon every man in that Force will have some effective form of weapon.'[15] He was obliged to backtrack within a week: 'the astonishing increase in the Force in the last fortnight I confess makes the arming of everyone less easy, but even so, I can say that now the essential blocks and vulnerable points throughout the whole country will be manned by armed men'.[16] He urged both patience and optimism:

> We can declare that every citizen enrolled in the Local Defence Volunteers can have his training and his allotted task in the formation with a reasonable hope that, in the not too distant future, he will have effective weapons to defend his post, to stop and, if necessary, destroy, as I honestly believe he can, any vehicles which may try to rush the posts, even the heavier type of vehicle.[17]

The chaos of the first weeks provided the cornerstone of the mythology of the Home Guard having poor and archaic weaponry. Langdon-Davies took a philosophical tone over the complaints:

> Of course, the Home Guard must grumble – especially at his equipment; otherwise there would be grave doubts as to whether he was a real soldier. The soldier who does not grumble at his equipment must be either dreaming, drunk or passed on to a larger existence elsewhere.[18]

In 1974 Norman Longmate used the supposed antiquated nature of the weapons issued to the Home Guard as part of his validation of the *Dad's Army* series which was subsequently accepted almost without question. In 1995 MacKenzie concluded that the Home Guard was equipped with 'weapons which in reality were of dubious fighting value, but which in all probability would never have to be fired in anger and could be presented as worthwhile'.[19] Dale Clarke's detailed study of the weaponry of the Home Guard in *Britain's Final Defence* (2016) finally put such tropes to rest. In a modern age of disposability and built-in obsolescence, the fact that the Home Guard was armed with weapons of First World War vintage was seen as evidence that it was laughably archaic but this is a fundamental error. The standard British Army rifle until 1943 was the SMLE which dated back in design to 1907, and the standard rifle of the Home Guard, the M1917 (Plate 14), was actually a later design. Even today, the British army rifle (SA80) dates to 1985 and went out of production in 1994, and although subsequently upgraded, it could be thought of as an older weapon in service than was the M1917 in Home Guard hands. MacKenzie's dismissal of the ad hoc artillery as being of dubious quality ignores the fact that, with the lack of anti-tank weapons in 1940, they were also issued to the army and RAF. The makeshift weapons have since become most closely associated with the Home Guard because it was later assumed that only they would dare use them.

The British Army almost doubled in size from 1939 to 1940 and in 1941 was three times the size of its 1939 equivalent but there was limited large-scale production of new rifles in the country (relying on a single factory at BSA Birmingham) as Britain had an empire-wide strategy for production with factories in Canada, India and Australia. The pre-Dunkirk complacency regarding the requirements for small arms is seen in the disinterest in an opportunity to buy substantial quantities of surplus rifles from the continent. Lord Boothby was sent to Belgium on 22 April by Churchill (then First Lord of the Admiralty) and at Liège he found 9,000 rifles, over 100 machine guns and 1,000 Schmeisser sub-machine guns ready for immediate delivery. At Amsterdam he was offered 200,000–400,000 Mauser rifles with 1,000 rounds each. In response, Dr Leslie Burgin, the Minister of Supply, brusquely informed Boothby that the rifles were not wanted.[20] This was before the loss of up to 300,000 rifles in the campaigns leading to the retreat from Dunkirk; combined simultaneously with the pressure to arm the new Home Guard, it caused a crisis in the provision of small arms in Britain.

The immediate situation was saved by the purchase of thousands of weapons from the US government (*see* Chapter Six). The speed with which these arms were distributed to the Home Guard varied considerably by region, and even from one platoon to the next. One complainant to the War Office in June 1941 noted 'one finds two adjoining villages, one with almost 100% arms and the other with less than 30%'.[21] One veteran from the Ashton-under-Lyne, Greater Manchester, Home Guard claimed that his unit had to rely on pick-axe handles for 12 months.[22] Yet his platoon formed part of a Zone which had received 600 rifles as early as 25 May 1940. A history of the nearby Wirral Home Guard maintains that by August 1940 they were fully armed with Ross rifles, replaced with the M1917 during the autumn, together with two BARs.[23] Overall, by 10 August some 75,000 Ross rifles, 484,930 M1917 rifles and 93,261 SMLE and P14 rifles had been distributed, arming 48 per cent of the current membership.[24] Another 109,000 SMLE and P14 rifles from the initial distribution had been withdrawn to equip regular forces. It was no mean feat. Over 653,000 men had been armed, twice the total strength of the First World War VTC and equivalent to over 70 per cent of the strength of the British army in September 1939. In strategic terms, the Home Guard had already moved well away from the image of hapless, ill-equipped men as fossilized in the *Dad's Army* television series.

Sir Edward Grigg, Under-Secretary for War, exaggerated when he claimed on 19 November: 'We have provided full armament for 1,000,000 men – twice the number anticipated when the Home Guard was first raised.'[25] Nonetheless, in January 1941, 990,357 out of a total of 1,613,189 volunteers in the Home Guard were indeed armed.[26] The main problem was in the lack of automatic weapons, but the numbers of these increased substantially in 1941, particularly with the introduction of sub-machine guns (Figs 6 and 7). Problems in providing a personal firearm to each volunteer continued throughout 1942, although it became less serious given the expanding range of duties that did not require a personal weapon and the fact that only 70 per cent of the Home Guard was expected to be able to mobilize on the first alert. An exception to the patchy distribution of weapons was in Ulster where, as part of the 'B Specials' of the RUC, the Ulster Defence Volunteers were already entitled to bear arms and were immediately fully issued with SMLE rifles (although some mounted units initially had .303 Martini Enfield carbines).

Over the summer of 1940 Tom Wintringham's 'Arm the People' slogan clearly struck a chord with the volunteers, who wanted to fight and wanted a personal weapon that clearly identified them to their neighbours as soldiers. For such men, the early shortages were deeply frustrating but before one laughs too loudly at images of the LDV parading with broomsticks, it is as well to ponder the fact that at least one regular army depot (Norton, Worcestershire) was also obliged to drill with broomsticks in June 1940.[27] On a tour of inspection in Lincolnshire on 24 June General Ironside found a Navy technical training base at Skegness with 4,000 recruits and just 1,000 rifles, and at a Royal Engineers School in Grimsby there were 'a lot of recruits without rifles'.[28] The difference was that the regular forces, unlike the LDV, were parading with broomsticks in their barracks, beyond the glare of publicity. Some of the most widespread images of the 'broomstick army' are those of the 'Civi-Corps' (Plate 1) which was formed in north-east England to relieve pressure on arming the LDV by providing drill to young men awaiting conscription.[29] One might also spare a thought for the volunteers of the Observer Corps, who might have had just a single rifle with 5 rounds to defend their post – 2 rounds of which were to be used to give the emergency signal for invasion.[30]

The memory of how long volunteers had to make do without adequate weaponry has tended to stretch over time. Those units within likely invasion areas naturally had priority. Having received the order on the evening of 17 May to have 1,500 of the new LDV on armed patrol the next day, Chatham Command provided 1,500 rifles and 15,000 rounds of ammunition. A further 2,000 rifles were provided on the following day.[31] They were SMLE rifles, fresh from storage and covered in grease. Some commanders were not prepared to wait and Major Witts at Margate was apparently not unique in going down to the harbour and collecting up discarded rifles and ammunition from the returning Dunkirk survivors. Eventually he was obliged to return them, but not before using up most of the ammunition in target practice for his 900 men.[32] In all, by 13 June there were over 30,000 armed LDV in XII Corps area. Here, the percentage of armed LDV rose to 53 per cent by 19 September at the height of the invasion threat (Fig. 5). This was just over the 50 per cent that C-in-C Home Forces believed was acceptable for the Home Guard.[33] Within Eastern Command 60 per cent of the Home Guard overall had been issued with rifles by 10 August 1940, but only 15 per cent in the capital (where it was assumed that regular troops would cover defences).[34] The overall progression of arming the Home Guard during 1940 and 1941 is shown in Figs 6 and 7.

Oral history frequently maintains that, even if they did have rifles, the men only had 5 rounds of ammunition, another potent symbol of how they had been prepared to stand against seemingly insurmountable odds. Yet 5 rounds was the allowance for guard duty outside the time of any invasion; individuals may not have been aware that there was a deliberate policy of holding back further supplies of ammunition from the men until it was needed in any invasion.[35] Substantial quantities of ammunition were held as a reserve so that it could be distributed where most needed, avoiding the problems of men holding scattered quantities of

Figure 5. Home Guard establishment in XII Corps, 1940. (*TNA WO 199/3247*)

w/e	Men	Rifles	Private Rifles	Shotguns	Machine Guns
13 June	87,081	27,167	44	2,880	
25 June	88,907	36,722	66	4,030	
1 Aug.	91,757	40,393	64	3,818	
8 Aug.	87,520	40,314	71	3,748	
15 Aug.	88,076	39,254	1	3,410	
22 Aug.	91,871	43,965	169	3,685	
29 Aug.	85,428	45,309	51	4,194	
5 Sept.	86,371	45,027		4,124	
12 Sept.	89,775	44,753		4,137	
19 Sept.	90,292	44,271		3,889	
15 Oct.	86,925	47,745	71	3,698	1,459
1 Nov.	86,775	53,423	1,027	3,424	2,034
15 Nov.	84,921	57,485	119	3,829	2,044
1 Dec.	83,810	54,997	126	3,832	2,074
15 Dec.	82,837	50,625	127	3,826	2,074

Figure 6. Fortnightly tally of arms held overall by the LDV/Home Guard in 1940. (*TNA WO 199/3247*)

w/e	Men	Rifles	Private Rifles	Shotguns	Machine Guns
13 June	1,166,212	226,830	7,626	48,409	
25 June	1,456,127	495,294	7,632	56,035	
1 Aug.	1,472,505	483,924	7,377	56,063	
8 Aug.	1,560,109	544,706	8,019	51,979	
15 Aug.	1,600,265	588,315	7,662	55,066	
22 Aug.	1,636,740	645,617	8,035	55,415	
29 Aug.	1,648,373	666,530	8,029	54,239	
5 Sept.	1,671,828	695,404	7,708	54,382	
12 Sept.	1,677,598	715,053	7,977	52,654	
19 Sept.	1,682,303	689,171	7,594	46,629	
15 Oct.	1,680,860	677,145	4,381	47,000	25,751
1 Nov.	1,675,833	707,249	7,752	43,317	29,933
15 Nov.	1,663,117	804,023	6,580	43,697	36,274
1 Dec.	1,648,581	827,341	6,326	41,620	39,965
15 Dec.	1,628,414	850,849	6,586	39,769	40,652

live ammunition at home.[36] Some battalion and company commanders reduced the ammunition issued even further to create an unofficial local reserve.[37] Each M1917 rifle shipped in July had been accompanied by 60 rounds and in August the War Office advised that 50 rounds were available for the M1917 'on man or with unit'.[38] In September the Home Guard Inspectorate confirmed that 50 rounds per man had been distributed for front-line Home Guard, with another 20 held in Command reserve, plus an additional War Office reserve.[39] Some ammunition for rifles was, however, reallocated to bolster the supply of the machine guns, where the allowance from 20 August was 750 rounds per weapon with a further 500 rounds held in reserve.[40] In December 1940, reflecting the

Figure 7. Monthly tally of arms held by the Home Guard in 1941. (*TNA WO 199/3247*)

w/e	Men	Rifles	Private .22 Rifles/ Other	Shotguns	Machine Guns	Sub-Machine Guns	Pistols	Northover Projector	Blacker Bombard	6pdr gun	Mortar 6″
8 Jan	1,614,876	838,866	6,732	40,437	40,679						
1 Feb	1,595,831	827,348	2,998	40,366	39,848						
1 Mar.	1,607,414	805,652	4,107	39,168	39671		1,807				
1 April	1,610,977	854,145	3,501	39,150	41,684	1,114	6,238				
1 May	1,606,900	831,687	2,731	39,078	42,470	4,452	6,921				
1 June	1,598,087	847,464	2,679	35,211	42,470	6,410	11,170				
1 July	1,603,133	834,057	3,704	32,384	42,108	7,707	11,404				
1 Aug.	1,592,953	842,152	1,792	34,922	43,524	10,166	12,984	6,630			
1 Sept	1,578,937	834408	3,465	33,189	43,684	13,084	12,948	8,584			
30 Sept	1,572,905	835907	3,705	34,119	43,025	16,993	13,445	9,300			
31 Oct	1,560,106	851164	3,754	33,391	42,959	17,990	14,203	103,74		2	
30 Nov	1,546,117	873019	3,186	32,048	43,107	20,660	15,747	118,99	2,153	14	
31 Dec	1,527,768	874285	2,541	33,623	43,626	26,591	19,864	13,661	4,305	24	7

reduced risk of invasion over the winter, the distribution was reduced to 40 rounds per rifle and 550 per light machine gun.[41] By February 1941 the Home Guard was holding 75.6 million rounds of .300 ammunition.[42] There remained a reluctance to release too much ammunition for training purposes and the supply of .300 ammunition was an enduring concern as all supplies had to be imported across the Atlantic from the USA.

The shortage of personal weapons was not unique to the Home Guard and in January 1942 there remained a shortfall of 400,000 personal weapons in the rest of Home Forces.[43] In addition, some (including Churchill's army guard at Chartwell) were still armed with Lee Metford rifles, dating back to 1888.[44] By the end of 1942 still only 40 per cent of Home Guard overall had a personal weapon but by then many were acting as gun crews to support weapons such as the Northover Projector or Blacker Bombard, or on AA or coastal artillery gun sites.[45] Another factor was that it was estimated that 30 per cent of the Home Guard might not be able to muster immediately upon 'Action Stations' due to their occupation or other responsibilities.[46] Such reasoning was of little comfort to those without firearms. The 73-strong platoon responsible for defending the wireless station at Sandridge, Hertfordshire, in May 1942 still had only fourteen M1917 rifles and six Thompson SMGs.[47] The widely held view of the individual volunteer remained that each man should have a rifle as the symbol of a professional soldier. The Duke of Sutherland complained in the House of Lords in February 1942:

> When the Home Guards were first formed at a time of great emergency, after the Dunkirk evacuation, we accepted quite naturally the great shortage of rifles, ammunition, etc., on the assurance that one day this would be made good. Now, after nearly two more years of war, when we have been told that our production output is both astounding and prodigious, we are in some units still in the same position as regards rifles and ammunition as we were in at that date, although it is true we have been given other weapons of different sorts since that date.[48]

The 'other weapons' that Sutherland alluded to included, by February 1942, 33,531 Thompson sub-machine guns. With this in mind, Lord Croft rejected the argument and commented 'There seems to be a feeling abroad that the rifle is essential as a weapon for all the Home Guard, and I should like to remind your Lordships that in the event of invasion in a great part of this country we shall be engaged in fighting of a close character.' Instead he highlighted the importance in urban warfare of bombing parties using hand grenades from ambush positions.[49]

Frustrated by a lack of personal weapons, the Home Guard made their own and it became a fascinating and diverting hobby. First World War veterans brought experience in making home-made hand grenades from food tins (using explosives from mines and quarries), piano wire and cheese wire were used to make garrottes, and carpenters' gimlets were converted into 'push knives'. One tongue-in-cheek letter to *Picture Post* even requested the magazine publish instructions on how to throw a boomerang on the basis that it could be used to knock out parachutists.[50] Commercial handbooks fed their enthusiasm, describing simple booby traps using clothes pegs to trigger electric detonators. The best-selling *New Ways of War* by Tom Wintringham and Levy's *Guerrilla Warfare*, promoted by national lecture tours, provided enticing details of pipe bombs, home-made grenades and mortars. The Osterley spin-off course at Hurlingham taught students how to make an anti-personnel fougasse, using a length of drainpipe packed with black powder and gravel.[51] The mammoth winter and spring lecture tours by John Langdon-Davies, taking in a hundred Home Guard battalions and published as *Home Guard Warfare*, explained how to make anti-tank traps using soup plates and blanket 'blinds' drawn across the street.[52] He hinted at how easy it was to make explosives from materials bought at the local Woolworths store.[53] With even less effort, the Fauldhead Colliery in Dumfriesshire provided explosives for 500 improvised grenades, and land mines containing 7lb of explosives were made up using old tins and electric detonators.[54] A horrified War Office tried to ban the production of home-made grenades but W.H. Tatham, the Deputy Assistant Director, Home Guard, complained that sufficient quantities of the promised official grenades had not yet been supplied, concluding that the Home Guards were becoming 'somewhat disturbed and restive' at the perpetual prospect of 'jam tomorrow'.[55] The War Office was unsuccessful in curbing the enthusiasm of the Home Guard and later pamphlets *What the HG Needs to know about Explosives* by Charles Knights (1942) and *Explosives for the Home Guard* by Captain Cronk (1943) both advised on how to dismantle the unwieldy Type 73 grenades to extract the explosives for other purposes.[56] In July 1941 Wintringham proudly published an article in *Picture Post* on how to build a drainpipe mortar that would fire a jam tin bomb over a distance of 350 yards (Plate 12).[57] Captain Simon Fine, invalided out of the Royal Fusiliers after being wounded with the BEF in France, became an instructor with the London Home Guard and described one of his colleagues thus:

> A local civil servant who sat in an office and spent your money and mine for us from nine till five every day. After five he came alive and developed nihilistic tendencies. I have sat through lectures and watched demonstrations by sappers and ordnance experts, but I never hope to meet again a man who loved explosives more, or who could handle any type of grenade with greater ability.[58]

The 'jam' promised to Tatham did arrive and by October 1941 Wiltsher could describe the wide variety of weapons now held by the Home Guard as 'somewhat perplexing'.[59] Contemporary cartoons now depicted the Home Guard weighed down with an increasing array of equipment.

Specific Weapons

Revolvers

One military weapon already in Home Guard hands were revolvers owned by former First World War officers, who had been expected to purchase their own side arms. The Home Guard Inspectorate was frustrated in an accurate audit of such weapons due to a reluctance of owners to declare unlicensed firearms, for fear of future confiscation; the 6,318 revolvers listed in the Inspectorate returns for October 1940 were, therefore, likely to be an underestimate.[60] Official issues, mainly of .455 calibre, were not reported until March 1941.[61] The .455 Mk VI Webley, the standard revolver of the First World War, remained an official issue in the Second World War but young officers found the new .38 calibre Webley or Enfield lighter to carry and with less of a 'kick', if a more insipid weapon. By September 1942 almost 13,000 handguns were in service with the Home Guard, issued to officers, dispatch riders and members of the operational patrols of the Auxiliary Units. The official ammunition allowance of 12 rounds was the same as for the rest of the army, as appropriate for a weapon of last resort for self-defence.[62]

Shotguns

Shotguns were the most common type of privately owned firearm in Britain and therefore the most immediately available for the Home Guard. In addressing leaders of the LDV on 5 June 1940, the C-in-C Home Forces, General Ironside, advised them when dealing with descending paratroopers to 'shoot them, shoot them, shoot them' and for this the humble shotgun would have been an effective, if messy, weapon.[63] By July 1940 there were 56,033 shotguns in service with the Home Guard.[64] For John Langdon-Davies, 'At night especially, the shotgun is far more dangerous in the normal HG hands than a rifle.'[65] Their widespread use by the US army in the First World War as 'trench guns' had been condemned by the Germans as being contrary to Article 23(e) of the Hague Convention 1907, which stated: 'It is especially forbidden to employ arms, projectiles or materials calculated to cause unnecessary suffering.' The German government issued a formal warning to the US Secretary of State in September 1918 that would have had brutal consequences if extended to include the Home Guard in 1940.

> The German Government protests the use of shotguns by the American Army and calls attention to the fact that, according to the laws of war, every prisoner found to have in his possession such guns or ammunition belonging thereto forfeits his life.[66]

Such warnings were disregarded by the volunteers. Clifford Shore's Home Guard platoon in Cheshire concluded:

> Quite a number of people held the opinion that if the Hun did arrive and perforce landed in wooded areas where he would probably escape detection much more easily, and where it would certainly be better for him to hide up, then the shotgun would be a better weapon than the rifle. There is no doubt that for very close quarter work the lethality of the 12-, 16- or 20-bore cartridge cannot be dismissed lightly.[67]

The War Office also ignored the German threat and made the shotguns more deadly by the production of 'lethal shot'. An official 'shrapnel ball round' for 12-bore shotguns was in production by 15 June 1940; the lead-alloy balls could penetrate the engine block of a vehicle and were accurate up to 100 yards, although lethal up to half a mile.[68] Subsequently other types of 'man-killing' shotgun ammunition were issued. SG shot contained several smaller lead balls, which were designed for a 3ft spread at 40 yards and could penetrate a triplex car windscreen at that range. In all, 1 million rounds of 'lethal shot' were distributed in June 1940 and 4 million by the end of January 1941.[69] Many Home Guard supplemented official supplies by making their own, using melted candle wax to bind together normal shot. The results could be gratifying:

> The firer took up his stance about 20 yards from the barn, put the gun to his shoulder and pulled the trigger. Most of the watchers were standing close to him and probably blinked at the noise of the explosion of the charge. They must therefore have been greatly surprised when, after the blink, they opened their eyes to find that the door had vanished! ... it was a most spectacular demonstration, and everyone went away very impressed with the terrific power of such a projectile fired from a 12-bore gun.[70]

Home Guard Instruction No. 27 (1941) made shotguns the preferred weapon for close-range house clearance and a sawn-off shotgun was still recommended into 1943, even after the introduction of the Sten gun. Home Guard Instruction No. 51 Part II: Battle Drill lists a shotgun as an alternative to a rifle or Sten gun for four of the eight members of a Home Guard squad, as well as the platoon sergeant and runner.[71] Modern counter-terrorism units still use such weapons to force rapid entry into premises.

Rifles

The rifle was culturally still seen as the mark of a soldier and 'the cleanest and noblest of all weapons'.[72] The provision of a rifle for every member of the Home Guard therefore became a fixation and could be taken to ridiculous lengths. Charles Graves describes how the 49th Battalion, Lancashire Home Guard borrowed Crimean-period Snyder rifles from the Belle-Vue Zoological Gardens in Manchester. The 11th Battalion, Shropshire Home Guard also acquired Crimean War carbines.[73] They were as useful as a broomstick for practising drill but otherwise of limited value.

An enduring disappointment was that the Home Guard was not going to be generally equipped with the standard army Short Magazine Lee Enfield rifle (SMLE). First coming into service in 1907, this was a familiar and well-liked weapon to many from the First World War. Relatively light, with a remarkable rate of fire of 15 rounds per minute from its 10-round magazine, it was perhaps the finest bolt action rifle of its era. What was worse, a general order was given in February 1941 for the withdrawal of those SMLE rifles distributed earlier to some Home Guard as the organization standardized on the M1917 rifle.[74]

The immediate alternative to the SMLE was the Pattern 1914 Enfield, popularly known as the P14. It shared the same .303 calibre as the SMLE but was based on a modified Mauser bolt action and had only a 5-round magazine. The P14 had been designed to replace the SMLE as there were fears before the outbreak of the First World War that the SMLE was not robust enough to withstand the rigours of war and had been disappointing at target trials. There was not time to convert production in Britain and the Empire before the outbreak of war and so it was decided to contract manufacture of the P14 to Winchester, Remington and Eddystone in the USA; production ceased in 1917. They were largely relegated as a training and sniper rifle following the unexpected success of the SMLE and since the end of the First World War they had been kept in storage in England. Over 677,000 were refurbished in August 1939 and they were issued to the RAF Regiment and anti-aircraft units throughout the war, as well as to the Home Guard. Although heavier than the SMLE, the P14 remained a respected army sniper rifle, being more accurate than the SMLE and with less of a kick, and it continued to be a favoured weapon of army shooting teams into the 1950s.[75] From Canada in late June came 75,000 M1910 Ross rifles in .303 calibre, which was an excellent target rifle but had been dismissed from front-line service in 1915 due to the ease with which its bolt action clogged in the Flanders mud. It is typical of the oft-repeated misinformation that one veteran could describe them as dating 'long before the First World War'.[76] However inadequate they were, part of General Alan Brooke's reasoning in December 1940 for issuing Thompson sub-machine guns to the Home Guard was that it would release the Ross rifles for redeployment to the field army.[77] By the end of July 1940, 495,294 rifles in .303 calibre had been supplied to the LDV, enough to have covered the total anticipated number of volunteers but only a third of the numbers needed to meet the aspirations of the actual number of volunteers who had enrolled.[78] The Vale of Evesham had a novel solution to the shortage of ammunition. In August 1940 local householders organized hot baths for the considerable number of troops still billeted in the area after Dunkirk – in return for 5 rounds of .303 ammunition per bath![79]

The answer for a supply of additional rifles came from the USA (*see* Chapter Six). In early June the sale of 500,000 M1917 Enfield rifles was agreed, at a price of $7.50 each. The first part of the shipment was distributed on 8 July 1940.[80] The M1917 rifle (Plate 14) was the main US rifle of the First World War but had been replaced by the 1903 Springfield, leaving thousands in US munitions stores. It was a modified Enfield P14, chambered for .300 calibre (using the 30–06 cartridge). Identical to the P14 in appearance and weight (and consequently commonly known within the Home Guard as the P17), it was similarly very accurate but shared the limitation of a 5-round magazine. Clifford Shore, who became an RAF Regiment sniper instructor after the war, commented: 'I could not have wished to use a better or more accurate weapon.'[81] To avoid confusion with the P14, a red band was painted around the fore-end, although it did not completely prevent all accidents with chambering the wrong-sized round. It was built by Winchester, Remington and Eddystone, although they were often referred to in the early days as 'Springfields' simply because they were American-made. Harold Taylor was a member of his village Home Guard when home on holiday from Eton and remarked on the difference in weapons. Eton School Home Guard had the JTC SMLE rifles but the village had 'very ancient American rifles, .300 calibre, very long things, but they were useable'.[82] Here was one origin of the myth of the 'ancient' M1917 rifle, actually ten years later in design than the SMLE, that has coloured the public perception of the Home Guard. Adding to the confusion, Longmate simultaneously described the 'cumbersome' rifle as the 'Springfield 1917' and the 'light, handy and accurate Remington'.[83] As well as the Home Guard, the M1917 was widely issued to AA Command and coastal artillery units.[84] In all, the heavy M1917 was well-suited to the Home Guard whose main role was envisaged as being sedentary and where every shot would count. Delivered in crates of ten rifles, they arrived straight out of long-term storage, covered in thick cosmoline and special mobile armourer units had to be created to advise and assist with the degreasing and to undertake minor repairs.[85] In Cambridgeshire it took 150 local women a fortnight to clean their first allocation of 8,000 rifles ready for action.[86] By 18 January 1941, 733,710 of the M1917 rifles had been distributed to the Home Guard.[87] The continuing value of the M1917 is clearly indicated by the suggestion in March 1942 that the Russians be asked to sell 50,000–1,000,000 of their Mosin-Nagant rifles with 150 rounds per rifle to arm the Home Guard and thereby release the already-issued M1917 rifles for army use.[88] As the Russians were thought likely to be unwilling to arm the Home Guard against what they saw as the now unlikely chance of invasion, the Home Guard were to be only identified as 'second line troops' in the request. Not surprisingly, nothing came of this initiative.

Amongst the miscellany of other rifles issued to the Home Guard were 64,000 M1903 Springfield rifles, also characteristically marked with the Home Guard red-painted band on the forward woodwork to denote their .300 calibre. It was the standard US battle rifle in the inter-war years until replaced by the Garand in 1938. Another source of rifles came from those reallocated from the French and Belgian troops who had escaped the fall of France. Several Belgian Mausers were rechambered to .300 calibre and issued to the Home Guard, including some in Worcestershire and London. French Lebel and Berthier rifles were similarly distributed, including to Cornwall and Devon Home Guard. To supplement the ammunition that came with these rifles, 8mm Lebel ammunition had to be purchased from Greek suppliers.

By 20 August 1940 the Home Guard Inspectorate claimed that 850,000 rifles of various types had been issued to the Home Guard – no mean achievement (but differing from the monthly returns, *see* Fig. 6).[89] From November 1940 there was also a trickle of privately donated arms for the Home Guard arriving from the USA (*see* Chapter Six), which were of mixed quality but did at least include some sporterized M1917 rifles and other hunting rifles of .300 calibre which could be easily assimilated into the Home Guard arsenal. The main problem with the rifles issued to the Home Guard, at least to the older volunteers, was simply that they were not the SMLE and were foreign (even if designed by Enfield). In December 1943 some Home Guard units began to be equipped with the new No. 4 Lee Enfield rifle, in line with the rest of the British army (Plate 30). It was essentially a simplified version of the SMLE, built for mass production, the early examples exhibiting poor quality control, and in many respects it was inferior to the Home

Guard's P14 and M1917. Nonetheless, to have the current British army rifle was, for many, at last a symbol of acceptance.

Bayonets, Knives and Cudgels

If he could not have a rifle, each man provided himself with a personal weapon of sorts. In *Invasion 1940*, Peter Fleming described how 'In Essex an unexpected windfall made possible the formation of a cutlass platoon, twenty-four strong, under the command of a former naval rating.'[90] In May 1941 German paratroops descended on Crete, exciting concern that the troops responsible for airfield defence had a serious shortage of weapons and ammunition.[91] Yet the first wave of paratroops had been badly mauled as they landed on Crete, by peasants armed with scythes and bill hooks. At the same time, with complaints from the Home Guard regularly appearing on his desk and in the press, Churchill had written to the War Office saying that 'every man must have a weapon of some sort, be it only a mace or a pike'. The War Office took Churchill's words literally and a consequence was the public relations disaster of the issue from June 1941 of the notorious 'Bayonet Standard', better known as the 'Croft Pike'. The War Office ordered 250,000 from the Ministry of Aircraft Production, each consisting of a 5ft-long steel tube with a bayonet welded to the end. Captain Godfrey Nicholson MP exploded in the House of Commons that the provision of pikes 'if not meant as a joke, was an insult'.[92] It was clear from the outset that there would be complaints and General Lloyd, Chief of the General Staff, stressed that it should be explained to Home Guard units that regular troops were also being issued with them and that they 'are a really useful supplement' to a unit's weaponry and not 'a makeshift alternative'.[93] Few were convinced. By May 1942, 100,000 had been distributed to Home Forces but many Home Guard officers refused to distribute them to their men. Lord Croft was the unfortunate minister who had to defend Churchill's idea in Parliament, arguing that if he were leading an attack in trenches or around buildings using grenades, 'then I should like to have a pike in order to follow up my bombing attack, especially at night. It is a most effective and silent weapon.'[94] The 'Croft Pike' has become an iconic element of the supposed absurdity of the Home Guard even though they received less than 50 per cent of the weapon: 85,000 were issued to Anti-Aircraft Command, the Royal Artillery, the RAOC and the RAF as compared to the 52,282 listed on the Home Guard monthly returns.[95] They have become particularly associated with the Home Guard only because they were the most public recipients and the most vocal complainants, and because there was a deliberate manipulation of the story to focus away from the problems of the rest of the armed forces. General Pile, head of Anti-Aircraft Command, admitted that due to the shortage of rifles his men, like the Home Guard, were issued with cudgels and pikes but 'we were asked to keep quiet about having them too'.[96]

The catchphrase 'They don't like it up 'em' of the elderly Corporal Jones in the television series *Dad's Army* was in praise of the bayonet and was an authentic attitude of the character's generation, which saw a long bayonet as necessary to protect infantry from cavalry. Nonetheless, the effectiveness of a bayonet had long been controversial. Tom Wintringham said in August 1940:

> The bayonet proved of little use in the American Civil War. It was ineffective in the Russo-Japanese War. It caused an infinitesimal number of the last war's casualties. Mechanization and automatic weapons leave it little scope. The bayonet is a myth, a cult, a superstition that has no longer even a symbolic value. It may cheer the hearts of semi-decrepit politicians and even of much less decrepit generals to see the bayonets of the sentries in Whitehall. But to those of us who have had some fighting on a modern scale in recent years, the bayonet is a picturesque survival like the claymore or the battle-axe.[97]

Ironically Wintringham himself ordered a bayonet charge at Jarama in 1937 just before he was wounded. John Brophy, although also maintaining that bayonet charges were out of date, pointed out that the bayonet still had a use in sentry duty and at least one unfortunate person was killed with a bayonet at a roadblock (*see above*, p. 25). Instead, Wintringham and many of the First World War veterans who had experienced trench warfare recommended the use of a stout knife instead of the standard 17in-long bayonet for close quarters combat. There was a rush on buying sheath knives but First World War veterans had already been used to cutting down discarded bayonets to make trench fighting knives. Now other First World War souvenirs were cut down. Trench clubs were another inheritance from the savage trench fighting of the First World War, and their use was transferred to the likelihood of close quarters house-to-house fighting or night fighting. Wooden truncheons or cudgels were weighted with lead and studded with nails or boot hobnails. The act of making such a crude weapon to make a personal stand against the enemy could be therapeutic. Longmate describes a pupil at Christ's Hospital 'lovingly whittling down a large piece of wood into a club, with string wound tightly round it to form a handle, and as the final touch, a set of heavy football-boot studs screwed into the "business" end'.[98]

In July 1941 the War Office circulated designs for cudgels made from 19in lengths of gas pipe with industrial gears or sprockets welded to one end, or from 15in lengths of rubber hose filled with concrete. In September Home Guard units were also circulated with the offer of a 14in lead-weighted rubber truncheon weighing 1.25lb, as also issued to the Auxiliary Units.[99] By the end of March 1942 there were 105,972 truncheons of various types in the possession of the Home Guard.[100]

Grenades

As with other weaponry, there was a shortage of the standard army grenades in 1940. The No. 36 fragmentation grenade weighed 1lb 11oz (765g) with a 4- or 7-second fuse, and was in use from the First World War until 1972. The serrations of the cast-iron, egg-shaped body were designed primarily to improve the grip rather than to assist fragmentation. The throwing distance was around 25–35 yards but the blast radius was up to around 100 yards, meaning that it must be thrown from behind cover.[101] Training accidents with them were frequent in the Home Guard – as they were in the army throughout the grenade's history. There was an understandable reluctance to issue grenades to local Home Guard until they had received training and there may have been more casualties but for an emphasis on repeated training with dummy grenades. W. Lockington, a platoon commander from the Isle of Man Home Guard, recalled repeatedly going through the drill for dealing with a dropped live grenade in the village hall one evening until they retired to the nearest pub in time for 'last orders'. The next day on the range a grenade was indeed dropped but the drill they had practised was carried out instinctively and no one was hurt. It was also Lockington's job to deal with any grenades that failed to explode, known as 'the longest walk'. The drill was to wait 5 minutes, then the officer would remove his helmet (to prevent it tipping over onto the grenade when he bent over it). A small charge of explosives had to be placed near, but not touching, the grenade, then the fuse was lit and the officer had to walk, not run, away from the grenade (to avoid any trips and falls).[102] By contrast, the No. 69 grenade was an offensive grenade, relying on short-range blast and shock for effect rather than shrapnel damage. It had a Bakelite casing and weighed only 13.5oz, fitted with a Type 247 'all-ways' fuse, which armed the grenade in flight. After removal of the protective cap, the grenade was thrown and a short length of weighted tape automatically unwound and pulled out the safety pin. It exploded on impact and was designed to be used to support an advance and particularly in house-to-house fighting. To supplement these official grenades, the Home Guard had the advantage of First World War veterans who passed on the skills of making home-made grenades from empty jam or food tins, filled with a stick of gelignite or gun cotton packed around with nails and other scrap iron and armed by a detonator and short length of fuse. Such grenades had been produced on an almost industrial scale at Gallipoli.

After Dunkirk the army had just 167 anti-tank guns in Britain and the War Office was desperate for any stop-gap solution, so turned both to crude 'sub-artillery' (*see below*, p. 104) and to specialized anti-tank grenades. The No. 68 anti-tank grenade, designed to be used from a cup discharger mounted on the muzzle of a rifle (and later from the Northover Projector), was already coming into service with the army. It was the first hollow charge weapon to be issued to the British army and had a range of up to 100 yards, capable of penetrating 2 inches (50mm) of armour, making it twice as effective as the disliked Boys anti-tank rifle. Given the paucity of other options, priority for the No. 68 grenade went to the army and it could only be issued to the Home Guard from 1942. It was responsible for one of the worst reported Home Guard training accidents. During a lecture in Rochester, ignoring orders that live ordnance was not to be used in demonstrations, a sergeant-instructor (aged only 22) removed the shear wire from a live grenade, remarking that 'This thing is quite safe; it would need a hard impact to make it go off.' He then hit the table with it and in the resultant explosion five were killed and three seriously wounded.[103]

The quickest solution to produce an anti-tank weapon on a large scale, for both Home Guard and the army, was to use petrol bombs ('Molotov cocktails') as used in the Spanish Civil War and the Finnish Winter War (Plate 18). Ironside wrote in his diary for 28 May: 'Local Defence Volunteers going well. I must get them armed with Molotoff [*sic*] cocktails in all the villages of England. The only way to deal with a tank.'[104] Anthony Eden was inspired by a *Daily Mirror* article by Tom Wintringham on 31 May 1940 which claimed that 'Anyone who fought in Spain knows how to stop German tanks.' Eden asked the War Office to explain the methodology used in Spain and its response was that large quantities of petrol bombs were in production and that MI(R) was also developing a 'sticky bomb' for use against tanks.[105] A leaflet was produced in June outlining the method of manufacture of Molotov cocktails and Royal Engineers travelled the country providing further training. Captain Prendergast of the Indian Army was in charge of one training unit of Royal Artillery Territorials and recalled using Tom Wintringham's *Picture Post* articles as their 'manual of instruction' for making and using the Molotovs.[106] This was not merely a Home Guard weapon and special note was made of the need for more Molotov cocktail matches for anti-aircraft units in June 1940. On 29 June there was concern over a lack of supply to the 2nd Armoured Division.[107] On 22 June Ironside stressed that all road-blocks, Home Guard or army, should have a supply of Molotovs.[108] In the Southern Area of Southern Command the Home Guard only received just over 50 per cent of the total supply.[109] Stephen King-Hall MP, the Chief Staff Officer to the new Defence Section of the Ministry of Aircraft Production, was not impressed. He reluctantly circulated details of the Molotov to Ministry of Aircraft Production factory Home Guard units but noted 'This bomb has been described as fool-proof. The Factory Defence Section draws your attention to the fact that it is not B. Foolproof.'[110] There were many variations, all based on a glass beer or spirits bottle containing two parts petrol, one part oil and one part liquid tar or a length of rubber hose (to act as a gelling agent to make the burning mixture stick to its target). Thinner-walled spirits bottles were preferred as they broke easily, with recommendations to score the glass of thicker beer bottles. The bottle was then sealed and a rag soaked in paraffin or a length of combustible celluloid film wrapped around the neck. Two matches, ideally the long-burning 'lifeboat' type, were to be taped to the bottle, ready to be ignited by a striker board. Detailed instructions were provided on where to aim them on a tank to cause maximum damage and in trained hands during street fighting they would undoubtedly have proved effective; it was suggested that six bottles would be enough to put a tank out of action. Instruction was also provided at the Osterley Training School on how to make simple chemical time-delay fuses that turned Molotov cocktails into incendiary sabotage devices. The Home Guard were never called upon to put their improvised tank-hunting methods to the test but *Volunteer for Liberty* in October 1941 recounted how the Russian Home Guard ambushed a convoy of eight tanks and twelve armoured cars in a Ukrainian town:

> The enemy were met with a hail of hand grenades and petrol 'hot bottles' from both front and sides. One tank and two armoured cars caught fire, and their crews were killed by machine-gun bullets as they tried to run for it.[111]

The 'Sticky Bomb' (officially the No. 74 ST bomb) had been under development by MI(R) since early 1940, originally for clandestine warfare, and consisted of a glass sphere containing 1.25lb (0.57kg) of nitro-glycerine and covered in a sticky stockinette, which was in turn encased in a protective sheet metal casing. When the user pulled a pin on the handle of the grenade, its casing would fall away. Pulling another pin would arm the grenade and, upon being thrown, a lever was released on the handle that activated a 5-second fuse. It was a short-range weapon best used from ambush positions, the idea being to stick the glass sphere against the target, but one risk was that the sticky cover could easily stick to the thrower's clothing. Its development history encapsulates the problems faced by the War Office in 1940 and the myths surrounding Home Guard weaponry. After his briefing on the Molotov cocktails and the ST bomb, Eden stressed in terms approaching panic that new anti-tank grenades for Home Defence were 'vitally urgent and should be available in very large quantities. I don't mind where they come from as long as we get them, home or abroad.' Churchill also leapt in to demand to know why there was a 'great sloth' in completing the ST bomb and demanded a report every three days.[112] To pacify Churchill, the War Office promptly ordered 1 million, even though full trials had not yet been undertaken.[113] The first rushed trial was unsuccessful, a fundamental problem being that the current adhesive would not stick to a wet or dirty tank! A difference of opinion resulted between the Anti-Tank Committee (which believed the ST bomb did not live up to the claims made of it) and the Director of Artillery (who maintained there was no better alternative).[114] Churchill was furious at the delays in finalizing the design but they could not be produced in any quantity until May 1941. Despite the association of the 'Sticky Bomb' with the Home Guard, most of the early production was sent to the 8th Army in North Africa (where it destroyed its first tanks soon after arrival in May 1941) and the Home Guard only began to receive small quantities from July.[115] Between 1941 and 1943 approximately 2.5 million were produced and, although the majority eventually came into Home Guard service, they continued to be used successfully in North Africa and Italy, and by the Australian Army during the New Guinea campaign.

At the same time as MI(R) was developing the 'Sticky Bomb', another experimental anti-tank grenade was being developed under the patronage of Section D of SIS by Albright and Wilson of Oldbury. The No. 76 Self-Igniting Phosphorous (SIP) grenade (or 'AW bomb') comprised a half-pint glass bottle sealed with a crown cap and containing white phosphorous stabilized under water, with benzine and a length of rubber tube (Plate 18). When the bottle was broken, the phosphorous would ignite the petrol and rubber forming a burning mixture that would stick to its target, releasing intense heat as well as a choking cloud of sulphur dioxide and phosphorus pentoxide. The first deliveries to Home Forces were made in mid-July 1940 but at the time no more than 25 per cent were allocated for Home Guard use.[116] By August 1941 over 6 million had been produced.[117] The SIP grenades were supplied in wooden crates each holding twenty-four of the glass bottles. Dire warnings were provided on the lids of the crates –

'Highly Inflammable. Do Not Drop. Handle With Great Care' – and inside an enamel plate advised that the cases of bombs should be stored in a cool place and preferably under water. Not surprisingly, many Home Guard platoons and Auxiliary Units patrols decided to bury the crates in a safe location until needed, or even submerged them in convenient ponds. By the end of the war the location of many of these crates had been lost and even in 2018 they are being regularly dug up on building sites. As a more stable alternative, some Home Guard units in 1944 received the new No. 77 phosphorous grenade, used as an incendiary and as a smoke bomb. It used the same fuse as the No. 69 grenade in a compact metal container.

Another anti-tank grenade designed in the panic of 1940 was the No. 73 grenade, issued from late 1940. It had an 11in-long cylindrical body, topped by a Bakelite Type 247 'all-ways' fuse, looking similar to that of a Thermos flask, hence the 'Thermos bomb' nickname. It was able to penetrate 2 inches (51mm) of armour and would blow off the tracks of a light tank but its 4.5lb (2kg) weight made it impractical to throw far enough to allow the Type 247 fuse tape to unwind and arm the grenade. The fuse was often removed and it was used instead as a demolition charge. There was also an official Home Guard satchel charge, comprising 3lb of explosive, a short length of fuse and a friction igniter, contained in a suitable bag or sandbag.[118]

A more successful anti-tank grenade was finally introduced in late 1941. The No. 75 Hawkins mine or 'Talcum Powder Bomb' (named for the rectangular tin shape of its metal container) contained 1lb (0.45kg) of explosives and would explode under the pressure of a 2cwt load; it was capable of snapping the track of a Mk IV Panzer. Several Hawkins mines were often tied together as a 'necklace' ready to be pulled across a road. The Hawkins mine was later widely issued to Allied airborne forces.

Sub-Machine Guns

The British army had not been interested in the development of a sub-machine gun prior to the outbreak of the Second World War. Small numbers of the Thompson M28A1 sub-machine gun from the USA appeared in British service in January 1940 when the War Office, realizing its mistake, also began to place contracts to buy up large-scale supplies from the USA. Some Home Guard units were briefly issued with the Thompson as early as September 1940. They appear in staged publicity photographs around this time but the early deliveries of the weapons to the Home Guard were quickly wrenched from their grasp and given to the regular army.[119] Nonetheless, in December 1940 General Alan Brooke, recognizing that any fighting in Britain was likely to be at close quarters, gave priority to the distribution of Thompsons in the Home Forces to the Home Guard, with an allocation of 30,000 Thompsons compared to just 10,000 to the field army. Progress was slow and it took a year to reach Brooke's target, with the first Thompsons not received by the Home Guard until March 1941, each with 750 rounds of ammunition (three months after the propaganda photograph shown in Plate 15) and first appearing in the monthly returns for April 1941, as shown in Fig. 7. The Auxiliary Units did not receive theirs until after May.[120] The 50-round drum magazine is the iconic image of the Thompson but it is heavy, rattles and takes time to reload. From May the normal Home Guard allocation was five 20-round magazines.[121] By April 1942 there were 43,017 Thompsons in Home Guard service but numbers declined thereafter as they were superseded by the mass-produced Sten gun.[122]

The seeming invincibility of the German army, widely equipped with the 9mm calibre Schmeisser machine pistol, made Britain realize it needed its own sub-machine gun that was cheap and could be easily mass-produced. The Sten gun (Plate 16), similarly using 9mm ammunition, cost just £3 compared to the price of $225 paid for each US Thompson sub-machine gun. It was a simple blowback design, weighing just 6.5lb, and at one point a single factory was producing 20,000 per week. This was nothing like the craftsman-built SMLE or Thompson M1928A1 SMG. 'The day our platoon was issued with Sten guns', remembered one Edinburgh Home Guard, 'I knew we were going to win the war. At last, I thought, we've ditched the fine British craftsmanship nonsense.'[123]

It was the issue of the Sten gun from March 1942, just a few months after its first issue to the regular army, that was taken as a final sign of the acceptance of the Home Guard by the military establishment. Eventually distribution reached a ratio of one per six men. Despite its reputation for misfires and accidental discharges, the Sten became the standard sub-machine gun of the British army and an iconic weapon of European resistance movements. An early myth was that it was specifically designed for the Home Guard – possibly because the crudity of what was nicknamed the 'Plumber's Nightmare' (some made by Lines Bros – the Triang toy company) seemed to be in the vein of the rushed designs of sub-artillery that became particularly associated with the Home Guard.[124] The Home Guard was issued with both the most common Mk II version and the simplified Mk III, which could be produced from just five man-hours of work and comprised only forty-seven different parts. Although widely derided by war-time troops as unreliable, largely because of poor quality control (especially of the magazines), a well-handled good example was more accurate and far lighter than the Thompson. Leiston Patrol (Suffolk) of the Auxiliary Units, who all worked for Richard Garrett & Sons' engineering company, confidently modified their Stens so they could be used safely in single-shot mode without switching to automatic of their own accord.[125] By November 1942 the Home Guard had 248,234 Sten guns, together with 34 million rounds of ammunition.[126] In one instance, extra ammunition was scrounged to experiment with rabbit-hunting using a Sten gun – not to be recommended as it left the poor rabbit so mangled as to be unfit to eat.[127]

Mines

Until regular army Mk I anti-tank mines began to be issued to the Home Guard from late 1940, soup plates were recommended as the basis of improvised mines and decoys. Laughable as that might seem, the technique was used successfully by republicans in Spain and by the British army on the retreat to Dunkirk. There, a company commander faced with the approach of a column of German tanks took five soup plates from the kitchen of a nearby house and laid them in the middle of the road. The first tank saw them and skidded to a halt, and the column then retreated and made a detour, causing a valuable half-hour delay before the position was finally overrun.[128] The method was consequently recommended in the War Office Instructions *Tanks and Tank Destruction: LDV Instruction Leaflet No. 8* (July 1940), the army manual *Tank Hunting and Destruction: Military Training Pamphlet No. 42* (August 1940) and also in the December 1943 SOE training syllabus.[129] Through a tank vision slit the plates would look similar to an anti-tank mine and might oblige a commander to stop to investigate, especially as the Germans would have had too few tanks when they landed to risk any being disabled. The deception could be improved by occasionally actually laying a plate with explosives and an improvised pressure switch, or a grenade hidden underneath to deter over-close inspection. Once stopped, the tank would be easier to destroy with petrol bombs. In the twenty-first century the caution of armoured columns on the roads of Iraq or Afghanistan when coming across anything which might possibly be a roadside bomb has clearly demonstrated the effectiveness of such improvised explosive devices. As an extension of the idea of deception, rumours were also spread that some post boxes had been sealed and filled with explosives ready for remote detonation. The Post Office was persuaded to seal some post boxes sited at road junctions that might be suitable places for ambush. There was also the McNaughton Torpedo or 'Bosche Bump', consisting of scaffolding tubes packed with explosives and buried under a road.[130] Suitable explosives could be obtained from mines and quarries or extracted from Type 73 grenades. Wilfrid Vernon, instructor at the Osterley Training School, went even further. Tom Hopkinson recounts how he passed Vernon in the kitchen and noticed him stirring 'some thick greyish substance' in a saucepan. Upon enquiry, Vernon explained that this was dynamite, reassuring Hopkinson that it would not explode by being heated. An unconvinced Hopkinson replied 'Yes – but are you sure it understands that?'[131] By late 1940 there was a plentiful supply of regular army mines to protect nodal points, with strict instructions that they were only to be laid by Home Guard trained by Royal Engineers instructors and they were not to be laid until attack was imminent. By December 1941 over 12,000 anti-tank mines and an equal number of Hawkins or Type 73 anti-tank grenades were held at the nodal points in Cambridge and Norfolk.[132]

Light Machine Guns

The initial US arms contract of June 1940 (Fig. 8) included a number of light machine-gun types that became standard in the Home Guard. As an example, by October 1940 Worcestershire Home Guard possessed a total of 152 Browning Automatic Rifles, 8 Hotchkiss Machine Guns, 30 Browning Machine Guns and 12 Lewis Light Machine Guns.[133] However, a notable omission from the list was the recently introduced British army light machine gun – the Bren gun. A popular, if polite, appeal came from Noël Coward's 1941 song *Could You Please Oblige Us with a Bren Gun*? The song takes the form of a letter written by the

CO of the local Home Guard to the Ministry of Supply. It includes the following two verses.

> Could you please oblige us with a Bren gun?
> Or failing that, a hand grenade will do,
> We've got some ammunition, in a rather damp condition
> And Major Huss has an arquebus that was used at Waterloo.
>
> With the Vicar's stirrup pump, a pitchfork and a stave
> It's rather hard to guard an aerodrome,
> So if you can't oblige us with a Bren gun
> The Home Guard might as well go home.[134]

The rejoinder came from Langdon-Davies, who commented 'If you in the Home Guard feel inclined to say rather bitterly: "Where is my Bren gun?", remember this answer – "Your Bren gun went to Libya"'.[135] The Bren gun was introduced to British army service in 1937 and was already respected for its accuracy and reliability, therefore it was naturally viewed with envious eyes by the Home Guard. It had a nominal rate of fire of around 500 rounds per minute, which was slowed by its reliance on a 30-round magazine. Noël Coward was writing for dramatic effect rather than strict historic accuracy. In June 1940 Britain had just 12,000 Bren guns but some had been acquired by the Ministry of Aircraft Production to equip the Beaverette armoured cars of its Home Guard factory units.[136] The War Office subsequently had some difficulty persuading the Ministry of Aircraft Production to release their Bren guns in exchange for .30 Browning machine guns, arguing that the Bren guns were urgently required by the field army.[137] A small number of Bren guns were later received by general service battalions of the Home Guard in 1942 for training purposes but there were still only 112 in its hands in November 1942.[138] Others were shared with the army. Crowle Home Guard (Worcestershire) shared anti-aircraft duties with the Regulars of No. 23 ITC from Norton Barracks on top of Whittington Tump (just to the east of Worcester), using a Bren gun on an anti-aircraft mount. If they lacked the Bren gun in significant numbers, the Home Guard was widely equipped with its unwieldy predecessor – the Lewis gun, mainly imported from the USA in .300 calibre as the US stripped-down aerial variant, with the distinctive cooling jacket removed and using a 97-round drum magazine. The 'Belgian rattlesnake' had first come into British service in 1915 and remained in service throughout the Second World War. The LDV Inspectorate estimated that 20 per cent of the volunteers were already trained machine-gunners and so would have been very familiar with this weapon.[139] In 1940 the British version in .303 calibre was a mainstay of British light anti-aircraft defences on land and at sea and is reputed to have accounted for 20 per cent of German aircraft shot down over London.[140] By 26 July 1940, 7,400 Lewis guns in .300 calibre had been supplied, each with 750 rounds of ammunition, supplemented with ammunition siphoned off from the allocation to the M1917 rifles.[141] Delays were caused by the difficulty in removing the thick storage grease, necessary refitting to make them suitable for ground warfare and the need to provide adequate training. New battle sights were fitted and where possible the spade grip was replaced with the standard wooden butt.[142] By February 1941 the Home Guard had been issued with 11,598 of the aerial variants and 2,277 of the ground variants. In Redditch, Worcestershire, Fred Dean of the Terrys Factory Home Guard manned an aerial-type Lewis gun mounted on top of the factory tower. Along with every other anti-aircraft gun in Redditch, he once engaged a Heinkel which bombed the BSA Works (and which was later brought down by a Spitfire). Without a cooling jacket, Dean's weapon overheated and the barrel 'blued', making it unserviceable.[143]

The Home Guard also had the US equivalent of the Bren gun, the M1918 Browning Automatic Rifle (BAR), which although seeing some service in the First World War was only generally introduced as the standard US infantry light machine gun in 1938 (and therefore more modern than its nomenclature would suggest, although the Home Guard tended to be supplied with early versions). It was lighter than the Bren gun but its effectiveness was limited by its lack of a quick-change barrel to avoid overheating in prolonged action and a smaller-capacity 20-round magazine. Over 20,000 BARs were in service with the Home Guard by February 1941 and it remained the most common light machine gun in Home Guard service.[144] Its key role is indicated by the distinctive Home Guard webbing ammunition pouches, sized to contain two BAR magazines (each man in the BAR group would carry two magazines as a supply for the squad BAR). The BAR remained in US service until the Vietnam war.

Other types of light machine gun included the Hotchkiss .303 machine gun which went into service with cavalry and yeomanry regiments in 1916 and was still in service with the remaining British cavalry at the start of the Second World War. The Hotchkiss weighed 27lb and had a rate of fire of 500 rounds per minute from a 30-round metal strip. The Home Guard also had a number of French Chatellerault FM 24/29 light machine guns, the standard light machine gun of the French army from 1930 until the 1960s, passed to them after Dunkirk.

Medium and Heavy Machine Guns

The standard British medium machine gun in 1940 was the Vickers, first introduced to service in 1912; it continued in service until 1968. This required a six to eight man team and had an effective range of 2000m with a rate of fire of 450 to 500 rounds per minute from a 250-round belt, capable (due to its water-cooling system) of prolonged sustained fire. Only a small number of British-made Vickers could be spared for the Home Guard, with the majority supplied from the USA in .300 calibre. The US equivalent of the Vickers was the Browning M1917A1 (Plate 17) and over 6,000 of them had been supplied to the Home Guard by November 1942, along with the Colt M1895 'Potato-digger' and its later development, the Marlin M1918 machine gun, also with a 250-round belt feed. London District Home Guard received forty Colt machine guns as a gift from US engineer A.P. Buquor; the guns were organized first as a machine-gun company to man river defence block-houses commanding the Thames river and then as a machine-gun battalion within 'R' Zone.[145] The Home Guard also had the aerial Vickers K gun, most famously used in the vehicles of the Long Range Desert Group and SAS.

The main use of the machine guns was as anti-aircraft defence for vulnerable points and factories. The Marlin machine gun was used for light anti-aircraft defence by both the Home Guard and the Merchant Navy. The Worcester City Battalion had eight, on two quadruple mountings, protecting the city power station; another pair was mounted on the Worcester Sheet Metal Company works on Hylton Road.[146] Some factory units had the luxury of being able to use the weapons produced in their factories for their defence. The Besa was a Czech-designed machine gun used in tanks and produced by the Birmingham Small Arms 'shadow factory' at Redditch, where its factory Home Guard acquired a number, with substantial quantities of ammunition, for light anti-aircraft defences. From March 1942 a small number of Hispano 20mm cannon, designed as aircraft guns, were also distributed across Home Guard commands for use in anti-aircraft defence; eighty-one were listed by November 1942 but the number was increased in the run-up to D-Day amidst the heightened fear of any interruption to the supply chain by the bombing of factories. The Hispano had an impressive rate of fire of 700 rounds per minute. The Workington Home Guard (Cumbria) at the High-Duty Alloys 'shadow factory' had a light anti-aircraft troop equipped with eight Marlin machine guns and nine 20mm Hispano cannon, while the neighbouring Iron and Steel Works was defended by eighteen Hispano cannon.

Boys Anti-Tank Rifle

The Boys .55in anti-tank rifle was first introduced into service in 1937. It was a bolt action rifle, heavy and unwieldy, with a strong recoil, and had a 5-round magazine. The Finns had used it to good effect against Soviet T-26 tanks in 1939–40 and it could penetrate the frontal armour of a Panzer I at 300 yards.[147] Although unpopular, it remained the principal British infantry anti-tank weapon until 1943. It began to be introduced to the Home Guard in small numbers from March 1942 but numbers increased to 10,000 by July 1943, following their replacement in the army by the PIAT.[148] Although increasingly ineffective against the heavier German tanks, it remained useful against soft-skinned vehicles and light armoured cars up to 100 yards. These were the reconnaissance vehicles the Home Guard were most likely to first face in any invasion or raid.

Sub-Artillery

The desperate shortage of anti-tank guns in 1940 was met by the invention of 'sub-artillery' pieces, whose main virtue was that they were cheap and, it was optimistically hoped, could be produced quickly without diverting resources from building replacement 2-pdr anti-tank guns. Their novelty appealed to Churchill but the sub-artillery was intended for army and Home Guard alike and should not be confused with the improvised home-made mortars cheerfully produced by the early Home Guard. The 'sub-artillery' did become particularly associated with the Home Guard, who had a lower priority than the army for early replacement of such weapons. One of the sacrifices in the rushed design and production was a lack of mobility but this was less important in the fixed positions of the Home

Guard's 'defended localities' and their requirement for multi-person gun crews was undoubtedly useful in resolving the criticism of the lack of personal weapons. Speaking of the three-man Northover Projector crew, Brigadier Whitehead of London Home Guard commented that 'they all feel it belongs to them, and forget, for the moment at any rate, that they have not got a rifle'.[149] Unfortunately, despite their apparent simplicity, the designs were plagued with problems which meant they came into service much later than intended, lessening their value as better alternatives became available.

The Northover Projector was designed as a means of increasing the range that a No. 76 SIP grenade could be lobbed and, like the latter, it was developed in conjunction with Section D of SIS. It was based on the design of Harry Northover (a Canadian gunsmith and Home Guard officer) for a clay pigeon trap, with one of its attractions being that it used little steel, the barrel being a 4ft length of standard 2.5in-diameter gas pipe.[150] Northover worked with Chester Beatty from Section D and during early trials it was known as the Chester Beatty Mortar; Beatty's Selection Manufacturing Company later redesigned the weapon. As well as the No. 76 SIP grenade, the Northover Projector could also fire the No. 68 anti-tank grenade, both to a range of up to 140 yards. Its main drawback was the use of a black powder propulsion charge that revealed the weapon's presence by a cloud of white smoke. The design was presented to Churchill in May 1940, with the first demonstration in mid-June 1940.[151] Beatty later briefed Desmond Morton, Lord Swinton and Professor Lindemann on progress:

> Today he [Beatty] showed me [Lindemann] a projector, something like the Stokes mortar, with which beer bottles can be thrown 140 yards with reasonable accuracy ... He thinks it should be possible to produce a thousand of these projectors a week and is anxious they should be placed in every village apt to be invaded by tanks ... He thinks in terms of tens of thousands of simple mortars to be produced in a few weeks against the War Office's hundreds.[152]

A later demonstration was given in front of the Prime Minister on 28 July 1940 at Hangmoor Ranges, Pirbright, Surrey. With no thought for health and safety, it was tested with No. 76 SIP grenades against a moving, manned, tank: 'The first went over the tank at about 120 yards range, whereas the second hit the visor of the tank and flame actually entered the tank, causing the driver to evacuate as quickly as possible.'[153]

Although simple, it was by no means the 'toy' that MacKenzie implies.[154] *Military Training Pamphlet No. 42, Tank Hunting and Destruction* of August 1940 gives advance notice of the weapon and makes clear it was intended first for the army and then for the Home Guard. But despite the optimism of the early trials, the Northover Projector was plagued with production difficulties and by the time it was ready for service, the supply of 2-pdr anti-tank guns for the army had improved. Most were therefore allocated to the Home Guard, although some were shipped to the garrison at Singapore. The first examples reached the Home Guard in January 1941 but did not enter general service until June 1941 (and were not included in the monthly returns until August, *see* Fig. 7). For the War Office this was, at last, a welcome means of dissuading the Home Guard from building their own drainpipe mortars (Plate 12).[155] In all, 13,000 examples of the Mk I version were made by Northover's Bisley Clay Target Co. Ltd and 8,000 of the redesigned Mk II version by Beatty's Selection Manufacturing Company Ltd (the main visible difference being it was supported by three rather than four legs, but the parts were not interchangeable).[156]

The 29mm Spigot Mortar (aka Blacker Bombard) was designed by Lieutenant Colonel Stewart Blacker of MI(R) in August 1940 as an anti-tank mortar, firing a 20lb anti-tank or 14lb high explosive round to a range of 100–200 yards (Plate 19).[157] There were the seemingly inevitable delays but the C-in-C Home Forces was sufficiently impressed by a demonstration in April 1941 to ask for production to be given as high a priority as possible and for it to be issued to anti-tank regiments, infantry brigades and airfield defence units, as well as the Home Guard.[158] The 29mm Spigot Mortar was not issued to the Home Guard until November 1941 (Fig. 7) but there were 18,000 in service with the Home Guard by the end of 1942. It was heavy and really suited only for fixed position defence, which made it unpopular with those in the Home Guard who were chafing for a more mobile form of warfare. Increased production of the 2-pdr gun (at the expense of retooling for the superior 6-pdr gun) removed much of the urgency for the rest of the army but a number were supplied to the 8th Army in the Western Desert and saw action at Tobruk and at El Alamein with the Indian, Australian and New Zealand divisions. Some 5,000 were also supplied to the Soviet Union. The design was developed into the highly effective anti-submarine 'Hedgehog' mortar of the Royal Navy and the PIAT anti-tank weapon. The Spigot Mortar was a muzzle-loading weapon, fired by a sprung steel rod striking a black powder charge on the base of the bomb. Its short range and the smoke again made it advisable to ensure a direct hit on the target with the first shot and from a well-concealed position. There was also a tendency for shrapnel from an exploding charge to fly back along its trajectory to the mortar position! It weighed 360lb, requiring a five-man crew to operate and manoeuvre, although GHQ stressed that it was designed to be used from fixed positions and resisted the distribution of mobile mountings.[159] The reinforced concrete base and stainless steel pintle of the Blacker Bombard emplacement is now one of the most commonly found memorials to the Home Guard, typically found in the undergrowth covering crossroads, bridges and other vulnerable points.

The largest, and strangest, invention in sub-artillery pieces was the Smith Gun (Plate 20), invented by retired major William Smith, Chief Engineer of the Trianco Toy Company. It was a 3in (76mm) smooth-bored anti-tank gun with a maximum range of 500 yards (460m) when firing the 8lb high explosive round but only 200 yards firing the 6lb anti-tank bomb. Accuracy was hampered by having to be fired at a high trajectory to compensate for the low muzzle velocity. It was mounted between two wheels which were tipped over onto their side to act as baseplate/turntable in the firing position. The design was initially rejected by the Ordnance Board but this was overruled by Churchill, not least because it cost just

£100 to manufacture. An order for over 3,000 Smith Guns was placed in April 1941 but they did not come into service with the Home Guard (other than a small number provided for training purposes) until June 1942. Priority had been given to the RAF Regiment for airfield defence and by the time production allowed them to arrive in Home Guard service they did look like a 1940 anachronism and were of increasingly limited practical value. In the end just over 2,000 Smith guns eventually came into service with the Home Guard. The weapon was heavy and awkward to manoeuvre and required a crew of four. It had a poor safety record with the solid tyres causing damage in transit, not least to the sensitive fuses of the shells, but nonetheless it was strangely popular with crews.

Field Artillery

The myth of obsolete weapons being issued to the Home Guard extends to the heavier guns. MacKenzie claimed artillery was issued 'for the sake of appearances' and described the 18-pdr and 2-pdr guns as only 'marginally less ineffective' than the Croft Pike![160] This is nonsense and is again grounded in the assumption that anything of First World War vintage used by the Home Guard was automatically functionally obsolete (as opposed to 'obsolete' used in War Office terminology as indicating replaced by a newer model). In June 1940 there were just 430 field guns in the country and every possible weapon was pressed into service. The Home Guard began to be issued with small numbers of field artillery guns from 1941 as they became replaced by newer models in regular army service, or as the Home Guard took over responsibility for weapons in installations vacated by regular troops. The priority went to those Home Guard units working with coastal artillery and there was a preference for those types (13-pdrs, 18-pdrs and 4.5in howitzers) with which ex-gunners of the First World War would already be familiar.[161] The total numbers are difficult to establish and even the War Office seemed uncertain in November 1943 as to the types held by the Home Guard.[162]

The most common artillery piece in Home Guard service was the Hotchkiss 6-pdr quick-firing (QF) gun which was originally designed in the late nineteenth century as an anti-torpedo boat weapon for use in the superstructure of Dreadnought battleships. From 1917 the weapon was mounted in the side sponsons of Mk IV male tanks and subsequently were put into storage. Several hundred of these guns had to be reconditioned in 1940 as a stop-gap anti-tank weapon for the Royal Artillery, which had lost most of its 2-pdr anti-tank guns in France. Many were deployed in fixed emplacements on the coast and on the stop lines, for which the Home Guard began to assume responsibility in the spring of 1941. They were also the main weapon of coastal armoured trains, manned by the Home Guard from 1942 (*see below*, p. 111). Consequently, the Home Guard used these weapons simply because they took over responsibility for the installations in which the weapons were sited, rather than the weapons having been considered too obsolete for regular troops. The quick-firing ability of the weapon was demonstrated by one Worcestershire Home Guard team, trained by an ex-naval gunner, who reputedly managed to get off eight shots in ten seconds.[163] By January 1944 the Home Guard were still responsible for 216 of the 6-pdr gun sites.[164]

The only other field guns supplied in quantity were up to forty-two of the US and British versions of the 75mm gun.[165] The British version was cobbled together from a shortened 3in anti-aircraft gun barrel, rebored/resleeved to the new calibre, mounted on a First World War field gun carriage. It had a range of up to 10,450 yards and was mainly intended for coastal defence. The US-built guns were probably part of a consignment of M1917 75mm field guns supplied to Britain in 1940. Ulster Home Guard also took over a number of 75mm anti-tank guns from the RAF Regiment in 1942, as well as several of the more modern 25-pdr field guns, when they took over responsibility for airfield defence and to bolster the defences of Belfast and Londonderry.

There were only a handful of other types of artillery piece. Haddington Company of East Lothian Home Guard acquired three of the eighteen issued 18-pdr field guns in 1942, training on them for two nights per week and every Sunday. In one exercise they fired 150 rounds on the Lammermuir Hills. Several Mk V 12-pdr QF guns, made at the Garrett Works in Leiston, Suffolk, and used on destroyers, armed merchant ships and for coastal defence, were given to the local Leiston Home Guard in permanent emplacements to defend the town and the nearby Sizewell Gap against enemy attack.

From 1943 the Home Guard was finally issued with the standard 2-pdr anti-tank gun, then being replaced in regular service with the 6-pdr anti-tank gun (Plate 21). In 1940 the 2-pdr gun could penetrate the armour of any German tank then in service up to a range of 500 yards. A deliberate decision was made to continue to rearm the army with 2-pdr guns after the losses suffered in France as the best way of maximizing production even at the expense of delaying manufacture of the much superior 6-pdr anti-tank gun, but even in 1943 the 2-pdr was still effective against lighter tanks, armoured cars and 'soft-skinned' vehicles – the types of target that the Home Guard might still expect to face. It was by no means as 'ineffective' as MacKenzie suggests, and remained as the main armament in British armoured cars throughout the war.[166]

Flame Throwers

Another answer to the shortage of anti-tank guns in 1940 was to turn to flame-based weapons and these were extensively used by the Home Guard as part of district defence plans. Flame traps (*flame fougasse*) were devastating weapons designed to engulf a passing convoy with flame and were not a weapon to be used in an ad hoc fashion. *Military Training Pamphlet No. 42, Tank Hunting and Destruction*, of 29 August 1940, stressed: 'This form of ambush should be prepared only where approved by general officers commanding-in-chief or such officers to whom they may delegate the authority.' Over 7,000 were carefully sited by Royal Engineer chemical companies in suitable defiles by June 1941 and were then operated by the Home Guard. Each trap consisted of a 40-gallon oil drum filled with a mixture of petrol and gas oil. An explosive charge at the rear of the barrel could be remotely detonated to throw the burning mixture forward and flood a 3m-wide stretch of road. Ideally they would be sited in batteries of four to maximize damage. A variant christened the 'Hedgehopper' was a drum set vertically with a small charge underneath, designed to be used in batteries of four, sited from behind cover. On firing, the 'Hedgehopper' would fly 3m into the air and 9m forward. On a smaller scale, by January 1941 the Home Guard had been issued with 2,000 of the standard, if rudimentary, British Army 'portable' Harvey flamethrower which could propel 22 gallons (1,000 litres) of burning creosote in a 10-second burst over a distance of 18m, using bottles of nitrogen as a propellant.[167] It was usually transported on a small trolley which allowed it to be manoeuvred into an ambush position. The Harvey was supplemented by a simplified Home Guard version comprising a 40-gallon drum of mixed petrol and diesel similarly mounted on a two-wheeled trolley; the fuel was projected from a hose using a simple rotary hand pump. The device had a range of about 14m and the flame could be maintained for about 2 minutes, after which the crew would beat a hasty retreat.

Armoured Cars

After Dunkirk the British army in Britain was desperately short of tanks and armoured cars. A wide range of makeshift vehicles were officially produced on commercial car and lorry chassis, using welded steel plate and concrete as armour, and were used by the army and RAF mainly for factory and airfield defence. The Beaverette was a commercially produced armoured car commissioned by Lord Beaverbrook to defend Ministry of Aircraft Production factories and airfields and became particularly associated with the Home Guard (Plate 22). General Alan Brooke was not impressed, accusing Beaverbrook of trying to raise a private army to defend Ministry of Aircraft Production factories:

> He acquired large proportions of armour plating for the production of small armoured cars called 'Beaverettes', with which he equipped Home Guard personnel of factories for their protection. This was at a time when I was shouting for every armoured vehicle I could lay my hands on with which to equip regular forces. The whole thing was fantastic.[168]

The Beaverette was built from June 1940 by the Standard Motor Company and was based around a Humber Standard or Super Snipe chassis with a simple riveted armoured hull, comprising 8–9mm steel plate backed with 3in-thick oak planks. Originally open-topped, it was armed with a Bren gun or aerial-type Lewis machine guns. Later versions were completely enclosed and had a turret-mounted machine gun. The Beaverette remained in production until 1942, by which time around 2,800 had been built and were in service with the British army, RAF and Home Guard. It was heavy, leading to metal fatigue on the chassis, and had a top speed of only 24mph. Confusingly, the name 'Beaverette' also became used as a general description of makeshift vehicles.[169] Publicity photographs show Home Guard in fleets of Beaverette armoured cars but in September 1942 GHQ sought to withdraw them because they encouraged a 'counter-attack' role that ran counter to the overwhelming concern for the Home Guard to defend fixed points.[170] It did not stop the Home Guard continuing to request their issue to mobile patrols, to the frustration of GHQ.[171]

The Beaver-Eel (officially the Leyland Type C Armoured Tender) was another improvised vehicle built in small numbers for airfield and Ministry of Aircraft Production factory defence. Home Guard crews even designed their own arm badge! It was an open-topped armoured lorry, based on the 3-ton Leyland 'Retriever', and mounted a variation of a 37mm Vickers anti-aircraft gun, a 20mm Hispano cannon or Lewis machine guns. Bisons were built by the Concrete Company Ltd to create mobile pill boxes on the back of a lorry chassis; a lighter version was designated the Armadillo. Both were primarily for airfield defence against paratroop landings and were initially used by the RAF, later passed to the Home Guard when it took on airfield defence duties. In Northern Ireland the Ulster Home Guard had the use of Lancia armoured personnel carriers, handed down to the police after the Irish War of Independence.

Many Home Guard units built their own armoured cars, armed with whatever weaponry was available, typically Lewis or Browning machine guns or Boys anti-tank rifles. Some were of dubious value and served mainly as morale-boosters but others were more practical and at least gave some protection against small arms fire. Colonel Tickler of the famous jam company in Maidenhead, Berkshire, built a series of armoured cars based on the Sunbeam and imported US Hudson chassis. King's Lynn Home Guard in Norfolk had a veritable fleet of armoured cars built on Alvis, Hillman, Railton, Rover and Ford chassis. London County Council built armoured cars on the chassis of the official fleet of Rolls-Royce cars. Stroud Home Guard in Gloucestershire built two open-topped armoured cars on the chassis of Morris Cowley cars and named them 'Daniel' and 'The Eagle'; they were armed with Hotchkiss machine guns. From as early as June 1940 Marton Platoon in Warwickshire had the 'Trojan', built on a Morris chassis provided by Parkside Garage in Coventry and fitted with welded armour plating by Cllr Sam Myers at his Warwick workshop; the armour was proof-tested against .303 rounds at 100 yards. It was used to carry a section of ten men but it was so heavy that when travelling uphill the men had to get out and push it. 'Trojan' was armed with a German sub-machine gun from the 1920s, later replaced by a Lewis gun. One of the most impressive armoured vehicles was built by the factory Home Guard of the Air Defence Research and Development Establishment at Sommerford in Hampshire (now Dorset). They used one of the Dodge-based armoured cars designed by Sir Malcolm Campbell to create a self-propelled gun, named 'Tubby the Tank Buster'. It was open-topped and equipped with a 6-pdr Hotchkiss gun. But not even this could compete with the Birmingham Carriage Company Ltd, Smethwick, which made A10, Valentine and Churchill tanks during the war and gave its factory Home Guard the use of six tanks.[172] Cambridge STC also retained their tank used for pre-war officer training.

With their appetite whetted by the assortment of vehicles produced in the aftermath of Dunkirk, and with an improving range of other weaponry, the Home Guard began to campaign for recognized armoured units. In the aftermath of the Cretan invasion, in June 1941 John Brophy called for 'Armoured Mobility' in the Home Guard.[173] As was typical, Churchill was enthusiastic in support of this large body of voters and in November 1941 he called for small specialist battalions equipped with Universal (Bren) carriers.[174] The War Office was less keen to have armoured units of the Home Guard roaming the countryside as yet another distraction from their role of defending fixed points. Margesson also made the point that the additional training for men serving only part-time and in reserved occupations was likely to impact upon their productivity and would divert still scarce resources from the army.

Armoured Trains

In 1942 the Home Guard took over the fleet of thirteen armoured trains that had been built at the Ashford Railway Works (Kent) in June 1940 and were previously manned by Polish units. They were typically formed by a small locomotive sandwiched between two supply wagons and a heavily armed armoured wagon at each end. The wagons were usually small, steel coal wagons with extra armour. The trains were used as mobile gun platforms on the coastal railway lines of south and east England from Cornwall to the Humber estuary, patrolling against the threat of parachute attacks and to reinforce any positions under attack. In Scotland the Home Guard from Glasgow, Edinburgh and the Highlands each took over the manning of an armoured train, covering the coastline of Fife, Edinburgh to Berwick on Tweed, and Aberdeen.

Each train was typically armed with a 6-pdr Hotchkiss gun, two Vickers machine guns, two Boys anti-tank rifles, six Bren guns, four Thompsons and a contingent of riflemen. They carried up to 38,000 rounds of ammunition of various calibres. The armoured train built for the narrow-gauge Romney, Hythe & Dymchurch Railway was more lightly armed, with each carriage armed with a Boys anti-tank rifle and two Lewis guns. In addition, over the winter of 1940 the Home Guard unit at the Experimental Establishment at Shoeburyness, at the mouth of the River Thames, refurbished a First World War armoured wagon with a 12-pdr gun and two 2-pdr pom-pom guns to be used as part of the anti-aircraft defence of Shoeburyness. It was christened 'HMS Terror'.

Other railway Home Guard made their own improvised armoured trains. In Middlesbrough reject steel plate from the shipyard was used to line the sides and ends of four-wheeled goods wagons, which were then furnished with a Lewis gun.[175] The railwaymen of the Worcester City Battalion were also reported to have had the use of an otherwise undocumented armoured train which was stored in sidings at Shrub Hill station.[176]

Home Guard Air Force

The Austin Aero Factory at Longbridge had two pilots in its Home Guard unit who had the use of two Hawker Hurricane fighters, supplied by the Ministry of Aircraft Production. They were kept on the works airfield at Cofton, on the edge of Worcestershire.[177] Although they flew on several patrols, to the disappointment of their pilots they never engaged the enemy.

Home Guard Uniforms

The men who volunteered in the first days and weeks following Eden's broadcast probably thought very little about the legality of their actions. All they really wanted was a gun with which to defend their country. The absolute priority of government in May 1940 was, however, to provide some sort of uniform to prevent the volunteers being classed as *francs-tireur* or terrorists. Langdon-Davies explained

> the laws of war, which must be obeyed by every British subject, whether or not they are obeyed by the Nazis, do not permit of civilians offering armed resistance, unless they are organized in a regular corps and wear a recognizable uniform. That is why people, who would otherwise be civilians, have to join the Home Guard and receive uniform.[178]

The first 'uniform' was a simple armband ('brassard') to be worn on the right arm, bearing the initials LDV, and from 22 July 'Home Guard'. In the First World War the Volunteer Training Corps' armbands were treated as legal documents, individually numbered, and recipients were issued with dire warnings to return them once their service was completed. By contrast, the LDV/Home Guard armbands were, in the main, unregistered and subject to local variations. Even by 23 July 1940 only 30 per cent of the LDV had been issued with the official armband and many were home-made, the letters stencilled onto white cloth.[179] In the film *Get Cracking* the narrator tells George Formby that his uniform is falling down – so he pulls his armband back from his cuff to upper arm! Officially, they were meant to be sewn onto the sleeve to prevent this eventuality. One of Eden's concerns when Churchill forced a change of name to the Home Guard was the cost of replacing the so-recently distributed LDV armbands, which might seem petty yet the minutes of the meetings of the Home Guard Inspectorate make clear the difficulties in 1940 of finding the resources for even this simple change. A bureaucratic argument then broke out as to whether 'Home Guard' or 'HG' was the correct form for use on the new armbands and the exasperated Quartermaster General made an arbitrary decision in order to get things moving.[180] It was stressed that 'the issue of these armbands and of uniforms was of even greater importance than the issue of rifles, as the German broadcasts were pouring out infective propaganda every night about the Home Guard being *francs-tireur*'.[181] By 10 September 1.8 million Home Guard armbands had been distributed, together with 1.1 million cheaper patches to sew over old LDV armbands or directly onto the new denim blouse.[182]

At the time there was a problem with supplying even the regular forces with battledress. Some of the BEF went to war in 1939 wearing 1922 pattern tunics and First World War webbing rather than the 1937 pattern battledress and webbing. The first proper uniform for the Home Guard was the shapeless denim work overalls newly introduced in 1939 as a second outfit to wear for fatigue duty over battledress. By 12 July 200,000 denim overalls had been distributed to the Home Guard but many were delivered without their removable buttons and buckles as these were issued from a separate source. Bottlenecks in local supply chains meant that although 933,382 overalls had been issued to depots by 20 August, along with 1,042,319 forage caps, there were difficulties getting them out to local units.[183] The continuing shortfall in uniform supply was partially resolved by taking denim suits intended for regular troops, who then had to be supplied with a more expensive second set of battledress to make up the difference.[184] Although derided for their lack of style, the denims were cooler in summer than the woollen battledress and were the favoured uniform of the 1944 D-Day assault troops as they dried out more quickly than the heavy woollen battledress. Nonetheless, an important step forward in image came when the serge battledress was distributed from January 1941.[185] The forage caps were the subject of particular complaint. They required one size above normal hat size in order to perch less precariously on the wearer's head and supplies of a decent size were in short supply. In late August George Orwell, who joined C Company of the 5th County of London Battalion, gave up waiting for one of the correct size and bought his own from a private outfitter.[186]

Uniforms were important to indicate to the men that they were being treated with respect and to cement their status as genuine soldiers within the community. When the West Indian George Roberts was refused entrance to the Grafton Hall dance hall in Liverpool, he returned in his Home Guard uniform to try (unsuccessfully) to embarrass the owner (*see above*, p. 17). In another status symbol, on 2 July 1940 the Home Guard Inspectorate confirmed that the badge of the county regiment would be issued. Nonetheless, a small number of units adopted a specific badge, as did the Upper Thames River Patrol and Rutland Home Guard. Printed cream on khaki Home Guard shoulder titles were officially approved in November 1940, but unofficial embroidered versions had already been widely produced and continued to be offered for private purchase. Ulster Home Guard also had its own pattern of county shoulder titles. The distinctive rectangular county and battalion flashes were authorized in February 1941 but were only issued on a large scale from late July 1941, and by 12 August 1941, 24 million had been supplied.[187] One of the continuing battles with the War Office resulted from the Home Guard's desire to demonstrate its professionalism by way of the standard army trade and proficiency badges. A proficiency badge, simple enough to be manufactured locally (a red felt diamond), was introduced in April 1941 but this did not stop the Home Guard from wearing other trade badges whether sanctioned or not.[188]

Another immediate problem was the supply of army boots. After discussion on whether to provide army boots or give an allowance for the wear and tear on men's existing boots (on the assumption that many were labourers who already possessed boots), it was finally agreed on 2 August that the War Office should provide a 100 per cent issue of boots.[189] They were distributed within days but there were suspicions that men were using them for everyday work or even gardening as they seemed to be quickly wearing out.[190]

Given the British plans to use poison gas on the invasion beaches, and the risk of retaliation, it was important to provide adequate gas masks but initially the Home Guard had to rely on civilian respirators in their flimsy cardboard containers. The first step was to provide better tin containers, but army respirators were only issued in large numbers from early 1941, with the failure to provide sufficient numbers still being raised in Parliament in April 1941.[191]

Another critical shortage was steel helmets, which was particularly hard to bear for Home Guard units working in London and other cities during the blitz. Remarkably, no thought had been given to issuing helmets when the LDV was founded, and a question was quickly sidestepped in Parliament, but some men bought helmets still available for private purchase in shops.[192] Again, the problem was that there was still a shortage of steel helmets for regular forces. Orwell was told in August 1940 that the army was still lacking 300,000 helmets.[193] In such circumstances it is not surprising that, when equipment allocated to the Home Guard was sent to army Ordnance depots for distribution, some material, including steel helmets, was 'acquired' for the regular army. It was in September that helmets began to be issued to the Home Guard on a regular basis but only at a rate of 6,000 per week (out of a total weekly national production of 30,000).[194] By the end of November 1940 only 214,595 steel helmets had been issued.[195] Many were the mild steel Mk II No. 2c helmets (identified with three holes to their brim) which gave them a reduced level of ballistic protection.

Whilst experiencing huge difficulties in providing even basic uniforms and equipment, it might seem strange that on 2 August 1940 the Home Guard Inspectorate discussed the need for a lapel badge. It harked back to the First World War when lapel badges were issued to prove that a man not in uniform was engaged on important war work. There had been complaints from newly arrived Dominion troops over the number of male civilians on the streets and physical proof that everybody was 'doing their bit' was clearly needed to reassure them.[196] Unofficial LDV lapel badges had already been produced in the short, seventy-day lifetime of that organization, both as a generic badge and as badges for individual units, including Vickers Armstrong, Bearsden (Glasgow) and Shepshed, Leicestershire. Although Churchill was in favour of an official Home Guard lapel badge, the War Office resisted the proposal. Instead, in the midst of resource and manufacturing shortages, a host of unofficial badges were produced.

The supply of other equipment began as a trickle but became a flood from September 1940 onwards. Home Guard units were not issued with the current webbing, which was in short supply, but instead were issued with the 1903 pattern leather belt, leather bayonet frog, mounted pattern leather water-bottle carrier and leather gaiters. A complication with the belts was that extra-large sizes had to be provided to cope with the non-military waists of middle-aged Home Guards. Before there were sufficient greatcoats, a distinctive serge cape was provided. By August there were calls for proper ammunition pouches to replace the flimsy 60-round cotton bandoliers that accompanied the delivery of the M1917 rifles from the USA. The distribution of the Browning Automatic Rifle (BAR) as the standard automatic weapon of the Home Guard section eventually led to the characteristic Home Guard webbing ammunition pouch, designed to carry either two BAR magazines, two grenades and 10 rounds of rifle ammunition or a cotton bandolier of 60 rounds of rifle ammunition (Plate 7). In the meantime, from November 1940 the Home Guard used the Pattern 1939 hard leather pouches originally intended as a stop-gap pouch for the Bren gun magazine and later used for Thompson or Sten gun magazines. Anyone throwing themselves on the ground risked serious injury! The BAR pouches did not finally arrive until May 1942. The distinctive Home Guard pattern haversack, made of rubberized canvas and worn over the shoulder or on the back, appeared in late August 1940 and 1.5 million had been delivered by the end of November. As the Home Guard were expected to fight in their own locality, it was considered that they did not need to carry the normal range of supplies carried by a soldier in a larger pack.

By the end of 1942 the Home Guard looked virtually indistinguishable from the regular army, except for their leather gaiters, BAR pouches and M1917 rifle. In December 1942 permission was even given for the Home Guard to wear the standard webbing gaiters (although in practice largely confined to officers). As the Home Guard were increasingly working alongside the army, this was a parity that they thought well-deserved.

Chapter Six

Aid from the USA

Struggling to rearm its forces after the retreat from Dunkirk, Britain relied considerably on being able to arm the Home Guard through the purchase of thousands of weapons from the US government. The cultural divide with the USA was, however, demonstrated by the ambivalence of the British government toward an unofficial US aid scheme, rooted in the mistaken assumption of US sympathizers that Churchill would want to arm the general population in the face of invasion. Instead, the work of the American Committee for Defense of British Homes (ACDBH) was tolerated as a useful propaganda exercise rather than as a serious attempt to bolster the defences of the country.

Official Aid

Official US support in 1940 depended on President Roosevelt being willing to bend the existing US Neutrality Laws that were intended to prevent the sale of arms by the US government to belligerent nations. (This did not affect sales by private companies to belligerents.) The Neutrality Act of 1935 had prohibited the export of 'arms, ammunition, and implements of war' to foreign nations at war but was modified in 1937 to allow belligerent nations, at the discretion of the President, to acquire any items except weapons from the United States, so long as they paid for such items in cash or gold and carried them on non-American ships. After a fierce debate in Congress, the 1939 Neutrality Act extended the 'cash and carry' provision to weapons, although the purchase had to be via a commercial third party. As Roosevelt intended, the change benefited Great Britain and France rather than Germany, as the only countries that had both the gold and the ships to make full use of the concession. To further assist the Allies, at the end of May 1940 General George Marshall, US Army Chief of Staff, was persuaded to declare substantial quantities of weapons and ammunition as 'surplus to requirements' and on 3 June the Attorney-General ruled that the sale of such guns and ammunition to Britain would be legal. Wasting no time, supplies were made ready for shipment on 6 June, ahead of a formal contract on 18 June, using the US Steel Export Company as the intermediary. Figure 8 shows the weapons in the initial contract, many of which were destined for the Home Guard.

After some adjustment, the total value of the first US arms contract increased to around $43 million.[1] The first consignment arrived in Britain on the SS *Eastern Prince* on 23 June and included 12,000 M1917 rifles, and over 37 million rounds of ammunition. These were shipped across the country on special trains to local Home Guards on 8 July. Between 16 and 22 June a further six ships were dispatched, carrying half of the contracted arms, with the shipments fully completed

Plate 1. The iconic 'broomstick army'. Members of the Doncaster 'Civi-Corps' drill under a former sergeant-major on 19 June 1940. The 'Civi-Corps' was a short-lived attempt in the North-East to relieve pressure on the LDV by training young men awaiting call-up. (© *Chronicle/Alamy*)

Plate 2. Southern Railway LDV before the issue of uniforms, showing off the first batch of newly arrived M1917 (P17) rifles. (© *Kent Messenger*)

Plate 3. Lye Platoon, 10th (Stourbridge) Battalion Worcestershire Home Guard in 1940. It clearly shows the youthful character of the Home Guard. Second row, fourth from right is Warrant Offic 'Black Joe' from the Caribbean. *(Courtesy Mick Wilks)*

Plate 4. Home Guard Mounted Patrol parading at Cowbridge, near Cardiff, in Wales. *(© IWM)*

e 5. Home Guard Canal Patrol in Edinburgh, mounting a Lewis gun on a motor launch. (© *IWM*)

e 6. Crosby & Co. (Farnham) Home Guard Bomb Disposal Unit in 1943, training with an SC 1000
mann' bomb. The bomb was used as a factory 'Gatekeeper' for several years and was then
ed. It was rediscovered during site redevelopment and caused a security alert, resulting in the
uation of part of Farnham! (*Author's collection*)

Plate 7. Home Guard on a commando course at the Commando Basic Training Centre at Achnacarry in the Scottish Highlands, July 1943. The characteristic 1903 pattern belt, BAR pouches and leather gaiters are all visible. (© *IWM*)

Plate 8. Auxiliary Units offices in the stable block, Highworth House, Coleshill. (© *Malcolm Atkin*)

e 9. Interior of the Auxiliary Units Operational Base in the grounds of Highworth House, eshill, used for training. (© *Malcolm Atkin*)

e 10. Part II Orders, 4th (Evesham) Battalion, Worcestershire Home Guard, 31 January 1942, iling members of Auxiliary Units patrols transferred from Company strength to Battalion HQ. *rtesy of the former Army Medal Office)*

2. <u>Transfers</u> (i) Internal.

s. The following members of Auxiliary Units are transferred to H.Q.,

12043, Vol. R. Wilkinson,
12333, " A.H.Packworth,
12344, " B.K.W.Tadman,
12964, " E.R. Shervington,
12980, " A.P. Harwood,
12997, " H.W. Wilkins,
35007, " C.H. Morris,
2002, " W. Purslow.

6 12044, Sergt. T.Holland-Martin
6 12334, Vol. W.J. Hall,
4 12963, " H.T.Curnock,
4 12969, " H. Plain,
4 12987, " C.H.Curnock,
4 22703, L/Cpl. A.H.Fernihough.
5 2049, Vol. W.H.B. Harley,

3 22645, Vol. G. Steele is transferred from No.3 Coy. to No.2 Coy., w.e.f. 9.1.42, list of clothing attached.

4 22739, Capt. H. Davenport Price M.C., is transferred from No.4 Coy. to No.1 Coy., w.e.f. 1.1.42.

Plate 11. Home Guard at the Osterley Training School in July 1940, learning how to blow up a tar
with Molotov cocktails, using a dummy tank towed behind a car. (© *NEA*)

Plate 12. Tom Wintringham (*left*) and Yank Levy (*right*) with a home-made 4-inch mortar firing a 'jam tin bomb' at the Denbies Training School. It had a range of 350yd, firing a 6lb bomb. In the 26 July 1941 issue of *Picture Post*, Wintringham proudly announced that such a mortar could be made for only 38*s* 6*d*. (© *Chronicle/Alamy*)

te 13. Home Guard demonstrating the art of camouflage at Denbies Home Guard Training
hool, July 1943. They wear 'sniper suits' made from painted denim overalls and camouflage
tting. (© *Associated Press*)

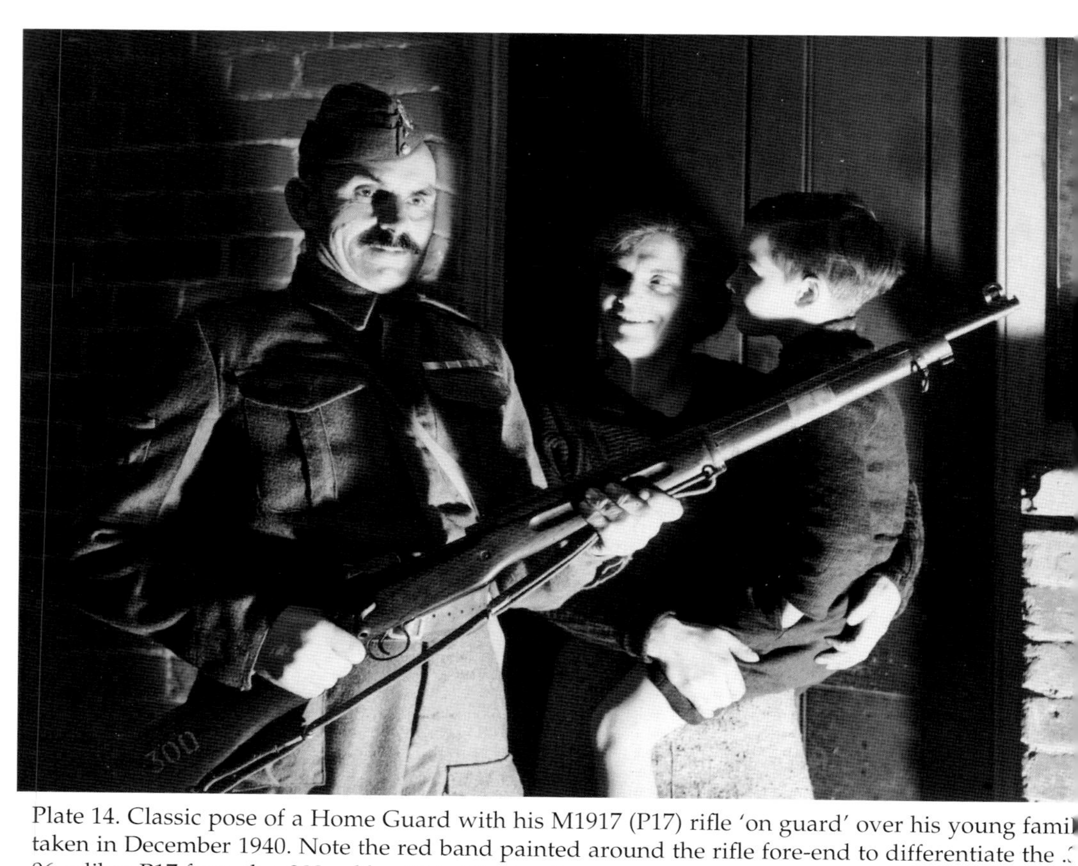

Plate 14. Classic pose of a Home Guard with his M1917 (P17) rifle 'on guard' over his young famil
taken in December 1940. Note the red band painted around the rifle fore-end to differentiate the .3
06 calibre P17 from the .303 calibre P14 rifle. (© *Chronicle/Alamy*)

Plate 15. A sergeant of the Dorking Home Guard cleaning a Thompson M1828A1 sub-machine gu
in his kitchen. One of a series of staged propaganda photographs taken around the Denbies Home
Guard Training School in December 1940. (© *IWM*)

e 16. Sergeant Bill Davies of Gresford Colliery Home Guard in North Wales says goodbye to his ly before going on evening parade in April 1943, armed with a Sten gun Mk II. Another typical aganda photograph showing the Home Guard as defenders of 'hearth and home'. (© *IWM*)

Plate 17. A youthful Browning Machine Gun team of Cheshire Home Guard at Holylake, the Wirral, June 1943. (© *IWM*)

Plate 18. Home Guard on exercise, with a wicker basket of Molotov cocktails (*front*), a wooden cr
of SIP grenades (*rear*) and BAR (*on right*). (© *IWM*)

Plate 19. A 29mm Spigot Mortar ('Blacker Bombard'), at No. 3 Home Guard Training School, Onibury, Shropshire, May 1943. The reinforced concrete plinth with stainless steel pintle is now t
most widespread memorial of the Home Guard. (© *IWM*)

e 20. Smith 3-inch gun, inspected in 1942 by Winston Churchill, with Sir Archibald Sinclair retary of State for Air), David Margesson (Secretary of State for War) and Lord Beaverbrook nister of War Production, formerly Minister for Aircraft Production). *(© IWM)*

e 21. 2-pdr anti-tank guns of Worcester Home Guard being demonstrated as a part of a 'Holiday Iome' event on the New Road Cricket Ground in 1943. *(Courtesy of A.E. Doughty via Mick Wilks)*

Plate 22. Beaverette II armoured cars of the Scottish Home Guard patrolling the Highlands, February 1941. The main weapon is a Lewis aerial variant machine gun. (© *IWM*)

Plate 23. Z rocket battery on Merseyside, July 1942. (© *IWM*)

Plate 24. Home Guard manning 40mm Bofo gun, November 1943. (© *IWM*)

SEND
A GUN
TO DEFEND
A BRITISH HOME

British civilians, faced with threat of invasion, desperately need arms for the defense of their homes.

THE AMERICAN COMMITTEE FOR DEFENSE OF BRITISH HOMES

has organized to collect gifts of

PISTOLS—RIFLES—REVOLVERS
SHOTGUNS—BINOCULARS

from American civilians who wish to answer the call and aid in defense of British homes.

These arms are being shipped, with the consent of the British Government, to
CIVILIAN COMMITTEE FOR PROTECTION OF HOMES
BIRMINGHAM, ENGLAND
The members of which are Wickham Steed, Edward Hulton, and Lord Davies

YOU CAN AID

by sending any arms or binoculars you can spare to

AMERICAN COMMITTEE FOR
EFENSE OF BRITISH HOMES
C. Suydam Cutting, *Chairman*
ROOM 100
10 WARREN STREET, NEW YORK, N. Y.

Plate 25. 'Send a Gun to defend a British Home' advert for the American Committee for Defense of British Homes in the November 1940 issue of *American Rifleman*. British government support is implied, although it tolerated the campaign merely as a propaganda exercise. The government particularly objected to the idea of weapons being distributed to civilians to defend individual homes.
(*Reprinted with permission of the National Rifle Association/American Rifleman*)

Plate 26. RAF personnel in November 1940 unpacking the first shipment of weapons collected by the American Committee for Defense of British Homes. Visible is part of the gift of 100 Remington rifles from a single donor. (© *IWM*)

Plate 27. Helen Parkins Gauntlett, Secretary of the British Civilian Committee for the Protection
Homes, presenting arms donated by the American Committee for Defense of British Homes campaign to the Mile End Hospital Home Guard, 28 June 1941. (© *Associated Press*)

e 28. Women being trained in rifle drill by Home Guard. Most of the rifles are dummies but e is one Martini Enfield and a number of M1917 (P17) rifles (presumably those of the 'uctors). (© *Trinity Mirror/Mirrorpix/Alamy*)

e 29. Members of the Worcestershire 'Nominated Women'/Women's Auxiliaries. They wear m overalls with Worcestershire Regiment cap badge, Home Guard shoulder titles and the tic Women's Auxiliary badge over left pocket. Two wear Two Year Service chevrons on the er right sleeve. (*Courtesy of Pershore Heritage Centre*)

Plate 30. A corporal in Kent Home Guard on exercise in October 1954. He wears the standard arr
1949 pattern battledress and webbing with a Second World War pattern helmet, and carries a Nc
rifle. Unlike the 1940s Home Guard, the 1950s iteration did have an older age profile.
(© *Thurston Hopkins/Picture Post/Getty Images*)

Figure 8. Agreement for US arms contract, 11 June 1940. [corrected for misprint for Cal., .30 Cal Ball, with thanks to Alan David] *(Hall 1955, p. 496)*

	Item	Appraisal Value ($)
LIST A		
130,000,000 rds	Cal., .30 Ball	3,900,000.00
17,000,000 lbs	TNT	2,550,000.00
6,693,000 lbs	smokeless powder 155G	3,651,060.00
1,000,000 lbs.	smokeless powder 155H	420,000.00
97,680 rds	Shell 3″ Stokes (used)	125,030.40
1,000,000 rds	75mm (CH) w/UK III fuzes	10,450,000.00
75,000 rds	75mm Shell, HE, Normal charge, complete with UK III fuzes	783,750.00
	Total Appraised value	21,879,840.40
LIST B		
500,000	Rifle, cal. .30, M1917 (used)	3,750,000.00
1,157	Lewis MG	39,245.44
7,071	Vickers MO	927,927.33
2,602	Marlin MG (tank)	193,458.70
15,638	Marlin MG (aircraft)	362,176.08
5,124	Vickers MG (aircraft)	173,806.08
38,040	Lewis MO (aircraft)	1,290,316.80
308	Mortar 3″ Stokes	3,850.00
20,000	Revolvers, cal.45	145,000.00
395	Guns 75mm M1917 w/ Limber	603,402.00
500	Guns 75mm M1897	2,243,750.00
1,350	Caisson for 75mm	168,750.00
1,350	Limber for 75mm	101,250.00
10,000	Guns B. MG M1917	2,154,900.00
10,000	Tripods M1918	260,000.00
100,000	Ammunition Belts	181,000.00
100,000	Ammunition Chests	360,000.00
10,000	Water Chests	129,000.00
10,000	Steam Condensers	19,600.00
3,333	Belt Filling Machines	163,283.77
25,000	Browning Automatic Rifle (BAR)	1,519,000.00
1,000,000	BAR magazines	950,000.00
	Total	15,739,716.20
	Add List A	21,879,840.40
	Total Contract Value	37,619,556.60

by the end of July.[2] Even as the first shipment was being made ready, on 10 June President Roosevelt went further and initiated the 'Charlottesville Program' with the twin aims of supplying resources to 'the opponents of force' and speeding up the rearmament of the USA.[3] Isolationists in the USA retaliated with the passage of the Walsh Amendment, which prohibited the sale or transfer of any vessels, weapons or munitions to any foreign government unless the Chiefs of Staff certified that they were not essential for national defence and were obsolete. General Marshall was undeterred by having to make such a commitment and, after a month's delay, the large-scale shipment of arms recommenced. On 9 August the British government requested another 250,000 rifles, followed by a personal message from Churchill to Roosevelt saying 'we have a million men waiting for rifles'.[4] In all, 784,930 M1917 rifles were supplied by mid-January 1941, 733,710 of them going to the Home Guard.[5]

By the end of November 1940 Roosevelt had agreed that Britain would buy up 50 per cent of the US munitions capacity, the British effectively funding US modernization of its armaments industry and paving the way for US industrial dominance from 1942 onwards. By early 1941 the British gold reserves were almost exhausted, but the financial consequences would be glossed over in the interests of Allied unity. In 1943 Churchill mis-stated the agreement when he broadcast:

> It was not until July that we ferried safely across the Atlantic the million rifles and one thousand field guns, with ammunition proportionable, which were *given to us* by the Government and people of the United States by an act of precious and timely succour.[6] [author's italics]

The American Committee for Defense of British Homes

> It was a motley collection, varying from long rifles used in the Louisiana Civil War of 1873, plus Teddy Roosevelt's favourite hunting rifle and a number of ancient buffalo guns, to modern pistols, revolvers and gangster's Tommy Guns.[7]

Amidst the debate over the legality of the US government supplying arms to Britain, many US citizens wanted to make a practical gesture of support by offering private arms to defend British homes. Isolated from the consequences of a modern invasion, there was a nostalgic folk memory of defending pioneer homesteads and, in their fervent belief in the Second Amendment of the US Constitution, they mistakenly assumed that the British government would wish to arm the whole populace. The official ambivalence towards the subsequent campaign to donate arms can only be understood by appreciating the British government's refusal to arm its civilians. Indeed, at the start of the war there had been an amnesty for all unlicensed firearms to be handed in to the police and most of them had been dumped in the sea or in local lakes. Leeds Police dumped more than 300 guns in Roundhay Lake.[8] The British government might take a cavalier attitude to encouraging the arming of civilian resistance forces in Europe but it was careful to protect the legality of its own combatant forces. Few in authority agreed with the devil-may-care attitude of Colonel Josiah Wedgwood MP, who was roundly criticized for encouraging terrorism by suggesting, on 7 May 1940, that civilians should be armed:

> They ought to be taught that they should not leave it to the regular forces to do the fighting but that they must fight themselves ... We should use them like *francs-tireurs*. They would no doubt be shot if they were taken, but they

> would be able to harass any small invading forces and not wait until some regular troops came to help.[9]

The result was a government press release which advised civilians that in the event of invasion they should leave the fighting to the army.[10] This was the immediate context to the formation of the LDV on 14 May as a means of channelling popular enthusiasm for an armed response into an official body protected by international law. At the War Cabinet meeting on 8 July Eden supported the belief of General Ironside, C-in-C Home Forces, that 'actual fighting should be restricted to the military and Local Defence Volunteers, and that no civilian who is not a member of these forces should be authorized to use lethal weapons'.[11] This advice was issued in the public information leaflet *Stay Where You Are*:

> Civilians who try to join in the fight are more likely to get in the way than to help. The defeat of an enemy attack is the task of the armed forces which include the Home Guard, so if you wish to fight enrol in the Home Guard.[12]

Although the principle of individual self-defence was accepted, there was no suggestion of arms being provided to make it more effective and *Beating the Invader* (May 1941) advised that if fighting broke out in the neighbourhood the population should 'Keep indoors or in your shelter until the battle is over.'[13]

Such a policy conflicted with the assumption of universal defence in the USA, with the Second Amendment of the Constitution declaring 'A well-regulated militia being necessary to the security of a free state, the right of the people to keep and bear arms shall not be infringed', written many generations before the USA ratified the 1907 Hague Convention, restricting the use of civilians in warfare.[14] Ignoring this, and fearful of attempts to introduce gun registration in the USA, the National Rifle Association would use the campaign of the American Committee for Defense of British Homes (ACDBH) as propaganda against what it saw as the results of disarming the British population through gun control. In September 1940 it declared: 'England, long the model for our *anti-gun reformers*, has now scoured the highways and citizenry for *guns to issue* to a gun-ignorant citizenry.'[15] [original italics]

Wintringham appeared to echo the tenet of the Second Amendment in his appeal to 'Arm the People' in *Picture Post*:

> It is in fact part of the British Constitution, and the *fyrd* of Anglo-Saxon times, the militia or volunteers of later periods, have often been called 'the Constitutional force', because it is part of the fundamental law of the country that each able-bodied citizen can and should bear arms for training for defence.[16]

This reflects Wintringham's idealistic view of history, and praising the forced obligation of military service in defence of one's lord was a strained argument for a socialist. The Bill of Rights (1689) established that Parliament would regulate the right to bear arms and it was the Firearms Act of 1920 which, by restricting private gun ownership, had, in the eyes of the American gun lobby, left the country defenceless in 1940 – rather than an inability to counter blitzkrieg tactics and a subsequent shortage of tanks and artillery.

The British government grudgingly accepted the propaganda value of an initiative that offered the private donation of arms in the hope that it might encourage greater support at a political level. But the naivety of the ACDBH campaign as a practical supply of weapons is illustrated by the plea of its British partner (the Civilian Committee for the Protection of Homes in Britain) in November 1940 for 100 'Tommy guns', claiming that the Thompson sub-machine guns were unobtainable in Britain.[17] In fact, the War Office had placed its first major order for Thompsons in January 1940 and by November 1940 Britain had taken up the whole of Thompson gun manufacturing capacity, having ordered around 150,000 guns.[18] By comparison, the ACDBH could only provide 110 Thompsons over its lifetime, including forty criminal weapons confiscated by police forces and supplied after December 1941.[19]

Following the overwhelming response to the appeal for volunteers to join the LDV, a public appeal was indeed made in Britain for citizens to 'lend' weapons for the LDV and some 20,000 guns were collected, mainly sporting rifles, shotguns and souvenir handguns from the First World War.[20] Nonetheless, the possibility of arming the LDV with sporting guns was scathingly dismissed by the Conservative MP Sir Archibald Southby. His words were a warning of the reaction to future US donations:

> It is idle to suggest that they will be adequately equipped if they have shotguns, and it is stupid to suggest that they should be armed with a variety of sporting rifles. They must be armed with Service rifles firing Service ammunition. It is no good if an attack takes place on a dark night in a wood for men to be armed with sporting guns – Mauser rifles, Mannlichers and .303 rifles, all using different ammunition. The confusion which would result would be appalling.[21]

The War Office still had not decided to use the new LDV as an integral part of the defence plan but Tom Wintringham had just launched his 'Armed People' slogan in the media. In June, soon after the fall of France, Wintringham dined with Edward Hulton and Tom Hopkinson, proprietor and editor respectively of *Picture Post*, to discuss how to better develop the LDV. They discussed the creation of a Training School at Osterley Park and, given the stated position of the government not to arm the LDV 'promiscuously' (*see* p. 81), identified the USA as a potential unofficial source of weaponry. Significantly, Hulton had latterly been working with Section D of SIS which was at the time acquiring non-attributable small arms from across the world for its agents.[22] The obvious body in the USA to organize the private donation of arms to Britain seemed to be the William Allen White Committee (aka the Committee to Defend America by Aiding the Allies), which had been formed only recently by the Kansas newspaper editor William Allen White and Clark M. Eichelberger of the League of Nations Association to campaign for official government support from the USA for the Allies. A branch ('Outpost') had been formed in London with Helen Parkins Gauntlett (Plate 27) as Secretary. Helen was an American who had settled in London with her new English husband. She was formerly Director of International Relations for the American Association of University Women and became Secretary of the American Eagle Club in London (for US citizens serving in the British armed forces). Hulton contacted her and then cabled William Allen White to raise the idea of a campaign to collect private arms for donation to Britain. The prime focus of the William Allen White Committee was to campaign at a political level for a Lend-Lease Act but ad hoc offers of arms were soon made to the British Purchasing Commission (BPC) in the USA. On 1 July 1940 the Director General of the BPC, Arthur Purvis, was pleased to notify the Ministry of Supply that they had received offers of sporting rifles free or on loan from across the country:[23]

> We believe that with little difficulty a large-scale movement could be stimulated amongst American sportsmen which would be productive of many useful sporting arms with adequate ammunition attached. Please advise immediately if in principle this is of interest to you.

Anticipating a negative reaction, Purvis pointed out 'We think you should bear in mind that to accept such offers as we have mentioned has the value of encouraging our supporters over here.'[24] The propaganda potential of such offers had its effect and the Ministry of Supply responded on 3 July: 'Offer of sporting rifles and ammunition much appreciated. Please proceed.'[25]

The William Allen White Committee could not risk compromising its lobbying influence by becoming directly involved in appealing for weapons so the American Committee for Defense of British Homes (ACDBH) was formed in New York (home of the most militant branch of the William Allen White Committee) on 31 July 1940, with wealthy explorer, property magnate and naturalist C. Suydam Cutting as its Chairman. Its headquarters were in the premises of Fiala Exploration Outfitters on Warren Street, owned by fellow explorer Major Anthony Fiala, who served as technical adviser. William Schmidt was Secretary and the Committee also included Colonel Douglas B. Wesson (Smith & Wesson), Albert Foster (Colt), Karl T. Frederick (NRA Director), Lowell Thomas (radio commentator), Dr Harold Anthony (American Museum of Natural History) and Claire Boothe Luce (author and political figure).

To try to ensure that the work of the ACDBH did not impinge on that of the BPC in sourcing weapons, Robert the Macneil of Barra (1889–1970) served with the Committee as an adviser and liaison officer. An American architect from Michigan, he had served during the First World War in the Royal Canadian Engineers and then on the United States War Trade Board, as well as inheriting the title of Chief of the Clan Macneil of Barra. Macneil had joined the BPC in early March 1940, in the Credit and Investigations Department of the Secretariat. His job was to liaise with US inventors before passing on potentially useful schemes to technical advisers, in August 1940 becoming Chairman of a new Inventions Board.[26] Despite this, he was described as 'a well-meaning, stupid man' with whom it was difficult to work, but seemed irremovable in the BPC.

He developed a proprietorial attitude to the ACDBH as his own 'special, semi-official child' and was 'very proud of it', even claiming to have founded the Committee, and this led to a conflict of interest with his work for the BPC and tension with the British arm of the campaign.[27]

The history of the ACDBH was beset with failures in communication across the Atlantic and confusion of intent. It could not appeal for arms until the committee had secured State Department agreement that its export scheme was compliant with the US Neutrality Act. But in the meantime one of its supporters in Britain made contact with Lord Beaverbrook, Minister of Aircraft Production, to try to secure his support. Richards Cotton was the American managing director of the Anglo-American British Rola Ltd in London and was another member of the William Allen White Committee 'Outpost'. Cotton wrote to Beaverbrook on 27 August but was not entirely honest about the state of the campaign. He first whetted Beaverbrook's appetite by claiming 'I have reason to believe that there will shortly be available at the docks in New York a considerable quantity of arms and ammunition which will have been donated by citizens in the USA for use by the Home Guard in this country.' In fact, campaigning for donations did not actually begin until 12 September! Cotton then made a blatant appeal to Beaverbrook's self-interest: 'I would like to ensure that this equipment is made use of by Home Guard units for the defence of Aircraft factories before it is allocated to other uses.'[28] The two men met on 29 August and the dynamic Beaverbrook lost no time in establishing his claim to any weapons or other equipment that might result from the campaign. Such eagerness was, however, at the expense of proper consultation with the rest of government and it is not even clear how far the rest of the ACDBH was aware of what Cotton had offered. Beaverbrook's Assistant Secretary, E.G. Compton, did consult the Foreign Office and US Embassy and although the Ambassador raised no objections, doubting if anything would come of the scheme, the Foreign Office warned of a possible breach of the Neutrality Act and advised the Ministry of Aircraft Production to consult with the British Purchasing Commission and the Central Office for North American Supplies. According to Compton, he 'disregarded that'.[29] Beaverbrook was already maintaining a distanced relationship with the BPC and other government departments, claiming the right to negotiate his own contracts in the USA.

The ACDBH gained a State Department permit to export arms on 3 September. It required the weapons to be delivered to a civilian receiving body, and in order to comply the ACDBH had invented the existence of the 'Civilian Committee for the Protection of Homes in Britain'. In excitement, but seemingly ignorant of Cotton's agreement with Beaverbrook just a few days earlier, the ACDBH consequently sent a message to the Ministry of Supply and the North American Supply Committee via Arthur Purvis of the BPC, urging that such a receiving committee be immediately established for weapons to be distributed to the 'civilian population'.[30] (Beaverbrook had assumed the weapons were being directly consigned to the Ministry of Aircraft Production Defence Section but the

ACDBH did not receive this information until 6 September.[31]) Adding more confusion, Macneil asked the Ministry of Supply to suggest suitable members of a committee and offered up suggestions of Chairmen from his Scottish connections. He was apparently unaware that, following his correspondence with William Allen White, Edward Hulton had perceptively formed an embryonic receiving committee in July as the Citizen's Defence Committee (pre-dating the formation of the ACDBH). Helen Parkins Gauntlett was its Secretary, with the other members being Lady Jersey and Tom Wintringham (representing an 'Osterley' connection), J.B. Priestley, Lord Davies (Welsh Liberal peer) and the writer Henry Wickham Steed. Ignoring the restrictions of the State Department agreement, Macneil also requested that the proposed British Committee should send an appeal to their US counterparts that could be used in US publicity.[32]

A flurry of irritated correspondence followed. William Gorell-Barnes of the North American Supply Committee in the Cabinet Office believed there was the possibility of a public relations disaster in the USA as the declared aim of the ACDBH in their 3 September communication of distributing weapons to the civilian population directly conflicted with British policy. He chided the Ministry of Supply, the Ministry of Aircraft Production and the Foreign Office for the lack of consultation: 'It would have been better, I think, if we had been consulted before the matter was taken quite so far on the other side [of the Atlantic]' and suggested that the proposal needed to be discussed by the Cabinet before it went any further. This exchange makes doubtful the later claim of the machiavellian Beaverbrook that the weapons were 'offered all over the place. The Americans got impatient because they could not persuade any responsible authority to take on their gift.'[33] (The War Office did not become aware of the scheme until 13 September.[34]) Gorell-Barnes' principal concerns were whether the Cabinet would agree to weapons being so distributed (especially by an unofficial committee) and whether a public appeal for arms in the USA might suggest an air of desperation that German propaganda could exploit.[35] At this stage all parties seemed unaware of Beaverbrook's agreement made with Cotton, on behalf of the ACDBH, to use the weapons primarily to arm Ministry of Aircraft Production factory units. On 6 September Sir Arthur Salter, Chairman of the North American Supply Committee, sent a telegram to Purvis which, whilst appreciating the enthusiasm being shown for the proposal in the USA, explained that it raised 'important and difficult questions' that needed to be discussed at a higher level. Salter urged Purvis to try to put a brake on the ACDBH, which was being driven by one of Purvis's own members of staff (Macneil).[36] Yet even as this warning was being issued, Cotton sent a telegram to the ACDBH, confirming his arrangement made with Beaverbrook.[37]

Into this fevered activity stepped Edward Hulton. On 5 September he had received a message from Evarts S. Scudder, an American author and liaison officer between the William Allen White Committee and its London 'Outpost' that 'all was ready' (i.e. State Department approval for arms shipments had been secured) and that he should meet with the British government without delay in order to secure the position of his committee.[38] On 7 September Hulton belatedly advised Gorell-Barnes of his committee's existence, before the government could act on Macneil's suggestions. Forcing the matter, Hulton claimed that the ACDBH was ready to begin shipments and therefore the need for a British receiving committee was urgent. Gorell-Barnes, and in turn Macneil, had little option but to recognize the Citizen's Defence Committee as a suitable receiving committee. Having been thwarted in his suggestions for a committee, Macneil's relationship with the Citizen's Defence Committee, and especially its secretary, Helen Parkins Gauntlett, remained tense for the rest of the campaign's history. Hulton was also asked to 'hold his hand' until the scheme had been further discussed.[39] Meanwhile Salter pointed out

> It seems undesirable ['quite out of the question' according to a marginal note] that lethal weapons should be issued to the civil population, at any rate by an unofficial committee.
>
> It seems equally undesirable that an appeal for the sporting rifles etc., should be made from anybody in this country, whether official or unofficial, to any person or body in the United States.[40]

The generous offer of donations could not simply be quashed and Salter proposed that, although the scheme had to be seen as an unofficial US initiative, the British committee should hand over the weapons to 'the proper authorities for distribution to the Home Guard'.[41] Gorell-Barnes only became aware of Beaverbrook's *fait accompli* two days later on 9 September. He bemoaned ruefully 'Much wasted labour but I do not think much harm done.'[42] State Department approval was on condition that the ACDBH delivered the weapons to a civilian body in Britain rather than to a government agency and as the ACDBH had already referred to a fictitious Civilian Committee for the Protection of Homes in Britain (CCPHB), Hulton's Citizen's Defence Committee simply changed its name to match (later changing again to the Civilian Committee for the Defence of Homes). In these confused circumstances, Beaverbrook did not become aware of the British Committee's role until 24 September.[43]

Cutting and Macneil had enduring difficulty in understanding the restrictions attendant on the State Department export permit and the wider context of the campaign. There was to be no appeal to the USA from Britain as the campaign had to appear as an unsolicited gesture of support from private US citizens.[44] The Home Guard also had to be presented by Cutting and Macneil as a civilian body but they did not understand its nature as part of the armed forces of the Crown.[45] The two men also glossed over the agreement made by Cotton on behalf of the ACDBH with Beaverbrook that the Home Guard units in question were defending Ministry of Aircraft Production factories rather than domestic homes. The Ministry of Supply and the Central Office for North American Supplies were not impressed by Beaverbrook's tenuous interpretation of a 'British home' that US donors thought they were helping to protect, not least because at the time Ministry of Aircraft Production Home Guard factory units were taking a very narrow view of their responsibilities (*see above*, p. 109). W.J. Hasler of the Central Office for North American Supplies was blunt:

> As you know, the 'homes' to be protected are situated in close proximity to aircraft factories. The scheme has become an MAP racket. I do not see how we can divert this particular stream of benevolence. The only ground of complaint might be from the Foreign Office on neutrality grounds since the appeal is on false pretences.[46]

Fundamentally, the ACDBH did not understand the British defence strategy. They consistently implied that the weapons were needed to allow civilians to defend their own homes, in order to strike a chord with the US Second Amendment. An advert in *American Rifleman* for November 1940 (Plate 25) claimed 'British civilians, faced with the threat of invasion, desperately need arms for the defence of their homes' and, whilst careful not to state that the scheme was in response to any official British appeal for arms, maintained 'These arms are being shipped with the consent of the British Government.' In Texas, a letter in the *Victoria Advocate* pleaded a typical argument:

> British civilians, for the most part, face this danger [of invasion] without weapons for the protection of their homes. Householders urgently ask weapons with which to defend their homes.[47]

Such statements were anathema to the War Office, which wanted defence to focus on the concept of 'nodal points', and it was concerned also that an uncontrolled influx of firearms into private possession might pose a future risk to the state, as well as contravening the Hague Convention. G.W. Turner of the Central Office for North American Supplies agreed with a comment of the Ministry of Supply that the work of the ACDBH was 'a little disturbing' and declared 'I thoroughly dislike this kind of appeal and agree with you that it might not have a good effect on American opinion. There are so many uses to which their energy could be put.'[48] He would later comment of Macneil that he was 'not quite right in the head and probably bogus'.[49] Unlicensed distribution of guns to civilians was illegal under the 1937 Firearms Act and a suggestion that Mayor Fiorello LaGuardia of New York should present a Thompson sub-machine gun to the Mayor of London led to a marginal comment 'My God, should this be allowed to continue?'[50]

Although resigned to accept the Citizen's Defence Committee/Civilian Committee for the Protection of Homes in Britain, the Cabinet Office wanted a 'more responsible' person than Hulton as Chairman. The official excuse was that it was thought inappropriate to have a newspaper proprietor as a figurehead.[51] Perhaps more pertinent was Hulton's association with Tom Wintringham, whose well-publicized demand was to 'Arm the Citizens'. Hulton's presumptive opening of the Osterley Home Guard Training School and subsequent reluctance to engage in correspondence with the War Office had not inspired confidence and there may have been concern that Hulton and Wintringham would use *Picture Post* to over-publicize the scheme and break the agreement with the US State Department.

Hulton was persuaded to stand down as Chairman in favour of the broadcaster and former editor of *The Times*, Henry Wickham Steed, latterly a lecturer in Central European history at King's College, London. At the end of the First World War he had served in Lord Northcliffe's propaganda department and toured the USA, becoming a frequent contributor to US newspapers. The 69-year-old Wickham Steed was a complex character who was virulently anti-Communist, anti-Semitic (endorsing the notorious *Protocols of the Learned Elders of Zion*) and anti-German. He had been a long-standing opponent of appeasement and supporter of an alliance with the USA, where his writing was well-known. Hulton remained on the committee and correspondence in late September makes it clear that the government still regarded Hulton as the prime mover in the scheme.[52] But he and Wintringham then appear to have taken little active part.

The appeal proved popular (although the results were on a smaller scale than contemporary propaganda sometimes claimed). By June 1942 the ACDBH had 364 branches across the USA; its local committees included representatives of veterans' organizations, local industries, schools, sports organizations and radio stations. They organized press coverage, public meetings and charity events to raise awareness and funds. Some confiscated weapons were given to the Committee by local police forces and the FBI. In March 1941 Newark, New Jersey, police force donated fifty weapons confiscated from criminals; in June 1941 Dallas Police announced that all confiscated pistols and revolvers, no longer needed as evidence, would be sent to Britain for the use of the Home Guard.[53] But the appeals were focused on a false premise. Scudder maintained in September 1940 that 'civilians in England are insufficiently equipped with small arms for defence in case of invasion'.[54] The *Scarsdale Inquirer* made a similar appeal in November, after the residents of Westchester had contributed fifty-nine weapons and binoculars 'distributed to civilians for use in event of invasion'.[55] Cutting continued the theme in the *Manassas Journal* on 6 February 1941 where he said: 'thousands of Americans have firearms which, though impractical for military purposes, would be invaluable in the hands of a British civilian in defending himself against marauders'.[56]

Yet Britain's real need was for military weapons, especially machine guns and anti-tank weapons, distributed strategically. Wickham Steed cynically contributed to the deception, carefully maintaining a distinction between the Home Guard and 'regular armed forces', claiming in a draft press statement provided to the Macneil of Barra on 13 December 1940 that the arms would be distributed 'to civilians for defence of their homes and not to His Majesty's armed forces', going on to claim the recipients 'will be bona fide civilian workers who act as Home Guards or roof-spotters after working hours'.[57] The illusion continued into September 1941 when Howard Bird, writing as a Home Guard officer in an Aberdeen factory unit which had received weapons through the campaign, wrote

> The thought of an individual American taking his own pistol, shotgun, rifle, binoculars, steel helmet, etc., and sending it over to an individual Englishman to defend his own home is magnificent.[58]

Bird was an American, the European Managing Director of the Chicago Pneumatic Tool Company, based in Aberdeen, and became Treasurer of Wickham Steed's CCPHB.[59] He had served with the New York National Guard in the Spanish-American War and then commanded a machine-gun company in France during the First World War.

The campaign continued to be used as a propaganda tool in the US domestic debate over gun control. A letter from the President of the Eaton Rifle Club in the *Times Herald* of Olean, New York, reflected the fundamental misunderstanding of the nature of the arms appeal: 'The sportsmen and gentlemen of England are brave, determined, and willing to defend their homes against the invader. But they have no guns! And they have no guns because the laws of their own land made it difficult for sportsmen to possess firearms.' Yet to claim that English sportsmen had no guns because of the firearms regulations was patently false. Shooting remained a popular sport. The letter went on: 'Let Americans learn from the sight of brave Englishmen begging for arms to defend their homes. Let Americans learn that anti-gun laws are not patriotic, but the exact opposite'.[60] This ignored the fact that the British government had not initiated the campaign and confused the offer of private weapons with the need for military ordnance. The National Rifle Association made similar confused claims:

> An England, *disarmed and gun-ignorant by reason of the same type of gun law that is now proposed for America*, is forced to turn to American arms plants and to American gun-owners for guns and ammunition for defense against invaders from without and criminals from within![61]

Arms donated from across the USA were collected in New York, with the first consignment including one of President Theodore Roosevelt's favourite hunting rifles (Cutting was a friend of Roosevelt). It took until November for the shipment to arrive in Britain and be distributed. A newsreel showed Home Guardsmen at a Vickers factory in Birmingham (close to the Castle Bromwich Ministry of Aircraft Production receiving depot) accepting part of the first shipment, parading in front of Lord Davies and Helen Parkins Gauntlett with Remington Model 341 .22 rifles that were reported to be part of a single donation of 100 rifles, together with 50,000 rounds of ammunition. A syndicated newspaper report of their arrival wildly exaggerated the scale of the campaign and claimed that these were the first of 'hundreds of thousands' being collected by Americans, who were making donations at the rate of 'more than 100 a day'. This was pure propaganda designed to bolster the morale of the domestic market.[62]

More honestly, Cutting estimated on 2 November that 1,300 gifts of firearms and binoculars, together with 91,092 rounds of assorted ammunition had been made.[63] The University of Pennsylvania Rifle Club's gift included twenty-five guns donated by T.S. Gates, President of the University.[64] Sidestepping the agreement not to make any appeal from Britain for the arms, in December 1940 Richards Cotton recorded a message of 'thanks and appreciation' to the USA as a US citizen. The BBC facilitated its transmission in the USA but was careful not to imply any endorsement.[65] In February 1941 Cotton also circulated a letter to US newspapers appealing for binoculars, explaining that in the factory he managed, productivity had been maintained through volunteer spotters being able to delay sounding the air raid warning until the last moment.[66]

The weapons were consigned to the 'Civilian Committee for the Protection of Homes, c/o Maintenance Unit, Castle Bromwich'.[67] This protected the identity of the receiving body from the US State Department as it was actually a Maintenance Unit of the Ministry of Aircraft Production. The weapons were unpacked by RAF personnel and then mainly distributed to the factory Home Guard units of the Ministry of Aircraft Production (Plate 26). Unsurprisingly, tensions were caused by what seemed to be empire-building by Beaverbrook, who told the rest of government that the work of the ACDBH was essentially a Ministry of Aircraft Production project.[68] In August 1940 General Alan Brooke, who believed Beaverbrook was already trying to turn the Ministry of Aircraft Production Home Guard into a private army, had described him as an 'evil genius'.[69] Sir Anthony Eden pointed out to Beaverbrook that it was he, as Secretary of State for War, who was in charge of equipping the Home Guard and for issuing import licences for arms, suggesting a compromise whereby the Ministry of Aircraft Production took the rifles and the War Office the (more useful) revolvers and binoculars.[70] Beaverbrook was in no mood to divide up the booty and on 3 October 1940 he replied saying 'I cannot divide the American weapons with you', going on to say 'nobody shall deprive me of the reward for well-doing'.[71] On 15 January 1941 Wickham Steed gave a progress report to Macneil, stating:

> All earmarked guns distributed. Others given to Home Guard units of factories on essential production in all parts country from Northern Scotland to Devon coast and London area besides American unit Home Guard. Some ordinary Home Guards in key areas also equipped.[72]

The government tolerated the campaign in helping to create a positive atmosphere that would assist the passage of the Lend-Lease bill. There were heart-warming stories such as that of a boy aged 12 from Lynchburg, Virginia, who raised $2.25 for the ACDBH by charging friends and family to sign his plaster cast after having broken his arm.[73] But once the Lend-Lease bill was passed in March 1941, the work of the ACDBH became redundant. The level of donations decreased but the ACDBH and CCPHB became even more desperate to win official signals of approval.[74] Macneil caused particular confusion in his dual role with the ACDBH and BPC, trying to persuade Wickham Steed to forward a press release stating 'British civilians need firearms for the defence of their homes'.[75] This was something the government could not allow.

The ACDBH remained bewildered by the lack of official British encouragement in raising the profile of the campaign. In May 1941 Macneil asked Wickham Steed to arrange ceremonies and press statements to accompany the presentation of an SMLE and a .58 calibre rifle to farmer David McLean, who had captured Rudolph Hess in Scotland.[76] Unwilling to publicize the scheme, the British government played down the event. It also sidestepped a request in June

1941 for Winston Churchill to make a public expression of thanks for the pair of binoculars (formerly belonging to Admiral Sims) that had been presented to him.[77] After the novelty of the first shipment in November 1940, and without any further official encouragement, the press lost interest although the agreement of the New York Senate to donate 'gangster guns' provided welcome fresh press appeal during March and April 1941. To spur interest, the CCPHB organized several shop window displays of material donated to local Home Guards with the advert for the Edinburgh display promising 'many prized personal possessions: rifles, shot-guns, revolvers, tommy guns, and automatic weapons, Webleys and Colts from the Wild West, German and French steel helmets – trophies of last war'.[78] The Sevenoaks Home Guard in Kent not only made a display of the donated items in a local shop but sent a letter of thanks for each item, accompanied by a Home Guard lapel badge.[79] By then, the reaction was mainly one of curiosity as the insatiable Home Guard were no longer impressed by antique arms but demanded more M1917 rifles, more machine guns and more artillery.

Only the self-interested Lord Beaverbrook had briefly broken with the official government position, making a broadcast to the USA in November 1940 and in December sending a message of support to the ACDBH in terms that he must have known were contrary to government policy. He had written: 'There is only one means of meeting the menace. It is by arming our people, by equipping the whole population to fight for liberty and the right to dwell as free men in a free land.'[80] Beaverbrook's attitude changed after he resigned from the Ministry of Aircraft Production and in June 1941 he refused to sign a proposed certificate of appreciation that could be distributed to donors.[81] In desperation, Macneil wrote to Wickham Steed requesting some form of message from the King, the Prime Minister, a Secretary of State or another important British personage. He went on tersely: 'If you desire American Committee to continue its work will you secure such messages this week.'[82] Wickham Steed patiently explained that Macneil underestimated the situation.[83] There was undoubtedly a hardening of official attitude against the scheme and the leaders of the ACDBH were accused of a 'lack of moderation'.[84] Cutting and Macneil did manage to persuade the British Ambassador in the USA, Lord Halifax, to write a letter of appreciation to the Chairman of the ACDBH which was published during June 1941 in the *Herald Tribune*, although there was relief in London that the newspaper had 'downplayed' the letter.[85]

Government disquiet came to a head in June 1941 when the ACDBH tried to use its substantial financial donations to purchase service weapons in bulk, which brought it into direct competition with the responsibilities of the BPC and Ministry of Supply and was complicated by Macneil's dual role. The Ministry of Supply handled the transmission of all cyphered telegrams between the British and US committees and on 2 June 1941 it saw a telegram from Cutting/Macneil to Wickham Steed which advised him that the ACDBH had the possibility of acquiring a large stock of US Navy revolvers, deemed surplus to requirements.[86] The Ministry of Supply acted immediately to purchase 10,837 of them directly through Lend-Lease rather than using funding from the ACDBH and thereby being tied to any restrictions on their distribution.[87] Helen Parkins Gauntlett regarded the intervention of the Ministry of Supply as 'unfair procedure'.[88] Wickham Steed accused the Ministry of poaching and Cotton implied to Beaverbrook that if it were not for the interference of the BPC, the weapons would have gone to Ministry of Aircraft Production factory Home Guard units. But Lord Beaverbrook was no longer Minister for Aircraft Production and his attitude had changed, maintaining that official contracts should take priority where any conflict over large-scale purchases occurred.[89] For their part, the Ministry of Supply was concerned as to why Macneil had not first made the BPC aware of the offer.[90]

The argument sparked a wider debate over the role of the campaign. According to Commander Hall-King (Ministry of Aircraft Production), the Ministry of Supply would now 'depreciate any encouragement of the American Committee' but at the same time saw no objection to it being given a public 'pat on the back' from some non-official person of standing, in recognition of its previous work, although 'not so high as to give its members swelled heads'.[91] On 18 June the Ministry of Aircraft Production and the Ministry of Supply agreed that the work of the committee was now 'superfluous' and should be discouraged.[92] Helen Parkins Gauntlett was persistent to the point of a blatant attempt at bribery to preserve the work of the campaign. On 17 June she sent a letter to Herbert Morrison, the Home Secretary, advising that he was being personally sent a consignment of two Krag rifles, a Mauser sporting rifle, a Remington sporterized M1917 and a Browning shotgun 'for allocation at your discretion or for your personal use' and suggesting that, in return, he might like to provide a message of appreciation and support for publication.[93] Although there was a consensus that the campaign should be wound up, no government department was prepared to defend this action in Parliament and risk any attendant bad publicity.[94] Nonetheless, Helen Parkins Gauntlett was warned that the government was considering whether the scheme now had any value.[95] This may explain the better cooperation over a subsequent offer on 22 July from the ACDBH to source 'reasonable quantities' of automatic pistols but accepting that the shipments would be distributed by the Ministry of Supply (who would then reimburse the ACDBH for around $10,000).[96] The Home Defence Executive (HDE) under Sir Samuel Findlater Stewart was now given the unenviable task of trying to control the enthusiasm of the British Committee as its new 'official guide, philosopher and friend', telling Wickham Steed 'his boys must lay off interfering with Service Department supplies. If he can round up odd rifles and binoculars this is OK and we will give him encouragement.'[97] Undeterred, Macneil still tried to elicit support from Lord Beaverbrook, who now followed the official line that the 'British Committee should limit activities to collection of arms and war material from private American donors and sources outside scope of British Purchasing Commission'.[98] Wickham Steed's committee would now provide the War Office with periodic lists of donated arms and the latter would then distribute them to Home Guard units in most need.[99] But donations were now on a much-reduced scale and Lord Halifax reported that the ACDBH now 'carries little weight' in the USA.[100] The indefatigable ACDBH, which was said to have 'more than the normal desire for publicity', next asked for a delegation of Home Guard to be sent to the USA to publicize the activities of the Committee.[101] The suggestion was rejected but the Committee later asked to formally make contact with a delegation of the Home Guard Directorate, which they learned was to go to the USA to advise on the possible establishment of a US Home Guard. It was patiently pointed out that the Home Guard would be received as part of the British armed forces and any joint appearance might impact upon the credibility, if not legality, of the ACDBH.[102] The Home Guard was no longer the ill-equipped body that had appeared in press photographs of 1940, an image still perpetuated by the ACDBH. Panic ensued, and any suggestion of a meeting with the ACDBH was withdrawn, but Macneil and Cutting had betrayed an ongoing lack of appreciation of the nature of the Home Guard.[103] Findlater Stewart was not impressed.

> Sir F. Stewart is beginning to be rather worried about the competence and reliability of the Macneil of Barra, who is showing signs of panic at the prospect that the fact that the Home Guard is definitely a military body may now be revealed in the US.[104]

In the event, the delegation was postponed but the charade maintained by the ACDBH of the Home Guard being a civilian body was already wearing thin.[105] As the Home Defence Executive wrestled with how to control the campaign, the US and British committees tried to inflate the significance of the campaign to ensure its survival. John Drew of the HDE had been told that the Home Guard had received around 50,000 weapons to date from the activities of the Committee and, on this basis, was prepared to see the scheme continue.[106] Findlater Stewart established that the actual figures were only 9,200 weapons up to June 1941 (4,000 rifles and shotguns and 5,200 revolvers).[107]

Relations between the US and British committees were deteriorating under the strain, centred around the ego of Macneil, who demanded to be recognized as the exclusive conduit of communications between the two committees. He first objected that a Home Guard unit in Derbyshire had independently sent a telegram of thanks to Cutting in January 1941.[108] He then protested that Helen Parkins Gauntlett (who had become the face of the campaign in Britain, touring the country handing out donated weapons in a series of local press opportunities), was communicating independently with the ACDBH, especially its publicity agent, was openly referring to the Home Guard in connection with the campaign, and risked conflicts in policy.[109] This was all taken as a slight against the independence of the British Committee and Wickham Steed protested.[110] Cutting naturally supported Macneil, stating that Macneil was the 'sole official liaison for H.M. Committee and I should appreciate all communication being sent through him'.[111] Macneil and Cutting then failed to enlist the support of Findlater Stewart in having Helen Parkins Gauntlett removed as Secretary of the CCPHB.[112] It was no surprise that Wickham Steed in turn described Helen Parkins Gauntlett as 'efficient and satisfactory' – a view with which Findlater Stewart diplomatically did not dissent.[113]

By October 1941 the level of donations had shrunk so that shipping costs (paid first by the Ministry of Aircraft Production and then by BPC from September 1941) had halved to just $500 per month. The British Committee was now running at a loss with 50 per cent of its expenses of £120–£130 per month having to be met through donations by its committee members and the rest through casual donations from factories receiving arms.[114] The British Committee had to ask for financial support from the government, which reluctantly agreed to pay the £16 10*s* monthly rent of its offices – although querying whether it was necessary for the London office to be on the prestigious Park Lane.[115] The entry of the USA into the war in December 1941 was the final straw for the campaign as US citizens now had more immediate concerns. In 1942 US National Guard and factory defence units also had to appeal for weapons in the *American Rifleman* and the US Navy made a public appeal for binoculars. The ACDBH staggered on until June 1942, when Cutting joined the US Army and the ACDBH was dissolved. By then it had secured, by donation or purchase, a total of 25,343 firearms. The supply of 2,993 binoculars and 379 stop watches is often overlooked but may have been the most valuable contribution of the scheme. As in the First World War, there had to be an appeal in Britain for the public to donate binoculars and telescopes and these were now particularly important to equip both the Royal Observer Corps posts which plotted the progress of enemy aircraft over Britain and the Fire Watchers who monitored the progress of air raids. By 10 April 1942 the scheme had provided binoculars to over 800 factories.[116] The stop watches allowed Royal Observer Corps spotters to time the flight of the German bomber fleets and a twenty-jewelled stop watch valued at £150 was donated by the US champion jockey Charlie Kurtsinger.[117] Over 16,000 steel helmets were also donated, mainly US, German and French types from the First World War, but in early April 1941 the Steel Materials Corporation of Detroit donated 4,800 desperately needed new helmets.[118]

The Weapons

The weapons donated to the ACDBH were a mixture of old and new, treasured possessions and unwanted cast-offs of dubious practicality; some were purchased from pawn shops. They included French army 1874 and 1894 rifles, a variety of Winchester and Savage lever action rifles, Springfield M1898 Krag, Springfield M1903, M1917 and Ross M1910 rifles, Winchester, Steyr and Marlin carbines, Mannlicher and Mauser hunting rifles, and Remington .22 rifles. There were assorted shotguns, nineteenth-century revolvers, modern .32 and .38 revolvers, and .22 automatic pistols. The .410 Handy Gun was a single-shot, breech-loading handgun produced from 1921 to 1934 by Harrington & Richardson but it was now illegal to own, and for US owners donation was a convenient way of avoiding prosecution. There were also 110 Thompson sub-machine guns and at least one Lewis gun and a Browning Automatic Rifle. The Imperial War Museum in London has a Winchester M1892, a Winchester M1894, a Remington No. 4 rolling block single-shot .32 rimfire target rifle, a Whitney rolling block single shot .32 rifle, a Springfield M1898 (Krag) .30–40 rifle, a Savage M1899 lever action rifle, and a Remington M1910 12g pump-action riot shotgun.[119] Other than .22 training rifles, there are few Second World War photographs that show Home Guard armed with such weapons and few mentions of the donations in unit histories. By the time they began to arrive, the Home Guard had much more practical, standardized, alternatives.

The *New Yorker* on 2 November 1940 maintained, somewhat unhelpfully, 'Any sort of firearm, with or without ammunition, is welcomed' and Anthony Fiala cheerfully announced 'Anything that goes off with a bang, we can use.'[120] The ACDBH later sensibly insisted that each weapon be accompanied by ammunition (50 rounds per rifles and pistols, 25 rounds per shotgun), but the wide range of calibres was problematic, as can be deduced from the appeal in the August 1941 issue of *American Rifleman*:

> The AMERICAN COMMITTEE for DEFENSE of BRITISH HOMES, 10 Warren Street, New York, N.Y., wants any quantity of the following cartridges. No soft points. Rifles, 22 L. R., .280 Ross, 303 Br., 30–06, 30–40, 30–30, 38–40, 38–55, 45–70. Automatics, 25, 30. 9mm. Luger, 30 Mauser, 32, 380, 38, 45. Revolvers, 32, 38, 38 Special S. & W., 44, 45 Colt. 20, 16, 12, 10 gauge buck or ball. Usable guns, steel helmets, stop-watches, binoculars. Ship pre-paid to above address.[121]

The oldest weapons needed black powder ammunition as the modern smokeless nitro-powder risked exploding the barrels, meaning that some of the shotguns could not be used with the 'lethal shot' issued by the War Office. Giving a householder an outdated weapon with just a few rounds of ammunition might fend off a desultory attack, but this was not the role of the Home Guard at the time the weapons began to arrive, whilst the mixed calibres in a unit were a supply officer's nightmare.

As with other Home Guard weapons, old designs did not necessarily mean that weapons were out-dated. The Winchester M1892 only ceased production in the 1930s and the Savage M1899 as late as 1998. The most useful weapons were the hunting or sporterized military rifles in standard .303 or .300 calibre, .22 rifles for training and the modern handguns. But the practical value of the donations was overwhelmed by the scale of commercial purchases of the British government during the same period. Between April 1940 and August 1942 the British government purchased 12,500 .22 training rifles from various sources and over 800,000 M1917 rifles from the USA.[122] Only 110 Thompson sub-machine guns were provided by the ACDBH up to June 1942 but by then the Home Guard had been issued with 31,828 Thompsons from War Office contracts and its replacement by the mass-produced Sten gun was under way.[123] Between May 1940 and June 1941, 49,764 Colt Official Police revolvers were purchased from the USA by the British Purchasing Commission.

The scale of the campaign was subject to considerable exaggeration. As early as November 1940 *Picture Post* claimed that 'tens of thousands of pieces' had already been collected.[124] The true figure was less than 2,000.[125] The *British Pathé* film *Arms for Britain* (1941) purported to show men loading large wooden crates full of rifles, carbines and shotguns, Colt and Smith & Wesson revolvers, Luger and Mauser automatic pistols and the .410 'Handy Guns'. The men in the film take little care in the packing, piling the guns so high that the lids do not close but beside the crates are cased quality hunting rifles and shotguns. The man supposedly making a tally of the weapons is clearly there only for effect. The crates are stencilled 'Ministry of Small Arms and Ammunition' – which would imply an official destination but it did not exist. This film appears to have been made for publicity purposes only. In March 1941 the *Daily Press* (*Newport News*) reported donations to date of 5,603 firearms.[126] The total had risen in June 1941 to 9,200 weapons but the number of *donated* weapons declined sharply after this point.[127] Only a further 2,680 weapons were donated before June 1942, although an additional 13,763 handguns were obtained by purchase. Nonetheless, Wickham Steed claimed in May 1941 that the arms had equipped 200 Ministry of Aircraft Production factories.[128] The final total in the June 1942 closing account is shown in Fig. 9, comprising 25,343 firearms and 2,042,291 rounds of ammunition. Over half of the weapons were handguns obtained using financial donations (totalling $71,839.03) after the level of physical donations had decreased.[129] The donations were also used to pay shipping costs within the USA, estimated at $4.63 per item. Although the military value of the weapons donations was negligible, each loaned weapon or financial donation gave the donor a small stake in Britain's survival.

The ACDBH was not the only source of privately donated arms from the USA and the scale of some contributions was extremely generous and targeted towards the actual needs of the Home Guard. In 1941 A.P. Buquor, chief design engineer for the Martin & Parry Corporation and one of the founders of the 1st American (Motorized) Squadron of the Home Guard, provided forty Colt machine guns for the London District Home Guard.[130] The 1st American (Motorized) Squadron received at least fifty Thompson sub-machine guns from supporters (*see below*, p. 137). The son of a former US Ambassador sent two Thompsons and a number of automatic pistols to Colonel Gubbins for the Auxiliary Units and in November 1940 Auto-Ordnance gave forty 'reconditioned' Thompsons to the British government.[131]

Figure 9. Material provided by the ACDBH by June 1942. (*Edwards, 1988, p.70*)

	Donated	Purchased
Rifles and Shotguns	5,133	
Thompson SMG	110	
Handguns	6,337	13,763
Binoculars and Telescopes	2,993	
Stop watches	379	
Helmets	16,322	
Rounds of ammunition	642,291	1,400,000
Belts		4,000
Holsters		5,000
Ammunition clips		30,000

Returning the Weapons

Few of the original owners of the 11,470 weapons donated to the ACDBH seriously expected to see their guns again, although this has become a *cause célèbre* on some modern US internet chat rooms. Reports and adverts in US newspapers clearly identify the weapons as gifts or donations rather than loans (Plate 25) and many were the result of police confiscations.[132] The *New Yorker* for 2 November 1940 clearly announced 'If any of the guns the Committee gets are obsolete or impractical, it trades them for other weapons, or sells them.'[133] The syndicated news reports of the first shipment delivered in November 1940 claimed that only one man had said his gun was on loan, to be returned after the war.[134] Each donation was supposed to be accompanied by two labels tied to it, one providing details of the item and the other the name and address of the donor. Richards Cotton's broadcast to the USA in December 1940 made it clear that these labels were to allow recipients to write a letter of thanks, rather than to facilitate a return, with the ACDBH claiming that such letters arrived at a rate of 500 per month throughout 1941 into 1942 (reflecting gratitude for the broad spectrum of donations).[135] The system was flawed: labels went astray during shipping and it was not until April 1941 that Wickham Steed asked Macneil to ensure that details of donor names and addresses were also included on packing lists.[136] Major John W. Hession of Connecticut took no chances with his generous loan of his M1903 Springfield target rifle, with which he had won the Olympic shooting event at Bisley in 1908 and the World 800yd Record in 1909. He mounted a brass plaque on the rifle prior to shipping: 'For obvious reasons the return of this rifle after Germany is defeated would be deeply appreciated.'[137]

Another post-war myth from disgruntled Americans is that most of the donated guns were either scrapped or dumped in the North Sea by the British after the war. Some instances may have occurred but Edwards' claim of 'photos showing ivory-handled Colt Frontiers and Starr double action percussion revolvers being shovelled into the furnace on police orders' in Britain have not been corroborated.[138] The implication has been that the responsibility for the failure to return the weapons was that of the British government but it steadfastly refused to accept any responsibility for the scheme which it neither sought nor encouraged, both during and after the war. Some of the losses were due to enemy action. In March 1941 three cases containing 8,000 rounds of ammunition were destroyed in an air raid. The first U-boat loss was in April when seventeen crates containing mainly rifles were lost at sea. Ten more cases were lost in the sinking of SS *Maasdam* in June 1941.[139] But in all, U-boats sank just four of the sixty-four shipments of US donations (amounting to 35 out of 795 crates) sent between September 1940 and June 1942. Some weapons were found to be unserviceable on arrival and others were useless due to their unusual calibre and, in the urgency of the war, many of them were indeed scrapped rather than scarce resources being spent on their repair. On 28 June 1941 Wickham Steed reported the arrival of 500 defective pistols (around 9 per cent of the donated total) and fifty defective shotguns, asking the ACDBH to forward $1,400 for the repair costs.[140]

Despite all the problems, after the war 146 crates of arms were handed back into the care of a reformed ACDBH, still under Suydam Cutting.[141] The continuing concern to maintain it as a private venture meant that responsibility for organizing the return was to be entirely at the expense of the ACDBH. It proved to be a fraught process: upon arrival in the USA the weapons were checked; damaged guns and those without any accompanying identification of donors were sold off, amounting to thirty-six cases of rifles and shotguns (sold for $980) and a large number of revolvers (sold for $6,149).[142] Another complication was encountered in shipping handguns across the USA, owing to differing State regulations. After the first returns Cutting realized the effort involved, and, believing few of the original donors had seriously expected to see their guns again, he decided that the remaining weapons in Britain should be sold and the proceeds donated to veteran charities.[143] Some of the proceeds went to the Royal Cadet Corps and the School for Orphans of the Merchant Navy.[144]

Nonetheless, many of the weapons were returned to surprised donors, pleased both at the condition of the arms and the fact that they had evidently seen some service. Some letters of thanks were forwarded to the British Embassy:

> I was delighted to receive back in good condition the Remington rifle which I contributed some years ago in response to the appeal from England. As a matter of fact, I had not supposed that I would see this rifle again. (*Cleveland, Ohio*)
>
> This morning the Express Company returned the Krag rifle that I contributed to you in 1940. It is in perfect condition and when I replace it in my gun cabinet I will do so with gratification of the use to which it was dedicated. (*San Francisco, California*)
>
> The weapon is in perfect order, with just enough signs of wear to suggest it was put to some use. I shall treasure it and the accompanying tag. (*New York City*)
>
> This rifle was received by me at my house yesterday, and it is in very good condition, with the exception of certain dents and scars on the stock, which indicate that it has undoubtedly seen service somewhere. I hope it has and that the 200 rounds of ammunition which I sent with it were effectively expended against the common enemy. I never expected to see the gun again, as I intended it as a gift and not a loan. I shall not part with it but shall keep it with its honourable scars intact. (*Minneapolis, Minnesota*)[145]

1st American (Motorized) Squadron of the Home Guard

A small but politically important and highly respected Home Guard unit was formed in July 1940 from fifty to seventy wealthy US businessmen and journalists living in London. The *Defiance Crescent News* of 23 July reported US citizens flocking to join the 'London Legion', equipped with 'tommy guns, fast cars and mills bombs'. This was much to the disapproval of the then US Ambassador, Joseph Kennedy Snr, a pessimist as regards the possibilities of Britain's survival, who claimed that it could cause all citizens of the then still-neutral US living in London to be liable to be shot by the invaders as *francs-tireur*.[146] Nonetheless, the 1st American (Motorized) Squadron was founded by engineer A.P. Buquor (*see above*, p. 134) and socialite Charles Sweeny (who became Adjutant and also founded the Eagle Squadron of the RAF in October 1940), with the assistance of Charles Lytle of the C.J. Lytle & Co. advertising agency. It was commanded by retired general Wade Hampton Hayes (1879–1956) who had fought in the Spanish-American War with the Virginia National Guard and served during the First World War on General Pershing's staff. He was captain of a US shooting team which visited England in the 1920s, and having settled in England became a prominent member of the Queen's Westminster Shooting Club. Hayes was originally in the advertising business but became an investment banker and a director of several regional electricity companies. Rebutting a furious Kennedy (who had threatened to revoke Hayes' citizenship), Hayes appeared on an early 1941 *Pathé News* to explain,

> We started the American Unit because our homes are here, and we wanted to show in some practical way that we were ready, with the British, to share the responsibility of defending their soil. We would have felt ashamed of ourselves if we had sat on the sidelines and done nothing.

He added, 'We believe we have a stake in this country hardly less than the British people themselves.' Hayes also said that he and his men had received many cables and letters from the United States indicating that Americans at home were fully supportive – 'short of war'. Relations were improved by the replacement of Kennedy as Ambassador by John Winnant in March 1941, with Winnant even inspecting the Squadron on parade, but there was a tacit agreement that the unit should not be asked to swear the normal oath of allegiance to the British Crown.

The Squadron had its headquarters at 58 Buckingham Gate, London, was organized in three troops and was well-resourced, all at the expense of its members (with some of the weapons supplied via the ACDBH; *see above*, p. 128). They provided eighteen of their own cars, including a Mercedes Benz roadster, camouflaged and fitted with wireless sets. An offer by Sir Malcolm Campbell to strip down six or seven cars and turn them into armoured personnel carriers at a cost of £2,000 each was, however, rejected.[147] The Scots Guards at Pirbright provided weapons training and the Squadron is usually shown armed with Winchester M1907 semi-automatic rifles (.351 calibre) and large, impressive, bowie knives. They also trained with the London Home Guard Colt machine guns and had a large number of Thompson sub-machine guns although the exact number is contentious. The first reference to Thompsons dates from the earliest reporting in the USA of the unit in July 1940 and the earliest explanation (1942) says that friends of Charles Sweeny at Oxford University paid for the importation of fifty Thompson sub-machine guns.[148] In 1990 Sweeny gave a different account, claiming he wired his father in New York, 'Can you obtain any sub-machine guns?' The reply came, '100 Tommy guns with 100,000 rounds of ammunition *en route* to you donated by the Thompson Company.'[149] Sweeny's unlikely account would almost equal the total number provided by the ACDBH over its lifetime and might have been expected to have attracted more publicity at the time. There may have been some confusion in the story from the forty reconditioned Thompsons donated to the British government by Auto-Ordnance in November 1940.

For the British government the Squadron was important in promoting the personal ties between the USA and Britain and in January 1941 Churchill, as part of his effort to influence American public opinion, gave the Squadron, then numbering seventy-two members, a special review in St James's Park (in stark contrast to the reticence shown to the ACDBH's publicity efforts).[150] Numbers rose to 128 members, and one of the Squadron's roles was to provide part of the guard of the HQ of C-in-C London District (Lieutenant General Sir Bertram Sergison-Brooke).[151] As such, it took part in several exercises with the Morris Detachment, responsible for royal protection. In one instance the Squadron was 'ambushed' by the Morris Detachment as it escorted Sergison-Brooke to lunch at Ascot. Sergison-Brooke, who had not been forewarned of the exercise, was dismayed by the liberal use of smoke grenades. The Morris Detachment looked forward to such exercises as afterwards they retired to the Squadron HQ for refreshments, where the British soldiers were treated to a feast of rare imported luxuries.[152] The Squadron also took part in wider Home Guard exercises with the army and on 22 July 1941 the *New York Times* described how 'Home Guard Unit Embarrasses Defence' when 'a score of middle-aged American businessmen' captured a Brigade HQ comprising 300–500 men defending an airfield. They used 'fifth column' tactics including a supposed 'golfer', a 'drunkard' and a man throwing sticks for his dog to spy out the defences, even taking photographs before storming the HQ building armed with 'tommy-guns, revolvers, tear gas and hand grenades'. Unfortunately, one of their flares set fire to the headquarters!

Although having little material impact, the unofficial shows of solidarity from the USA for the British war effort were important symbols of support and added to the atmosphere that allowed the passage of the Lend-Lease Act. But in terms of assistance to the Home Guard, the critical decision had already been made before such campaigns came into being and that was Roosevelt's determination to bypass the Neutrality Act and allow Britain to buy huge quantities of arms on a 'cash and carry basis'.

Chapter Seven

Training the Home Guard

> Suicides' academies have apparently been set up all over Britain. The head-masters are cunning blackguards, who teach the inmates how to make bombs at the modest cost of 2 shillings each, how to poison water supplies by throwing dead dogs into streams and how to kill sentries noiselessly from behind.
>
> *William Joyce (Lord Haw-Haw), broadcast over Bremen Radio, 2 August 1940*[1]

Around 40 per cent of the volunteers in 1940 had pre-existing military training, mainly from the First World War. As the Home Guard became younger, this advantage decreased and the training had to adapt to its changing roles. Given the unexpected flood of volunteers and the uncertainty over the Home Guard's role, there was confusion on the best way to train the new force for the present war. Some senior officers disputed the need for any training to defend fixed positions in what was envisaged as a short term, if not suicidal, role. George Orwell recorded attending a lecture given by Brigadier James Whitehead, CO of the London Home Guard, in late August:

> Dilating on the Home Guard being a static defensive force, he said contemptuously and in a rather marked way that he saw no use in our practising taking cover, 'crawling about on our stomachs', etc., etc., evidently as a hit at the Osterley Park training school. Our job, he said, was to die at our posts ... These wretched old blimps, so obviously silly and senile, and so degenerate in everything except physical courage, are merely pathetic in themselves, and one would feel rather sorry for them if they were not hanging round our necks like millstones.[2]

Wintringham also encountered Whitehead:

> Soon after the school was founded an officer high up in the command of the LDV requested Mr Hulton and myself to close the school down, because the sort of training we were giving was 'not needed'. This officer explained to us with engaging frankness that the Home Guard did not have to do 'any of this crawling round; all they have to do is to sit in a pill-box and shoot straight'.[3]

Brigadier Whitehead, aged 60, had left the army in 1927 and then joined the Metropolitan Police until retiring in 1938. In 1940 he became commander of the London Home Guard and was the epitome of the 'blimp', with equally strident views against women joining the Home Guard. Fortunately, wiser views prevailed at the War Office. The simplest way of harnessing the energy of the volunteers whilst waiting for official instructions and weapons was to engage in traditional parade-ground drill. Conflict then arose between traditionalists who believed that drill was an essential prerequisite for any soldier to learn discipline and the automatic response to orders, and those, frustrated by the thought of imminent invasion, who wanted more exciting, action-packed training. In his LDV enrolment form one Worcestershire volunteer tried to qualify his application by saying that he would not undertake drill but only wanted to fight off any invasion.[4] In *New Ways of War* Wintringham was dismissive of the value of traditional drill:

> But to take perfectly good young men and give them weeks on end of barrack-square, knocks out of them not only any 'instincts' for fighting they may have, but also their ability to think about all orders received and to use their own judgement. Independence, initiative and intelligence are all ground out of the recruit at the average training.[5]

In fact, the War Office stressed that the necessary drill as recommended in LDV Instruction No. 5 of July 1940 was basic, consisting only of 'Attention, stand at ease; fall in three lines; right turn; left turn (keeping the ranks); move off to a flank in threes; keep step; left wheel; right wheel; halt; right turn (keeping the ranks).'[6] The real problem came at a local level when units were commanded by traditionalist officers who saw smartness in drill as an objective in its own right. John Brophy captured the confusion in approach:

> Some will urge that Arms Drill and Marching Drill are unnecessary ... Others will have it that not enough drill is described here ... Discreet inquiries have shewn that these two extremes are being followed in different parts of the country, sometimes in different parts of the same area.[7]

In the absence of any other immediately available training material, 100,000 copies of Wintringham's *Picture Post* article of 15 June 'Against Invasion: the lessons of Spain' were distributed by the War Office as the first training leaflet for the Home Guard, effectively giving official sanction to Wintringham's position as public strategist for the Home Guard.[8] As a longer-term solution, on 27 June the Home Guard Inspectorate discussed the desirability of weekly training pamphlets and a flood of training instruction leaflets was soon under way (Fig. 10).[9] To coordinate these efforts, on 19 July Field Marshal Lord Gort (former C-in-C of the BEF) was appointed as Inspector of Training for the LDV. Churchill had specifically requested him, as representing a modern general who had come directly from active service.

The nine LDV leaflets were simple and functional. Subsequent Home Guard Instruction Leaflets were expanded to include fieldcraft, map-reading, camouflage, enemy tactics, enemy recognition, use of weapons, street fighting, defence of towns, first aid and drill, and the number of lecture tours, demonstrations and training courses soon mushroomed. From August 1942 the focus in training changed towards greater emphasis on battle inoculation with live fire and other field training, often in conjunction with the regular army – battle exercises in which neither side showed mercy! Such training was aimed at the increasingly

Figure 10. List of LDV Training Leaflets, June–July 1940.

No. 1	Road Blocks
No. 2	Role and Status (June 1940)
No. 3	German Parachute Troops
No. 4	Training Instructions
No. 5	Elements of Training
No. 6	Relations between Civil Defence services and LDV
No. 7	Field Defences
No. 8	Tank Hunting
No. 9	Grenades
No. 10	Home Guard General Instructions (replacing LDV Instructions No. 1, 2 and 4) (August 1940)

youthful members of the Home Guard before they were conscripted into the armed forces. The limited time for training and its impact on the labour force had been recognized when there was early grumbling that men were not turning up for evening parades:

> We have to realize that in the villages, especially in the small villages, the whole of a platoon, or it may be a section, is drawn from the agricultural labourers, who have been working all day long, and if you expect them – as we do whenever there is a warning – to be on duty at their block, it is really more than we can ask of them that, in addition, they should turn up at numerous parades at eight o'clock or eight-thirty in the evening.[10]

Despite the difficulties, the Home Guard were eager to improve their skills and demonstrate their commitment, which was psychologically important for men who, for whatever reason, were unable to serve in the regular forces. Publishers soon realized there was a profit to be made from their voracious appetite for training literature and one of the first commercially available manuals was a reprint of the First World War booklet for the VTC on *Rifle Training for War* by Captain Ernest Robinson. Despite paper rationing, over 150 commercially available manuals and other related Home Guard literature were produced over the course of the war. Official army manuals tended to be dry and dull, but unofficial publications could be far more exciting, deliberately written for an amateur audience. They offered important information on unfamiliar techniques of street fighting that would be crucial to the role of the Home Guard in defending nodal points, and cheerful instructions on how to make home-made mortars, or dismantle service grenades to extract the explosives for more 'useful' devices. Notable was the 'blood and thunder' approach of left-wing journalists, many of whom had the cachet of having served in the Spanish Civil War (or had at least been in Spain). They wrote with enthusiasm and evangelical zeal, with, as Brophy admitted, 'certain informalities of outlook and phrasing' that kept the Home Guard engaged.[11] The War Office was driven by the scale of unofficial publications to publish a list of half a dozen books which had been submitted to them for approval and which were deemed useful. As a measure of their acceptance by the establishment, the list included Tom Wintringham's *New Ways of War* and Hugh Slater's *Home Guard for Victory*, both of which promoted an offensive state of mind rather than one of siege mentality.[12]

One of the most prolific writers of manuals was John Brophy (who also appeared on the War Office approved list). He had served throughout the First World War, joining up at the age of 14. Brophy became a successful author and literary critic and was a company commander in the Middlesex Home Guard. His *Home Guard: a manual for the LDV* was a bestseller by September 1940 and had been reprinted nine times by March 1942 (when it was republished as the *Home Guard Handbook*). With the publishers sensing a ready market, it was followed by *A Home Guard Drill Book & Field Service Manual* and in 1941 by *Advanced Training for the Home Guard*. In 1945 he displayed his left-wing roots in *Britain's Home Guard: a character study*, with iconic portraits of working-class Home Guard provided by Eric Kennington.

Colonel George Wade (of the famous Wade pottery family) was one serving army officer who managed to write in an engaging and informal style. He had enlisted with the South Staffordshire Regiment in August 1914 and was commissioned and seconded to the Machine Gun Corps. He served in France and Egypt before being demobilized in 1919. At the start of the Second World War he returned from the TA Reserve, still aged only 48, to command the Birkenhead garrison in Western Command. Despite a lack of recent army experience, he wrote a remarkable series of practical and engaging guides for Gale & Polden: *Fire Control*, *Defence of towns*, *Defence of Houses*, *Defence of Villages & Small Towns*, *Road Blocks*, *House-to-house Fighting*, *Factory Defence*, *The Art of Prowling*, *The Fighting Patrol*, *Fighting Patrol Training* and *Fighting Patrol Tactics*. His most extraordinary manual was *The Defence of Bloodford Village*, published in late November 1940, with a short foreword by the first Director General of the Home Guard, Major General Eastwood. It is written as a *Christmas Carol*-esque parable, illustrating through a series of dreams by the Home Guard commander what might happen if proper preparations were not made for the village's defence. After each disaster caused by an error in planning, he revisits the scene to correct the weakness. In one instance, the protagonist even 'watches' as he is shot dead and his body hung from the village's old gibbet as a result of one of the blunders! Ultimately, a successful defence plan emerges and the description of the quintessential idyllic village now at peace has many comparisons with the opening scenes of the 1942 film *Went the Day Well*.

For the first time radio could also be used as a medium for spreading information. One broadcaster was Lieutenant Sydney Carter of Wickhamford, Evesham, who had served in the First World War with the RFC and RAF and then became a pioneering documentary film-maker on farming topics. He was working for the BBC at its secret broadcasting station at Wood Norton but after attending a course at Osterley he not only established a local training school but also hosted the popular Sunday afternoon programme *For Home Guards Only* on the BBC with his Cromwellian catchphrase 'Keep your powder dry'. It was a conspiratorial title, designed to increase their sense of community, and featured answers to questions sent in by listeners to the BBC in London.

While the War Office tried to confine the Home Guard within a strategy of defending nodal points, the writings of Wintringham and like-minded enthusiasts offered a more imaginative approach that, in 1940 at least, seemed more appropriate to their need for improvisation. Wintringham's *Deadlock War* of March 1940 had already challenged the convention of rigidly holding a position at all costs in favour of the principle of an 'elastic web of defence', and also stressed the need to encourage initiative in the lower ranks, predicting a need to fight independently in small units with 'a new spirit and discipline in the army, a release of the initiative and independent energy of the men who are our soldiers'.[13] John Langdon-Davies wrote encouragingly in similar terms in his regular 'Home Guard Parade' column from October 1940 in the *Sunday Pictorial*: 'The best Home Guard section is not necessarily the one with the best shots; it is the one which has grasped the adventure, the need for using the imagination, that has had to be called into existence to destroy Nazism.'[14] Such publications played a major part in elevating the conventional harrying role of the Home Guard to an independent 'guerrilla' strategy.

The War Office lagged behind the unofficial training schools that sprang up across the country but the latter were soon absorbed into official regional and local networks of training centres. The first training school was formed in early June 1940 at Claverley near Draycott in Shropshire by Lieutenant Colonel Robert Otter-Barry, formerly of the Shropshire Light Infantry and Royal Sussex Regiment, who had served on the staff of the School of Musketry at the end of the First World War. It was originally housed in a tent supplied by the Royal British Legion in a local sand quarry and focused on rifle training in 10-hour courses each Sunday. In early 1941 official recognition came with the appointment of three Permanent Staff Instructors and funding provided by the TAA, its syllabus extended to training with grenades and then with the new spigot mortars. The course moved into two huts, with eighty students attending each Sunday and additional weekday evening courses. Widely used by the Shropshire and Staffordshire Home Guard, it had a travelling wing providing courses throughout the neighbouring counties. From June 1942 Claverley became a training school for Home Guard officer and NCO instructors, with a lecture hall, office, canteen and stores buildings and courses extended over the whole weekend. Otter-Barry was awarded the OBE in 1945 for his initiative in providing training facilities.

The most famous Home Guard Training School was opened at Osterley Park on 10 July 1940, with Tom Wintringham as Chief Instructor. It was funded by Edward Hulton, the owner of *Picture Post*, on land provided by Lord Jersey, whose only condition was that they not blow up the house! The training, mainly for Home Guard officers, was carried out in the park but two houses were rented on an adjacent street to house the trainees, packed with straw mattresses, blankets and catering equipment, with additional refreshments provided by a YMCA mobile canteen.[15] There was an hour off for lunch at the local pub just outside the lodge gates and their custom no doubt consoled the publican when bombs from the home-made mortars occasionally landed in his car park. Two adjacent streets of condemned houses were also used to practise street fighting – a unique feature of the training at the time, made more urgent due to the BEF's recent experience in the defence of Calais and a necessary component in the War Office plan for the Home Guard to hold the 'defended localities' to the last.

Wintringham's flair for publicity and the backing of Hulton's *Picture Post* gave this innovative course an international reputation, assisted by the mystique of instructors who had served in the Spanish Civil War, although, other than Hugh Slater and three Spanish refugees, their actual combat experience in that war was more limited than the legend suggests. Wintringham had devised the syllabus during a War Office lecture tour in June while his wife Kitty sorted out the administrative arrangements, including securing the instructors. It had a lively 'blood and thunder' approach that the students found a welcome change from the traditional parade drill taught in many Home Guard units. Over a two-day course the students were given unique instruction in how to deliver the Home Guard role of harrying the enemy, using camouflage, improvised explosives, street fighting and ambushing techniques. One prime objective was to 'debunk the tank' and the fear of what seemed to be the invincible German Panzer. Mollie Panter-Downes, an English journalist writing for the *New Yorker*, watched a demonstration of an ambush with a dummy tank made of corrugated iron being towed behind an old car (Plate 11). Boy scouts on bicycles acted the role of motorcycle troops. A barricade was pulled across the road, the 'tank' hit a landmine pulled into its path and was then attacked with Molotov cocktails.[16] The War Office reaction to the school was mixed. To the irritation of the LDV Inspectorate, the first they knew of the school was a letter from Edward Hulton which they received two days after the school opened. On 16 July the Inspectorate was told that 'While approving of the school in principle, the London District Assistant Commander did not think the Instructors were of a suitable type.'[17] The reasons were later amplified: 'The report was adverse not so much as regards the School but owing to the Communistic tendency of the Instructors.'[18] MI5 noted 'General Whitehead, the local LDV commander (who objected to the very principle of Home Guard training), has refused to have anything to do with the school' but disapproval was not absolute and the War Office 'seem to have given it some very half-hearted recognition'.[19] Mollie Panter-Downes also remarked that the War Office smiled benignly on the school but had not given it official backing:

> It is possible that high military circles take the cautious attitude that a people's army trained and armed for a people's war might be too much like placing dynamite near that sacred body of law, the British constitution.[20]

The Secret Intelligence Service may not have shared this ambivalence as the Inspectorate also reported on 19 July that 'MI Branch' (as opposed to MI5) was interested.[21] Hulton had already carried out work for Section D, and the techniques taught followed the methodology of its Home Defence Scheme.[22] By the end of July over a hundred men were attending each course. In all, some 5,000 students were taught at the school until its close in late September. Inspired students returned to their localities and set up local versions of the school, so disseminating the ideas even further. The school received high-level deputations of MPs as well as a meeting with Sir Ronald Adam, the Deputy Chief of the Imperial General Staff, Sir John Brown, the Deputy Adjutant General, and Major General Augustus Thorne, the commander of XII Corps, whom Wintringham briefed on irregular warfare and 'political combat'. As a result, the army sent officers on the course from the Brigade of Guards, the Royal Armoured Corps, and various infantry regiments, and there were even students from a Naval shore establishment.[23] Senior Auxiliary Units officers also visited, with one believing the training provided at Osterley was better than what they themselves could provide at the time (*see above*, p. 64). It is tempting to speculate that some of the army attendees were the Guards officers from the tank-hunting platoons of the 3rd Division, who trained the early Auxiliary Units. Wintringham exploited the growing popularity of the term 'guerrilla warfare' – a label not used in *New Ways of War* or even in his 'Arm the Citizens' article in *Picture Post* of 29 June – for almost any small-scale action, but the school also taught the principles of guerrilla warfare proper (*see above*, p. 78). The term captured international attention and *Life* magazine announced:

> As deadly as Army snipers are the former book-keepers, cricketers and civil servants, including the phlegmatic ex-Ambassador to Germany, Sir Neville Henderson, who attend the unofficial Home Guard Training School for Guerrilla Warfare. On Lord Jersey's estate near London they practise garrotting, stabbing and strangling.[24]

Wintringham was the Chief Instructor. His main strength was as a strategist and motivator and he exaggerated the practical experience of the instructors from the Spanish Civil War to emphasize the modernity of the teaching. In September Mollie Panter-Downes found 'a more flexible method of warfare evolved in the Spanish Civil War by men with plenty of courage and ingenuity but little equipment'.[25] Yet the British Battalion of the International Brigades had not engaged in guerrilla warfare and Wintringham's own combat experience was limited, having been wounded on the second day of the battle of Jarama in February 1937. Hugh Slater (formerly Chief of Operations in the International Brigades) was more experienced. He joined the school in August and was a specialist in street fighting and tank hunting as well as campaign strategy. Mollie Panter-Downes described Slater as having a 'pleasantly brisk and humorous manner'.[26] In describing what were at the time still novel techniques of house-to-house fighting, he exhorted students 'Don't be rash, either; you may feel a bit of a fool crawling on your stomach over a nice pile carpet in some total stranger's drawing room, but you'd feel a lot worse with a bit of lead in your guts.' He gave the benefit of his experience in such situations with 'Tommy guns' (a loose term at the time for any sub-machine gun):

> 'other people may have different opinions about them for fighting at close range in a limited space – say, in a bathroom – they're useful things. I know what I'm talking about, because I once had to fight in a bathroom with a Tommy gun,' he said, smiling gently. 'It was useful – very.' The military gentlemen gazed at him doubtfully, as though slightly shocked by the idea of battle in such unorthodox surroundings.[27]

Bert 'Yank' Levy taught unarmed combat and knife fighting. He brought the romance of involvement in Central American revolutions and cultivated an eccentric air, frequently wearing an old flying helmet. His skills were those of a tough street fighter and boxer in the USA, but his credentials from Spain were also limited, having been captured at Jarama. There were three refugee Spanish miners who, as well as their practical experience in making home-made grenades, brought an international flavour and a gritty sense of realism from men who had lost their country to fascism. Charles Graves explained how the Spanish miners became idols of the LDV and 'even a nodding acquaintance with them carried more prestige among the LDV than a close friendship with a Hollywood film star would have done in peace time'.[28] Ricardo was 'Slight but wiry, he would throw a dummy bomb and then scuttle away, looking rather like a keen, intelligent terrier.'[29] Kitty Wintringham explained to Mollie the love of the Spaniards for Molotov cocktails and described the attack on some Universal (Bren gun) Carriers that had been brought to the school when a party of MPs visited for an inspection:

> The other day we had some real tanks down here and the boys simply couldn't resist it. A Molotov bottle just happened to fly out of someone's hands as a tank went by. It made a swell blaze, but Tom was awfully worried.[30]

Not all the high-ranking visitors approved. Mollie Panter-Downes reported,

> One old boy – looked like a general or something – snorted, 'That's not the clean, British Army way of fighting, sir.' Well, my friend chuckled softly, 'this isn't a clean war, either. If the Germans try to come over here, it's going to be as dirty for them as we can make it.'[31]

Former Soviet spy Wilfrid Vernon (*see below*, p. 160) lectured on improvised explosives, how to build anti-glider obstacles and the use of rifle fire against dive bombers, using a model aeroplane on a zip wire. Roland Penrose was a leading Surrealist artist and a Quaker who had served with the Friends Ambulance Unit in the First World War. He had broad left-wing sympathies, had organized the Artists' Refugee Committee in 1938 helping artists to escape the Nazis, and helped set up the British tour of Pablo Picasso's *Guernica* in 1938–39. This was enough to put him under low-level MI5 surveillance. Upon the outbreak of the Second World War he co-founded the Industrial Camouflage Research Unit to advise factories on how to camouflage their works, and then taught camouflage skills at Osterley, playing on its disreputable reputation. 'To an old soldier, the idea of hiding from your enemy and the use of deception may possibly be repulsive. He may feel that it is not brave and not cricket.'[32] As a teaching aid, he would sometimes produce a naked Lee Miller from her concealment under camouflage netting. Penrose subsequently joined the Middlesex Home Guard and wrote the *Home Guard Manual of Camouflage*, which provided practical guidance on the use of colour and texture, especially for protection from aerial reconnaissance:

> A mixture of soot and flour will make a good paste which sticks to the skin. By some who live in the country districts cow-dung has been advocated, and for those who have the courage to use it, it can be highly recommended in spite of its unpleasantness, since it retains good colour and texture when dry.[33]

In June 1942 Penrose joined Langdon-Davies at the Burwash Fieldcraft School before being commissioned into the Royal Engineers, and was appointed Senior Lecturer at the Eastern Command Camouflage School in the Assembly Rooms, Norwich. Other instructors included Stanley White, Chief Instructor of the Boy Scouts, who taught the skills of stalking and observation. Captain John Hay, on sick leave from the Indian Army General Service Corps, lectured on fieldworks and how to make effective road-blocks. Taking lessons from the French campaign to heart, he stressed that any concern for private property should be ignored:

> You must get out of the idea that there's any such rubbish as private property in this war! When the invasion comes, such a thing won't exist. All you've got to think of is what will happen if these filthy Nazis come and beat us.[34]

With some relief, on 10 September 1940 General Pownall (Inspector-General of the Home Guard) announced that 'the school at Osterley was gradually being taken over by the War Office'.[35] This was a means of controlling the syllabus and enthusiasm of the instructors as well as Wintringham's flair for publicity but the first stage was a mere token, finding an unemployed former officer on the Emergency Reserve List to become nominal commandant of the school. Captain Roy 'Peter' Wyatt-Foulger had served in the First World War with the RASC in France and Palestine but in September 1940 was an unemployed commercial boiler salesman on the Officers' Emergency Reserve List. He taught techniques of anti-aircraft rifle fire at Osterley but he was not directly employed by the War Office and was not transferred to Denbies with the rest of the school. Having been recommissioned in February 1941 and becoming a staff officer, from January 1942 he served again as a training officer at Denbies. Osterley was finally closed on 30 September and relocated to Denbies House, Dorking, designated as No. 1 Training School under Major Hugh Pollock (Royal Scots Fusiliers), who had edited the serial publication *Battle Training* in 1939, to which Wintringham was a contributor. To avoid the rebellious image cultivated at Osterley, Denbies was explicitly ordered to keep a lower public profile.[36] There were practical advantages to the new site. Osterley did not have covered provision for the winter, and training was carried out in the grounds surrounding the house, whereas Denbies had covered training facilities and students could also be accommodated on-site.[37] It was also able to offer more comprehensive, five-and-a-half day courses to Home Guard officers. In a return to traditionalist attitudes, because of restrictions on space they were asked not to bring servants![38] The Osterley instructors still dominated the course, with Slater carrying much of the workload. He taught the tactical role of the Home Guard, street fighting tactics, reporting, fieldworks and fortifications, and (with 'Yank' Levy) field manoeuvres. Wilfrid Vernon again taught anti-aircraft musketry, use of smoke screens, bombing and bomb-making. Roland Penrose continued to teach camouflage and Stanley White taught stalking. Wintringham's contribution was more constrained, being confined to anti-tank warfare and unable to exploit his talent for publicity. Frustrated, he resigned in June 1941 while Slater was undergoing officer training. Slater briefly returned as a newly commissioned second lieutenant but later became an instructor in a Scottish Command officer training school. Levy eventually returned to the USA to help train the US equivalent of SOE – the Office of Strategic Services (OSS). Some problems of enforcing War Office discipline remained but were ironically caused by the CO himself, who seemingly encouraged the students to decide for themselves whether to follow the War Office focus on defended areas. On 5 November 1940 the Home Guard Inspectorate was annoyed to discover that:

> I.G. [Inspector General] said it had come to his notice that the commandant of the School in a lecture was telling students that it was dependent on the interest shown by them which would decide in what role they are to be employed, either static or outside their own area. This has created consternation and he thought it was a dangerous statement to make. There is no intention of altering the role of Home Guards.[39]

The course began to change after Wintringham left and by the time A.G. Street attended the Denbies course in January 1942 it was heavily oriented toward weapons training. He found the course exhausting, from dawn to 9.00pm, and at the end Street described himself as suffering from 'mental constipation'. 'We learned the ins and out and tricks of every weapon already issued to the Home Guard, and also those soon to be issued ... In addition the tactical use of each weapon was explained.' By then the instructors were a mixture of regular army officers, Home Guard and civilians. Pollock was still Commandant, described as someone who 'fairly doted on sub-artillery'. There were still said to be veterans of the Spanish Civil War, 'experts in dirty tricks or thuggery' and those who 'apparently slept each night from choice with live bombs as bedfellows'.[40]

In September 1940, with the War Office trying to take over Osterley, Hulton founded a second school at No. 2 Polo Ground, Hurlingham, Fulham, run by two former Osterley instructors, Captain John Hay and Captain Crisp. It ran until December 1940 and although it was again discouraged by the authorities, General Gough, Zone Commander of the Chelsea & Fulham Home Guard, funded the publication of its lecture notes.[41] Repeating the message of Osterley, the lectures warned students 'you may have to kill British citizens in order to get at the Huns ... if the Germans use civilians as a human shield, there must be no hesitation in opening fire'.[42] It called for flexibility in defence, combined with offensive action that required 'far more trained initiative and discipline than just "staying put" in a blockhouse'.

John Langdon-Davies had been a conscientious objector during the First World War and then became a well-travelled writer who warned about the threat of fascism. He covered the Spanish Civil War for *News Chronicle* and wrote *Behind the Spanish Barricades* as a plea for British and French intervention on behalf of the Republic; he also became a relief worker and founded a Home and Foster Parents Scheme for Refugee Children (now *Plan International*). He was later a war correspondent in the Finnish Winter War. Langdon-Davies supported the Spanish Republic but had little confidence in its military ability. Although attracted to the Spanish anarchists in 1938 as 'superb, loveable human beings', he felt they were too disorganized to mount an effective defence against the Nationalists.[43] He criticized the anti-Stalinist Partido Obero de Unificación Marxista (POUM), which he felt was undermining the Republican war effort, and also became an outspoken critic of the Communist Party because of the Hitler–Stalin Pact – such broad criticism probably made him more acceptable to the establishment than Wintringham. After Wintringham was silenced by his move to Denbies, Langdon-Davies began to fill that void. He established a weekly 'Home Guard' column for the *Sunday Pictorial* from October 1940 to March 1942, which both explained and gently challenged War Office policy towards the Home Guard, capitalizing on this with a mammoth lecture tour of Home Guard units over the winter of 1940 and the spring of 1941 (the lecture was published in *Home Guard Warfare* in 1941). With Wintringham-esque enthusiasm, he repeated the stories of Spanish militia stopping tanks using improvised explosives, blanket blinds, soup plates and pieces of railway track rammed into the tracks; his appeal for imagination and ingenuity suggested that 'we, adults though we are, are sometimes called upon to behave in a way in which we longed to be able to behave when we were boys of thirteen and fourteen'.[44] His hugely popular *Home Guard Training Manual* (December 1940) had a strong emphasis on fieldcraft and Langdon-Davies, now with the rank of captain in the Home Guard, followed this up in March 1941 by founding a fieldcraft school on his farm, Bowman's at Burwash, Sussex, staffed initially with help from the local Home Guard. Within six weeks five local schools had been formed by former students. When the Burwash school was taken over by the War Office in December 1941 as the South East Command Fieldcraft School, training Home Guard instructors, Langdon-Davies was promoted to major and continued in command. It was an immersive course based around camouflage and stalking, with unshaven students expected to move throughout the day as if they were under enemy fire and always to carry their rifle.[45] After spending one night in the relative comfort of a barn or other outhouses, the students were expected to make their own shelters in the woods where they were taught the skills of taking cover, moving silently, guiding and reconnoitring for the army and camouflage (Plate 13). From June 1941 the school also gave training to regular army officers, who eventually made up one quarter of the intake on its weekend courses.[46] Langdon-Davies wrote in a quiet but engaging style that dealt with practicalities and avoided politics; his school had an on-going influence throughout the war. Unlike Wintringham, Langdon-Davies was formally recognized for his work with the Home Guard, being awarded the MBE. Wintringham's Penguin publications have provided a lasting legacy but Langdon-Davies' more ephemeral weekly pages in *Sunday Pictorial* from October 1940 were eagerly read by thousands and his lectures were equally popular. He even claimed miners wrapped their lunches in his newspaper articles so that they could discuss the contents at work.[47]

The creation of No. 1 School at Denbies was followed by No. 2 School at Kinnaird House, Larbert, Falkirk, in June 1941 where the course was again five-and-a-half days long.[48] In 1942 came No. 3 School at Stokesay Court, Onibury, Shropshire, which trained company and platoon officers, had a leadership course for junior officers and NCOs, and a specialist training course for adjutants. As the demand increased, in March 1941 the first 'travelling wing' of three officers, three warrant officers and three drivers was administered by the Denbies Training School. They provided both weekend and mid-week courses to train local instructors, covering Eastern, Southern, South-Eastern and London District Commands. In July 1941 a similar travelling wing was attached to No. 2 Training School at Kinnaird House covering Scottish, Northern and Western Commands. By November 1941 they had expanded to two travelling wings from Kinnaird and three from Denbies. In addition there were more specialized regional training schools, including weapons training schools at the Western Command Training Centre at Altcar, Lancashire, and the West Riding Training School at Harrogate. The emphasis on the defence of nodal points gave a particular importance to street fighting, first pioneered at Osterley. In Scotland there were regional town fighting schools at Glasgow, Leith and Aberdeen. The Glasgow school was based in a row of ruined miners' cottages at Dixon's Blazes offering weekend courses for 'guerrilla fighters'.[49] The course included throwing live grenades and firing Northover Projectors, and was also used by the British and US armies. Meanwhile, the Leith school was said to help avoid 'the more elementary forms of suicide'.[50] The Town Fighting School in Birmingham, in existence by September 1942 and continuing until late 1944, was based around a disused former Unitarian chapel on Bristol Street and the adjacent bombed-out streets, and at the Blind Institute, Edgbaston. Students came from across the country with the Chief Instructor being regular army officer Captain Albert Edwards, who had first joined the Lincolnshire Regiment in 1919 as a boy soldier. The six-day course covered the theory and organization of street fighting with lectures, films and demonstrations, followed by exercises in the techniques of crossing obstacles, defending and clearing buildings and streets, mouse-holing, high-toggling and patrolling. Given modern media's fixation on either the comedic aspects of the Home Guard or its 'secret' activities, the *Birmingham Post* in February 2016 managed to combine both stereotypes by describing the training school as a 'secret Birmingham base' where 'those of advanced years learned to engage the Nazis in grim close combat'. Far from being secret, a report on the school was published in the *Birmingham Evening Dispatch* on 4 September 1942, following a demonstration provided for Viscount Bridgeman.[51]

Students took the lessons from such schools back to their units, and local training schools proliferated across the country. Their efficiency was greatly assisted by the appointment of regular army NCOs as Permanent Staff Instructors attached to the Home Guard from the summer of 1940, initially on a regional basis but eventually extending to battalion level. A key feature from 1942 onwards was battle inoculation using live-firing exercises. Although the possibility of the Home Guard having to fight in Britain had decreased, such training was increasingly useful for the teenage Home Guard who were awaiting call-up and would shortly be fighting overseas. In many cases it meant that they arrived at their army unit already proficient in musketry, grenades and the Sten gun. The constant cycling of such men out of the Home Guard did, however, mean that there was an endless need to train new recruits. Evesham Battalion had formed its own training school following the attendance of Lieutenant Sydney Carter at Osterley and in 1943 it established a battle inoculation course at The Dingle, Elmley Castle. As each squad made an assault up the side of the hill, machine-gun fire would be directed as close to their heads as safety would allow, while mines exploded around them and they fired live ammunition at targets set in various locations on the hill. Captain Collett used a Hotchkiss light machine gun to fire many thousands of rounds during these exercises but confidently 'firing to miss 'em'.[52] Bromsgrove Battalion ran a similar course in a wooded dingle to the south of the Hampton Lovett rifle range, where Bill Allington laid explosive charges of guncotton wired back to a central control panel, allowing him to explode varying patterns of simulated shell fire as the Home Guard participants made their way around the wooded course, following a safe path marked by white tapes.[53] Increasingly, there were also exercises with the regular army which could be on an enormous scale. One in Birmingham, staged in March 1943, involved 10,000 members of the Home Guard with units from Staffordshire and Worcestershire attacking Birmingham from the south and west; as with exercises with the Jedburgh teams (*see above*, p. 45), they were designed to benefit both sides before the army units were posted overseas. Southern Railways Home Guard Group had its own training centre at Gomshall, Surrey, and released men to attend both weekday and weekend courses without loss of pay. Created during the blitz, it partly provided some relief for railwaymen in more peaceful surroundings and continued to have a relaxed atmosphere. One notable feature seemed to be frequent provision of mealtimes! It was described as 'a holiday camp in the sense that the best holiday is a change of work'.[54]

After the effort that went into training, the Home Guard naturally wanted some recognition for their hard work. The War Office was reluctant to allow the Home Guard to wear the standard arms and trade qualification badges (although this restriction was widely ignored) but an official proficiency badge (a simple red felt diamond), issued from April 1941, was awarded after completion of a test that included general knowledge and demonstrable skills with a rifle, 'other weapon', No. 36 grenade, battlecraft and map reading (*see* Appendix 1.10).

The need to train a new army almost overnight, using local instructors often with only limited training themselves, inevitably led to accidents. Naturally, the memoirs of the Home Guard volunteers tend to place an emphasis on training accidents as they involved their own friends and neighbours. For many Home Guards a range accident was also the nearest they came to being under fire and such incidents were, therefore, particularly memorable, each incident being then duly recorded by subsequent historians, whereas the same incident might not be so noteworthy to a soldier who had been through Dunkirk, El Alamein or Normandy. Such accidents should not detract from the fact that the Home Guard who served with Anti-Aircraft Command, Coastal Artillery or with field artillery, at least, were judged as being of equal competence to their comrades in the Royal Artillery. Accidents typically happened during grenade practice or in the accidental discharge of rifles and the infamously temperamental Sten gun. Some were a result of poor instruction or range discipline. Out of 137 gallantry awards, 25 were a result of accidents on grenade ranges. But many of the recorded casualties were the result of motor accidents whilst on duty, due to driving at night in the blackout on unlit country roads. It is difficult to compare the casualty figures with those of the regular army or to justify MacKenzie's claim that 'the chances of a Home Guard dying on duty from causes that had nothing to do with the enemy were at least four times those of a regular soldier' – not least because around two-thirds of the British army were employed in administrative and support roles not comparable with the duties of the Home Guard.[55] In all, 1,206 Home Guard personnel died on duty, out of a force of up to 1.8 million men at any one time, but a total of 4 million passed through its ranks. Reflecting its position in and around 'Hellfire Corner', Kent Home Guard's casualties included two officers and forty-three other ranks who were killed by enemy action up to 30 November 1942.[56]

Chapter Eight

A People's Army?

> It so happens that this war, whether those at present in authority like it or not, has to be fought as a citizen's war ... it has been found necessary to bring into existence a new network of voluntary associations such as the Home Guard ... They are a new type, what might be called the organized militant citizen.
>
> *J.B. Priestley*[1]

The term 'People's War' was used widely, if loosely, in the Second World War and the Home Guard became its armed front as the 'People's Army'. The term implies a democratic spirit and egalitarian approach to defending the country but the Home Guard was not the nation in arms. Apart from the obvious fact that women were never enrolled as full members, many men were excluded, including some members of the Labour Party who had previously taken an anti-war stance, and people of Irish origin were treated with particular suspicion. Sir Edward Grigg pointedly ignored the patron saint of Ireland (St Patrick) when he claimed

> It is Britain incarnate, an epitome of British character in its gift for comradeship in trouble, its resourcefulness at need, its deep love of its own land, and its surging anger at the thought that any invader should set foot on our soil. That is the make-up of the Home Guard. St. George, St. Andrew, St. David – yes, and St. Crispin – are alive and marching in its democratic ranks.[2]

Also under suspicion were those of immigrant families from countries with which Britain was now at war, including Jewish refugees. Controls on the vetting of such groups was only relaxed in 1943. Nonetheless, the stipulation that members of the LDV should be British subjects was deleted on 4 September 1940 and there was a distinct international aspect to some units: the 7th Battalion Shropshire Home Guard included Belgian, Russian, Polish and Dutch nationals and men from the Dominions and colonies.[3] Evesham Battalion had Dutch and Spanish volunteers. There was a squadron of US nationals in the London Home Guard (*see above*, p. 136) and the 10th Battalion Surrey Home Guard had a platoon of Norwegian exiles.

It was a volunteer army of voters who were not afraid to break the chain of command and complain directly to the press, their MP or to the Prime Minister. General Pile, the CO of AA Command, later ruefully noted 'The Home Guards were quite uninhibited by thoughts of going through the usual military channels. Their complaints went straight to Parliament or the local Press, and the first I would hear of it would be either in reading my morning paper or in receiving a disapproving letter from above.'[4] In this respect, at least, it has a claim to being a democratic army, although the TAA's comment in July 1940 that 'the LDV is a citizen force organized on the same principles of equality of service and status as other volunteer services' was soon to be outdated.[5] On 12 August 1940 General Pownall, Inspector General of the LDV, complained 'The HG are voters first and soldiers afterwards ... What they think they need, if they say so loudly enough, they will get.'[6] For the government in 1940 it was approaching anarchy, albeit officered by the gentry. The government was unpopular in June 1940 – the army had been forced to retreat from Norway, the Low Countries and France, and the bestselling *Guilty Men* by 'Cato' (Michael Foot, Frank Owen and Peter Howard) pointed the finger of blame at those politicians associated with earlier appeasement but still in government. The popular enthusiasm that accompanied the creation of the LDV risked being negated by government indecision as to its purpose and into this discordant atmosphere came Tom Wintringham, who used his platform in the press to become the unofficial chief publicist for the Home Guard. Wintringham tapped into the widespread frustration with an optimistic message of aggression and improvisation, but unashamedly tied to a Marxist message. In the bestselling *New Ways of War*, Wintringham called for a people's army, the arrest of those who wanted a negotiated peace, the removal of the 'Guilty Men' in government, the establishment of workers' councils to share power and the nationalization of resources.[7]

Wintringham's fiery writing, along with that of George Orwell, tried to give a political slant to the Home Guard, but theirs were isolated voices, their socialist message negated by the twists and turns of the Communist Party of Great Britain (CPGB) and the unwillingness of the Labour Party to engage in political campaigning whilst part of the government of national unity. Ironically, the concept of a 'people's army' was resisted most strongly in 1940 by the very same organizations that had supported the Spanish Republic in its war against the Fascist coup. The CPGB and the International Brigade Association took cover behind the dogma of demanding a people's government before supporting the war effort, dismissing the 'current propaganda that the present bloodstained scramble for colonies is a "People's War"'.[8] They derided the Home Guard as a fascist organization, founded by the capitalist state to suppress workers' movements, and forbade their members to join, whilst conducting 'a vicious campaign of libel' against Wintringham and the other Osterley instructors and simultaneously expressing outrage when their members were prevented from joining.[9] George Orwell had been a member of the Independent Labour Party and had served with the anti-Stalinist Partido Obero de Unificación Marxista (POUM) in Spain. He then joined the St John's Wood Home Guard and became a sergeant and instructor. Unlike the popularist Wintringham, Orwell wrote for the socialist intelligentsia in the USA and Britain and complained that the Labour Party, with elements still hesitant as to whether it was an 'imperialist' war, was not engaged enough to give the Home Guard political direction:

> For the first time in British history the chance exists for Socialists to have a certain amount of influence in the armed forces of the country. The

> Home Guard is trembling in the balance, uncertain whether it wants to become a real People's Army or a not-very-good imitation of the pre-war Territorials.[10]

Orwell returned to this theme in January 1941: 'A year hence, if it still exists, it may be a democratic army capable of having a strong political influence on the regular forces, or it may be a sort of SA officered by the worst sections of the middle class.'[11] The task, therefore, was to ensure that 'the rifle hanging on the wall of the working-class flat or labourer's cottage is the symbol of democracy. It is our job to see that it stays there.'[12] For Orwell, the Home Guard was 'an astonishing phenomenon, a sort of People's Army officered by Blimps'.[13] His goal was clear:

> Only revolution can save England, that has been obvious for years, but now the revolution has started, and it may proceed quite quickly if only we can keep Hitler out. Within two years, maybe a year, if only we can hang on, we shall see changes that will surprise the idiots who have no foresight. I dare say the London gutters will have to run with blood. All right, let them, if it is necessary. But when the red militias are billeted in the Ritz I shall still feel that the England I was taught to love so long ago for such different reasons is somehow persisting.[14]

The government was well aware of the possibility of infiltration and subversion in the Home Guard by left or right. Prospective volunteers were vetted, albeit inconsistently, by the local police and an order of 27 May 1940 equally banned active Fascists and Communists from joining. Even so, membership alone of the British Union of Fascists and the Communist Party of Great Britain was not an automatic bar to service but it did lead to additional scrutiny to establish if the person was actively working to subvert the war effort. Given the Hitler–Stalin Pact, the Communists were seen as a particular threat. Whereas the British Union of Fascists had a membership of only 8,700 (their main danger was in their strong connections to the establishment), the CPGB had a membership of around 20,000 with its influence extending into the 90,000-strong mass circulation of the *Daily Worker* and a base within industry.[15] Not all the British volunteers who had served in Spain with the International Brigades were Communists, but the Brigades had been organized proprietorially by the Communist Party and it is hardly surprising that MI5 regarded any former Brigader as a potential agent of the Comintern (Communist International).

The policy of the CPGB was directed by Stalin's need to preserve his pact with Hitler and thereby delay a German invasion of the Soviet Union. On the outbreak of war the CPGB had issued a gut-level manifesto which argued for a fight against Fascist Germany and against the appeasement policy of the British government. But on 14 September a telegram arrived from Moscow declaring it to be an imperialist conflict and the *Daily Worker* on 7 October duly had the headline 'Stop the War!' with the Party putting much of the blame on Britain and France.[16] The new LDV was derided by the *Daily Worker* on 29 May 1940 as a 'means of establishing an armed force directly under the control of the hunting-shooting-fishing oligarchy'.[17] In June 1940, after the fall of France, the Communist *Labour Monthly* denounced the principle of national defence as the 'mutual extermination of the workers for the profit of the shareholders'.[18] The International Brigade Association dutifully followed the policy of the CPGB and disparaged comrades who sought to work with the Home Guard as 'helping the ruling class' while at the same time, like the CPGB, expressing righteous indignation when International Brigade veterans were barred from joining as examples of victimization.[19] The publisher Victor Gollancz asked a former member of the International Brigade whether he and his comrades would help to train LDVs in the methods of the Spanish War. He replied 'No, we don't support the war yet.'[20] A despairing Wintringham later wrote,

> Because revolutionaries had the experience of Spain they had an opportunity that is not likely to recur of proving themselves better, and better because of their politics, at doing a job that millions of people wanted done. The British Communists turned down this opportunity, refusing to allow Party members who are Brigaders to work at Osterley when they were invited to do so and offered a 'free hand'.[21]

Bill Alexander, former CO of the British Battalion, therefore only told one side of the story when he wrote 'there was official opposition to the employment of Brigadiers in the forces'.[22] But International Brigade veterans did have to undergo additional vetting to establish whether they were likely to carry out subversive activities on behalf of the CPGB.[23] The official policy had been made clear in a secret instruction of January 1939, advising that army recruiting authorities had been warned that any would-be recruit who was a former member of the International Brigade would require vetting from MI5. A ban was not automatic and it was stressed that 'These instructions should be regarded as secret and care should be taken that no man reported should become aware that he is viewed with suspicion, as it is not desired to prejudice any recruit who may have merely gone to Spain out of a sense of adventure and not become imbued with revolutionary doctrines.'[24] Supporting their fears, the *Daily Worker* had acknowledged that some International Brigade members had been selected for training in subversion prior to their return from Spain.[25] Justification of MI5's concerns came in April 1939 when the policy towards the International Brigade veterans was leaked to the CPGB, together with secret material relating to the expansion of the Territorial Army by Ted Edwards, a former Brigader and CPGB activist in Sheffield. In March 1939 he had obtained a job as a civilian clerk with the Territorial Army in Sheffield but a neighbour reported that Edwards was removing secret documents and copying them in the local CPGB office. Incriminating documents were found in his home and Edwards was sentenced to 18 months' hard labour with a recommendation that he should not then be accepted into the armed forces.[26] Upon release, he became a full-time official for the CPGB in Manchester but still managed to join the local Home Guard. MI5 initially recommended that he be kept under surveillance but not dismissed:

> While I do not think his Communist record is sufficient to warrant his being removed from the Home Guard, nevertheless I think he should be watched. The Police do not appear to be aware that he is in the Home Guard.[27]

Senior officers, however, declared him 'undesirable and dangerous' and pointed out that MI5 had better things to do than organize a continuing watch on him if he remained in the Home Guard.[28] The tale then became bizarre as in November 1942 Edwards was conscripted into the Pioneer Corps but was discharged almost immediately when MI5 became aware. Undaunted, Edwards volunteered for the Royal Engineers and his presence at the Transportation Training Centre at Longmoor was only discovered through the intercept of a letter to Sam Wild, former CO of the British Battalion and a CPGB organizer. Edwards was again discharged in May 1943 and the *Daily Worker* tried to make him a *cause célèbre*, professing outrage at his dismissal, whilst Edwards feigned uncomprehending innocence. The *Daily Worker* carefully failed to mention Edwards' conviction under the Official Secrets Act.[29] But he was nothing if not determined, and in September 1943 further intercepted correspondence suggested that Edwards had rejoined the Manchester Home Guard, although MI5 was unable to find confirmation.[30] The official opposition of the International Brigade Association to the war in 1939–40 and the Edwards case made the government distrustful of giving a position of responsibility to any International Brigades veteran.[31]

Despite their opposition to the war, the creation of factory Home Guard units put the CPGB in a quandary as, even in an 'imperialist war', it could not resist the opportunity to call for factory defence to be under the control of workers' committees, with a consequent concern over the possible infiltration of Home Guard factory units. On 11 July the *Daily Worker* reported that the Cambrian Combine Committee of Welsh miners was to consider the formation of a volunteer battalion under the control of the Committee. A resolution for the democratic control of the LDV was also put before the Mineworkers' Federation of Great Britain in the following week with the *Daily Worker* suggesting that the alleged exclusion of trade union militants was to allow the LDV to be used by the Establishment 'not for defence but for their own reactionary purposes'. One delegate said 'The control of the LDV is essentially in the hands of the gentry class. With a Workers' army in this country we can meet any aggressor and resist any tyranny.'[32]

Such bursts of enthusiasm to infiltrate the Home Guard were undermined in August when the CPGB was instructed to follow the Moscow policy of 'revolutionary defeatism' and that 'no steps should be taken to oppose a German landing in this country since a short period under a Nazi regime would be the quickest way of bringing about a Communist revolution'.[33] Orwell railed against the 'holier than thou' anti-war attitude of the Independent Labour Party and Communist Party:

> The Communists, ILP and all their kind can parrot 'Arms for the Workers' but they cannot put a rifle into the workers' hands; the Home Guard can and

> does. The moral for any Socialist who is reasonably fit and can spare a certain amount of time (6 hours a week, perhaps) is obvious.[34]

Many CPGB members and International Brigade veterans ignored party policy and joined the forces and Home Guard. Only 25 per cent of the British veterans of the International Brigades had joined the IBA and many had returned from Spain already disillusioned with the Stalinist discipline of the Communist Party. Welsh miner Tom Jones fought in Spain with the anti-tank battery and machine-gun section. He was badly wounded and captured in 1938, but was eventually repatriated. Jones drifted away from the CPGB and IBA but his injuries meant that he was ineligible for call-up. He joined the Rhos LDV, eventually being commissioned as a second lieutenant in the Home Guard.[35] George Fletcher, born in Swindon but raised in Manchester, had served fifteen years in the Lancashire Fusiliers, rising to sergeant, but joined the CPGB in 1935. He became adjutant and one-time CO of the British Battalion of the International Brigades and was wounded three times. Back in England, he got a job with the new Rolls Royce factory at Crewe, Cheshire, and in July 1940 joined the factory Home Guard. He did not declare his service in Spain on his enrolment form and the local police raised no objection. He was promoted to sergeant but was dismissed on 3 March 1941 as 'services no longer required' (*see* Appendix 1.5 and 1.6). One might presume that the local Special Branch, smarting from their failure to monitor Ted Edwards, had finally caught up with his enrolment. By November 1941 he was no longer a member of the IBA and in March 1943 he was back as a second lieutenant in the factory Home Guard (*see* Appendix 1.7).[36]

Most significant of the small group of former International Brigaders who rejected the policy of the IBA and the Communist Party were Tom Wintringham, Hugh Slater and Yank Levy. As instructors at the Osterley Home Guard Training School, they (together with George Orwell) created the short-lived spectre of a socialist influence in the Home Guard beyond anything the rhetoric of the CPGB could achieve. Wintringham's writings contain the most overt socialist content in promoting the Home Guard, especially if, as seems likely, he was responsible for the political content of Levy's *Guerrilla Warfare*. His focus was on enlarging and fully arming the Home Guard to create a 'People's Army' of up to 4 million men and, in so doing, to form the basis for a future revolutionary militia. Nothing could be further from the vision of a cosy middle-class Home Guard as depicted by the television series *Dad's Army* than the government concern in 1940 that it might be hijacked as a revolutionary socialist militia. Although the ever-suspicious MI5 took the risk seriously, the War Office took a more relaxed attitude to the supposed threat, which proved illusory. Wintringham had drifted away from the Communist Party over its ruthless Stalinism and dismissal of the 'popular front' and was expelled from the Party in 1938, the excuse being his refusal to put the Party above his then mistress, the American journalist Kitty Bowler, who was accused of being a Trotskyist spy (the standard accusation against any opposition). Nonetheless, Wintringham remained a Marxist, differing from the CPGB programme only tactically, believing it was necessary to work with the capitalist British government to defeat fascism. He wrote in 1941:

> Politically I rediscovered democracy, realizing the enormous potentialities in a real alliance of workers and other classes ... I was disgusted by sectarian intrigues and by the hampering suspicions of Marty and Co. ... I came out of Spain believing, as I still believe, in a more humane humanism, in a more radical democracy, and in a revolution of some sort as necessary to give ordinary people a chance to beat Fascism. Marxism makes sense to me, but the 'Party Line' doesn't.[37]

Foreseeing the impending outbreak of war, in *How to Reform the Army* in April 1939 he had accepted the need to work for 'defending British democracy, in something like the shape it is, against Fascism, by means of an efficient army'. As well as proposing a small Home Guard-type organization, his proposals for army reform included an end to recruiting officers from the aristocratic class and the provision of 'commissars' as adjutants.[38] The booklet was largely ignored by the general population until his profile rose in 1940, with 10,000 copies selling in June 1940 alone. While his political views hardly endeared him to the officer class and he was undoubtedly an irritant to the War Office, he was not the outcast sometimes imagined. Immediately before war broke out, Wintringham was commissioned to write two articles for the serial publication *Battle Training in Word and Picture*, which was officially approved by the War Office. MI5 blocked his appointment to a post in the Transport, Mechanical Section of the War Office during September 1939, on the grounds that it might give him access to confidential information, but during June and early July 1940 and again in the autumn, he was engaged on lecture tours on behalf of the War Office.[39] His bestselling *New Ways of War* was one of the few Home Guard books recommended by the War Office.[40] The book combined inspiring and practical advice sandwiched between sections (that could be ignored or not) arguing the case for political change: 'What we need, in order to be strong, is a planned use of men, machines and factories: in other words what we need is socialism.'[41]

The fear of MI5 was that Wintringham might have remained a deep cover agent for the Comintern and would use Osterley as the basis of political indoctination. Wilfrid Vernon, a fellow instructor at Osterley, had already been convicted for improper possession of secret documents as a Soviet agent and Hugh Slater, a former commissar in Spain, had long been under intense surveillance. MI5 reported 'We are taking steps to find out exactly what goes on at Osterley Park. There is always the possibility that Wintringham might like to build up something in the nature of a future Red Army.'[42] One of the MI5 officers sent to keep Osterley under surveillance during August was Henry Brocklehurst, the noted explorer.[43] Worryingly from their point of view, Wintringham was proposing that the Home Guard develop as a completely independent force, warning: 'Home Guard Units must organize themselves into completely self-contained armies ... Be prepared to fight through to the end without help from the Regular Army.'[44]

Wilfrid Vernon was the explosives expert at Osterley. A major in the RAF at the end of the First World War, Vernon then worked as a technical officer at the Royal Aircraft Establishment (RAE) Farnborough. He came under MI5 surveillance as an active Communist from 1933 and in 1935 was implicated in encouraging sedition and desertion within Aldershot army camp. He contacted Wintringham, then editor of *Left Review*, in 1936 and in 1937 was convicted of improper possession of secret blueprints, for which he was fined £50 and subsequently dismissed from the Civil Service. Unsurprisingly, his application to rejoin RAE Farnborough was refused in March 1940 but he then appears as an instructor at Osterley and continued at Denbies until December 1942, still under MI5 surveillance. In September 1943 MI5 blocked an application for him to be a civilian lecturer to the forces and he worked thereafter as an adult education lecturer in Portsmouth and Bournemouth.[45] He was Labour MP for Dulwich from 1945 to 1951 but in 1952 he admitted having been a Soviet agent.

The contributions of the other two International Brigade veterans at Osterley to political debate were muted. Hugh Slater had been educated at the Slade School of Art and was a promising avant-garde artist before taking to politics. He was arrested three times in London during 1931–34 for obstruction of police and wilful damage during anti-Nazi protests and was also involved in street fights with the Nazis in Berlin during a visit in 1932. He joined the CPGB in 1933 and wrote for the Comintern newspaper *World News and Views*. Slater began corresponding with Wintringham in 1934 over the new 'Union of Revolutionary Writers' and was arrested a further four times between 1933 and 1937 for incitement to riot, wilful damage, obstructing the police and, in France, for contravention of the policy of non-intervention in Spain. Slater went to Spain as a journalist for the Communist monthly *Inprecor* in August 1936 and then served with the International Brigades until October 1938, becoming the Chief of Operations. He was described in Soviet files as 'a leader almost of genius', although he was regarded by many of the men as a middle-class ideologue. But by the time he left Spain, like Wintringham, he may already have become disillusioned with the Stalinist Communist Party, as his 1947 novel *The Heretics* suggests. In 1939 the Air Ministry briefly employed him as an Aerial Survey Officer to advise on camouflage but, unsurprisingly, like Wintringham, he failed his MI5 vetting and was dismissed. Despite intensive Special Branch surveillance, they could find no evidence of any further subversive activity but to their horror Slater enrolled at a government training centre for munition workers in Bristol. MI5 tried to arrange his dismissal, but Wintringham beat them to it and asked for his release so that he could become an instructor at Osterley. In August Slater became an instructor and Officer-in-Charge of the Outside Advisory Department of the school, lecturing on street fighting and the use of smoke screens. Slater moved with Wintringham to the Denbies training school in September, with MI5 still regarding him as an 'active and ardent Communist'.[46] Slater was, however, expelled from the CPGB on 7 January 1941 for being 'actively associated with the Wintringham group'.[47] He was about to publish *Home Guard for Victory* and the CPGB did not want to be associated with it. The book has little political content, although he wrote:

> It is a people's army. Its purpose is a democratic one – to win the war against Fascism. The Home Guard must, therefore, be thoroughly permeated with democratic ideas, methods and attitudes.[48]

MI5 remained suspicious and later explained, 'At that time we thought the expulsion might be a blind and that both he and Wintringham might be working underground for the party.'[49]

Despite MI5's concern that Slater was too dangerous to be allowed into the armed forces, in December 1940 he was conscripted into a Light AA training regiment. Wintringham was as angry as MI5, believing that his being conscripted as a private was a waste of his talents; he did not realize this was a device of the Directorate of Military Training, which evidently did not share MI5's worries, as the first stage in getting Slater commissioned as an army instructor. Slater also had support from the Secretary of State who believed that he should 'have the opportunity of earning a Field Marshal's baton'. Obliged to accept Slater's commission in the Border Regiment, MI5 at least wanted Slater confined to working with the Home Guard. He duly returned as an instructor to Denbies as a second lieutenant, but to MI5's further dismay he was posted, on the specific request of General Thorne, as an instructor at the Company Commanders' Training School of Scottish Command and was promoted captain in 1943. Their final horror came when Slater was recommended for a transfer to the Intelligence Corps, with the Director of Military Intelligence raising no objection! Slater failed the interview, although one must wonder if some influence was not brought to bear on the selection board. It was only in July 1943 that MI5 finally accepted that both Wintringham and Slater had severed their links with the CPGB.[50]

Bert 'Yank' Levy was born in Canada in 1897 but moved to the USA and became a professional boxer, serving during the First World War in the Merchant Navy and a Royal Fusiliers battalion of the Jewish Legion. How far his colourful career was directed by any intellectual Marxist analysis or a desire for adventure is debatable. He took part in the Mexican revolution and briefly became a gun smuggler for the Sandanista in Nicaragua but then served five years in prison for a bank robbery in the USA before becoming a leader of the Canadian unemployed workers' movement. His service in Spain was limited: not long after arriving in Spain in late 1936 he was captured at the battle of Jarama (February 1937), and eventually released in a prisoner exchange and returned to Canada. On the outbreak of war he worked his passage to England on a merchant ship and then lectured at Osterley on unarmed combat and knife fighting, subsequently touring Britain giving lectures and demonstrations. He was the only Osterley instructor who had any practical experience in guerrilla warfare and his best-selling *Guerrilla Warfare* was published in 1941. It seems likely, however, that as well as writing the Introduction, the political content was ghost-written by Wintringham. Levy then returned to Canada and the USA where he helped train OSS in guerrilla warfare.

These socialists were outnumbered by the non-political instructors at Osterley and they lacked any coherent political focus or organized left-wing support, shunned by their former comrades in the CPGB. MI5 finally concluded that, with only a weekend course, there was no evidence of overt political indoctrination and any direct political content usually only appeared in the closing questions and answers part of the course. A student would be primed to ask how war could be prevented, giving Wintringham an excuse to expound his socialist vision. Orwell concurred: 'Their teaching was purely military, but with its insistence on guerrilla methods it had revolutionary implications which were perfectly well grasped by many of the men who listened to it.'[51]

The War Office was less suspicious than MI5 and both *New Ways of War* by Tom Wintringham and *Home Guard for Victory* by Hugh Slater were part of the select War Office approved reading list for the Home Guard.[52] The CPGB and IBA had a complete *volte-face* following the German invasion of the Soviet Union on 22 June 1941 and Wintringham later took pleasure in pointing out that the defenders of Leningrad used methodology taught earlier at Osterley Park, whilst again bemoaning the lack of interest from the British left:

> 'LENINGRAD, Sunday. Every factory is training its reserves. The men learn to handle a rifle, throw grenades and fire bottles. Special attention is paid to anti-tank warfare.'
>
> That is from the *Soviet War News* of August 26. The training described is exactly that given at Osterley fifteen months ago. The only difference is that in Russia 'every factory' is learning. Fifteen months ago I was fighting for a Home Guard 4 million strong, which would necessarily have included men from every factory. That fight did not succeed, and we need not now discuss why it did not succeed.
>
> But when Douglas [G.D.H. Douglas, editor of the IBA *Volunteer for Liberty*] writes that I am 'obsessed with guerrilla tactics' I do not feel like denying it. It is not a bad thing for socialists, and particularly for revolutionaries, to be obsessed with the tactics suitable for, and attainable by, the masses of the population, while leaving it to others to specialise in the tactics of the knights in armour.[53]

The CPGB sought to take advantage of the new pro-Soviet atmosphere in the country and in November 1942 GHQ London District received a report from Special Branch that secret instructions had been issued by the CPGB to its members to 'permeate' the Home Guard to obtain military training and weapons. It was further stated that in the case of at least two factories in London a considerable number of active Communists had enlisted in the Works Company of the Home Guard, some of them boasting quite openly of their motives for so doing. MI5 believed that some on what was a short exclusion list of CPGB activists were now being admitted to the Home Guard.[54] But by now the left had lost its most fervent champion of a socialist Home Guard. Reined in by military discipline at Denbies, by May 1941 Wintringham had become intensely frustrated by his inability to effect change in the Home Guard and the conscription of

Slater (not knowing the War Office planned to give the latter a commission) became a convenient excuse to resign. Wintringham was unaware that, despite the opposition of MI5, the War Office had also agreed that he should be commissioned as a major in the Home Guard, but his resignation made this impossible. He became a volunteer in the Dorking Home Guard and continued to give lecture tours to Home Guard units but (in contrast to Otter-Barry at Claverley and Langdon-Davies at Burwash) never received any official recognition of the significant contribution that he made to the development of the Home Guard.

Chapter Nine

Women and the Home Guard

The First World War had forced an acceptance in Britain that, at least in times of emergency, women had a role within the support services of the armed forces but there remained a firm gender divide in that only men were expected to take part in combat. Some women had demanded a more active role although it was widely derided as 'khakism'. The Women's Volunteer Reserve (WVR) was founded in late 1914 by suffragette Evelina Haverfield and demanded the right for women to bear arms in the defence of their families and homes. They trained in first aid and signalling, and drove motor vehicles, working closely in many areas with the Volunteer Training Corps, whose members provided weapons training. After the war ended official support for women's military organizations evaporated but as the European political situation deteriorated, in 1938 the government established a new women's army service, the Auxiliary Territorial Service (ATS), which served with distinction as part of the BEF.[1] From 1939 women also served as full-time members of the Women's Royal Naval Service (WRNS) and the Women's Auxiliary Air Force (WAAF). In January 1939 the Mechanized Transport Training Corps (later the Mechanized Transport Corps) was also founded to provide a role for volunteer women drivers outside the full-time ATS, as a uniformed civilian service. But none of these services was expected to have a combat role, and the MP for Streatham, David Robertson, was not alone (amongst both men and women) in his opinion that 'a woman's duty is to give life and not to take it, and the training which your Movement [Women's Home Defence Corps] gives in unarmed combat, signalling, fieldcraft, and musketry, is abhorrent to me'.[2]

The distinction between combat and non-combat roles in women's services became more indistinct as the Second World War progressed and many women would perform duties that fell just short of 'pulling the trigger'. Nonetheless, the distinction was fiercely protected and indeed it was only in 2017 that women were allowed to train for a full combat role in the infantry and Royal Armoured Corps.

The participation of women in the Home Guard on the same terms as those serving in the ATS should not have been controversial, but became so because of government antagonism towards Dr Edith Summerskill, Labour MP for Fulham West. Her relentless media campaign to revive the spirit of the First World War WVR and arm women in the Home Guard risked a wider precedent that the government was unable to contemplate. For Summerskill, the right for women to bear arms in the Home Guard was a matter of gender equality but she was careful to choose her battleground on the topic and did not challenge the role of women in the ATS, WAAF or WRNS in the same way. The Home Guard was uniquely rooted in the community, with the power of the vote and outside military discipline that normally precluded dissent from official policy. Summerskill's critics argued that they were not dismissive of the value of women in the war effort but rather that women were more usefully employed elsewhere than in the Home Guard, and that her campaign offered an easier option from either full-time service in the forces or work in industry or Civil Defence. The Defence (LDV) Regulations of 17 May 1940 explicitly stated that the volunteers should be male (Appendix 1.3).[3] Nonetheless, many hundreds of women were unofficially involved from the outset, particularly in the administration of the LDV/Home Guard. Edna Selwyn, a secretary from Birmingham, recalled: 'I went straight round there as soon as Anthony Eden finished. [The police sergeant] was quite horrified and said "I had no idea there'd be any women".'[4] The sergeant gave Selwyn the job of helping him to enrol volunteers, and thus she became one of the first women volunteers in the LDV, later becoming secretary to the West Midlands Home Guard Zone Commander. In Chelsea General Sir Hubert Gough recruited his daughter as secretary while the local doctor's wife, Mrs Genge-Andrews, provided her car and acted as his driver.[5]

For those women able to serve full-time, the uniformed ATS, WAAF and WRNS had to accept the limitations of their allotted roles. In the rushed formation of the LDV there was no similar allowance for a distinct women's section of 'non-combatants' and if women were to be given this privilege within the existing Home Guard, some in the War Office saw a possible risk of male conscientious objectors demanding the same rights. More seriously, some women demanded the right to be armed alongside the men, reviving the aspirations of the First World War WVR. At a time when the concept of policewomen having powers of arrest was still novel, the possibility of armed women guarding road-blocks with the authority of lethal force clearly challenged the contemporary assumption of masculine superiority.[6] Any such revolutionary concession to the Home Guard would then have had profound implications for the scope of the full-time women's services in the armed forces. It was the specific point of bearing arms rather than the employment of women *per se* that made it a controversial issue and it can be argued that Summerskill's vocal campaign prevented an earlier official role for women, on a par with the ATS. It has also had the effect of devaluing the work with the Home Guard undertaken by existing women's groups, particularly the Women's Voluntary Service (WVS), which were more prepared to accept the social conventions of the day. Ironically, by the time that limited official status was granted in 1943, interest from women was waning because there were many other options for national service and the agreed quota of women serving in the Home Guard was never realized.

Without having considered the need for a distinct women's section in the fraught negotiations of May 1940, the first government response in June to the requests for women to join the LDV was a knee-jerk announcement that women could not be enrolled.[7] Within the male-dominated society, any possibility that some of the limited supply of arms might be taken from men and given to women would have added to the woes of an already unpopular government. On 25 June 1940 the government spokesperson was evasive when answering a question from

Frederick Cocks MP, who claimed that 'hundreds of women in this country who are expert in the use of a rifle are absolutely furious because they are not allowed to join the Local Defence Volunteers'.[8] Claiming that 'hundreds' of women were clamouring for arms was not likely to have much sway when thousands of male Home Guard currently did not have a rifle. It is also an indicator that Summerskill's media campaign may have exaggerated the level of interest in the issue.

On 2 July 1940 Edith Summerskill used Churchill's famous words to suggest the need for national defence based upon a true reflection of society, whether man or woman: 'May I ask the right Hon. Gentleman how we are to fight in the hills, in the streets and in the houses, as envisaged by the Lord President of the Council on Sunday, if women are excluded from the Local Defence Volunteers?'[9] The objection to the use of women in the LDV was only that they should not be armed and therefore given a different status from that of the ATS. The LDV Inspectorate was already supportive of women taking over clerical and other support duties as 'it should be remembered that in addition to the total numbers required to bear arms in an emergency, additional personnel will be necessary for clerical and similar administrative duties'.[10] Home Guard Circular No. 6 (December 1941) stressed that such non-combatant roles were vitally important, with Viscount Bridgeman pointing out to his men that in an infantry battalion there were around 210 men who were not required to handle a weapon and that the Home Guard equally required signallers, dispatch riders, orderlies, clerks, stretcher-bearers and cooks. He went on to make a comment that Summerskill could not accept: 'It is wrong to suppose that a volunteer who is detailed to any of these duties is being asked to do a job of less importance than the man who handles a weapon.' To that end, the first women's organization to work with the Home Guard was the Women's Voluntary Service (WVS), formed in 1938 after the Home Secretary had requested that Lady Reading establish a women's organization that would assist the government and local authorities if war were declared; it was to be considered an official state service, but would be operated by volunteers. Lady Reading proposed in July 1940 that the WVS should be recognized as the formal women's arm of the Home Guard, providing similar services to those they provided for other areas of Civil Defence. The WVS did not challenge the role of women in the same way as would Summerskill and the future Women's Home Defence Corps (WHDC), but their contribution to the war effort in Civil Defence must not be overlooked. A million members organized emergency rest centres and mobile canteens, performed first aid, assisted evacuee organization and ran blood transfusion depots.

Even as the Home Guard Inspectorate and WVS were heading towards the provision of a non-combatant women's arm of the Home Guard with similar scope to the ATS, politicians were becoming nervous about the high-profile interventions in Parliament and in the press by Summerskill to press for an armed role for women. Discussions with the WVS began to unravel because of the fear that any official opening-up of the Home Guard to women would be exploited by Summerskill as the first stage in a campaign for a full combat role. Adding to the confusion, Churchill wavered on the issue with the War Cabinet, at first appearing to be supportive, recording at its 10 July meeting: 'The position of women was mentioned. It was urged that those who wished to do so should be provided with uniforms and allowed to use arms.'[11]

In this positive atmosphere the LDV Inspectorate meeting on 19 July received a proposal that 10 per cent of the enrolled personnel of the LDV should be non-combatant women, which would allow the overall number of Home Guard to be maintained whilst reducing the need for weapons by an equivalent 10 per cent.[12] But on the same day at the Defence Committee, Churchill reversed his earlier position and said there were 'many reasons', including the lack of weapons, against enrolling women in the Home Guard, whilst Anthony Eden, Secretary of State for War, questioned whether there was any real demand. The Committee therefore would not recommend the enrolment of women in the Home Guard and in a futile effort to avoid controversy, considered that no public statement on the subject should be made unless forced by public demand.[13] Just days after an agreement seemed to have been reached with the WVS, a puzzled meeting of the Home Guard Inspectorate on 9 August reported that the question of women's involvement in the Home Guard 'appeared wrapped in mystery' and that it was believed that Eden was now adverse to the proposal.[14] A few days later, on 13 August, the Home Guard Inspectorate had to report 'they [the government] are trying to kill this question'.[15] As a delaying tactic it was reported that any decision would be postponed until the autumn, by when the main threat of invasion would have been over for the year, allowing more time for debate.[16]

The Ministry of Information film *Miss Grant Goes To The Door*, made at the height of the invasion crisis in August 1940, appealed for both men and women to be prepared to do their part in resisting the invader but there is a subtle message against arming women. The Grant sisters have followed government advice and immobilized their transport, showing that women can participate in defence without having to carry a gun. Miss Grant confronts a German spy with a revolver, staring him down with steely determination whilst in her dressing gown, but the message of gender equality collapses when she is disarmed. Reassuringly for the audience, the male LDV efficiently dispatches the enemy paratroops and ultimately, therefore, even determined women had to rely on men for protection.

Usually a master of the biting riposte in Commons debates, on 3 November 1940 Summerskill did her argument no good by implying that women should be allowed to join the Home Guard in order to relieve their boredom, claiming 'in villages up and down the country there are women who have very little to occupy their spare time and who waste it very often in doing knitting and things of that nature'. In reply, Sir Edward Grigg,[17] Under-Secretary of State for War, pointed to the existing opportunities for women in Civil Defence and also to the continuing practical difficulties of supplying the Home Guard as it then stood:

> We have given consideration to that question, with every desire to give such opportunity as we can to the many women who want to serve, but we have been deterred by two things. In the first place, there is a tremendous demand

for the services of women in the Civil Defence Services and, in the second, it is not much use recruiting women into one of the military Auxiliary Corps unless you can give them uniforms. As the Hon. Lady knows, we have already been finding difficulty in providing uniforms for the Home Guard as it is. Perhaps later on it may be possible to do something.[18]

In 1940 the shortage of cloth to make uniforms was real enough (*see above*, p. 112). The battle in Parliament between the government and Summerskill went on. On 19 November 1940 Grigg tried to draw a picture of age-old heroism and resolution but Summerskill was quick to note that it was an essentially masculine heroism and after Grigg produced a litany of male saints – St. George, St. Andrew, St. David, St. Crispin – she was quick to call out 'What about Boadicea?'[19] She went on to demand equal rights for women and challenged the government priority for women to serve in Civil Defence, leaving the Home Guard to the men:

> I want to make it clear that I am not asking for women to be included solely as cooks and clerks in the Home Guard but in the same capacity as men, with equal rights and no privileges ... Who will dare to define women's work to-day? We have only to look around the country to find women working in all the industries ... a healthy woman can do picketing and patrol work just as well as a healthy man.[20]

Summerskill had made an argument that went beyond the immediate issue of recruitment to the Home Guard, challenging the whole basis of male prejudice in the forces and the government could not accept it without major upheaval across the fighting services.

Many women in the summer of 1940 had felt the understandable need to defend themselves and joined rifle clubs in order to learn to shoot, or formed their own local self-defence groups (Plate 28). The Amazon Defence League in West London was founded by Marjorie Foster, a poultry farmer who had taken up small-bore rifle shooting at the age of 8. During the First World War she served with the Women's Legion, training women drivers and servicing vehicles. After the war she joined the South London Rifle Club and in July 1930 became the first woman to win the King's Prize at Bisley. She went on to work with Summerskill in the Women's Home Defence Corps (*see below*) and then joined the Auxiliary Territorial Service, commanding a transport company. The Women's Home Defence Corps (WHDC) was first formed by Miss Watson-Williams and Mavis Tate, the Conservative MP for Frome, as a local organization in Bristol.[21] In December 1940 it became a national organization with Marjorie Foster as Treasurer and Edith Summerskill as Chairman. Training included practice with firearms and in unarmed combat, often with local sympathetic Home Guard as instructors. The activists organized a high-profile media campaign but this in itself cannot be taken as a measure of the real popularity of the cause. The Home Intelligence reports of the Ministry of Information in 1940 showed no great desire from women to join the Home Guard and in January 1942 there were still only thirty branches of the WHDC.[22]

Support, or opposition, for an armed role for women in the Home Guard transcended gender and politics. Some of the most influential advocates of the Home Guard were ambivalent. Supporters of the right of women to bear arms frequently cited the Spanish Civil War but Tom Wintringham, coming out of the tradition of the Communist Party and International Brigades which had banned women from combat, only paid lip service to the idea. In the first of Wintringham's classic articles in *Picture Post*, 'Against Invasion: the lessons of Spain', he declared 'Today we need the powers and abilities of every fit man and woman in these islands.' He then made an explicit call to arm women: 'Many do not wish arms; others desire them, and should have them if they are available. Whenever a people has been fighting for its life, the women have joined in. You can't keep them out.' But this endorsement of the idea of the nation in arms was superficial and the text and illustrations of the article were essentially addressed to men.[23] His subsequent articles 'Arm the Citizens' and 'The Home Guard Can Fight' were entirely written in male terms. In *New Ways of War* Wintringham defined what he meant by a 'People's War' and it was a male preserve:

> It does not mean the indiscriminate arming of everyone. It means that the efforts of our army for the defence of this country should be supplemented by some training and some arming of about 4 million men.[24]

Similarly, Wintringham's fellow instructor at Osterley, Hugh Slater, a former International Brigade Commissar, declared that women in Spain had been 'appallingly foolhardy' but 'there were plenty of ways in which a corps of determined housewives could make themselves a nuisance to the enemy without actually fighting'.[25] John Langdon-Davies could not avoid a patronizing tone in his lectures to a male Home Guard audience when supporting the call for a Women's Home Guard Auxiliary: 'In due course we became the LDV and our wives were privileged to sew on armlets to that effect.'[26] He believed, probably correctly, that many in the Home Guard shared his view that

> I think the average Home Guard has joined it because he wants to protect his hearth and home, and he would feel a bit annoyed if the hearth and home insisted upon coming along with him and doing some of the protecting.[27]

It was an entrenched male view which would survive long after the war and one he believed not worth challenging in the interests of male morale: 'It may be an idle boast, "My wife never had to go out and earn any money," but many Home Guarders still like to feel "our wives have never got to go out and handle a rifle".'[28]

Langdon-Davies explicitly attacked Edith Summerskill in his *Sunday Pictorial* column and was ready to accept that Summerskill would condemn his attitude as 'old-fashioned' prejudice but he believed, like Slater, that women could have a more useful role than taking up a rifle:

> The problem is bigger than the one that interests Dr Summerskill. There is not the slightest need for women doing men's jobs in the Home Guard,

> but there is every need for the women's jobs in local defence to be better understood.[29]

He gave as an example of a useful role the collection of foodstuffs and their removal to a place of safety prior to an attack or destroying them to prevent them falling into enemy hands. Women might also tear up floorboards in houses and otherwise make passage through them difficult for the enemy, prepare blanket screens, make Molotov cocktails or act as messengers. Without the protection of a uniform and formal status, Langdon-Davies' division of labour was unlikely to have protected women from being shot as *francs-tireur*.

Lieutenant General J.R. Eastwood, the first Director General of the Home Guard, was spurred by a petition received from a hundred supporters of Bristol WHDC, calling for separate women's sections of the Home Guard, to determine in December 1940 that a formal policy towards women's employment was required.[30] He agreed with the C-in-C Home Forces that it was useful to have women volunteering as clerks, telephonists and drivers, but the barrier to formal enrolment in the Home Guard was the weapons issue:

> Under no circumstances should women be enrolled in the Home Guard ... it is undesirable for women to bear arms in the Home Guard, and I do not think anyone should be enrolled in the Home Guard who is not under an obligation to bear arms when called upon to do so. (In any case, as the HG still requires 350,000 rifles to arm the men enrolled, there would be none for women members for a long time to come.)[31]

Arriving at a policy was easier said than done. WVS members continued to provide canteen and clerical services for the Home Guard and under Eastwood's successor from May 1941, Viscount Bridgeman, discussions over a formal agreement with the WVS were renewed. But in June 1941 Bridgeman had to explain to Lady Reading that it was not possible to provide official recognition of the role of the WVS, whilst stressing that the value of the services they provided was appreciated.[32] Behind the hesitancy was the risk of opening the way for Summerskill's WHDC to demand similar privileges and use any official status to further its campaign to bear arms. Instead, Regional Commands were urged to make best use of the WVS for support services, and their provision of administrative support especially was becoming ever more important under the weight of War Office paperwork. Brigadier Currey, Commander of the Surrey and Sussex Home Guard, pointed out that the Home Guard relied heavily on women volunteers for such services. Colonel Harold Wernher of South East Command added that the transfer of clerical and cooking duties to women would free up 20 per cent of men for combat duties.[33] Major General Brownrigg, London R Zone Commander, wanted to go further and proposed that uniformed women should be fully integrated into the Home Guard but only in a non-combat role.[34] He said all they would require was a skirt instead of battledress trousers and, he supposed, stockings. Brownrigg also believed there should be no compulsion to recruit women volunteers so as not to antagonize misogynists in Home Guard commands. In reply, Bridgeman stressed that a separate women's section would be necessary to overcome the difficulty that all other Home Guard were expected to bear arms and suggested that the Mechanized Transport Corps (MTC) might fulfil that role, but pointedly made no mention of the WHDC.[35] The overwhelming consensus of senior officers in Home Forces and the Home Guard was that women were needed but only in a support role, comparable to that of the ATS. By now women volunteers working with the Home Guard were unofficially wearing a mix of uniform elements according to the imagination of the volunteers or the whim of the commanding officer, including army denims, ARP-type dungarees, khaki shirts and skirts and the standard forage cap. Some even began wearing Home Guard shoulder titles and regimental cap badges, to the particular concern of the War Office.

The encouragement to avail themselves of WVS support was published in Home Guard Information Circular No. 5 in November 1941 but by then the Home Guard Directorate had finally sought advice from the ATS on how to proceed further, and a report of October 1941 identified a need for women clerks, orderlies, telephone operators, dispatch riders, cooks, drivers, nursing orderlies and instrument operators on AA and coastal artillery sites.[36] At last there seemed to be movement towards official recognition and the Vice Chief of the Imperial General Staff was ready to submit a proposal to the Army Council in November 1941 for a 'Women's Auxiliary Home Guard' but any agreement had to be first sanctioned by those Ministries more widely responsible for allocating labour for the war effort, and they were unsympathetic.

Summerskill realized that the WHDC was at risk of being shut out of any formal role in the Home Guard. On 30 October 1941 and again on the following day she wrote to Churchill to press for a women's section of the Home Guard, whose members would be taught how to shoot a rifle. Summerskill pointed to the spread of the WHDC groups across the country as indicating a popular desire for such action and forwarded a suggestion from Major Gavin Jones of Letchworth Home Guard that women could be employed on static guard duty, thereby freeing men for more offensive roles.[37] Churchill again wavered and copied the letter to the War Office, minuting 'I favour the idea.'[38] But the hackles of the War Office had been raised by a sensationalist article in the *Daily Mail* on 29 October claiming that since August a fifty-strong uniformed women's section of the Home Guard at Mollart Engineering in Tolworth, Surrey, had been parading with the men and learning rifle drill. The headline might suggest that they were training for combat but the article went on to explain that their catering, first aid and clerical sections only meant that 'every man in the factory's Home Guard company will be able to take his place in the firing line'. Their function was therefore in line with the current consensus within the Home Guard high command but they were providing their own uniforms of khaki blouse and pleated skirt with forage cap, and wore Home Guard shoulder titles. Sergeant Major Stevens enthusiastically but undiplomatically commented, 'Although the girls are not officially recognized as Home Guards, they go on manoeuvres and train the same as the men. Four nights a week they go on parade. Their keenness and spirit are magnificent.'[39] Bridgeman was obliged to remind the GOC London District that women could not parade or train with the Home Guard.[40] In response, the Works Director rolled-back the story and explained that the women were 'entirely separate' from the company Home Guard and were not connected to any outside body (i.e. the WHDC). He also downplayed their arms training: 'What little firing they have done is with a .22 on the Works' own miniature range.'[41] After an enquiry, the Zone Commander categorically denied that the women ever paraded with the men but the very fact that they were wearing Home Guard insignia was a breach of War Office instructions. To clarify the situation, on 29 October a message was sent out to all army commands and was made public in *The Times* of 12 November:

> The training of women as Home Guards has not been authorized by the War Office. Weapons and ammunition on charge of the Army or Home Guard Units will not be used for the instruction of women. The use of the word 'Home Guard' by unofficial bodies is not permitted for any purpose.[42]

Summerskill next tried to get the War Office to agree to a deputation of ten local Home Guard commanders to meet the Secretary of State for War (now David Margesson) to press her case – a breach of military protocol that was swiftly refused.[43] The renewal of the debate in the press and Summerskill's lobbying greatly complicated Bridgeman's plan to form a women's section and the controversy may have been engineered by Summerskill, who had realized she had been outflanked by the WVS and did not wish to see a 'lesser' scheme implemented. But the most serious objections came from those responsible for allocating labour for industry and Civil Defence. The October proposal was rejected by the Ministries of Home Security and Labour on the grounds that it would divert women away from higher priority needs in the Civil Defence services and industry.[44] There were also strong demands for a cap on the overall numbers of males in the Home Guard, to limit the impact on factory production caused by exhausted workers. They believed the strategic imperative was for male and female workers to replace men called-up for active service in the expanding war industries and this was especially true when the conscription of single women aged from 20–30 (under the National Service No. 2 Act) in December 1941 reduced the available pool of labour.

Compromise with the WHDC finally seemed to be in the offing when on 21 January 1942 Dame Helen Gwynne-Vaughan submitted a WHDC petition to the Secretary of State for War, supporting, in essence, Bridgeman's scheme. Gwynne-Vaughan had joined the WHDC in July 1941 but had different ambitions from Summerskill. She had been a suffragette who became Head of Botany at Birkbeck College, London, in 1909. At the outbreak of the First World War she joined the Red Cross but in 1917 she was appointed Controller of the Women's Army Auxiliary Corps in France and then became Commandant of the Women's Royal Air Force (WRAF) from September 1918 until December 1919. In these two posts she made a major contribution to changing the attitude towards women in the armed services. She returned to Birkbeck College after the war but from 1939 to 1941 was Director of the new ATS with a reputation as an efficient organizer and inspirational speaker but she was also a strict disciplinarian who was increasingly resented by her younger staff. Gwynne-Vaughan insisted on equal status and conditions for the ATS when taking over the duties of men in the army, but she did not challenge the scale of those duties as laid down by the War Office. She was eventually dismissed as presenting an old-fashioned image of the ATS but then became secretary to Lieutenant General Brownrigg, with whom she had worked when he was Director General of the Territorial Army and who was now Commander of the R Zone Home Guard in London. Based on her ATS experience, she began to develop a scheme for a Women's Home Guard Auxiliary which, she believed, could take over 14 per cent of the work of the male Home Guard. At Brownrigg's suggestion, she also joined the local WHDC branch and became its President, as well as having a place on the national committee.[45] Brownrigg may have seen Gwynne-Vaughan's recruitment to the WHDC as an attempt to create an organization more acceptable to the War Office and not as wedded to Summerskill's views on women taking on a combat role.

Gwynne-Vaughan's petition sought the official enrolment of women in the Home Guard for duties 'similar to those performed by women serving with the regular forces'. By definition, this would exclude a direct combat role and reflects Gwynne-Vaughan's vision of a uniformed equivalent of the ATS. It was signed by twenty men and women, including six Home Guard officers (notably Langdon-Davies), two leading members of the WVS, retired generals, an admiral and marshal of the RAF and several academics.[46] Summerskill signed the petition but clearly did not approve of the limitations, adding a note to the copy that she signed 'any other duties which may appear necessary in an emergency', and immediately sabotaged the initiative. At a meeting between Sir James Grigg, Secretary of State for War, and Summerskill on 27 February 1942 it was recorded:

> Dr Summerskill made it quite clear that she is not in the least concerned with the question of fetchers and carriers. What she wants is the acceptance of the principle that women should be enlisted into the Home Guard as fully combatant members ... The S.o.S [Secretary of State] made it clear to her that he would not accept any such proposal.[47]

Gwynne-Vaughan's efforts at compromise would not have been helped by the 14 February 1942 issue of *Picture Post* whose cover showed a Canadian soldier teaching a woman how to fire his SMLE rifle, and also gave a progress report on the WHDC, announcing that 'The question of whether women should or should not be allowed to join the Home Guard has caused so much discussion and brought so little result, that the women have finally taken matters into their own hands.'[48]

The article claimed that there were more than fifty units of the WHDC in London alone 'learning how to fire rifles, revolvers and tommy guns, how to load and reload without waste of time, how to throw hand grenades, how to pot at an enemy from behind cover, how to shoot at a parachutist'.[49] Such weapons could only come from illicit cooperation with local Home Guard, who had been banned from offering musketry instruction to women.

Bridgeman reworked his proposal in February 1942 but the Ministry of Home Security was still concerned about the shrinking Civil Defence workforce and Summerskill's renewed offensive had hindered discussion. Her meeting with Sir James Grigg on 27 February had been uncomfortable and it was during this period that Summerskill records Grigg exploding that he wanted to hear no more about 'your bloody women'.[50] Grigg's patience had expired and he tried to block Bridgeman and the Home Guard Inspectorate from having any further discussion on the matter.[51] Bridgeman persevered and by mid-March believed he finally had the support of the Ministry of Home Security and the Ministry of Labour for a formal partnership scheme.[52] Bridgeman singled out the WVS and MTC as exemplars for their existing cooperation with the Home Guard and also included the Women's Institute, Red Cross and Women's Legion. Summerskill would not admit defeat and on 29 March 1942 repeated her demands to Grigg, claiming that there were now around 135 units of the WHDC in the country.[53] A few days later the government took advice as to whether it could suppress the WHDC as being an illegal armed body. Civil servant Frederick Bovenschen (who had objected to the initial creation of the LDV) provided the legal advice:

> The training which is being given by Women's Home Defence appears *prima facie* to be contrary to the law which prohibits 'All meetings and assemblies of persons for the purpose of training or drilling themselves or being trained or drilled to the use of arms ... without lawful authority from His Majesty or the Lieutenant, or two Justices of the Peace, of any county.'[54]

There was, however, concern over the scale of public protest if it was decided to ban the WHDC and a problem that in at least one instance a JP was a leading member of the WHDC. Summerskill continued to press her case but on 1 May 1942 Sir James Grigg wrote uncompromisingly to her:

> I think I made it clear to you at our meeting in February that I am not prepared to allow the enlistment of women in the Home Guard for either combatant or non-combatant duties ... I don't think that the enrolment of women for ancillary duties would satisfy you in the least, as I gather that what you are chiefly interested in is the employment of women on combatant duties.[55]

Trying to avoid being shut out of any final settlement favouring the WVS, Summerskill changed tactics in May 1942, making the extraordinary claim that she had never wanted women to perform combatant duties but only for women to be able to release men for combat, while requesting the ability to be trained in the use of arms for self-defence.[56] She tried to convince Parliament that she had simply been misunderstood. 'I stressed the point that women did not want rifles. I knew there were not sufficient to go round, but I asked that they should be taught how to use a rifle.' Still determined to reach some conclusion on the matter, in early July 1942 the persistent Bridgeman repeated his March 1941 proposal that women from recognized women's organizations, specifically the WVS, MTC and WI, should formally provide support services for the Home Guard, wearing a Home Guard armband but without War Office funding. The *persona non grata* WHDC was still excluded from this list. The effort failed but Summerskill was desperate to try to recover a position for the WHDC and at a meeting of the Inter-Parliamentary Home Guard Committee on 21 July she stressed her new position that she did not want women to take part in combat operations, or even to be given weapons, but merely to be trained in their use. In a remarkably condescending statement, she also argued that enrolment in the Home Guard would not detract from other duties as the WHDC members only had 'simple' jobs. The meeting supported the creation of Women's Home Guard Auxiliaries but not their use of arms.[57] The next step was a consultation of this proposal in August with the army Regional Commands, organized by Lieutenant General Paget, now C-in-C Home Forces. Unsurprisingly, the conclusion was firmly against women having any sort of combat role and showed a clear preference for organizing women volunteers through the WVS, with either a badge or brassard, rather than having a uniformed women's section of the Home Guard. Only Eastern Command (Major General K.J. Martin) was in favour of direct enrolment of women into the Home Guard, but only for those over the age of conscription and employed as cooks, drivers, telephone operators and clerks. Scottish Command (Lieutenant General Andrew Thorne) did not think that the WVS should have a monopoly but believed they should be the coordinating body for women's Home Guard services. As a result, Paget wrote to Duncan Sandys MP, Finance Member at the War Office, to say that he was not in favour of directly enrolling women into the Home Guard, but that he wanted more tribute paid to the supporting work of the WVS.[58] He followed this up with a letter to Sir James Grigg, Secretary of State for War, suggesting that interested women volunteers should be enrolled into the WVS as its own Home Guard section, with a badge.[59] In a last-ditch effort to avoid being left out of any formal agreement, the WHDC organized a letter-writing campaign from local branches to MPs and the Prime Minister, seeking official recognition. David Robertson MP angrily wrote to Ernest Bevin (Minister of Labour) believing 'it is quite wrong that a Movement of this kind should be tolerated at this time' and suggesting that women wanting part-time work should be directed towards factory work or nursing.[60] Bridgeman confirmed in early October that 'it is not proposed to mention specifically the Women's Home Defence as one of the voluntary organizations through which this assistance should be afforded'.[61] But further progress on creating a formal women's section was still being blocked by the Minister of Labour and the Home Secretary, who believed the proposals were a means of circumventing the cap on Home Guard numbers. Herbert Morrison in January 1943 thought the proposals would have a net effect of draining 100,000 people from the part-time labour pool. The Ministries wanted a firm commitment that the Home Guard would only recruit women aged over 45 to protect younger women for fire-watching duties, with a clear understanding that service with the Home Guard would not mean exemption from any other national service.[62]

Summerskill met Bridgeman on 27 October 1942, to again stake the claim of the WHDC to be recognized alongside the WVS and MTC as an official partner in working with the Home Guard. By now, there were 251 branches of the WHDC.[63] On Merseyside the Wallasey Unit had a membership of up to fifty who 'combined work and family with evening defence duties'.[64] They each had to make a weekly contribution of *6d* towards the costs of the meeting room, with extra costs for insurance and ammunition. The local 16th Cheshire Home Guard provided instructors in drill and weapons handling. By April 1943 the WHDC claimed 30,000 members but this included women's units that only used the badge as a proficiency award. In Colwyn Bay members of the Ministry of Food women's section of the 11th Battalion (Ministry of Food), Denbighshire Home Guard who attended 75 per cent of the lectures were awarded a WHDC badge. In practice, the duties that the WHDC performed were identical to those of the other women volunteers (i.e. cooking, driving, first aid, signalling and administration) and Bridgeman privately acknowledged to Grigg that the work of the WHDC members 'appears welcome' to the Home Guard.[65] Unfortunately, by focusing its media messaging exclusively on weapons training, the WHDC could be presented by opponents as more self-indulgent than the WVS or MTC.

Summerskill's reluctant acceptance of a non-combatant role for women as what she termed the 'thin edge of the wedge' did not inspire confidence in how the WHDC would be able to work on a formal basis with the Home Guard.[66] The irony was that at the time (as Summerskill would have been well aware) the Home Guard was under strain in providing enough members for the demanding AA duties and an influx of women into support roles on the same basis as the ATS would therefore have been welcome. Her change in position had convinced no one and Morrison later referred to Summerskill as 'wants a gun, not a dishcloth', who only saw the present proposals as a stepping stone to her original objective.[67] Into this suspicious atmosphere came the release of the Ealing film *Went the Day Well* (December 1942), which offered a more positive message of women taking up arms than the 1940 *Miss Grant Goes To The Door*. Two Land Girls vie with each other for how many Germans they have shot, the post-mistress kills one with an axe and Nora executes an unarmed fifth columnist. This commercial film was designed to appeal to a wide audience, men and women, but by then such female aggression was firmly out of step with government priorities, which were to direct women either into industry, or to join the services on a full-time basis or volunteer for Civil Defence.

On 8 December 1942 another attempt in Parliament to obtain formal recognition for the WHDC had to be sidestepped by Sir James Grigg as being part of a 'much larger question'.[68] The resulting publicity organized by Summerskill in favour of the WHDC tested the patience of Lady Reading, who wrote to Grigg complaining that the long-standing arrangement with the WVS was being overlooked. Grigg wrote to Morrison: 'Most of what you have read in the newspapers on the subject is untrue – particularly that part (nearly the whole in fact) which derives from our Amazonian colleague Summerskill.'[69]

Summerskill was relentless but the Secretary of State refused to meet a deputation of the WHDC, leaving a reluctant Bridgeman to take on the task on 25 January. Bridgeman stonewalled and Summerskill's argument that membership of the WHDC was declining because of the absence of recognition only came as a welcome relief to the government.[70] After further delay, the concerns of the Ministries of Home Security and Labour were finally overcome and to Bridgeman's enormous relief, an approved scheme for women in the Home Guard was presented to Parliament on 20 April 1943:[71]

> It has been decided that a limited number of women, proportionate to the strength of the Home Guard, may be nominated for service as auxiliaries with the Home Guard to perform non-combatant duties such as clerical work, cooking and driving. Women between 18 and 65 will be eligible for nomination, but instructions have been issued that Home Guard battalion commanders should give preference to those over 45 or those who are not liable to direction to other work. Women nominated will wear a badge brooch. The shortage of women-power for part-time duties is such that it will not be possible to exempt women nominated for service with the Home Guard from being directed to any other form of full-time or part-time service. The nomination of individual women will be permitted, but Home Guard commanders are being instructed wherever possible to make use of existing women's organizations which indeed have in very many places been performing services to the Home Guard on an unofficial basis. I am very pleased to have this opportunity of acknowledging the valuable and devoted services which they have performed.[72]

Service with the Home Guard would therefore form the lowest priority of part-time war work for women. In practice the agreement gave official recognition for those women already working with the Home Guard. They would be 'nominated' by the local Home Guard commander for service, preferably from existing women's organizations rather than as individuals. 'Nominated Women' would be recruited to a maximum number of 80,000 and to give them a measure of legal protection they were given the archaic designation of 'civilians who follow the Armed Forces of the Crown' (*see* Appendix 1.9). It was envisaged that most women would come from the WVS and whilst it was hoped that the WHDC would assist on the same basis as other women's voluntary organizations it was specified that 'no training in the use of arms will be given to women auxiliaries'.[73] Their roles would be resolutely non-combatant (mainly clerical, telephony, cooking and driving) and so excluded some duties that women had been undertaking since 1940, including signalling duties in the field and first aid roles, arguing that they duplicated the efforts of other Civil Defence first aid services. Both restrictions continued to be widely ignored at a local level. Although not actually enrolled in the Home Guard, the title of 'Women's Home Guard Auxiliaries' was eventually officially conceded. There was no official uniform and no personal equipment was provided, only a plastic badge (*see* Appendix 1.16). It is clear that the government did not want to offer anything that might increase the status of the 'nominated women' as compared to other Civil Defence services, or make it an attractive alternative to full-time service in the ATS. Also ignoring this restriction, many local units continued to provide uniforms, as they had since 1940, sometimes wearing the WHDC badge as a cap badge or pinned to a tie. Women attached to the Intelligence section of Redcliffe Home Guard in Bristol and some Worcestershire Women's Auxiliaries wore denim overalls with collar and tie, battalion badges and the county regiment cap badge in their forage caps (Plate 29).[74] Unsurprisingly, this long-awaited but uninspiring final recognition of women did not produce any significant increase in numbers from those women already working with the Home Guard. The refusal to allow women to officially engage in activities such as signalling and first aid, as well as weapons training, removed much of the appeal of service, especially when they were not even provided with an official uniform. Recruitment of the 'nominated women' never came close to the agreed ceiling of 80,000. There were just 21,683 in December and still only 31,753 at the November 1944 stand-down.[75] By then, there were many other avenues of service available to women in civil defence or in the armed forces, and the wider Home Guard was in a period of low morale and resentment over the continuing burdens of service.

As in other aspects of the Home Guard, the situation at a local level was often distanced from the political wrangling in Whitehall. Even without a formal agreement, by February 1943 some 60,000 women were serving with the Home Guard, including units in the War Office, Air Ministry and Ministry of Food. Local officers had connived to issue uniforms and even provide a degree of weapons training, whether for serious purposes or as a social activity is not always clear (Plate 28).[76] In the heart of the War Office, Colonel Menertzhagen of the departmental LDV had unofficially taught women how to shoot and make Molotov cocktails.[77] The Upper Thames Patrol established shore patrols in June 1940 to cover a 3-mile band each side of the river, and recruited forty women drivers who wanted something more exciting than what they termed the 'colourless activities' of the WVS and admitted being 'blissfully ignorant' of the official ban of women in the Home Guard.[78] Other women crewed the patrol boats. Phyllis Woodham and seven other women volunteered to cook for Sussex LDV during a weekend exercise and were later trained in intelligence and signalling duties.[79] In Shropshire Joan Harborne and Betty Reiman, who worked for the Ministry of Aircraft Production at the Radio & Gramophone Development Company at Bridgnorth, took shifts in mounting night guard on 'The Tump', Ellesmere, during July 1940.[80] At Benhall, Suffolk, women volunteers took on the role of watching for parachutists during the day, whilst the male members of the LDV were at work. They wore armbands with an embroidered WO (Women Observer). In Surrey Lieutenant Colonel Ralston of the 51st Malden Home Guard recalled how in August 1941:

> one Sunday morning, a young lady (now Sergeant G) appeared, requesting to be allowed to assist the Battalion in First Aid. This was granted, and today we have a fully trained women's First Aid Section under the title of Women's

> Auxiliaries. They are equipped with a uniform ... consisting of khaki skirt and shirt blouse, F.S. cap (no badge) with shoulder flashes with the word 'Medical'. All this clothing had been purchased privately out of funds derived from concerts and dances, etc., the women generously giving up their clothing coupons for this purpose.[81]

The BBC Home Guard had a hundred women members performing duties in cooking, signalling, telephony, intelligence and 'handling ammunition'.[82] In January 1943 the Ministry of Food's Home Guard, evacuated to Colwyn Bay, Wales, also formed a women's section.[83] They affiliated to the WHDC and their training syllabus included lectures on the role of the Home Guard, discipline, military vocabulary, general knowledge of the area, map reading, anti-gas drill, first aid and drill. Whilst they received lectures on the weapons used by the Home Guard, there was no expectation that they would use them and training was essentially theoretical, thus 'they took part in almost every phase of Battalion work with the exception of actual infantry training'.[84] After the establishment of the official 'nominated women' (Women's Auxiliaries), the unit was organized into six sections: administration, communications, guides, intelligence, transport and catering. Photographs show them wearing dark blue Civil Defence-type battledress with the plastic Women's Auxiliaries badge on the tunic and berets with the cloth badge of the Ministry of Food Home Guard. The London Air Ministry Home Guard also included a detachment of ten to twelve women, uniformed in blue dungarees and army forage caps. They were given rifle practice at a local airfield and practised grenade throwing in St James's Park.[85] The Commanding Officer of the Air Transport Auxiliary at White Waltham, Kent, in 1943–44 formed a shooting team of his 'nominated women' and told them that their role, if attacked by a parachute raid, was to climb onto the roof of the aircraft hangars and shoot the paratroopers as they descended.[86]

The WHDC officially disbanded in December 1944. Summerskill had challenged the existing role of women in the armed forces through her campaign, but her fervour had the effect of hindering the formal recognition of the work that thousands of women had been quietly undertaking in the Home Guard in less socially challenging roles since 1940. Summerskill had mounted a well-orchestrated media campaign to elevate her demands; by comparison, the practical work of the WVS, which did not challenge convention, could seem routine, 'colourless' and of little importance. Writing from a twenty-first-century perspective, Summerfield and Peniston-Bird unfairly characterized tension between the WHDC and the WVS as a conflict of 'rifle-training versus tea-making', thereby dismissing the important contribution of women to the hard-pressed administrative needs of the Home Guard. They even reversed the chronology by claiming that the WVS somehow 'displaced' the WHDC.[87] In any case, many Home Guard would have disputed the unimportance of a cup of tea whilst on duty (*see above*, p. 29).

The failure to reach an agreement on a defined role for women with the Home Guard until 1943, or to give them an official uniform as a mark of respect, was followed by a difference in their letter of thanks at the stand-down. Whereas the male Home Guard received a certificate of appreciation from the King, the certificate for a 'Woman Home Guard Auxiliary', belatedly issued in 1945, was only signed by the Secretary of State for War (P.J. Grigg), which seemed to be a clear signal of their lesser importance (*see* Appendix 1.15 and 1.16). Officially marginalized, culturally there were few references to women's service with the Home Guard during the war and no mention was made of their contribution in John Brophy's 1945 history *Britain's Home Guard: a character study*. Women were again becoming invisible. Most had probably worked in HQ offices and it is telling that out of fifty Home Guard veterans interviewed by Austin Ruddy in Leicestershire, only one was aware of the existence of the Women's Auxiliaries.[88] The rapid exclusion of women from the mainstream story of the Home Guard and its subsequent male-oriented reminiscences in pubs and Home Guard rifle clubs gave no collective focus for their stories. Their memories faded and in most cases were replaced by experiences that seemed more valuable. They could not even hang their memories around television's *Dad's Army* because women were almost totally absent from the series.

Some progress was made in official thinking by the time a revival of the Home Guard was considered in 1951, when it was accepted that women would be able to join and even be commissioned. The ban on combat duties remained but excited virtually no comment. The issue was raised only briefly in a House of Commons debate in November 1951 but Edith Summerskill did not respond to the request for her opinion on the subject, and she took no part in any of the debates over the role of the revived Home Guard (*see* Chapter Ten). It would be a battle for a future generation to continue. In a rare tribute, during a debate on the reformation of the Home Guard in 1951, Conservative MP Sir T. Moore commented:

> I can only say from personal experience that the two most efficient members of the battalion which I had the honour to command were women. One ran the whole of the transport arrangements of the battalion, and the other ran the whole of the food arrangements, and these two were the most efficient departments in the battalion.[89]

Chapter Ten

The 1950s Home Guard

The earliest Home Guard Old Comrades' Association was formed in Tooting in October 1943.[1] A great camaraderie had built up in the Home Guard, through shared experiences and local roots. But even as the Home Guard was being stood down in December 1944, its value seemed to be questioned. An obvious means of retaining the sociability of their service seemed to be to join the main veterans' organization, the Royal British Legion; after all, they had borne arms and were entitled to the Defence Medal, but following discussions at branch meetings across the country during late 1944, the Royal British Legion at its AGM in May 1945 refused to allow Home Guard veterans to become members and use its facilities. The argument was that the government had not formally designated the Home Guard as 'ex-servicemen' and they had not seen active service. Their work in Anti-Aircraft Command, coastal artillery and bomb disposal was disregarded. Resentment was expressed that some Home Guard had to be conscripted from 1942 onwards and that this was considered a 'comfortable' option of national service.[2] There may even have been a sense of quixotic, wasted effort given the lack of an invasion. Such attitudes contributed to the lack of attention given to the Home Guard until the *Dad's Army* series brought it back into the popular consciousness, and it took until 2002 for Home Guard veterans to be allowed to take part in the annual Royal British Legion Remembrance Day parade. In the first contingent was Jimmy Perry, writer of *Dad's Army*. As an alternative, Home Guard veterans set up their own social and shooting clubs; twenty-four Home Guard rifle clubs had been formed in Worcestershire alone by June 1945.

Despite such negativity, noises soon began to be made about requiring a revival of the Home Guard.[3] As early as 1946 Winston Churchill, now Leader of the Opposition, was warning about the threat from his former ally, the Soviet Union, and in March 1948 Lieutenant General Sir Gerald Templar, Vice Chief of the Imperial General Staff, raised the spectre of a Communist fifth column based in the trade unions. This was followed by hesitant thoughts in May towards reconstituting the Home Guard.[4] Military thinking envisaged a rerun of the 1940 crisis; in December 1948 the Director of Military Operations at the War Office suggested that Russia might quickly overrun Western Europe, try to bomb Britain into submission and then mount a full-scale invasion, aided by a Communist fifth column. A Home Guard might therefore once again be required for guard duties and anti-aircraft defences, freeing the army to fight in Europe.[5] An ECAC report of February 1949 even harked back to the Auxiliary Units, suggesting that 'special elements of the force could play a valuable part in organizing a resistance movement in areas of the country temporarily overrun'.[6] Bill

Allington, a company commander in the Worcestershire cadre of the new Home Guard, recalled an approach being made for him to form such a force locally, but he declined.[7] There is no confirmed evidence of any success in reviving the Home Guard Auxiliary Units or creating a resistance organization. Instead, the role of hidden guerrilla units was held by the re-formed 22 SAS Regiment and its new territorial army regiments (21 and 23 SAS), which were training to go to ground in north Germany, if not within Britain, using a version of the Second World War Auxiliary Units hides.

If the Home Guard in 1940 had been characterized by a lack of forethought and planning, the same could not be said of the protracted discussions about a revived force in the 1950s. A working party was established in June 1949 to consider proposals but in August came the shock of the Russian atomic bomb test, which, for many, made preparations for conventional warfare irrelevant. Nonetheless, in January 1950 the War Office proposed a new Home Guard with a target strength of 1.75 million, based on the maximum strength of the Second World War Home Guard, and the onset of the Korean War in June 1950 then showed doubters the continuing threat of conventional warfare.[8] It was estimated that the new force would require 1.25 million rifles (with 25 million rounds of ammunition), 0.5 million Sten guns (plus 50 million rounds of ammunition) and 7 million grenades, which, together with the necessary uniforms and steel helmets, would amount to a cost of £50 million. With the chaos of 1940 still in mind, prior planning and resource allocation would attempt to avoid conflicts in training and supply with the regular forces. Recruitment to the Civil Defence Corps was already proceeding and in November 1950 the Defence Committee finally agreed, in principle, that a Home Guard was needed. Considering the fragile economic state of the country it was proposed that, until the 'precautionary stage' of an emergency, only paper planning should proceed, confining recruitment to the earmarking of battalion commanders. Further, in the first month of war recruitment would be confined to a force of no more than 200,000 Home Guard (an odd consideration given the expected speed of attack).[9]

Unlike 1940, there was little political consensus over the need for a Home Guard, and as the Labour government had only a slim majority it faced repeated arguments between opposition Tory hawks and left-wing Labour back-benchers, as well as inter-departmental disputes within the government. As one of the main perceived threats was Communist subversion, the need to exclude known Communists or suspected 'fellow-travellers' was an obvious priority but in September 1951 both MI5 and the Home Office, without any direct threat as faced in 1940, baulked at the scale of vetting that would be required.[10] Churchill saw the issue as a means of reviving the memory of his glory days and the creation of a Home Guard became part of the Conservative Party election manifesto. In election meetings the spectre was raised of landings by 20,000 Russian parachute troops and the consequent need to mobilize a Home Guard to defend against them.[11] It was only in March 1953 that Churchill asked the Chiefs of Staff to consider whether such an invasion was really feasible and they promptly dismissed the suggestion, with or without the deployment of atomic weapons.[12]

Churchill returned to power after the October 1951 general election and the intention to create a Home Guard was announced in the Queen's Speech, the reading of the Home Guard bill being scheduled for 22 November. But shades of the chaos of May 1940 then re-emerged when the Chiefs of Staff maintained that they did not see the point of a large force, only wanting 50,000 men to guard vulnerable points (in effect a return to the original 'armed special constabulary' of May 1940). As a compromise, a peacetime cadre of 125,000 men was proposed – but this would still cost £2.5 million to arm and it was discovered that there were no available uniforms, all manufacturing capacity being devoted to the needs of those called up for National Service and the planning for a rapid mobilization of the Territorial Army. With *déjà vu*, in the initial stages the Home Guard 'uniform' would be an armband (this time yellow and green with Home Guard shoulder title overstitched) worn on the left arm and an early Second World War pattern steel helmet upon which would be painted the badges of rank.

After last-minute negotiations, Minister of War Anthony Head was able to announce plans to raise a Home Guard peacetime cadre of 125,000 men aged 18–65, in anticipation of a total mobilized strength of 900,000.[13] They would be volunteers, engaging for two years but able to resign on a month's notice, and they would not be subject to military law until mustered for training, or on duty. There would be a minimum commitment of 15 hours' training per quarter and weapons were not to be stored at home. The new Home Guard would be more centralized than that of the Second World War, with no expectation that platoons would be formed in every village or town. There would be two categories of unit, with 162 'Category A' battalions in the south and east of England (on a line from Flamborough Head to Selsey Bill, and the area judged at most risk from invasion) recruiting 60 per cent of their projected wartime strength to a total of 100,000 men. In addition, 397 'Category B' battalions would be established on a skeleton cadre basis of fifty men (20,000–25,000 men in all), which could then be expanded as necessary. Given that National Service for younger men was already in operation there was, this time, a genuine age bias. Members of the Territorial Army Reserve of Officers over the age of 51 and all members of the Z Reserve (those men who had served in the latter stages of the Second World War and up to 1948) and who were over 46 were able to join automatically. Younger members of the Z Reserve needed War Office approval. Parliament was unenthusiastic and Labour Party MPs were particularly concerned that the emphasis on countering a Communist fifth column might be extended to using the Home Guard for strike-breaking – Anthony Head had raised the suggestion in an earlier House of Commons debate.[14] There was little sense of the 'nation in arms' and Wilfred Fienburgh, Labour MP for Islington North and a serving Territorial Army officer, christened it 'a Praetorian Guard of elderly Tory buffers'.[15] The reaction from the press was mixed, with even *The Times* coming out in objection to the proposals.[16] A Home Guard coordinating conference organized in December by the Director of the Territorial Army could not find consensus and the Home Office and Chief Constables in January 1952 again strongly objected to any role in vetting volunteers for left-wing sympathies, saying that, in a time of peace, 'the police are not concerned with the politics of individuals but with the enforcement of the law'.[17] The idea of mass vetting was subsequently dropped, leaving MI5 to vet only those who would be responsible for planning the guarding of vulnerable points. In one positive move, women were to be admitted under separate conditions of service following an amendment to the bill from Labour MP Emmanuel Shinwell to delete the word 'male' from the description of the force, but they would still not be permitted to bear arms. Shinwell's objection to this restriction was supported by the Conservative Sir T. Moore, who asked 'I would like to hear in this debate the views of the right Hon. Lady the Member for Fulham, West [Edith Summerskill], because she took a very prominent line in advocating that women should also be trained in the use of arms.'[18] However, Summerskill did not have the appetite to take up this battle again and took no part in any of the debates on the Home Guard. Without her, there was no campaign in the press or Parliament for women to be given equal status. Social attitudes had not greatly changed in the aftermath of the Second World War and now there was no champion for women's equality. In 'A Word to the Women', an article in the *Sussex Express and County Herald* for 5 September 1952 suggested there was much for women to do in the new Home Guard 'particularly in welfare and hospital work', reassuring them that they did not need much training, 'for the part of "ministering angel" is one that every worth-while woman is already equipped to play'. The enrolment of women up to 4 per cent of the personnel of all Home Guard battalions was authorized for administrative and other non-combatant roles but was only finally implemented in April 1954. They would be uniformed and given ranks, and a limited number would be commissioned. One problem came in their use of regimental cap badges but a compromise was accepted that where regimental colonels objected, the women would be allowed to wear the General Service cap badge. By February 1955 only 1,000 women had enrolled, with 1,500 on the reserve roll.[19]

The statutory basis for the new force was the Home Guard Act of 7 December 1951. It was again to be unpaid and men were not required to give whole-time service or live away from their homes until mustered, or to carry out duties in connection with an industrial dispute. It was to be mustered only in defence of the UK against an actual or apprehended attack and, as in the Second World War, would be administered by the Territorial Army Associations. An appeal for recruits was made on 25 January 1952 but, without an immediate threat to the country, there was little public appetite to volunteer. As early as 8 April 1952 the Labour Party called on the government to 'abandon this foolish scheme'.[20] In response, the CIGS, Field Marshal Slim, hero of the Burma campaign, urged recruitment on the not terribly encouraging grounds that 'if the horrors of atomic bombing fall on this island one of our first needs will be a force of steady, disciplined, armed men throughout the country'.[21] In a recruiting campaign for Worcestershire, Lieutenant Colonel J.H.L. Beard, CO of the new 3rd Battalion of the Worcestershire Home Guard, tried to stress that this was something new, claiming 'The Home Guard of today is a very different organization from that associated in the public mind with the dark days of the early 1940s' – an indication of how deeply the 'broomstick army' image of 1940 had become established. To reinforce this, he suggested that a new name was needed and a small bounty paid to its members on the lines of the Territorial Army. As a name, he suggested the 'Territorial Reserve' or the 'Reserve Army'. Following the precedent of both the First and Second World Wars, he believed that in the event of a new war, the regular and Territorial armies would all be overseas. Home defence would therefore be left to the Home Guard.[22] The scenario remained unappealing.

The regulations for the new Home Guard were issued by the War Office on 14 March 1952. There was to be no fixed war establishment, but on mobilization battalions would average in numbers 1,500 all ranks. The main tasks were likely to be the same as in 1940: defence against airborne or small-scale seaborne raids, anti-sabotage protection of key points, assistance to Civil Defence, and defence against invasion. To make volunteering more attractive, Churchill eventually decided 'upon consideration to draw upon our mobilisation reserves to the extent necessary to clothe at least the first 50,000'. The uniform subsequently issued was the standard 1949 pattern battledress with collar and tie, with dark blue beret (or a Balmoral bonnet for Scottish battalions), which was to be worn only when on parades or duties. There were red shoulder titles with county codes and battalion numbers. In November 1952 the War Office gave approval for the issue of white metal lapel badges to the volunteers. Some were still armed with the SMLE but most had the now standard No. 4 Lee Enfield rifle (Plate 30), while officers and NCOs were to be issued with the Sten gun. The first Stens were reputedly issued to the 61st Surrey Home Guard in September 1952 whilst they still had only the brassard as uniform.[23] They also had the Bren gun, as well as Vickers heavy machine guns, the recently obsolete PIAT anti-tank projector and 2-in mortars. Apart from helmet and greatcoat, the only other equipment provided was the normal Bren pouches, with no haversack, waterproofs, water bottle or entrenching tool. In these respects they were less well equipped than the Home Guard of 1940. With recruitment failing, the Army Council in September 1952 recommended abandoning trying to recruit the active battalions in favour of cadres of just a hundred men across the country, moving the overall total closer to the small force useful for guarding vulnerable points that the Chiefs of Staff had wanted in the first place.[24] It seemed too much like defeat for the scheme and in November Head announced a compromise to Parliament reducing the active battalions to a cadre of 300 men.[25] One problem was the preponderance of officer volunteers in the permitted age range. In early 1953 there were just 20,000 other ranks – but 9,000 officers (*see* Appendix 1.17)! To raise interest, the rationale of the force began to shift towards assistance for Civil Defence but a recruiting drive over the summer of 1954 again failed and by October the strength was still only 36,143 with a reserve roll of 34,830. Making matters worse, men who had volunteered in the early months were coming to the end of their engagement.[26] Lieutenant General Sir Francis Festing, GOC Eastern Command, in December 1954 commented 'It is a fact that the ordinary man in the street does not believe in the danger of war. He is hardened to crises and sees no reason for joining the

Home Guard.'[27] Kenneth Allsop of the *Picture Post* contrasted the situation in 1940 when 'you could smell the gunpowder in the wind' to the 1950s when the war-weary population 'with a garden to tend and a novel to read, doesn't feel ready to be stampeded into khaki'.[28] In echoes of Wintringham's earlier criticisms of 'blimps', Allsop complained of the preponderance of officers in the establishment and also of the permanent staff adjutants 'drawing £670 p.a. and spending most of their sparse hours on duty at crosswords'. Allsop also claimed there was falsification of records to automatically include the names of Home Guard who had served in the Second World War and complained that Eastern Command were 'all under strength and high in age'.[29] Although accepting the need to have a cadre ready for mobilization if necessary, he believed that the Home Guard should divest itself of 'delusions of grandeur' and not persist with its unsuccessful attempt to recruit to any larger number.[30] The lack of interest must also be seen in the wider context that some men who had served in the Second World War were not finally demobbed until early 1948 and there was a general war weariness. Albert Squires of Blackpool recalled how he spent almost ten years at war: 'What with joining the Home Guard and then being called up for Army Service and fighting in Palestine until I was demobbed in 1949, it took half my childhood and all of my teenage years ...'[31]

Young men – 17 to 21 years old – were liable to National Service and were disinclined to take on an additional burden before they were called up.[32] National Service was portrayed in the comedy series *The Army Game* (1957–1961), in which a group of hapless conscripts try to get through their term of service by doing as little as possible. Like the later *Dad's Army*, it is a partial impression, which reflected the boredom and seeming futility of National Service at home, but ignored the real risks for those called to active service. National Service personnel faced service in the Malayan Emergency (1948–60), the Korean War (1950–53), and the Mau Mau Uprising in Kenya (1952–60). In addition, during 1951 and 1952 a total of 250,000 Z Reservists were called-up for refresher training. For older men who had served in the Second World War, the memories were still raw and, with no comparable enemy massing on the coasts of France, they felt they had 'done their bit'. The government was also trying to recruit volunteers for the Civil Defence Corps, focusing on what seemed to be the more immediate need to make preparations for the aftermath of a nuclear attack. Given such pressures, Allsop maintained that few men under 45 years were free of other obligations that allowed them to join the Home Guard.[33]

There is little evidence for practical activity in the new Home Guard. In Hertfordshire a weekend exercise near Whitwell in September 1952 by fifty members of the 1st Hertfordshire Home Guard, designed to give instructions in minor tactics and fieldcraft, caught the attention of the national media because local officers, as a self-deprecating joke, had called it 'Operation Lumbago'. The *Daily Graphic* was scathing: 'Would it persuade you to give up your time if a poster said, "Are you an old crock? Then join the Home Guard."' The War Office and Churchill were not amused by this reinforcing of the prejudices against the force, even more so because the forty Home Guard defenders of a supposed munitions works were wiped out by just ten attackers in the exercise.[34] The most popular activity amongst the new Home Guard was inter-army shooting competitions, possibly because there was a surfeit of .303 ammunition after the war. Some still used the old P14 as the preferred target rifle.

By the autumn of 1953, with little public enthusiasm for the force, the Labour Opposition was continuing to press for its abolition whilst the likelihood of cuts in the defence budget put a priority on protecting the existing army commitments. The main argument for retention was that the Home Guard avoided the need in an emergency to disperse Territorial Army units to guard vulnerable points against sabotage and provided a disciplined force to assist Civil Defence. The Cabinet meeting of 29 October 1953 concluded that the Home Guard should be retained, adding that 'The decision to retain it should be announced boldly.'[35] There was then a renewed recruitment drive to bring cadres up to strength and increase the numbers on the reserve roll for recruiting in an emergency. As an incentive to morale, it was decided to formally affiliate Home Guard battalions to their county regiment, rather than just allowing them to wear the cap badge. But in March 1954 the Opposition described the Home Guard as a 'complete fiasco' and even Harold Macmillan, when he became Minister of Defence, asked in December 'Is the Home Guard any good?'[36] Although membership had risen to 37,000 in active battalions and 39,000 on the reserve roll, the Home Guard budget was cut by £22,000 for the year 1955–56. The only thing keeping the Home Guard alive was the personal interest of the Prime Minister but after Churchill resigned in April 1955, to be replaced by Sir Anthony Eden, the Home Guard lost its most fervent supporter and interest waned further. The Strath Report of 1955 concluded that an attack on Britain using hydrogen bombs would result in the immediate death of around one-third of the population and all other defence provisions paled into insignificance. The outcome was substantial cuts in the regular army and in the reserves. On 20 December 1955 the Minister of Defence announced that the Territorial Army was being scaled down to two divisions and that the Home Guard would finally stand down. By 8 June 1956 most of those who were in the cadres had been transferred to the Home Guard reserve roll, leaving just a small cadre of officers to keep up-to-date all arrangements for future mobilization. The Home Guard was finally disbanded on 31 July 1957.

Chapter Eleven

The Home Guard in Wartime Popular Culture

Published accounts of the home front written during the Second World War were controlled by censorship, voluntary or enforced, that established a deeply embedded consensual memory of the British community and fighting spirit, standing united across class divisions. A pride in their stoical suffering, in which all classes shared and 'mucked in', came to define post-war Britain's self-belief in the face of a changing world order that saw the collapse of the Empire and the rise in economic power of the USA. In taking comfort in what was, overall, a genuine wartime communal spirit, less comfortable evidence of an inequality of experience and suffering, continuing social divisions and an explosion of looting and racketeering were put to one side. Home Guard stores offered a new source of weapons for criminal activity. In 1941 two boys aged 14 and 15 escaped from Wallington Remand Home and broke into the Home Guard store at Upper Norwood, stealing one of the new Thompson sub-machine guns and 400 rounds of ammunition. In March 1943 three 17-year-olds held up the cashier at the Ambassador cinema in Hayes with three loaded Sten guns that had been stolen from the local Home Guard store; they later admitted to taking part in forty-three other robberies in London.[1] Such problems aside, the Home Guard became a visual expression in local communities of what became known collectively as the 'Dunkirk spirit', uniting soldiers and civilians of all classes in a common cause. 'Jimmy' Taylor, who served in both his Eton College Home Guard and that of his home village, recognized the apparent change in the social order: 'for the first time I got to know the villagers'.[2] Examples of workers holding superior rank to their managers in the Home Guard, or retired generals who accepted service in the ranks, were proudly held up as proof of the egalitarian spirit at a local level, despite the clear evidence that senior officers were overwhelmingly of the gentry or aristocratic class (*see above*, p. 14). The determination to resist the invader with broomstick and pitchfork formed a key element of a mythology that was actively cultivated, ignoring the later well-armed Home Guard, and less attention was given to stories of Home Guard weariness and prosecutions for non-service.

It should be understood that, aside from formal group photographs (Plate 3) and privately taken pictures of Home Guard proudly showing off their uniform in their back garden, most of the surviving images of the Home Guard are censored press photographs and therefore present a controlled image. An instruction of 31 May 1940 made clear that published photographs were not allowed to show the men at their war stations, nor any details of defences.[3] Restrictions were later placed on showing their weaponry:

> All stories about the Local Defence Volunteers should be submitted for Censorship. Instances of what should not be printed are: details as to their strength in any particular formation or locality, their organization or their equipment.[4]

One consequence was that many photographs had to be staged out of context, which explains the sometimes awkward still images reconstructing Home Guard exercises, including those of dummy tanks and disguised 'fifth column' at road-blocks. The propaganda intent of some photographs is obvious. Photographs of the Osterley Home Guard Training School were syndicated worldwide, showing a ruthless preparation for invasion, including lectures on how to make explosives, Molotov cocktails and home-made mortars, or demonstrations on how to ambush a tank (Plates 7 and 8). A common motif was of the Home Guard literally defending 'hearth and home' and Plate 14 is a dramatic image of a Home Guard at his doorstep, posed to shield his wife and child with his M1917 rifle. There is a similar intention behind Plate 15, showing a veteran Home Guard sergeant, wearing his First World War medal ribbons, sitting at his kitchen table cleaning a Thompson sub-machine gun while his wife sits quietly in the background knitting. It is a highly contrived image to demonstrate settled harmony and quiet resolve. But this photograph was taken in December 1940 as part of a series of propaganda photographs (now in the IWM collections) showing members of Dorking Home Guard armed with Thompson sub-machine guns and a Bren gun before these weapons were actually issued to the Home Guard. The sergeant's Thompson was probably swiftly removed on completion of the photoshoot. The intention of the series was to imply that the Home Guard was now as well-equipped as the regular army, ready to meet any renewed invasion threat in the spring. Still pursuing this theme, but more honest, was the 1943 image of a Home Guard miner carrying a Sten gun, saying goodbye to his family (Plate 16). If the photographic image of the Home Guard was manipulated and censored, this begs the question of why earlier photographs were allowed showing the LDV drilling with broomsticks (Plate 1). They were, like photographs of the 'blitz spirit', a symbol of unity with men, young and old, standing together, determined to protect the country at whatever cost, and were, at least in part, directed towards an international audience. The message for the Germans was that the tentative peace negotiations were unlikely to succeed, and that invasion would not be easy. It was the men's spirit rather than their weapons that was the key message. For the Americans, such images were an appeal to extend the existing 'cash and carry' arrangement and supply arms to a desperate nation. The lack of uniform or the egalitarian denims were also elements that countered criticism of a class-ridden Britain being engaged purely in a war between rival imperial powers. No similar images of the army training with broomsticks could be published as this would have had a more negative impact.

In literature, an all-pervading theme was the defence of Britain as the romantic 'green and pleasant land', steeped in a community spirit that transcended contemporary industrialized society, which took inspiration from a literary heritage, particularly the works of Thomas Hardy set at the time of the Napoleonic threat. Such nostalgia bore little relation to reality but the cosy 'nationalist collectivist myth' allowed the contemporary divisions in society between classes and between town and country to be overcome.[5] Even left-wing writers demanding social and political change could not escape using sentimental images which became *de rigueur* across popular literature, with the Home Guard placed at the centre of this construct. *Watching Post* by Cecil Day-Lewis (who had left the Communist Party in 1938 and was a member of Musbury LDV in Devon) was written in July 1940. It powerfully evokes an image of traditional England, symbolically jointly defended by an intellectual poet and a farmer from the Home Guard:

A hill flank overlooking the Axe valley.
Among the stubble a farmer and I keep watch
For whatever may come injure our countryside –
Light-signals, parachutes, bombs or sea-invaders.
The moon looks over the hill's shoulder, and hope
Mans the old ramparts of an English night.

In a house down there was Marlborough born. One night
Monmouth marched to his ruin out of that valley.
Beneath our castled hill, where Britons kept watch,
Is a church where the Drakes, old lords of this countryside,
Sleep under their painted effigies. No invaders
Can dispute their legacy of toughness and hope.

Two counties away, over Bristol, the searchlights hope
To find what danger is in the air tonight.
Presently gunfire from Portland reaches our valley
Tapping like an ill-hung door in a draught. My watch
Says nearly twelve. All over the countryside
Moon-dazzled men are peering out for invaders.

The farmer and I talk for a while of invaders:
But soon we turn to crops – the annual hope,
Making of cider, prizes for ewes. Tonight
How many hearts along this war-mazed valley
Dream of a day when at peace they may work and watch
The small sufficient wonders of the countryside.

Image or fact, we both in the countryside
Have found our natural law, and until invaders
Come will answer its need: for both of us, hope
Means a harvest from small beginnings, who this night
While the moon sorts out into shadow and shape our valley,
A farmer and a poet, are keeping watch.[6]

The Stand-To, written in September 1940, is in similar vein and was offered to the Ministry of Information as a 'vigorous patriotic verse'.[7] The setting is again one of tranquil rural life into which the war intruded and made everyday heroes of the thirty roadmen, farm labourers and masons in Day-Lewis's platoon, but they are not the nameless masses. Each one of the 'ragtag fighters of lane and shadow' is named, putting them on a par with the famous generals and politicians of the war, including Spot the darts player, Ralph the ploughman and Whiller the lorry driver, united in comradeship and all 'faithful as bone to bone'.[8] The reduction of the war effort to the steely determination of a single community, emphasizing the constituent trades and occupations that reflect its diversity, would later form the essence of the 1960s–70s *Dad's Army* series.

The most influential of the socialist intellectuals was J.B. Priestley, whose evening *Postscript* series on the BBC had an audience of around 16 million. His third *Postscript* on 16 June, shortly after Paris had fallen to the Germans, related his impressions following his first night on duty with the LDV on the South Downs. The imagery was familiar. 'There we were, ploughman and parson, shepherd and clerk, turning out at night, as our forefathers had often done before us, to keep watch and ward over the sleeping English hills and fields and homesteads.' Self-conscious of the stereotype he was creating, Priestley admitted feeling he had wandered 'into one of those rich chapters of Thomas Hardy's fiction' but felt 'a powerful and rewarding sense of community; and with it a feeling of deep continuity'.[9] But, to the discomfort of the government, he went beyond such conventional imagery, insisting that the sacrifice of the people in war had to be rewarded by social reform in the subsequent peace. On 21 July 1940 he argued:

> We can't go forward and build up this new world order, and this is our real war aim, unless we begin to think differently ... we must stop thinking in terms of property and power and begin thinking in terms of community and creation.[10]

Priestley was sacked by the BBC in March 1941 after attacking the 'sentimental speeches' of politicians praising merchant seamen without offering them a 'square deal' after the war. Graham Greene wrote that Priestley 'became in the months after Dunkirk a leader second only in importance to Mr. Churchill. And he gave us what our other leaders have always failed to give us – an ideology.'[11]

The romantic harking back to an illusory past was not merely for domestic consumption but was intended to appeal to US audiences and their stereotype of 'Olde Worlde England'. It must be remembered that Churchill's 'We will fight on the beaches, we shall fight on the landing grounds ... ' speech of 4 June 1940 ended with a plea to the USA in the hope that 'the new world, with all its power and might, steps forth to the rescue and the liberation of the old'.[12] Margery Allingham's *The Oaken Heart* (1941) was written in the winter of 1940, based around her experiences in the Essex village of Tolleshunt D'Arcy (alias 'Auburn'). An established detective novelist when war broke out, she found herself at the heart of local war preparations as the village billeting officer and first aid organizer; her house also became the ARP Post. The book was explicitly written to show an American audience what the war was like for ordinary British people, in the classic vein of other wartime propaganda, and the hypothetical fate of 'Miss Jane' and 'Miss Ethel' in attempting to slow the progress of the invader was later echoed in the film *Went the Day Well*. The villagers adjust to the war, by turns confused, frightened and then fatalistically determined. Scenes of rural tranquillity at the time of the Munich crisis, including the quintessential annual village cricket match, contrast with the later villagers stoically accepting the possibility of death in defending their village, armed with pitchforks and antiquated weapons.

The most cynical example of this expression of British tradition came from travel writer and Home Guard officer H.V. Morton in 1942. He too drew comparison with ancient times, speaking of the Home Guard sentry on the church tower, whose 'forage cap might have been a Norman helmet or a medieval casque':

> I think that a more peaceful bit of old England could not be found than this village of ours. Yet in every cottage sleeps an armed man. If I rang the bell now, they would come running out with their rifles, ready to defend their homes. Such a thing has not happened in Britain since the Middle Ages.[13]

He wrote of his fellow Home Guard,

> that should the rest of England fall, our own parish would hold out to the last man. The responsibility of defending our own village has given to that village a gigantic significance in our eyes. To us it seems the main objective of any invader, if all villages throughout England think as we do, what a hedge of opposition they present to anyone who dares to set an invader's foot upon this island.[14]

In reality, Morton was an anti-Semite and anti-democrat who, in his private diary for October 1940, described his fellow Home Guard as 'ungrateful yokels'. In February 1941 he noted 'I don't for a moment regard the HG [Home Guard] as more than a good publicity stunt,' railing against democracy and Jews, whilst maintaining that 'Nazi-ism has some fine qualities'.[15]

What gave credibility to the small group of socialist activists who to varying degrees tried to promote a political significance to the Home Guard was their practical engagement with the Home Guard, rather than political theorizing. Tom Wintringham's *New Ways of War* drew on a militaristic, rather than pastoral, English tradition, taking the ancestry of the Home Guard back to the Anglo-Saxon *fyrd* and relating the struggle to the seventeenth-century Levellers. His fervent pursuit of a revolutionary socialist agenda was couched within a nationalistic patriotism:

> There are those who say that the idea of arming the people is a revolutionary idea. It certainly is. And after what we have seen of the efficiency and patriotism of those who ruled us until recently, most of us can find plenty of room in this country for some sort of revolution, for a change that will sweep away the muck of the past. But arming the people is also completely part of the tradition of the British.[16]

Wintringham's laboured attempts to call upon an egalitarian past was nowhere near as effective as his coining of the stirring slogan in the 28 May issue of the *Daily Mirror*: 'An Aroused People, An Angry People, An Armed People' in demanding the need to arm the populace in the spirit of the Spanish Civil War. In vain, he tried to exploit the newly fashionable label of guerrilla warfare as an expression of revolutionary warfare that celebrated the independence and initiative of men and their NCOs against the control of an officer class dominated by the gentry: 'Guerrilla warfare is essentially the weapon of free men – a guerrilla band functioning efficiently under compulsion is inconceivable.'[17]

The film *The Dawn Guard* (1941), with its debate between Home Guardsmen Bernard Miles and Percy Walsh, took the approved Ministry of Information motif of defence of a 'green and pleasant land' as its starting point but extended it more into the territory that Priestley, Wintringham and Orwell were proposing – that military victory needed to be accompanied by social change. But as Orwell later rued, such philosophizing over the nature of war and society was rare in the Home Guard and had little direct impact.

An exception to the usual romantic literary expression of the Home Guard was Graham Greene's June 1940 short story 'The Lieutenant Died Last', written in the immediacy of the invasion threat and published in *Collier's Weekly* magazine. In Greene's story, the hero is a drunken old poacher who thwarts the German landing in the village of Potten with only his Boer War vintage rifle and just six rounds of ammunition, but just as importantly, he is able to use his fieldcraft skills. Written for a still-neutral American audience not yet ready to demonize the enemy, the Germans are treated sympathetically. They are polite, shoot to wound rather than to kill and their officer entreats the captured villagers to remain quiet as their imprisonment is only temporary. As typical in such stories, the villagers are slow to realize that the men wearing strange uniforms and cutting telephone lines are Germans. Even Bill 'Poacher' Purves does not immediately appreciate the significance of the descending parachutes. Having finally realized the situation, Purves ambushes the German saboteurs, his last round hitting the charge of explosives the Germans were laying on the railway line. All but the officer are killed; he, badly wounded, asks Purves to put him out of his misery. 'Old Purves always felt pity for broken animals' and so obliged, using the lieutenant's own revolver. In a matter of fact way, Purves then collects two snared rabbits from his traps before returning to the village and freeing his neighbours. In a demonstration of the continuing rule of law, Purves was promptly arrested for poaching. His only reward was to be let off with a caution by the magistrate and given 'a cold commendation'.[18]

The Home Guard was quickly absorbed into the British way of life and soon found its way into popular culture. It features in two crime novels: *Home Guard Mystery* by Belton Cobb (1941) and *Murder in the Home Guard* by Ruth Adam (1942). *Home Guard Mystery* is a simple crime novel but follows the accepted wartime convention of different classes working together in a spirit of national unity ('good fellows, every one of them') but has an effortless authenticity. An ex-major was now a corporal, serving under a former NCO who was an obsequious grocer by day but whose 'infallibility [was] put on with his uniform'. The novel captures the discomfort and boredom of nightly guard duty, the unreality of training exercises, an accidental discharge of a rifle as civilians try to adjust to becoming soldiers, but then the excitement at the possibility of invasion: 'Streuth! ... That'd be a bit of orl right.' In 1941 these sentiments would all have been relatable to the reader. The murder victim is the pompous sergeant, Cunningham, written in the mould of what would become Compton Mackenzie's Captain Waggett or Jimmy Perry's Captain Mainwaring, but an altogether less attractive person, involved in a complex love triangle. Ruth Adam, who worked for the Ministry of Information, uses *Murder in the Home Guard* more overtly as a propaganda tool, exploring the impact of the war on a cross-section of society in a community that is reluctant to engage in the national war effort, exposing and challenging negative attitudes to refugees and evacuees. The Chief Constable of the town mused:

> He pictured Longmarket as a town of ants under a huge stone, with each little ant scuttling about its important business, heedless of the fact that the stone had been lifted off, and that a gigantic human monster hovered over it, ready to crush it to pieces. Last night the German war machine had hovered for a moment over its thousand homes, but the little ants below had gone on blissfully running about on the adventures of their own little lives just the same.

Adam dedicated the novel accusingly to 'those who sat tight in safe areas'. *Murder in the Home Guard* is set in a small rural town where, after a rare air raid, the body of a young Home Guard is found shot dead, after he had reported what appeared to be lights flashing signals to the German aircraft. The twist is that the murderer turns out to be the Home Guard commander who, in a warped patriotism, signalled the German bomber to bring down an air raid on his narrow-minded community and so jolt the people into a more unified wartime spirit. As with the film *Went the Day Well*, there is here also a warning to be aware of 'fifth columnists' in positions of authority, even in the Home Guard.

Faced with the prospect of imminent death, the Home Guard took solace in the long British tradition of self-deprecating humour which was encapsulated in Robb Wilton's famous radio monologue of 1942, 'The day the war broke out'.

> an' I came down into the kitchen an' the missus looked at me an' she said, 'What are you supposed to be?' I said, 'Supposed t' be! ...' I said, 'I'm one of the Home Guards!' She said, 'One of the Ho ... what are the others like?' And then the missus said, she said, 'Well, what do you do in the Home Guards?' I said, 'I've got to stop Hitler's army landing!' She said, 'What ... you?' I said, 'No ... there's Harry Bates and Charlie Evans and ... ' I said, 'there's seven or eight of us altogether.' I said, 'We're in a group.' I said, 'We're on guard in a little hut be'ind *The Dog and Pullet*'. She said, 'Now what's the good of being on guard in a little hut behind *The Dog and Pullet*?' she said, 'I suppose that was your idea!' I said, 'Aye ... and that Charlie Evans wants to claim it, as 'is!'

Humour was central to the character of the Home Guard and when publishers realized that the members offered an opportunity for mass sales like no other, they also appreciated that collections of humour were likely to make souvenir histories more marketable than simply producing a war diary of reporting endless nights of boredom whilst standing on guard. As early as 1941 Basil Boothroyd published a collection of cartoons and stories from *Punch* magazine as *Home Guard Goings-On*. The Preface stated:

> What they are reading, though not wholly fiction, is not the whole truth either. If the note is gay rather than grim it is only because the author has preferred the chaff to the wheat, not because the Most Amazing Army in the World lacks any part of the Churchill spirit.[19]

Here was an admission that the story of the Home Guard was already being tweaked to make it more humorous at the expense of strict accuracy. In 1942 came *Laughs with the Home Guard*, a compilation of Giles cartoons and short stories by S. Evelyn Thomas. The affectionate title was laugh *with* rather than *at* the Home Guard and was in the spirit of the First World War trench cartoons of Captain Bruce Bairnsfather and the cartoons that satirized the First World War Volunteer Training Corps.[20] Carl Giles was a corporal in the Middlesex Home Guard. British humour has very little reverence for either politics or institutions but taken out of their immediate context and raised to new heights of absurdity, such stories became an important inspiration for the *Dad's Army* series of the 1960s–70s. Thomas saw one of the greatest assets of the British as the ability to laugh at themselves:

> We laugh at the people and the things we love. It is a laughter of sympathy and understanding, and those who make us laugh join with us in our merriment ... So I am sure the Home Guard will appreciate this book, they will see in these occurrences that have given rise to laughter situations wherein they themselves might have been the victims – these things might have happened to them! ... There is little enough time for laughter in the serious business of winning the war. Few of us nowadays have time to read, and most of us are too busy for ordinary relaxation and entertainment. I hope this little book will help us to bridge that gap, and that, in overcrowded trains and noisy buses, it will not only amuse its readers, but also help them in some small way to weather the present storm.[21]

A comedic aspect of the Home Guard even extended to comforting nursery stories. In *Hare Joins The Home Guard* (1941), Alison Uttley interprets the Second World War for 5-year-olds with the gentle woodland animals facing an invasion from the cruel, and seemingly invincible, army of weasels. The woodland community stands united and cleverly ambushes the enemy, with the weasels vowing never to return. 'Courage, Fight for Freedom,' sing the victorious heroes.[22] Hare is the representative of the Home Guard and his task is made clear to the young reader: '"You must defend Grey Rabbit's house and all our homes with your life," said Mole.' But Hare is also the comedy character who, as determined as the rest of the fighters, mistakenly catapults his sandwiches, rather than stones, into the enemy. For an adult, Hare might seem a pompous coward, but the message for the children was that the Home Guard, the armed soldiers on their doorstep and sitting in their kitchen, were friendly and not terribly fierce, but they were there to keep them safe.

In the chaos of the initial stages of the Home Guard's formation there were undoubtedly many incidents that bordered on the farcical. Such stories have been given added potency because, unlike other military units, the participants were tied to the local community and so the incidents, although not confined to the Home Guard by any means, were easy to record and formed a part of local folklore, told and retold in pubs and social clubs until fact and exaggeration merged. Many were published in souvenir histories towards the end of the war, inserting a note of humour in what are often dry records, aimed at the veterans who understood the context, but subsequently given a prominence out of all proportion to their scale, especially after the *Dad's Army* series when the reporting of such stories became the accepted norm in portraying the Home Guard. Memories became selective, timescales flexible, and there was evident pride from veterans in the fact that, in the first weeks of existence, the Home Guard was prepared to stand and fight the common enemy with minimal equipment. Mavis Rennison remembered her father commenting that 'if Hitler had come early in the war we would certainly have won because all his troops would have laughed themselves to death at the sight'.[23]

Even though the threat of invasion decreased during 1942, the government still wanted to maintain an air of alert amongst the general population, not least because the 'invasion spirit' helped bind the country together. Graham Greene's 'The Lieutenant Died Last' (*see above*) formed the loose basis of Alberto Cavalcanti's masterful 1942 film *Went the Day Well* (in turn, the inspiration for the Jack Higgins novel and 1976 film *The Eagle Has Landed*). The sleepy, idyllic English village of Bramley End, reminiscent of G.A. Wade's 'Bloodford', looked backwards from a time of ultimate victory to when German paratroopers, disguised as British soldiers, set up an advance post for a planned invasion.[24] As in Graham Greene's story, there is a lack of watchfulness. The audience is reminded of the dangers of the fifth columnists (the village did not realize that the commander of the local Home Guard was a traitor) and the duped Home Guard pass on their defence plans to the disguised German officer. They then ignore the warning chimes of the church bells, which leads to their deaths. The necessary ruthlessness in war is demonstrated by the local post-mistress killing a German guard with an axe, whilst in the finale a young woman shoots her Home Guard friend who had turned out to be a Nazi collaborator. Fortunately, despite the tragic early failure of their own Home Guard, their comrades in the neighbouring Home Guard return with the army to efficiently dispatch the enemy. In Jack Higgins' post-war *The Eagle Has Landed* (1976), the German characters were treated more sympathetically and it was the American army that saved the day!

The nature of the Home Guard changed from 1942 when service became compulsory and arguably more demanding, and morale began to slip. There was less scope for humour. Instead, members began to look back at the more chaotic, independent days of 1940 with some fondness, and comic representations of the 1940 LDV became popular elements of public entertainments. In 1943 three very different films included reference to the Home Guard, all of them to varying degrees with a comedic element. The classic propaganda film was *Millions Like Us*, written and directed by Sidney Gilliat and Frank Launder, in which all members of an 'ordinary' family are shown 'doing their bit' within a multitude of references to wartime shortages, stresses and sacrifice. Comedic relief is provided by Jim, the father (Moore Marriot), who struggles with the changes to traditional domestic life. Brought up to expect the womenfolk to look after his every need, he is suddenly obliged to cope with managing the home after his daughters leave to work in the aircraft factory or join the services. As a lesson that the war effort was not just for the young and fit, he too serves his country by joining the Home Guard.

The film *Get Cracking* is a vehicle for the musical comedy style of George Formby, who portrays a Home Guard lance corporal. With a sense of relief that the threat of invasion was over, it was possible to make a comedy around the preparations that had been made. The opening scenes could have been taken from any 1940 press photograph of the LDV 'broomstick army' and engagingly portray the build-up of equipment. Much is made of the presence of First World War veterans in the ranks as the narrator reels off the list of battles in which they served, which was to engender pride in the battle-worn experience of the volunteers. This then serves as a stark contrast to the sudden appearance of the hapless Formby in the ranks. The Home Guard is shown as an all-male preserve with the female characters fulfilling conventional gender stereotypes, providing humour and a love interest. The story depicts the rivalry between the Home Guard platoons of neighbouring 'Major Wallop' and 'Minor Wallop'. In the end Formby builds his own tank (as did many Home Guard units) and is promoted to sergeant; the rivalry between the two village platoons is ended and they unite against the common foe – the neighbouring village of Midgeley. Despite the wartime theme, this is a story of rural England in its own self-contained bubble and it is told with an affectionate humour:

> Lorry driver: 'Are you a soldier?'
> George Formby: 'No, Home Guard.'
> Lorry driver: 'Never mind – we've still got a Navy!'

Something any Second World War soldier could relate to was the misery of night-time guard duty but it was particularly apposite to the Home Guard for whom guarding vulnerable points throughout the war must have seemed an endless duty. George Formby commemorates this in the song 'Home Guard Blues', albeit singing it incongruously in the middle of the day with a broad cheeky smile on top of a corrugated iron tank:

> On sentry go in the night
> If it's wet the water trickles down your neck to where it tickles,

And the raindrops ooze through your socks and shoes.
If you're feeling on the black side with the wind around your earholes
Then you'll get those Home Guard Blues.[25]

The plot of inter-village rivalry was not fanciful. Sir Frederick Morgan, GOC of Western Command, wrote of the rivalry between the Cornwall and Devon Home Guards: 'For to the men of Devon those of Cornwall were damned foreigners who, like as not, would welcome the Germans: while the Cornishmen reckoned those of Devon to be a soft lot who could be relied upon in no way to resist the enemy.' He believed they were more interested in putting up defences on the county border than on the potential landing beaches! After suggesting at a public meeting that there needed to be close collaboration between the towns of Dartmouth and Kingswear, Morgan reported 'an indescribable uproar' and he had to be hustled from the building![26] For the Cambridgeshire Home Guard their neighbours from Suffolk were cousins rather than brothers – 'and sometimes distant cousins at that'.[27]

A more unsettling humour was contained in *The Life and Death of Colonel Blimp*, inspired by the *Colonel Blimp* cartoons by David Low, which dated back to 1934 and satirized the pomposity and jingoism of the British Establishment. The film by Michael Powell and Emeric Pressburger was a romantic drama with an underlying dark message about the difficulties of adjusting to the realities of modern war. Ex-general Wynne-Candy (Roger Livesey) had become a senior commander in the Home Guard but was old-fashioned in his outlook, becoming a figure of pity and reflecting the complaints of Wintringham and others who referred to the 'Blimp' mentality of senior officers as being stuffy and lacking in imagination. In particular, Wynne-Candy was reluctant to accept the view of his exiled German friend that the age of chivalry was dead and that war had to be fought by whatever means were necessary. The sympathetic portrayal of a German was unusual and the international exposure of the rather pathetic Wynne-Candy/'Blimp' character struck a raw nerve in the War Office. Wynne-Candy's early military career was based on that of the historical consultant for the film, General Brownrigg of London Home Guard, but his attitudes as a later Home Guard commander were more akin to those of Brigadier Whitehead, who had opposed the concept of Home Guard training and rejected the introduction of women into the Home Guard. With twisted irony, the film shows Wynne-Candy's photograph pasted into the *Picture Post* illustration of the instructors at the Osterley Training School. Released in a period when Home Guard morale was slipping, a film that showed the Home Guard as poorly led and ineffective was unwelcome to the War Office and Churchill tried unsuccessfully to have the film banned. Compton Mackenzie's story of the Home Guard on a remote Hebridean island in *Keep the Home Guard Turning* (1943) was in gentler vein but still had the theme of a pompous officer outwitted by the 'common man'. In real life the Commanding Officer of the Barra Home Guard, Mackenzie dedicated the book to his former comrades in the Inverness-shire (West) Home Guard, praising them for solving with laughter so many of the problems which beset them.[28] The follow-up to the book in 1947 was *Whiskey Galore*, which in 1949 was turned into a successful film and provided much of the inspiration for *Dad's Army*.

By 1943 the Home Guard had become a cultural institution, not only referenced in books and films but also defining its own cultural history. It used its role within morale-building entertainments to illustrate the changes in the organization from the desperate days of 1940. Home Guards were increasingly called upon to provide entertainment at local fetes to support campaigns such as 'Warship Week', 'Wings for Victory Week', and 'Salute the Soldier Week', all organized to persuade the public to help finance the war effort by purchasing war bonds and later for 'Holiday at Home' events. There was usually a comic element which was later echoed in the television series *Dad's Army*. On the evening of 18 May 1941 a company of the Stourbridge Battalion, Worcestershire Home Guard, entertained some 3,000 members of the public at a fete in the grounds of Field House at Clent. They began with a slapstick representation of the mounting of the first LDV post at Milton's Seat with the guard, dressed in civilian clothes, arriving with blankets, bottles of beer, etc. One of the sentries caused considerable laughter by 'shooting a rabbit'. The performance was designed to reinforce how quickly the Home Guard had become a well-equipped and organized force and so the LDV display was followed by a representation of a current, more efficient, Home Guard post, followed by skilled demonstrations of an attack in open formation, bayonet fighting and a bombing attack on a strongpoint. The means of mounting a road-block were also explained, including the arrival of a car full of 'refugees', who milled about the road in comic confusion, illustrating the importance of keeping the roads free of civilian refugees during an invasion. A 'fifth columnist' disguised as a British soldier then attempted to blow up the road-block, but was overpowered. The finale was the defence of a strongpoint by a detachment of the enemy, who were all wiped out to great applause![29]

Christmas 1943 saw the publication of *Home Guard Rhymes* by Lieutenant A.H. Watkins. It was full of gentle humour and proud reflections on their patriotism, with a recognition that the Home Guard was entering its final phase. 'A Patriotic Ode' chided those who moaned about the management of the seemingly endless war but avoided duty themselves, whilst *They Also Serve* reflected on their own patient service and tried to establish the Home Guard's place in the nation's defence:

Not ours the Nation's loud acclaim to share
With those who served at Sea, on Land, in Air;
Not ours to venture, or to give our all
For Honour, Freedom, Truth, at Duty's call.
No glorious deeds recorded in our name
Shall be emblazoned on the Book of Fame;
But this we ask: That it may be related
We also served, though we but stood and waited.[30]

There was also the obligatory tribute to their willingness to serve in the months of inadequate supply, represented by the *Legend of Bill Brown's Boots* and the efforts of a demented quartermaster to find a pair that fitted for a pernickety 'old sweat'.

Remarkably, histories of individual Home Guard units were published from as early as 1942, marking the changes brought about by the introduction of compulsory service but they mushroomed in 1944–45.[31] They share a quiet, self-deprecating humour with anecdotes intended to reinforce the bonds of comradeship in what were mainly seen as local souvenirs for members of the force. They are an important source for modern historians but should not be used uncritically; they were censored and many authors admitted taking a comedic licence with the truth to make the books more entertaining; without realizing it, they were preparing the way for a major rewrite of Home Guard history. A.W. Churchill admitted in his history of 7th Battalion, Shropshire Home Guard: 'What you are about to read is not wholly the truth but mainly the whole truth plus a little fiction added to taste.'[32] The year 1943 saw the first attempt at a national history of the Home Guard as *The Home Guard of Britain* by Charles Graves but the War Office carefully edited out Carden Roe's critical account of its confused role in the formation of the LDV (*see above*, p. 9):

> I am sorry to say that in the final expurgated edition of Charles Graves' book on the Home Guard, the censors have for some unknown reason removed entirely your dramatic story and also any mention of your name. I have told Charles Graves I personally consider this latter very unfair but he says he can do nothing about it until after the war when he can say what he likes ... I hope that in the course of time truth will out, but at the moment the War Office can suppress anything they want to and one cannot do much about it.[33]

With this in mind, the book unsurprisingly took a schoolmasterly tone with Tom Wintringham and the Osterley Home Guard School, criticizing Wintringham and Edward Hulton for being 'inclined to make a political issue of their admirable enterprise'. The section 'Who Inspired the LDV?' makes no mention of Wintringham and already the groundwork was being set to manipulate the 'authorized' version of the Home Guard within an acceptable vision of a country united, displaying humour in the face of overwhelming odds, and with no place for socialist radicalism.[34]

Wintringham and Orwell in 1940–41 had failed in their attempt to develop the Home Guard as a socialist militia due to their isolation from the organized political parties. Another chance to use the Home Guard for political ends came at the close of the war in the run-up to the general election of July 1945. The most famous end-of-war summary of the Home Guard was *Britain's Home Guard: a character study* (1945) by John Brophy, now remembered largely because of the gritty, albeit romanticized, portraits of Home Guardsmen by Eric Kennington. Brophy had written a number of bestselling Home Guard training manuals but was now able to express his political views. Published in January 1945, this was an elegiac account of the Home Guard as part of a wider campaign to give credit for victory to the sacrifice of ordinary working men and women, who thereby deserved a proper say in the conduct of the peace via a new Labour government. Kennington's portraits were not originally produced for this book. Politically conservative, he had been an official war artist in both world wars and the pastel portraits were originally commissioned by the War Office in 1943 for an exhibition and proposed booklet to encourage Home Guard recruitment.[35] Brophy reused them to escape the 'green and pleasant land' trope of early war propaganda and instead created an idealized vision of working-class volunteers going about their everyday jobs but, with steely-eyed determination, they also quietly served their country in the Home Guard. This is personified in the shepherd, Sergeant Stokes of Huntingdonshire Home Guard, leaning on his crook – but with his M1917 rifle and battledress casually visible in the background. There are older men, proudly wearing their First World War medals, such as Private Ockenden of Hampshire Home Guard, stoically reflecting that he has to go through war again – the ribbon of his Victoria Cross almost lost in the shadows as the epitome of the quiet hero. The political message was clear. On facing pages are images of a tough-looking young man, portrayed as 'Melvin Jones, Miner' and 'Melvin Jones, Corporal, Monmouthshire Home Guard'. The same device was also used in the film *One Man, Two Jobs* (1943), produced around the same time that Kennington was painting his portraits. The book was not well-received by a war-weary and cynical media, who found the illustrations overly romantic and overly dramatic. The *Manchester Guardian* was left with 'an uncomfortable doubt as to where art leaves off and propaganda begins'.[36] The book does, however, capture the spirit of the 1940 Home Guard in a way that few academic books have done:

> Most of them calculated that their personal task would be sacrificial; the utmost they could hope for was to fire a few shots from behind a hedge or a wall – perhaps, if they were lucky, to throw some petrol-bomb grenades and see a German tank or lorry catch fire – before they were blasted out of this life.[37]

Brophy had captured the mood of the country and on 5 July the Labour Party secured a remarkable landslide victory, despite the continuing personal popularity of Winston Churchill. The Home Guard had never been politicized as an institution but the shifting trend of the country to the left is clearly seen in the 1945 history of the Ministry of Food Home Guard, within the establishment bastion of the Civil Service. The author, Henry Smith, not only used the by now obligatory nationalist image of 'free men' defending the country from the Elizabethan militias onwards, he also offered a more modern internationalist context in 'this spontaneous rising of free men to defend their freedom against Fascism', placing the Home Guard in the spirit of the 'untrained and half-armed People's Army of the Spanish Civil War', and invited comparison with the French Forces of the Interior and the Yugoslav and Soviet partisans, who went into battle 'half-armed, half-trained and ill-equipped in defence of their freedom'.[38] Smith's personal politics, including an amnesia over the Hitler–Stalin Pact, are given away in his statement 'For many, to whom the only justification for war was the championship of the democratic way of life, the Russian alliance was a final confirmation of the ideological basis of the war, while the record of popular resistance emphasized the effectiveness of the part which the Home Guard might play in the war against Fascism.'[39]

As the world order began to change, with the economic dominance of the USA and the onset of the Cold War, a rose-tinted nostalgia for the idea of Britain standing alone, united and defiant, in 1940 quickly developed. The Home Guard offered a comfortable image of a once-united country. In his review of *Britain's Home Guard: a character study*, the veteran war reporter Henry Hamilton Fyfe (who had served in the Home Guard until it was discovered he was over 70 years of age) wrote in strangely enthusiastic terms of the 'warm, cloudless, delicious summer days of 1940' and provided a summary of the role of the Home Guard:

> The value of the Home Guard was that it prevented nuisance raids by parachute troops, which might have done a great deal of damage. It formed the second line of defence behind a very thin front line. It gave us more confidence, it strengthened our resolve never to give in, and don't forget that in 1940 all the world, not only the French but the Americans, not only the friends of Hitler but our friends, everywhere, believed that we should have to give in. The Home Guard was the answer we gave to those gloomy forebodings.[40]

There were some dissenting voices to this cosy interpretation. An article entitled 'Birth Pangs of the Home Guard' by Carden Roe was rejected by *Army Quarterly* in 1946 on the grounds that revelations of the conflict between the Home Forces and the War Office over the role of the Home Guard would be embarrassing.[41] Instead, the War Office cultivated the legend of the broomstick army and a manuscript History of the Home Guard produced for the War Office during the Cold War included a wholly inaccurate statement which harked back to a more innocent time and became part of later misunderstanding:

> for the first 12 months, no uniforms, arms or equipment were available but these began to be issued in 1941, in the meantime men wore their own clothes and boots, made do with shot-guns and .22 rifles, any old revolvers were dug out, broom handles were used for drilling purposes where rifles could not be borrowed from school armouries etc., but it was accepted with good humour and spirit as 'part of the game'.[42]

In March 1946 Winston Churchill created the powerful image of the Iron Curtain dividing former Allies and Europe. Wintringham's vision of the 'People's Army' was now an unwelcome reminder of the revolutionary threat of the early Home Guard and his contribution to the early development of the Home Guard was almost completely written out of the official version of events. Wintringham died in August 1949 and his passing was largely ignored. Even the *Daily Worker*, of which he had been founder and editor for many years, made no comment. Alan Wood wrote a despairing tribute in the *Tribune*:

> Here was a man who, during the war, was known to millions through *Picture Post*, the *Daily Mirror* and Penguin Books; as the prophet of the Home Guard his was an essential part in our finest hour. Could not one newspaper editor at least see an interest in the leader of that select band of Englishmen who had the honour of actively fighting for Spanish democracy? That is something for which he will always be remembered.[43]

By the late 1960s, following the jaded dismissal of its 1950s iteration, the Home Guard had drifted into dim memory, leaving a comfortable image of quiet pluck and determination, laced with cheerful good humour. The Home Guard of 1940 had become part of the iconography of Britain at war to the complete exclusion of its later history. Here was the broomstick army standing resolute against seemingly insurmountable odds as part of the same nostalgic image of cheerful Londoners carrying on their lives during the Blitz, or defeated 'Tommies' returning from Dunkirk with big smiles, the 'thumbs up' sign and a cup of tea. What was certainly not wanted in the period in which *Dad's Army* appeared on our television screens were stories of British volunteers being trained in how to make home-made bombs or mount a ruthless guerrilla warfare. This sounded rather too much like the terrorists that Britain was now confronting, and condemning, across the world.

Chapter Twelve

The 'Dad's Army' Effect

Today the Home Guard is commonly known as 'Dad's Army' but few realize that this term was entirely the invention in 1967 of Michael Mills, BBC television's head of comedy. Without the *Dad's Army* series, the existence of the Home Guard might have passed from popular memory, much as its First World War predecessor had done. Writer Jimmy Perry exaggerated only slightly when he claimed 'The Home Guard had never been discussed for twenty years before I got the idea of Dad's Army.'[1] *Dad's Army* ran for eighty-three episodes from 1968 to 1977. There was also a film (1971), a radio series of sixty-seven episodes (1974–76) and a musical stage play (1975). A revival film was released in 2016 but failed to repeat the magic. Jimmy Perry, a former Home Guard himself, relied heavily on 1940s reminiscences and wrote it in a spirit of affectionate tribute to his former comrades – but inadvertently created a legend of stereotypical characters that risked becoming more memorable than the originals. Danny Buckland wrote in the *Sunday Express* in 2014:

> Bumbling, comic and about as threatening as a jam roly-poly with custard, the Home Guard in the Second World War has been portrayed as a feather duster of a fighting force that could never make Hitler think again ... Seen through the prism of *Dad's Army*, it is hard to imagine the last line of defence as anything but a token effort likely to be swept aside by marauding Nazis ... The TV show's exquisite scripting of the antics of the platoon guarding the fictional seaside town of Walmington-on-Sea was so powerful that it now passes as an unofficial history of the Home Guard.[2]

Many veterans seethed at being apparently reduced to a comedy act. Maurice 'Peter' Bradshaw, who worked during the war in the Supermarine factory and as a member of Newbury LDV, remembered the initial phase of bayonets tied onto broomsticks, old rifles and shotguns but was adamant: 'The Home Guard, a lot of people I think have got the wrong impression from a certain television programme. Because it was never like that. They became quite a professional unit.'[3]

Perry had served in the Watford Home Guard as a teenager for two years from late 1941 whilst working in a munitions factory and until conscripted into the Royal Artillery in late 1943. He admitted that the character of 'Private Pike' was based on himself, whilst 'Corporal Jones' was based on an old French polisher who had served at Omdurman in 1898.[4] Perry captured the wartime cultural fiction of the Home Guard defending a timeless rural idyll of the 'green and pleasant land', although this time transferred to a quiet seaside town. He skilfully combined this with attacks on pompous authority and the class system in the spirit of the new medium of satirical television. In a period of seemingly endless industrial disputes, the series offered a 'feel-good' sense of national pride in a nostalgic memory of Britain's 'finest hour'. As written sources, he could draw on the wartime histories of Graves (1943) and Brophy and Kennington (1945), together with the comedic collections of Boothroyd (1941) and the quiet humour of Street (1942). He grew up with the radio broadcast of Robb Wilton's monologue 'The Day the War Broke Out' (*see above*, p. 194), whilst from the cinema came the farce of *Get Cracking* (1943). Although Perry cited the 1937 film *Oh Mr Porter* as an inspiration for the dynamics of the main characters, the Home Guard in *Whiskey Galore* (1949) was a clear influence. The latter has the pompous commanding officer in the form of Captain Waggett (Basil Radford), his ineffectual second-in-command George Campbell (Gordon Jackson), dim-witted private Angus MacCormac (Duncan Macrae) and the wily rest of the platoon. Street's *From Dusk Till Dawn* includes a discussion on the pomposity of some Home Guard officers but at the other extreme (as a clear precursor of *Dad's Army*'s 'Sergeant Wilson'), Street was warned not to try giving orders using well-bred civilian politeness, in the form of 'I say, old chap, would you mind attacking that fellow.'[5] Perry may also have remembered the futility of the 1950s Home Guard and was cognizant of the 1960s audience, sceptical of official institutions and bound up in the Vietnam War protest movement that had contributed to Joan Littlewood's 1963 anti-war stage play *Oh What a Lovely War*.

> Dad's Army became a metaphor for valiant but self-important leadership and incompetent soldiering that was applied critically to numerous political and military developments from the late 1960s onwards.[6]

After the first episodes, a wave of correspondents shared their humorous stories of life in the Home Guard and some were incorporated into later storylines. These veteran contributors were pleased that the Home Guard was at last getting a mention in popular culture and realized full well they were contributing to a comedy series, which influenced the experiences they chose to share with the writers. Criticism only emerged in the 1990s after the programme had taken on a wider cultural significance and was being treated as a satirical history of the Home Guard. 'Dad's Army' had now become a synonym for the Home Guard and a metaphor for military pomposity and incompetence.

The portrayal of the Home Guard for the television series had to be selective and sanitized to fit the comedic format. The basic setting for the series is the church hall as a convenient open space for the set, but the smoke-filled back room of the local public house would probably have been more appropriate as the HQ. In an interview for the BBC in 1990 Perry admitted that the platoon of elderly bunglers he scripted deviated in many respects from his own experience in the Home Guard. Most of his Watford platoon were young men waiting to be called up into the services; his platoon evolved into 'a very efficient guerrilla force' and he was part of the commando section of that platoon. As early as 1943 Charles Graves had pointed out that the average age of the Home Guard by then was just under 30 years but the myth of the old age pensioner Home Guard, as epitomized by 'Corporal Jones' of *Dad's Army*, became so strong that this fact was greeted as a stunning new discovery by the media when reported by the National Archives in the twenty-first century.[7] Former Home Guard Fred Woolford from Romford, Essex, knew better:

> So many people soak up that silly programme called *Dad's Army* but in truth it should have been called *Kid's Army* for that is what it was. The majority of our company were youngsters like myself and my kid brother who was 15 at the time.[8]

There were undoubtedly many old soldiers in the early stages of the LDV/Home Guard, before they were weeded out as part of the increasing professionalism of the force and before the physical training took its toll. They were often extolled as examples of the indefatigable British fighting spirit but, in any case, the time-span between the First and Second World Wars was short enough for a veteran of the former to be still very useful in 1940:

> In a high percentage of cases the toughs in any given units were not the young but the older men, between forty-two and fifty, who had seen active service. They might not have been so fast on their feet, but they knew what to do and knew when to stick their toes in.[9]

The small percentage of men who had served in the Boer War or even earlier captured public imagination and they were eminently newsworthy, being given undue prominence in the contemporary press. The hero of Graham Greene's 'The Lieutenant Died Last' (1940) was a wily Boer War veteran who still held a grudge against the 'Bojer' (Boer) ambushes.[10] 'Private Pike' is the representative of the younger volunteers in the *Dad's Army* series but even he is a young professional, working at the local bank. There was no sign of Fred Woolford's 'Kid's Army' and the 16-year-olds who helped man searchlight sites, and this age bracket has received nothing like the attention given to the older ex-soldiers. The tacit approval of the War Office to allow boys in their mid-teens into the ranks of the Home Guard was a norm at the time, when the school-leaving age was still only 14. George Orwell's complaint about the Spanish Civil War's anti-Stalinist Partido Obero de Unificación Marxista (POUM) militia involving children as young as 11 was not about the morality of the situation, but about the stamina of the 'wretched children of my section'.[11]

The pomposity of 'Captain Mainwaring', who automatically took his commission through his civilian status as the local bank manager, was undoubtedly reflected in many Home Guard units of the time, where the local social order was transferred to military rank. The Mainwaring character is deferential to higher authority but in reality one of the great problems for the War Office was that Home Guard officers, some of whom had held far higher rank in previous service, were not afraid of telling professional soldiers how to do their job and, especially in 1940–41, ignored the normal chain of command to raise complaints in the press or in Parliament. The quality of officers improved from November 1940 when officer selection boards were established and Simon Fine then praised the Home Guard for its democratic process:

> While I was at Group I saw a gate porter advanced from corporal to platoon commander over the heads of his civilian bosses. I watched a lieutenant rise in eight months to become battalion commander. I do not know his civilian salary, but I am certain that it can be counted most easily in hundreds. He took command of a battalion in which at least six men in the same service as himself held rank under him, while their salaries could be counted by the thousands. This scrupulous impartiality on the part of the selecting officers worked a miracle.[12]

Confusion over the authenticity of the television series was enhanced by Perry's use of a 'constructed' realism, as described by Morgan-Russell, which deliberately confused wartime fact and 1960s fiction. The series uses a modern theme song (written in a 1940s style by Jimmy Perry) but sung by wartime icon Bud Flanagan. The opening credits for the first series used mock 'wartime' footage of the Walmington-on-Sea Home Guard with a commentary by the wartime newsreel commentator E.V.H. Emmett.[13] The uniforms, equipment and settings *looked* very authentic but for purists there were a number of errors, notably the use of binocular cases rather than proper Home Guard ammunition pouches. (This error was faithfully reproduced in the 2016 *Dad's Army* film.) Nonetheless, for most viewers, the series had an authentic feel and it entered the psyche almost as a documentary of the Home Guard, although this was never the original intention. It was not a problem faced by another comedy series of the BBC set in the Second World War. *'Allo, 'Allo* (1982–92) is a pantomime representation of the French Resistance (a parody of the BBC series *Secret Army*) that could not possibly be mistaken for the real thing. By contrast, in *Dad's Army* the outline narrative of an episode is usually based on a nugget of historical information, but the comic scenarios within this drive the story to the limits of absurdity.

Dad's Army thereby managed to be a series that was simultaneously absurd but had an authentic feel. There was the chaotic rush to volunteer following Eden's broadcast, issues of rationing and the black market, shortage of weapons, and conflicts in the contemporary class system. The platoon veered between being heroic and patriotic or inefficient and futile. Admirers can point to its authentic origins whilst critics can despair over the dominant sense of absurdity. One of the reasons for the enduring popularity of the series is that in its essence the Home Guard plot line was simply a device for exploring relationships between a disparate group of individuals. For Graham McCann, 'Dad's Army, deep down, was not really about the war. It was about England, it was about us.'[14] It appealed to the British fondness for amateurism and improvisation, to anyone who at one time or another had suffered a pompous or an ineffective boss or had tried to contain the enthusiasm of an elderly relative. It spoke to the British fascination with the class system and social status (note the classic contemporary 'Class sketch', featuring John Cleese, Ronnie Barker and Ronnie Corbett, from *The Frost Report* of 1966). All this was achieved in the format of a single community, in the spirit of wartime propaganda.

Dad's Army coincided with the start of the Irish 'Troubles' and the gentle humour was more comfortable than any reminder that the Second World War Home Guard had been trained in the skills of ambush, roadside bombs and improvised explosives, or that the Auxiliary Units had been taught how to create terror by the mutilation of German sentries. It seemed best not to acknowledge that Britain was prepared to use terrorist tactics in 1940. Women had a minor role in the series, being either incidental to the plot or used as a device to create conflict between the platoon and the outside world. In the episode 'Mum's Army' (Series Four), three women try to join the platoon, but they are represented as a sexual distraction in subservient and disruptive roles that reflect many wartime cartoons of women and the Home Guard. The original 1940s humour ignored the complexities of the contribution of women to the Home Guard and *Dad's Army* might be taken as accurately representing this dismissive attitude, although a chance was lost to offer a better representation of women's service.

The episodes meshed the nostalgic concept of the British 'stiff upper lip' and fondness for the inspired amateur with some of the more desperate aspects of the Home Guard in 1940–41. One memorable scene occurs when the early LDV crouched behind a rickety barricade and waited to meet the enemy with 'Mainwaring' and 'Wilson' discussing how best to use their two rounds of ammunition. The atmosphere reflected genuine experience in the summer of 1940, when gallows humour was a way of coping with the anticipation of imminent death. Yet in the 1960s and 1970s the comedy outweighed the historic context. A film version of *Dad's Army*, set in 1940, was released in 1971 but had little of the innocent charm of the series. McCann concluded: 'The move from one medium to the other had been ill-conceived: the cinema framed the situation comedy, it gave it a beginning, middle and end, whereas television allowed it to flow.'[15] Although the television series took the Walmington-on-Sea platoon of the Home Guard from 1940 to 1944, the uniforms changing along the way, the writing remained locked in the chaos and desperation of the 1940 invasion scares as providing the best comedy potential, ignoring the increasing professionalism of the later Home Guard, in which the older members of the *Dad's Army* platoon would not have been tolerated and nights of endless guard duty were a poor basis for comedy.

It became difficult for modern viewers to appreciate the original context of the humour. The editor of the *Bystander* in the First World War put the problem well in introducing the first issue of Captain Bruce Bairnsfather's biting collection of cartoons, *Fragments from France* (1916): 'Here is the great war reduced to a grim and gruesome absurdity. It is not fun poked by a mere looker-on, it is the fun felt in the war by one who has been through it.'[16] The anecdotes told by veterans of the Home Guard took on a different aspect when viewed out of context by a different generation, and since the series first aired the publishing industry has sought a comic interpretation in virtually any story relating to the Home Guard, to tap into the huge *Dad's Army* market. One of the first books that the series spawned was Norman Longmate's 1974 *The Real Dad's Army*. It was the first modern history of the Home Guard and it has had an enduring influence, republished in 2016 to accompany the second *Dad's Army* film. It was intimately connected to the BBC television series and validated its comedic image of the Home Guard, rather than presenting an objective history of Britain's last line of defence. Instead the publisher promising on the dust-jacket 'a wealth of hilarious anecdotes as well as all the unlikely facts to produce the first popular history of the Home Guard to be written since the war'.

The book was originally commissioned to accompany an exhibition at the Imperial War Museum that was, in turn, to coincide with the start of the seventh series of the *Dad's Army* television series. Longmate was a journalist and a producer of history programmes for the BBC. The book was written in just two months and relied mainly on published sources from the 1940s, notably Graves (1943), together with anecdotes that had accumulated since the launch of *Dad's Army*, rather than from original archival research, and was imbued with the atmosphere of the first six series. It also reflected the weariness and frustration suffered by a once-teenage conscripted member of the Home Guard in 1943:

> And yet, smile as one may at the excesses of its fire-eating commanders, begrudge as one may the millions of man-hours that might have been more profitably or pleasurably spent, there is about the Home Guard (especially in its early days) a touch of nobility as well as absurdity, that makes one almost proud to have belonged to it.[17]

Almost proud – but not quite! Longmate was remarkably dismissive of their record, acknowledging that some accused the Home Guard of merely playing at soldiers in 1940.[18] Yet any argument as to whether they would have been useful in stopping the invasion misses the brutal point – they were *expected* to die for the sake of buying time for the regular forces. For Longmate, however, their contribution in 1940 was merely psychological – to provide 'an outlet for the eager patriotism of many men'.[19] He ignores both the practical contribution to a defence in depth and its political importance in helping to retain the confidence of the US government in the ability of Britain to resist invasion. By contrast, the 1941 survey of the Home Guard undertaken on behalf of the US War Department was highly complimentary and advised its use as a model for a similar body to be created in the USA.[20] Longmate also concluded that in the later years of its existence, when service was compulsory, it probably did 'more harm than good' in tying up resources and exhausting its members (of which he was one).[21] He described the fear of enemy parachute landings in 1944 as 'complete nonsense, as British intelligence must have known'.[22] In fact, British intelligence had been very concerned in 1944 about this threat (*see above*, p. 45). There is a selectivity about Longmate's chosen anecdotes and illustrations that suggests a deliberate effort to present an image that matches the television series rather than offering an objective history. The weaponry is misleadingly represented as archaic. Longmate uses staged photographic stills from Home Guard exercises that, reproduced out of context, can easily seem ridiculous. One famous image shows a 'German spy' dressed as a woman pushing a 'pram' who has just wiped out a lax guard post. In isolation this might seem a laughable pantomime but the exercise of which it was part was serious enough. The men were being trained where to best place men to guard against being caught unawares at a checkpoint and avoid being caught in a crossfire. The tableau was a memorable reminder of what might occur if they dropped their guard. Such images have been frequently used only for their comedic value rather than appreciating the underlying motive. Similarly, Simon Morgan-Russell in 2004 commented on a suggestion from the *Home Guard Training Manual* of Langdon-Davies:

> Home Guard training manuals . . . themselves read like handbooks for Dad's Army's comic plotlines. Anti-tank exercises, for example, call for the construction of a simulated German tank from wood and sacking mounted on a car.[23]

In the understandable absence of a convenient tank as a practice target, the construction of a simple dummy version as a teaching aid on how to organize an ambush was an obvious and effective solution (Plate 11). It was the placement of the ambush party that was the key element of the exercise rather than the nature of the target. The 1941 Instruction for the Home Guard on how to construct road-blocks explains the importance of the careful positioning of the ambush team:

> As the enemy approach the block they should see NO ONE. The vehicles should be attacked from unseen positions by bombs and any other suitable weapons which are available. If a vehicle tries to turn or drive off the road it should be trapped by hidden ditches, anti-tank mines (if available), etc. If they try to get out of the vehicle they should be shot at from unexpected directions by unseen riflemen.[24]

Longmate regards as a joke the idea of stopping a tank by laying down soup plates to try to fool the Panzer commanders into believing they were anti-tank mines.[25] He ignores the fact that this was a method proven in the retreat to Dunkirk (*see above*, p. 101) The only positive lesson he reports from the Osterley Training School was that they were taught how to 'live off the country' by boiling potatoes in one's steel helmet.[26] There is no mention of the training in making improvised explosives, techniques of street fighting and the use of camouflage, or the fact that the regular army recognized the Osterley School as a pioneer in the instruction of street fighting and irregular warfare. In line with the emphasis of the television series, the role of women in the Home Guard gets barely two paragraphs. The interpretation of the Auxiliary Units as having no real connection to the Home Guard (as published by David Lampe in 1968) is accepted without question.

Longmate made the claim that the Home Guard was in 'a unique position as the only army in history to have killed more of its countrymen than its enemies'.[27]

This jibe referred to the dangers of failing to stop at checkpoints but ignores the point that the sentries, whether army or Home Guard, would have been derelict of duty if they had not followed their orders and opened fire. The accusation fails to consider the active service role of the Home Guard in anti-aircraft and coastal artillery and there are no figures of how many lives were *saved* by the hazardous work of the Home Guard bomb disposal teams or their participation in Civil Defence. The first award for gallantry to a Home Guard was on 17 September 1940 when a Military Medal was awarded to Glyn Jones for his actions during an air raid on 12/13 July. Two posthumous George Crosses were awarded. The first was in May 1941 to Section Commander George Inwood for self-sacrifice during a Birmingham air raid on 15/16 October 1940 when he rescued two men from a gas-filled cellar. The second was to Lieutenant William Foster, who threw himself onto a live grenade after it had rebounded into the firing position, saving the life of his comrades. Other awards included 3 further George Crossed, 13 George Medals, 408 BEMs, 396 MBEs and 129 OBEs.

Longmate's book was seriously flawed but it provided a pseudo-academic justification for the vision of the Home Guard as presented in the television series. It remained the best-known published source on the Home Guard until S.P. MacKenzie's *The Home Guard: a military and political history* (1995) and was still popular enough to be republished in 2016 with new cover artwork. Therein lay a problem. Few reviewers in the popular press appear to have realized that the text dated back to the 1970s and was now considerably out of date. The old myths risked being reborn:

> Do Panic! How the real Dad's Army never had a hope: Robert Hardman looks inside a new book about the much-loved military institution which has been a national joke for years ... a new book charting the overzealous, trigger-happy capers of the Home Guard, with comparisons drawn to those documented in the BBC show ... Norman Longmate, who was a real-life Private Pike having joined his local unit aged 17, researched some of the most farcical tales of the wartime volunteer service for his book – *The Real Dad's Army*.[28]

The need to associate with one or another of the *Dad's Army* characters was typical of many veteran reminiscences of the time and poses a problem in establishing an accurate narrative of the Home Guard. The image that the television series presented became self-perpetuating and correspondents would write saying they recognized elements of 'Private Pike' or 'Captain Mainwaring' in their platoons, providing appropriate stories. But where were the stories of the women Home Guard or the local versions of Tom Wintringham? Such stories were not perceived at the time as being part of the required canon. The problem of relying on oral history was not new, as Peter Fleming had recognised in 1957, warning that 'The stories they tell of the period have become better, but not more veracious, with the passage of time. Rumours are remembered as facts, and ... the sequence of events is blurred.[29] The problem was worse when Jimmy Perry and

Norman Longmate began to gather anecdotes after another ten years. The problem of over-reliance on oral history was discussed again in the early 2000s when Penny Summerfield and Corinna Peniston-Bird were conducting interviews with the diminishing number of former Home Guard volunteers for the book *Contesting Home Defence*. They highlighted the issue that 'Individuals borrow from versions of the past that circulate in the public domain, when making sense of and expressing their personal pasts.'[30] Authentic memories of the 1940s were being distorted and modified by false memories derived from what they saw on the television screen or read in books – or what they believed the researchers wanted to hear. Memories are important cultural sources but they are not necessarily accurate histories.

A reaction against *Dad's Army* slowly developed in academic circles: Keith Gulvin's study *Kent Home Guard* (1980) is noticeably less peppered with humorous anecdotes and contains more detail on organization and equipment, and the photographs of battle exercises look altogether more realistic. A new era of research began in 1995 with the publication of S.P. MacKenzie's *The Home Guard: a military and political history*. For the first time it was based upon original archival research and academic analysis. The review by the *Bulletin of the Military History Society* praised the work as being the definitive history of a neglected subject and there is perhaps an implied criticism of Longmate (1974) in the comment 'the writing is refreshingly free of oral and anecdotal evidence'.[31] The book for the first time tried to analyse the military and political impact of the Home Guard. Even here, the writer could not escape the gravitational pull of *Dad's Army* and one flaw was the author's continuing assertion of the archaic nature of the weaponry. The Introduction felt obliged to credit the authenticity of *Dad's Army*, albeit heavily qualified:

> As my research progressed, I came to suspect that in some ways at least the fictional platoon of Walmington-on-Sea was not as far off the mark as I had once thought: full of exaggeration, of course, emphasising the absurd, but nevertheless not that distant from reality in at least some respects.[32]

Dad's Army had become a powerful marketing brand that few could avoid. Fact and fantasy were further blurred with the production of a spoof Home Guard training manual, written by 'Captain Mainwaring' (Guy Adams) with his own backstory.[33] Stephen Cullen took up this point in 2011 when apologizing for the title of his book *In Search of the Real Dad's Army*:

> The term 'Dad's Army', which was not used during the war, has a high recognition value. A number of books on the force have used 'Dad's Army' in their titles, and the marketing department of Pen and Sword Books was insistent that it be used again in the title of this book.[34]

Confusion reigned between *Dad's Army* the television series and 'Dad's Army' as a modern nickname for the Home Guard. The name has now become a metaphor for any sign of military incompetency. The two were entwined in Graham

McCann's 2002 *Dad's Army: The Story of a Classic Television Show*, which assumed that the real Home Guard was inherently ridiculous and that this was encapsulated in television's *Dad's Army*. McCann dismisses the anti-aircraft role of 'some of the more able-bodied' of the Home Guard as allowing them to finally engage the enemy 'if only at five miles up'. McCann concluded that 'if Hitler had invaded in strength, it is unlikely that the Home Guard, casting around for lengths of tram line to incapacitate tanks, or hurling lethal glassware at motor-cyclists, would have lasted long'. Again this ignores the simple fact that in the chilling anti-invasion strategy, the Home Guard was acknowledged as being essentially suicidal. With hindsight, the British strategy in 1940 might seem cruelly laughable – but it was no joke to those expected to implement it.

In 2011 the remarkable diary of Rodney Foster was published, after being found in a car boot sale and then sold on e-Bay.[35] It is the diary of an ex-Indian Army lieutenant colonel who was 58 when he joined what was then the LDV. It is a story of everyday life under the constant threat of bombing on 'Hellfire Corner' in Kent. Never intended for wartime publication, it is unfettered by the need to please the censors. His comments are honest and pithy; he considers Churchill to be a windbag and blunderer, and is cynical about British propaganda; he is disturbed by the area bombing of Cologne, he believes that Churchill's abandonment of Poland to the Russians, as agreed at the Yalta Conference, is a disgrace. Within this wider context are his experiences in the Home Guard. There are initial moans about disorganization (of the country as a whole, not just the Home Guard), stories of exercises and mock battles, but the overall impression is one of the workaday with Foster preparing guard rosters, and collecting and returning equipment. It is the 'ordinary' content of the diary which makes it so interesting to a historian but it was difficult for modern publishers to escape the promotional value of *Dad's Army*. The Introduction feels obliged to state 'These diaries may only now have come to light, but they could easily have been the inspiration for the television series.'[36] The popular press still had enormous difficulty in being able to consider the Home Guard without recourse to the easy stereotypes provided by *Dad's Army*. The review of the Foster Diary by the *Daily Mail* twisted the text to a remarkable degree:

> The Home Guard was more farcical than the comedy sitcom Dad's Army which ribbed the antics of their real-life counterparts, a diary has revealed.
>
> The newly unearthed journal, sold at an Exeter car boot sale, has lifted the lid of the real Home Guard. And it makes Captain Mainwaring and his platoon of hapless recruits look positively professional.
>
> The journal kept by a Home Guard officer called Rodney Foster features a string of incidents that could well have come straight from the TV scripts.[37]

Significantly, no attention is drawn by the publisher or reviews in the popular press to other stories in the book, which, if connected to the Home Guard, would no doubt have been automatically characterized as hilarious or incompetent. On 3 July Foster claimed that Hurricanes 'flew in the wrong direction' and, on 4 July an explosion which put out all the lights in the town proved to have been caused by an officer of the Royal Engineers demonstrating a new type of anti-tank bomb on top of the main gas main! On 22 September there was a tragic incident when an RE sapper trod on a mine that he had laid the previous day. Even worse, on 24 February 1941 an RE sergeant led a party of infantrymen into the beach minefield, resulting in the deaths of seven soldiers and injuring five more.[38] No mention is made of these incidents in reviews because they do not relate to the television series. A rare social history of day-to-day life in wartime Kent is thereby marketed more as an adjunct to a television series than as a primary source in its own right. Similarly, the publication in 2010 of a new edition of the 1945 *Home Guard Humour* by 'HHT' has a new introduction by Campbell McCutcheon that states 'This little booklet of Home Guard Humour shows that the japes and scrapes that the Walmington-on-Sea platoon got into were no different from that of any other unit of the Home Guard.'[39] With the *Dad's Army* image firmly in mind, one review described it as the story of 'a bumbling group of ill-equipped soldiers', but even in a book of cartoons depicting the Home Guard, the text is a light but factual account of the Home Guard with no pantomime stories. Cartoons, by their very nature, are designed to exaggerate and caricature ordinary events for comic effect and the incidents were not exclusive to the Home Guard. Some are reminiscent of the cartoons drawn by Spike Milligan to illustrate his disorderly Second World War service in the Royal Artillery. Here again is a desperate need to put anything connected with the Home Guard into the framework of *Dad's Army*. What is true is the original conclusion to *Home Guard Humour*: 'Whatever happens, the humour which seeped through every hard circumstance will be remembered long after grim days have been dimmed by time.'[40]

The work of MacKenzie, and the launch at the same time of the English Heritage *Defence of Britain Project*, inspired a new wave of research, largely focused on county histories and with a particular interest in the Auxiliary Units (*see* Chapter Four). The extent of official documentary evidence contained within the National Archives was realized and for the first time local anecdotal evidence could be tested against detailed analysis of documentary evidence. The humour could at last be properly set within the reality of the Home Guard. Researchers were all too aware that the opportunities to interview veterans were slipping away but there was now a different tone to the stories, with a clear reaction from both researchers and veterans against the image of the Home Guard as presented by *Dad's Army*. One of the most detailed studies was Austin Ruddy's *To the Last Round: the Leicestershire and Rutland Home Guard 1940–1945* (2007). The Introduction had a section headed 'Setting the Record Straight':

> Nowadays the Home Guard has become synonymous with *Dad's Army* and is rarely mentioned without reference to its satirical offspring. The much-loved, classic BBC sitcom has become as much a part of British folklore as the organization it mimicked. And not without reason. Many Home Guard veterans recall amusing anecdotes that would not have been out of place in *Dad's Army* ... But the comparison ends there. *Dad's Army* was conceived with comic intent; the Home Guard was conceived in desperate times with

> deadly serious intent. This key point seems to have been all but lost and forgotten in the shadow of the programme's success and, to a certain degree, has tarnished the Home Guard as a light-hearted joke itself.[41]

But the *Dad's Army* vision was hard to kill. For Midge Gilles in *Waiting for Hitler* (2006), 'Every unit had its own cast of comic characters ... *Dad's Army* ... was a sitcom waiting to happen.'[42] In 2016 the *Telegraph* dismissed the contribution of Osterley: 'As it turned out, Osterley's greatest legacy was not the skills it taught, but the material it provided for British comedy.'[43]

One particular consequence of the comedic impression of the Home Guard as provided by *Dad's Army* was that the oral history of veterans from the secret commando organization of the Home Guard – the Auxiliary Units – over-emphasized their distinction from the parent body and also played on the interest of many researchers on the dramatic, not to say gory, aspects of their role. In turn, this helped create the myth of the Auxiliary Units as a secret resistance rather than as a commando force designed to operate only during the actual invasion. It was not until 2004 that Hugh Purcell in *The Last English Revolutionary* managed to revive the story of Tom Wintringham as a guiding spirit of the Home Guard.[44] By this time Wintringham had been almost completely written out of history. His ambition of turning the Home Guard into a 'People's Army' and a ruthless guerrilla force had been an irritation to the War Office, one that the Establishment had tolerated in 1940 but would rather forget. In the late 1960s revival of interest in the Home Guard, his story did not fit with what became an entrenched vision of *Dad's Army* as the bumbling Home Counties stereotype.

In recent years historical re-enactment has become a popular means of trying to both entertain and educate the public and the Home Guard has become a growing element. Unfortunately it is not always clear what exactly the groups are trying to portray. Some groups explicitly represent the television series, 'Private Pike's' scarf and all. Others focus on nostalgia rather than historic integrity. Some have been evangelical in trying to present a more accurate impression of the Home Guard, although the public invariably arrive with cries of 'Don't Panic', 'They don't like it up 'em' and other *Dad's Army* catchphrases. An event organizer once asked a group to make the drill more like *Dad's Army* as the re-enactors were taking it too seriously! By contrast, Bill Allington, formerly of Worcestershire Home Guard, was unimpressed by another re-enactment's group attempt at drill, pointing out that an ex-Guards NCO had trained his unit. Derek Pearson similarly remembered his training by 'old sweats' being much better than that which he later received from the Worcestershire Regiment at Norton Barracks.[45] When done properly, re-enactment can inform families of their relative's contribution to the war effort, and veterans have commented that they are pleased to be at last treated with respect.

The repackaging of old texts such as Norman Longmate's *The Real Dad's Army*, or retitling works such as Arthur Ward's 1997 *Resisting the Nazi Invader* as the 2013 *Churchill's Secret Defence Army*, means that old ideas are recirculated without it being obvious to the reader that they have been superseded by fresh research. The first line of enquiry is now often the internet but many websites referring to the Home Guard and the Auxiliary Units have relied on out-of-date texts that are rarely referenced or dated as a guide for the reader. Old ideas are given a false modernity and become an ever-more entrenched part of the cultural psyche, creating their own orthodoxy. Visions of the bumbling Home Guard and the icy Auxiliary Units have become cherished elements of the British national culture and there is a reluctance to acknowledge any argument that casts doubt on either image.

Conclusions

We also served, though we but stood and waited.[1]

The Home Guard occupies a unique place in the history and mythology of the Second World War Home Front, whilst its First World War predecessor, the VTC, has been almost completely forgotten. The most important single reason for this difference is undoubtedly the interest generated by the popular television series *Dad's Army*. The extent to which an objective history of the Home Guard has been distorted by vagaries of memory and shaped by modern media is a salutary warning as to how quickly, and how deeply, historical myths can become entrenched and become the new orthodoxy.

Histories of the Home Guard have been dominated by a 'bottom-up' approach, relying on the personal reminiscences of individual volunteers and wartime local histories, often full of humour and set within a carefully manipulated wartime image. But the local perspective can differ considerably from the more strategic concerns of the dry official records. Each source has its own validity but must be combined to offer a balanced assessment. The impact of the television series *Dad's Army* introduced a third element to the Home Guard story. Its popularity was such that no subsequent history could avoid referencing the agenda set by the writing of Jimmy Perry. At first, veterans were keen to be part of the television image and selected reminiscences to match, trying to see an element of the television characters in their own experiences. A change was apparent after the huge popularity of the series accidentally gave it the status of a semi-documentary history of the Home Guard. Snippets of historic fact had been elevated to comic absurdity for the purposes of entertainment but the absurdity itself came to be regarded by the public and the media as the truth. Historians were not immune to the gravitational pull of *Dad's Army* and the supposed archaic weaponry and bumbling incompetence of a body of pensioners became the automatic starting point of new histories. One consequence of the dismissive attitude towards the Home Guard was that veterans of the Auxiliary Units began to rewrite their own history to distance themselves from the general service battalions; the levels of secrecy were over-stressed and their skills, including as ruthless assassins, exaggerated. They were assumed to be the home front equivalent of the French resistance and SOE, even inventing the title of 'British Resistance Organization' – a romantic interpretation that came at the expense of misunderstanding their role within the wider strategy of anti-invasion defence. Tropes have been repeated from one publication to the next, reliant on oral history and received wisdom. Any material that did not fit the orthodox image, including the criticism of the organization in Nigel Oxenden's contemporary official history of the Auxiliary Units, was ignored.

The *Dad's Army* series almost completely ignored the relationship of women to the Home Guard. In many respects it was an accurate reflection of the attitude that had existed during the war and beyond. Women had volunteered for the LDV from the outset and served unofficially throughout the war in administration (in which their role was especially valued), first aid, intelligence, signalling and catering sections. Viscount Bridgeman, the Director General of the Home Guard, deserves considerable credit in trying to put such roles on an official basis but he had to face opposition not only from the Ministries of Labour and Home Security, which wanted to see women directed into other forms of national service, but also from those women who would accept nothing less than a full combat role in the Home Guard. The War Office avoided drawing any public attention to the work of the women volunteers to avoid controversy and at a local level the men, whilst appreciating the assistance of women, did not see them as a core element of the Home Guard. Women were, therefore, barely acknowledged in most wartime local histories of the Home Guard and their contribution began to be forgotten. Consequently, there was little in the published record for Jimmy Perry to draw upon as a source for *Dad's Army*. It is only recently that interest in the women who worked with the Home Guard has been revived. In redressing the balance, however, there has been a tendency to view the subject in isolation and from the perspective of the twenty-first century, focusing on the demands for gender equality, as represented by Edith Summerskill and the Women's Home Defence Corps demanding a combat role for women in the Home Guard. Yet in the wider context, most women sought parity with the existing women's branches of the armed services (the ATS, WAAF and WRNS), none of which had a direct combat role. As a consequence, modern research has tended to devalue the practical contribution of organizations such as the MTC and WVS that did not challenge the status quo in the same way.

Many of the problems surrounding the Home Guard arose from its rushed formation, with no clear idea in the War Office or government of its intended purpose, whether special constabulary, observer force or militia. The confusion extended to Churchill, who particularly wavered over the role of women. Even in the immediate aftermath of Dunkirk, General Ironside (C-in-C Home Forces) did not regard the LDV as an important element in his anti-invasion plan. If this was a 'People's War', it was still to be fought by proper soldiers, a perspective that was to cause great confusion for sympathizers in the USA, where the American Committee for Defense of British Homes collected weapons on the mistaken assumption that the British government would want to arm individual householders. This campaign had more propaganda than practical value but it provided a tangible way for US citizens to show support for the Allied cause and help build a political climate that allowed the passage of the Lend-Lease Act in 1941.

The volunteers quickly became impatient over the problems of strategy and supply, simply wanting a gun to defend the country against invasion and a more aggressive role than the War Office originally envisaged. In their individual frustration over the lack of a rifle, it was difficult for them to appreciate how rapidly thousands of weapons were being imported from the USA and distributed on a strategic basis. It was also difficult to explain that the War Office did not necessarily see the need for them all to have a weapon! The image of the 'broom-stick army' has dominated the popular perception of the Home Guard. Any and every weapon issued to the Home Guard seemed incapable of being described in other than comedic terms, despite the similar shortfalls in the rest of the army. This has obscured the scale of the British army's reliance on makeshift weapons after the losses at Dunkirk. All home defence forces in 1940 were supplied with the Molotov cocktail and SIP grenade, not just the Home Guard; the Royal Artillery was obliged to use cobbled together nineteenth-century naval 6-pdr guns as anti-tank weapons before passing them on to the Home Guard; RAF and army Anti-Aircraft units were issued with the majority of 'Croft Pikes'; the 8th Army received the 'Sticky Bomb' before the Home Guard; and the RAF Regiment had priority over the Home Guard for the unique Smith gun. The Northover Projector and 29mm Spigot Mortar were designed for both army and Home Guard use, although delays in production led them to be issued primarily to the Home Guard as second-line troops.

General Brooke elevated the Home Guard to a core part of the anti-invasion strategy from late July 1940 by putting them at the heart of the defence of 'nodal points'. The Home Guard constantly strained against the limitations of what was essentially a static defence, trying to re-establish the concept of the First World War VTC in guerrilla warfare. Any consideration as to how effective the Home Guard might have been in opposing an invasion must first dispense with the idea that the Home Guard was a body of pensioners as represented in *Dad's Army*. In the main, it was a force of fit teenagers and men in reserved occupations, including dockers, railway workers, miners and agricultural labourers, many with previous military experience. But in any invasion they were not expected to win battles – they were expected to die while buying time, through constant harrying of the enemy, for the regular forces to regroup. The men were well aware of their sacrificial role in 1940–41, making their readiness to face the invader with whatever weapon they could lay their hands on even more remarkable. In the shadows the hidden patrols of the Auxiliary Units were part of that same plan; they too were expendable after completing their allocated primary demolition targets. Everything was subservient to buying precious hours for the armour of the field army to concentrate for a counter-attack. In those circumstances the Home Guard chose to literally laugh at danger and their humour has become one of their enduring legacies.

As the realistic chances of invasion diminished, the Home Guard provided what might have been their most useful service in the war – taking over duties in Anti-Aircraft Command, coastal artillery and bomb disposal, guarding against the possibility of enemy 'spoiling' raids prior to D-Day whilst simultaneously providing a necessary 'enemy' for troops training for Allied operations, all of which allowed regular forces to be deployed overseas and to train for D-Day. Thousands were effectively on active service. After most had carried out a full day's work, they spent endless nights on guard duty and, for many men, boredom and a continuous struggle against exhaustion were now the main threats. Beyond their practical value the Home Guard also had a political and propaganda importance. Churchill continued to use the Home Guard, located within every community, as a visible reminder of the threat of invasion long after any real danger had passed, helping to maintain national unity in the face of increasing hardship. The Home Guard also had a sense of adventure, mixed with improvisation and innovation, that, unfettered by military discipline, had wider applications. The training school at Osterley became a pioneer of guerrilla warfare, anti-tank warfare and street fighting that meant even regular army officers signed up for its courses. The greatest compliment to the unofficial Home Guard training schools at Osterley and Burwash was for them to be taken over by the regular army.

The fear of MI5 that the Home Guard might turn into a revolutionary socialist militia proved illusory; the small group of left-wing intellectuals centred around Tom Wintringham and the Osterley Training School were isolated and the Home Guard never developed any particular political character that challenged the status quo. Instead it managed to mesh nationalist patriotism and the tradition of the volunteer militias with more modern democratic tendencies and anti-Nazi sentiment. It was borne out of a particular threat, and there was little public appetite for its reformation in the war-weary 1950s, by which time, in the age of the nuclear threat, the Home Guard seemed to many people to be an anachronism.

All Home Guard, including the Auxiliary Units' operational patrols, were eligible for the Defence Medal (as long as they completed the necessary three-year term of service) and a number of Home Guard were awarded gallantry and good service medals. Over 1,200 Home Guard had been killed on duty through enemy action, training or other accidents. Their serious contribution to the war effort should not now be relegated to background information for a television comedy series. Sadly, there are just a handful of memorials to the work of the Home Guard, although the reinforced plinths of the Blacker Bombard (Plate 19) can still be found in many places; they are covered in overgrowth and lie neglected beside crossroads or bridges – in some ways a metaphor for our understanding of the Home Guard.

Home Guard

Four years ... And still you do not shirk
The weary round of watch and work.
Four years ... And still from bank or bench
You man the Tommy gun or trench
Four years ... And still when others pause
You give your Sundays to the cause
Today you wait the final fray;
We wish you 'No Returns' to-day:
But may the spirit, may the flame –
Live on forever, with your fame –
The greatest army mustered yet
That never asked what it would get.[2]

Notes

Introduction

1. Orwell (1940), p. 36.
2. Fleming (1957), p. 9.
3. Shaw (1990).
4. Scott (2011).
5. MacKenzie, S.P. (1995), pp. 37–8.
6. Longmate (1974).

Chapter 1: Forming the Home Guard

1. Churchill, A.W. (1946), p. 9.
2. Information from Mick Wilks' research in the Army Medal Office, Droitwich.
3. Ironside to CIGS, 11 June 1940: TNA CAB 106/1202.
4. Wintringham (1939), p. 74.
5. Memo of Churchill to Home Secretary, 7 October 1939, quoted in Churchill (1954), p. 393.
6. Speech to Conservative Party, Central Hall, Westminster, 4 April 1940.
7. The Legion of Frontiersmen was a pre-First World War organization, founded with the intention of serving as a field intelligence unit, with branches throughout the then Empire. In the First World War it had battalions within the Canadian Expeditionary Force and the 25th Battalion Royal Fusiliers, but in the Second World War most members simply joined other services and the Essex example is unique.
8. Graves (1943), p. 15.
9. Lansdale to Southern Command, 12 May 1940: TNA WO 199/1885.
10. MacKenzie, S.P. (1995), p. 28.
11. 'The Volunteer Force During the Great War', March 1940: TNA WO 32/10615.
12. 'Birth Pangs of the Home Guard', p. 1 in IWM Carden Roe Papers 77/165/1.
13. 'Birth Pangs of the Home Guard', pp. 1–2 in IWM Carden Roe Papers 77/165/1.
14. 'The Volunteer Force During the Great War', March 1940: TNA WO 32/10615.
15. Broad (1955), p. 143.
16. 'Home Guard (Local Defence Volunteers) Origins', Major John Maxse, undated: TNA WO 199/3236.
17. Minutes of War Cabinet, 9 May 1940: TNA CAB 65/7.
18. Minutes of Chiefs of Staff Committee, 11 May 1940: TNA CAB 79/4; Minutes of War Cabinet, 11 May 1940: TNA CAB 65/7; Collier (1957), p. 106.
19. Carden Roe to Walter Kirke, 21 December 1942: IWM Carden Roe Papers DD/77/165/1.
20. Minutes of War Cabinet, 13 May 1940: TNA CAB 65/7/15 f.72.
21. Minutes of War Cabinet, 17 May 1940: TNA 65/7/21 f.103.
22. Carden Roe to Walter Kirke, 21 December 1942: IWM Carden Roe Papers DD/77/165/1.
23. Carden Roe to Walter Kirke, 30 December 1942: IWM Carden Roe Papers DD/77/165/1; Order in Council, Defence (Local Defence Volunteers): TNA WO 199/3237.
24. Supplementary War Office Instructions, 18 May 1940: TNA WO 199/1885.
25. Bond (1974), p. 5.
26. Circular letter from Alexander Maxwell to Chief Constables, 14 May 1940: TNA HO 45/25009.
27. Circular letter from Alexander Maxwell to Chief Constables, 15 May 1940: TNA HO 45/25009.
28. Points from Regions, 5 June 1940: TNA INF 1/264 (published in Addison & Crang (2011), p. 81).

29. House of Commons debate, 21 May 1940: *Hansard*, vol. 361, c.8.
30. Gough (1954), p. 239.
31. 'Public Opinion on the Present', 15 June 1940: TNA INF 1/264 (published in Addison & Crang (2011), p. 116).
32. House of Commons debate, 18 June 1940: *Hansard*, vol. 362, c.62.
33. *North-Eastern Gazette*, 22 and 27 June 1940; *Newcastle Journal and North Mail*, 15 July 1940.
34. Churchill to Secretary of State for War, 13 August 1940: TNA PREM 3/223/13.
35. Sir Edward Grigg, House of Commons Debate, 19 November 1940: *Hansard*, vol. 365, c.1887.
36. Churchill to Eden, 22 June 1940: quoted in Churchill (1954), p. 147.
37. Minutes of War Cabinet, 1 July 1940: TNA CAB 65/8/2 f.29.
38. Bridgeman (1942), 'The Home Guard', *Royal United Services Institute Journal*, 546(87):141.
39. Quoted in MacKenzie, S.P. (1995), p. 78.
40. House of Commons debate, 7 August 1949: *Hansard*, vol. 364, c.224.
41. Morgan (1961), p. 147.
42. Graves (1943), p. 16.
43. Gough (1954), pp. 244–5.
44. Street (1942), p. 11; Churchill, A.W. (1946), p. 11.
45. *Sunday Post*, 7 December 1941, quoted in Osborne (2009), p. 123.
46. Wintringham (1941c).
47. Orwell (1941a), p. 496.
48. Langdon-Davies, *Sunday Pictorial*, 20 July 1941.
49. Lieutenant Colonel Brian Kimmins (GHQ) to BGS, 2 July 1941: TNA WO 199/361.
50. Gough (1954), p. 249.
51. Supplementary War Office Instructions, 18 May 1940: TNA WO 199/1885 reproduced in Appendix 1.4.
52. Memo of Sir James Grigg, 31 May 1940: TNA WO 32/10615.
53. Graves (1943), p. 60.
54. Minutes of War Cabinet, 17 June 1940: TNA CAB 65/7/65 f.321.
55. Undated letter to F.W. Bentley from Group Commander, LDV, Orpington (in private possession).
56. MacKenzie, S.P. (1995), pp. 37–8.
57. Shaw (1990), p. 39.
58. Shaw (1990), p. 57.
59. Verlander (2010), pp. 30–1.
60. *Defence: the Services' Magazine*, August 1943, p. 26.
61. *Liverpool Daily Post*, 2 August 1944, p. 3.
62. Ruddy (2007), p. 70.
63. Wynn (2006), pp. 339–40.
64. *Report on Osterley Park LDV Training School, 5–6* August, 1940 by J. Pilling: Wintringham archive in King's College London Military Archive.
65. ACI 468/1941.
66. Whittaker (1990), p. 13.
67. Minutes of the Home Guard Inspectorate, 30 July 1940: TNA WO 165/92.
68. Fisk (1983), p. 269.

Chapter 2: The Role of the Home Guard, 1940–41

1. Gough (1954), p. 243.
2. Minutes of Meeting, 10 August 1940: TNA PREM 3/223/13.
3. *Official History of VTC*, 1920.
4. *VTC Regulations*, 1916.
5. Draft history of the formation and organization of the Home Guard, 1940: TNA WO 199/3243.
6. LDV Training Instructions nos 2 and 5, June and July 1940: TNA WO 199/3243.
7. LDV Training Instruction No. 2, June 1940.
8. DGHG to Regional Commands, 3 November 1941: TNA WO 199/362.

9. *Sunday Pictorial*, 16 February (1941); published in Langdon-Davies (1941), pp. 179–84.
10. Langdon-Davies, *Sunday Pictorial*, 30 March 1941.
11. Gough (1954), p. 244.
12. Lord Croft, House of Lords debate, 11 July 1940: *Hansard*, vol. 116, c.930.
13. Wintringham (1941b), p. 46.
14. Western Command Operation Order No. 21, 31 August 1940.
15. Game to Sergison-Brooke, 1 July 1940: TNA MEPO 2/7013.
16. Sillitoe (1955), p. 147.
17. Ruddy (2007), p. 27.
18. Graves (1943), p. 84.
19. LDV Instruction No. 5, 1940, p. 5.
20. LDV Instruction No. 5, 1940, p. 5.
21. Headmaster, Charterhouse School to Southern Command, 28 May 1940: TNA WO 199/1886.
22. Scott (2011), p. 37.
23. Fleming (1940), p. 68, note 2.
24. MacKenzie, S.P. (1995), p. 59.
25. *Evening Despatch*, 20 September 1940, p. 5.
26. *Evesham Standard*, 16 August 1941, and *Kidderminster Times*, 30 August 1941.
27. *Pers comm.* to Mick Wilks from Egbert Ganderton at an interview on 16 December 2002.
28. Shropshire Archives, SA 1024/203, quoted in Lowry (2010), p. 7.
29. WOL 20/HG/26 23 August 1940: TNA WO 199/3236.
30. Bousfield (2014), pp. 24, 59, 62, 80, 84, 94.
31. Colin Cuthbert interview, IWM SA 15803.
32. MacKenzie, S.P. (1995), pp. 60, 62.
33. Diary entry for 12 July 1940 in Colville (1985), p. 192.
34. Langdon-Davies (1941), p. 49.
35. Cited in Purcell & Smith (2012), p. 194; Norman MacKenzie, *New Statesman* journalist. In June 1940 he was a member of the Independent Labour Party and was in the second batch of Home Guard to enrol at Osterley.
36. *Daily Mirror*, 28 May 1940.
37. Quoted in MacKenzie (1995), p. 50.
38. Ironside Diary, 30 May 1940, p. 345.
39. 'Local Defence Volunteers', Notes of a Meeting on 5 June 1940: published in Graves (1943), pp. 70–5.
40. Ironside to CIGS, 11 June 1940: TNA CAB 106/1202.
41. Ironside to CIGS, 11 June 1940: TNA CAB 106/1202.
42. Undated draft speech by Josiah Wedgwood MP (following a secret report to Parliament, 8 June 1940): TNA CAB 106/1202.
43. GHQ to Regional Commands, 23 May 1940: TNA WO 199/1885.
44. Wintringham in Howard & Endicott (1941), p. 9.
45. 'Local Defence Volunteers', Notes of a Meeting on 5 June 1940: published in Graves (1943), pp. 70–5.
46. Quoted in MacKenzie, S.P. (1995), p. 42.
47. 'Points from Regions', 1 June 1940: TNA INF 1/264 published in Addison & Crang (2011), p. 64.
48. Street (1942), p. 27.
49. GHQ Operational Instruction No. 3, 15 June 1940: TNA ADM 223/484.
50. Vice-Chiefs of Staff Committee, 26 June 1940: TNA CAB 63/167, f.159.
51. Petherick to Sir James Grigg, 7 May 1942: TNA WO 199/363. As well as being an MP he was also head of the Special Duties Branch of the GHQ Auxiliary Units and his return address was their HQ, given as c/o the Post Office, Highworth, Swindon.
52. 'Two Million Resolute Men', Churchill broadcast from the USA, 14 May 1943, published in the *Listener*, 20 May 1943, p. 589.
53. Bert Northwood interview in Whittaker (1990), p. 12.
54. Carroll (2002), p. 75.

55. Minutes of the LDV Inspectorate, 21 July 1940: TNA WO 165/92.
56. Rowe (2010), p. 53.
57. Brophy & Kennington (1945), p. 26.
58. German radio, 16 May 1940. Ironically, in 1944 the Germans sought assurances from the British Foreign Office (through neutral diplomats) that the Allies would regard their own version of the Home Guard, the *Volkssturm*, as legal combatants. As a gesture of conciliation, in October 1944 the Wehrmacht was ordered to treat the French Forces of the Interior as legitimate combatants provided they wore their tricolour armband with the cross of Lorraine. In November Britain, followed by the USA, agreed to recognize the *Volkssturm* as long as they abided by the Hague Convention.
59. Quoted in *Picture Post*, 10 August 1940, p. 3.
60. Ironside diary, 6 July: Macleod & Kelly (1962), p. 383.
61. GOC Western Command to GHQ, 7 May 1941: TNA WO 199/360.
62. Home Guard General Instruction No. 10, 1 August 1940, p. 1.
63. Alan Brooke diary, 22 July 1940: Danchev & Todman (2001), p. 94.
64. GHQ Operational Instruction No. 3, 15 June 1940: TNA ADM 223/484.
65. Home Guard Instruction No. 51 part IV, *Organised Home Guard Defence*, 1943, p. 1.
66. Home Guard Instruction No. 51 part IV, *Organised Home Guard Defence*, 1943, p. ii.
67. ACI No. 924/40, 15 August 1940. The word 'static' was omitted for its reissue as ACI No. 872 in 1942: TNA HO 45/25009; WO 199/3236.
68. Home Guard General Instruction No. 10, 1 August 1940, p. 2.
69. Watts (1916).
70. Levy (1941), p. 74.
71. J. Piling, *Report on Osterley Park LDV Training School*, 5–6 August 1940, pp. 1, 4: Wintringham Papers.
72. William Joyce broadcast, 2 August 1940.
73. Anon (1945b), pp. 17, 59.
74. *Home Guard Instruction No. 14 Winter Training*, September 1940, p. 1.
75. Quoted in Graves (1943), p. 126; Viscount Bridgeman, *The Times*, 15 August 1941.
76. Kerr (1940), p. 91.
77. *Guerrilla Warfare: Military Training Pamphlet No. 54*, pp. 2–3, War Office.
78. Langdon-Davies, *Sunday Pictorial*, 30 March 1941.
79. Activities of SOE in the Balkans, June 1941: TNA HS 8/957.
80. Draft instruction leaflet, September 1941: TNA WO 199/361.
81. Langdon-Davies, *Sunday Pictorial*, 30 March 1941.
82. Wintringham (1940a), pp. 176–83.
83. Miksche (1941); Slater (1941).
84. Grace left the Home Guard to become Director of Education for the Canadian Army.
85. Appendix A, 2 Corps Letter Z/1546 (HG), May 1942: TNA WO 199/2489.
86. TNA WO 199/360.
87. DGHG to Regional Commands and TAAs, 10 May 1941: TNA WO 199/360.
88. Minutes of Chiefs of Staff Committee, 12 June 1941: TNA CAB 80/28.
89. Langdon-Davies, *Sunday Pictorial*, 25 May 1941.
90. John Brophy, *Sunday Graphic*, 8 June 1941.
91. H.F. 301/Ops (VP), 13 June 1941, referenced in TNA WO 199/2489; HF 3010/Ops, 30 June 1941: TNA WO 199/361; *Home Guard Instruction No. 36. Mobile Patrols for Action Against Airborne Troops*, August 1941 (referred to in 'The Role of the Home Guard', 30 April 1942): TNA WO 199/363.
92. Home Guard Instruction No. 51 Part II, Battle Drill, pp. 3–4 and Part IV, The Organization of Home Guard Defence, pp. 10, 12.
93. Paget to Fisher, 15 December 1941: TNA WO 199/362.
94. Minutes of Defence Committee, 21 October 1941; Margesson to Churchill, 22 January 1942: TNA PREM 3/223/9.
95. 'Local Defence Volunteers', 8 June 1940: TNA CAB 106/1202.

96. Minutes of Home Guard Inspectorate, 16 July 1940: TNA WO 165/92.
97. Minutes of meeting on 10 August 1940: TNA PREM 3/223/13.
98. Commissioning of Officers in the Home Guard, 23 January 1941: TNA WO 199/3238.
99. The Role of Home Guard Factory Units, July 1942: TNA WO 199/2489.
100. Graves (1943), pp. 68–9.
101. Notes on Southern Command Home Guard conference, 28 April 1942: TNA WO 199/363.
102. GOC Western Command to GHQ, 7 February 1941: TNA WO 199/360.
103. A.E. Bagwell Purefoy, Western Command, 20 July 1941: TNA WO 199/361.
104. GHQ to Regional Commands, 18 March 1941: TNA WO 199/360; Home Defence Committee report to War Cabinet, 1 September 1941: TNA CAB 67/9/88 f.318.
105. Ransted (2017).
106. Ransted (2017), p. 148.
107. Ransted (2017), pp. 149–50; TNA HO 250/11/455.
108. *London Gazette*, 11 March 1941.
109. Ransted (2017), p. 151.
110. Ransted (2017), p. 172.
111. HF 3010/Ops (VP), July 1941: TNA WO 199/361.
112. Mills & Carney (2001), pp. 85–6.
113. Wilks (2014), p. 120.

Chapter 3: Integration with the Army, 1942–44

1. Viscount Bridgeman in Smith (1945), Foreword, (no pagination).
2. Minutes of Cambridge District Coordinating Conference, 6 November 1941: TNA WO 166/1193.
3. ACI 2100, 27 October 1941.
4. 'Salute the Home Guard', *Save for Victory Appeal*, July 1943.
5. Radnor (1945), p. 122.
6. Lord Croft, Under-Secretary of State for War. Speech at Guildhall, 15 January 1942.
7. Memo of Secretary of State for War, 15 December 1941: TNA CAB 67/9/150 f.417.
8. Graves (1943), p. 139.
9. Shaw (1990), p. 13.
10. *Kidderminster Times*, 30 September 1944; Report of the TAA meeting of 10 April 1942, quoted in Wilks (2014), p. 96.
11. Anon (1945a), p. 69; William Bently Capper, 'Home Guard Recessional', *Defence Magazine*, October 1944, 12(107):15.
12. ACI No. 872, April 1942: TNA HO 45/25009.
13. HF 4022/12/G (SD), 2 July 1942: TNA 199/2489.
14. Shropshire Archives SA 1474/59: quoted in Lowry (2010), p. 44.
15. Quoted in Connelly & Willcox (2006), pp. 4, 19.
16. Pers. comm. by Morris Jephcott during an interview with Mick Wilks on 23 April 2009, with thanks to Mick Wilks.
17. Street (1942), pp. 95–8.
18. Eastern Command Ops Inst No. 37, Defended Places, 26 January 1942: TNA WO 199/2489.
19. Lord Croft, House of Lords debate, 4 February 1942: *Hansard*, vol. 121, c.705, quoted in *Western Daily Press*, 5 February 1942, p. 3.
20. Letter to Major General Gregson-Ellis: TNA WO 199/364. Although filed with papers of autumn 1942, the letter is most likely to have been written in early 1942 by Colonel Bill Major, before he left in February 1942 to form the RAF Regiment. He had formerly been a staff intelligence officer for Eastern Command.
21. A Shropshire Home Guard attendee of the lecture quoted in Lowry (2010), p. 98.
22. GHQ to Regional Commands, 22 April 1942: TNA WO 199/363.
23. Marshall-Cornwall to Swayne, 27 April 1942: TNA WO 199/363; Marshall-Cornwall (1984), p. 197.
24. GHQ to Marshall-Cornwall, 1 May 1942: TNA WO 199/363.

25. Cambridge Area Operational Instruction No. 16, 16 December 1941: TNA WO 166/1193.
26. Walker, 'Guerrilla Warfare and the Home Guard', 30 April 1942: TNA WO 199/363.
27. Home Guard Progress Report No. 2, April 1942: TNA WO 199/363; GOC instructions to Corps Commanders – Operational Role of the Home Guard June 1942: TNA WO 199/1869.
28. CGS to Regional Commands, 2 November 1942: TNA WO 199/364 and TNA 199/2489.
29. District Instruction on Operational Employment of Home Guard, GS 15/60, 28 December 1942.
30. Home Guard Instruction No. 51 Part IV, *The Organization of Home Guard Defence*, November 1943, p. 11.
31. S.P. District Home Guard Instruction, 28 October 1943 and January 1944: TNA WO 199/1869.
32. 'Future of the Home Guard', DGHG, December 1942: TNA CAB 123/204.
33. Oxenden (2012), pp. 14–15.
34. TNA KV 4/194, f.16; The Brandenburg Regiment was Hitler's English-speaking special forces unit who were trained to operate in Allied uniform.
35. 'Two Million Resolute Men', Churchill broadcast from USA, 14 May 1943: published in the *Listener*, 20 May 1943, p. 590.
36. Instructions for 'Exercise Curb', 2 May 1944: TNA WO 166/14516.
37. Instructions for 'Exercise Lash', 27 May 1944: TNA WO 166/14516.
38. Home Guard Information Circular No. 15, September 1942, pp. 1–2; 'Future of the Home Guard', DGHG, December 1942: TNA CAB 123/204.
39. Anon (1945b), p. 58.
40. The Earl of Elgin, House of Lords debate, 4 February 1942: *Hansard*, vol. 121, cc.697.
41. Memorandum for the guidance of Invasion Committees, Northern Civil Defence Region, 5 January 1942: TNA WO 199/1415.
42. Shaw (1990), p. 61.
43. Wilks (2014), pp. 104–5.
44. Thomas (1942), p. 15.
45. Thomas (1942), p. 22.
46. Circular Minute of Prime Minister, 5 March 1943: TNA CAB 123/204.
47. Brophy & Kennington (1945), p. 41.
48. Pile (1949), p. 225.
49. Memo of Lord President of Council, 25 November 1941: TNA CAB 67/9/137 f.386; Minutes of War Cabinet, 28 November 1941: TNA CAB 65/20/14 f.90.
50. Stichelbaut (2009), p. 236.
51. Carroll (2002), p. 69.
52. TNA WO 199/3247.
53. Pile (1949), pp. 256, 385.
54. CGS to Regional Commands, 19 September 1941: TNA WO 32/9757.
55. HF 4022/9/G (SD), 'Equipment of Home Guard in Coast Artillery', 19 September 1941: TNA WO 199/361.
56. Chief of General Staff (Home Forces) to Regional Commands, 23 September 1941: TNA WO 32/9757; Mills & Carney (2001), pp. 87–92.
57. Lidstone (1945), pp. 103–5.
58. *Defence: The Services' Magazine and Home Guard Monthly*, September 1944, p. 13.
59. *Defence: The Services' Magazine*, August 1943, p. 39.
60. GHQ to Regional Commands, 6 September 1944: TNA WO 199/1869.

Chapter 4: The Secret Home Guard

1. Shropshire Archives SA 486/1/1, quoted in Lowry (2010), p. 14.
2. Wilks (2014), p. 40.
3. ADRDE Home Guard files of August 1941: Wilks (2014), pp. 40–1.
4. The history of XII Corps Observation Unit and the Auxiliary Units is considered in depth in Atkin (2015), and the relationship of the Auxiliary Units to SIS in Atkin (2017). The present study focusses on the relationship of these two bodies to the Home Guard.

5. MI(R) War Diary: TNA HS 8/263. Fleming had originally been recruited to MI(R) in August 1939 to investigate the potential of assisting Chinese guerrillas against the Japanese. He was the brother of 'James Bond' author Ian Fleming.
6. MI(R) War Diary: TNA HS 8/263.
7. Hart-Davis (1987), p. 234.
8. Arnold (1962), p. 53.
9. Fleming (1952), p. 13.
10. Memories quoted on www.kentauxiliaryunits.org.uk.
11. The SIS multi-layered system of resistance organizations and the relationship of the HDS to the Auxiliary Units is discussed in detail in Atkin (2015) and (2017).
12. Conclusions of War Cabinet, 17 June 1940: TNA CAB 65/7/65 f.321.
13. Macdougall to Ismay, 22 June 1940: CAB 21/1473.
14. Peter Wilkinson interview in Sutton, S., 'Farmers or Fighters. Dissertation on the existence and function of Britain's "secret army". Auxiliary Units in southern England during 1940–44'. Unpublished BA dissertation 1995, Canterbury Christchurch College. (BRO Museum Archive).
15. The intelligence wing of the Auxiliary Units, the Special Duties Branch (SDB), operated on parallel but separate lines to the Operational Branch with a continuing SIS influence. but with no connection to the Home Guard. Its history is consequently beyond the scope of the present book, but see Atkin (2015), chs 9 and 10.
16. DMI to Ismay, 24 June 1940: TNA CAB 21/1473; Atkin (2017), pp. 188–91.
17. Gubbins to LDV Area Commanders 5 July 1940: TNA CAB 120/241.
18. Gubbins to LDV Area Commanders 5 July 1940: TNA CAB 120/241.
19. Gubbins, circular letter to LDV Commanders, 5 July 1940: TNA CAB 21/120.
20. Gubbins to Colonel Hall, Southern Command, 20 September 1940: TNA WO 199/2151; Atkin (2015), p. 69.
21. General Paget to Captain Sandys, 30 July 1940: TNA CAB 120/241.
22. TNA CAB 120/241.
23. Oxenden (2012), p. 1.
24. D Section Early History to September 1940, pp. 17–18: TNA HS 7/3.
25. Report VIII, July 1940: TNA HS 8/214.
26. Atkin (2015), chapter 11.
27. Great Britain's Only Successful Experiment In Total Warfare, by Laurence Grand, August 1940: TNA HS 8/214.
28. Report VIII, July 1940, p. 23: TNA HS 8/214; Turner (2011), p. 96.
29. Oxenden (2012), p. 2.
30. Gubbins, ''Auxiliary Units, Home Forces', 26 July 1940: WO 199/738.
31. Oxenden 2012 (typescript 1944), p. 7.
32. War Establishment report of 26 July 1940, quoted in Warwicker (2004), pp. 67–8.
33. Grigson-Ellis to Glanusk, 10 September 1942: TNA WO 199/738.
34. Lowry & Wilks (2002), p. 55.
35. Oxenden (2012), p. 5.
36. Oxenden (2012), p. 6.
37. Oxenden (2012), p. 9.
38. Lindsay (1987), p. 142.
39. Oxenden (2012), p. 4.
40. The 'Phantom' unit of the BEF had received the first examples in January 1940.
41. Scout Patrols, 28 March 1941 and August 1941 training timetable: BROM Archive.
42. Oxenden (2012), p. 4.
43. CGS Home Forces to Regional Commands, 5 September 1940 and Southern Command to 5 Corps, 10 September 1940: TNA WO 199/1891.
44. Skennerton (1988), pp. 21–2.
45. Angell (1996), p. 35.
46. Oxenden (2012), p. 12.
47. Lampe (1968), p. 78.

48. Oxenden (2012), p. 23.
49. Atkin (2015), p. 83.
50. Mick Wilks Home Guard interview file with Tony Barling.
51. Warwicker (2004), pp. 97, 100.
52. Mick Wilks, Home Guard interview archive.
53. Lowry & Wilks (2002), p. 65; Diary entry for 12 July 1940 in Colville 1985, p. 193.
54. Atkin (2017), p. 25; Calvert in a post-war radio broadcast, recounted in Warwicker (2008), p. 68.
55. Colville (1985), p. 193.
56. Mark Seaman interview with Wilkinson in 1993: IWM Interview Cat. No. 13289, reel 5.
57. Letter of Brigadier Richie, HQ Southern Command to Major General Gammell, 3rd Division, 1 August 1940: TNA WO 199/2151.
58. Record of a meeting between Colonel Hall, HQ Southern Command, and Major Beyts, Auxiliary Units, 9 August 1940: TNA WO 199/2151.
59. Thanks to Richard Thorpe for passing on this information.
60. Auxiliary Units, Progress report for period ending 1 September 1940: TNA CAB 120/241.
61. Wilkinson (2002), p. 104.
62. Oxenden (2012), p. 7.
63. Gubbins, 'Auxiliary Units, Home Forces', 26 July 1940: TNA WO 199/738.
64. Letter of Forbes to Warwicker, January 2002: BRO Museum Archive.
65. Quayle (1990), p. 230.
66. Quayle (1990), p. 230; Letter of Forbes to Warwicker, January 2002: BRO Museum Archive; Patrol Leader's Course Notes: BROM Archive.
67. Oxenden (2012) , p. 13.
68. Oxenden (2012), p. 13.
69. Oxenden (2012), p. 23.
70. Warwicker (2004), pp. 107–8.
71. Colonel Douglas, 'Economy in Manpower', June 1944: TNA WO 199/738.
72. TNA WO 199/738.
73. Beyts to DCGS, 'Function of IO headquarters', 19 May 1942: TNA WO 199/738.
74. Oxenden (2012), pp. 17–18.
75. Oxenden (2012), pp. 14–15.
76. Wilkinson (2002), p. 104.
77. Auxiliary Units, Home Forces. Organization, July 1940: TNA CAB 120/241.
78. Peter Wilkinson interview in Sutton, S., 'Farmers or Fighters. Dissertation on the existence and function of Britain's "secret army". Auxiliary Units in southern England during 1940–44'. Unpublished BA dissertation 1995, Canterbury, Christchurch College. (BRO Museum Archive).
79. *Target for Tonight* lecture notes 1941: BRO Museum Archive.
80. Lowry & Wilks (2002), p. 83.
81. Wilks (2014), pp. 207–8.
82. http://www.sixtownships.org.uk/the-secret-army-page-1.html.
83. Duncan Sandys to Churchill, 8 August 1940: TNA CAB 120/121.
84. DGHG to TAAs, 22 May 1941: TNA WO 199/3251.
85. Warwicker (2008), p. 109.
86. Letter from DGHG to county TAAs, 20 January 1941: TNA WO 199/3251 and TNA WO 199/3238; *see also* Atkin (2015), Plates 42 and 43.
87. DGHG to TAAs, 30 March 1942: TNA 199/3251.
88. Correspondence of Colonel L. Bain with Captain Stewart, Auxiliary Units, November 1943: TNA WO 199/2892.
89. Letter to IOs and regional TAAs, 21 August 1942: TNA WO 199/3265; Letter from DGHG to TAAs, 25 August 1942: TNA WO 199/3251.
90. War Office to Reading TAA, 2 October 1942: TNA WO 199/3265.
91. Worcestershire Home Guard Part I and II Orders, formerly held by the Army Medal Office, Droitwich, until its closure in 2005; Worcestershire Regiment Museum Archive.
92. TNA WO 199/3389.

93. Cowgill to Comyns Carr, 28 April 1941: TNA KV 4/205.
94. DGHG to Regional Commands, 9 March 1941: TNA WO 199/3238; War Office to Reading TAA, 2 October 1942: TNA WO 199/3265.
95. Letter of 15 May 1944 from the CO of the Banff Home Guard: TNA WO 199/2892.
96. Warwicker (2008), p. 110.
97. 'Reduction in Auxiliary Units', CGS, War Office, 6 January 1943: TNA WO 200/738.
98. Oxenden (2012), pp. 17–18.
99. TNA WO 199/936.
100. War Office to Major General Callander, GHQ Home Forces, 25 April 1944: TNA WO 199/738.
101. Memo of War Office to Colonel Douglas, 17 May 1944: TNA WO 199/738.
102. TNA WO 199/3251.
103. TNA ADM 179/456.
104. *Contra* Searle (1989), p. 112; account of Herbert Bowman of Thorpe St Andrew Patrol on CART website (http://www.coleshillhouse.com/the-auxiliers-go-overseas.php, retrieved January 2019).
105. Lowry & Wilks (2002), pp. 65, 85, 98, 103.
106. The PLUTO pipeline was never expected to supply the initial landings, which would rely on the shipment of 4-gallon jerrycans, but the scheme was plagued by delays and it was not until 22 September that fuel began to flow from Sandown, by which time several channel ports were in allied hands. Despite the engineering achievement, it proved to be a costly operational failure.
107. Simak & Pye (2013), p. 59.
108. The movement orders are contained within TNA WO 199/294.
109. G(Ops), GHQ Home Forces to MGGS, 21 July 1944: TNA WO 199/294.
110. *Newcastle Evening Chronicle*, 25 April 1968.
111. *Morpeth Extra*, February 2011.
112. Reproduced in Hall (2015), plate 5, p. 16.
113. Clarke (2016), p. 12.
114. Pryce-Jones (1975), p. 184.
115. Wilkinson & Astley (1993), p. 74.
116. Progress Report on Auxiliary Units for period ending 1 September 1940, by Peter Wilkinson: TNA CAB 120/241.
117. Atkin (2016), passim.
118. Preliminary orders for the badge were taken as early as July 1944; Hall, Ian (2015), p. 11.
119. SIS blocked the issue of medals to the SDB on the basis that those civilians had performed much the same function as their Section VII resistance, who would not be able to receive public recognition. See Report of Sir Robert Knox, Central Honours Committee: TNA WO32/21918.
120. Fleming (1957), p. 270.
121. Collier (1957), pp. 130, 297.
122. Lampe (1968), p. 78.
123. Lampe (1968), pp. 75, 78. Plastic explosive was being distributed by Section D of SIS to foreign resistance groups from November 1939 and Thompsons were used by the BEF from February 1940.
124. Searle (1989), p. 111; repeated on CART website 2018.
125. Stuart Edmundson, quoted in Warwicker (2004), p. 93.
126. Hoare (2002), p. 199.
127. Warwicker (2008), p. 82.
128. Ward (2013), p. xii.
129. Wilkinson (2002), p. 104.
130. Ward (2013), p. xxii.
131. Preliminary Notes on Regional D Scheme, 4 June 1940: TNA HS 8/255; Atkin (2017), p. 184.
132. Wintringham (1941b).
133. Wintringham (1941d), p. 15.
134. Piling, J., *Report on Osterley Park LDV Training School*, 5–6 August, 1940: Wintringham Papers, King's College London Archive.

135. Levy (1941), p. 36.
136. Ruddy (2007), pp. 143–8.
137. *See* Atkin (2015), Chapter 11 for a wider discussion of Section VII.
138. Lowry & Wilks (2002), p. 113.
139. Lowry & Wilks (2002), pp. 113–15.
140. *Newsletter* No. 3, 1999, British Resistance Organization Museum, Parham, p. 2.
141. Correspondence between author and Eric Nussen in 2015.
142. Atkin (2017), p. 149.
143. Atkin (2015), p. 148.
144. Ruddy (2007), p. 149.

Chapter 5: Arming and Equipping the Home Guard

1. A history of the formation and organization of the Home Guard: TNA WO 199/3243; War Office Telegram 15 May 1940.
2. Minutes of War Cabinet, 17 June 1940: TNA CAB 65/7/65 f.321.
3. Allingham (1941), p. 176.
4. Allingham (1941), p. 177.
5. House of Commons debate, 22 May 1940: *Hansard*, vol. 361, c.243.
6. 'Local Defence Volunteers', Notes of a Meeting on 5 June 1940: published in Graves (1943), pp. 70–5.
7. Home Intelligence report, 19–20 May 1940: TNA INF 1/264, published in Addison & Crang (2011), p. 14.
8. ACI Nos. 114, 115 and 116 of 1941: TNA WO 199/3238.
9. *Midland Daily Telegraph*, 27 June 1941, p. 6.
10. It had previously been owned by Harry Fowler of Fair Hills, New Jersey. Purcell with Smith (2012), p. 205.
11. Millgate (1998), p. 44.
12. Minutes of War Cabinet, 5 June 1940: TNA CAB 66/8/24.
13. Wiltsher (1946), p. 17.
14. Wiltsher (1946), p. 31.
15. Lord Croft, House of Lords debate: *Hansard*, 3 July 1940, vol. 116, c.771.
16. Lord Croft, House of Lords debate: *Hansard*, 11 July 1940, vol. 116, c.930.
17. Lord Croft, House of Lords debate: *Hansard*, 11 July 1940, vol. 116, c.931.
18. Langdon-Davies (1941), p. 19.
19. Longmate (1974), p. 73; MacKenzie, S.P. (1995), p. 177.
20. Boothby (1978), pp. 140–1; Edwards (1988), p. 37.
21. Peter I. to Brian Kimmins (War Office), 26 June 1941: TNA WO 199/361.
22. Shaw (1990), p. 97.
23. Jager (1945), pp. 13, 19.
24. 'Home Guard rifles, approximate position on 10 August 1940': TNA WO 199/3249.
25. Sir Edward Grigg, House of Commons debate, 19 November 1940: *Hansard*, vol. 365, c.1886.
26. Note of January 1941, Director General Home Guard: TNA WO 199/3249.
27. Birdswood (1952), p. 235.
28. MacLeod & Kelly (1962), p. 370.
29. *North-Eastern Gazette*, 22 and 27 June 1940; *Newcastle Journal and North Mail*, 15 July 1940.
30. Wood (1976), pp. 80, 88.
31. Gulvin (1980), pp. 9–12.
32. Hylton (2004), p. 48; Graves (1943), p. 224.
33. Viscount Bridgeman, 'Future of the Home Guard', December 1943: TNA WO 32/9423.
34. TNA WO 199/3249.
35. DGHG, 31 March 1941: TNA WO 199/3249.
36. Minutes of Home Guard Inspectorate, 13 August 1940: TNA WO 165/92.
37. DGHG to ACIGS, 31 March 1941: TNA WO 199/3249.

38. Minutes of LDV Inspectorate, 23 July 1940: TNA WO 165/92; War Office to Commands, 20 August 1940: TNA WO 199/3249.
39. Minutes of Home Guard Inspectorate, 3 September 1940: TNA WO 165/92.
40. Note, 20 August 1940: TNA WO 199/3249; Minutes of Home Guard Inspectorate, 10 September 1940: TNA WO 165/92.
41. Small arms ammunition for Home Guard, 19 December 1940: TNA WO 199/3249.
42. ACIGS to DGHG, 3 February 1941: TNA WO 199/3249.
43. C-in-C Home Forces to Under-Secretary of State for War, 31 January 1942: TNA WO 199/3249.
44. Clarke (2016), p. 85.
45. Viscount Bridgeman, 'Future of the Home Guard', December 1943: TNA WO 32/9423.
46. DGHG to Regional Commands, 11 November 1941: TNA WO 199/362.
47. Memo of GOC Eastern Command, 6 May 1942: TNA WO 199/2489.
48. Duke of Sutherland, House of Lords debate, 4 February 1942: *Hansard*, vol. 121, cc.686.
49. Lord Croft, House of Lords debate, 4 February 1942: *Hansard*, vol. 121, c.702.
50. Letter from Norwich, *Picture Post*, 19 October 1940, p. 35.
51. Anon. (1940), p. 12.
52. Langdon-Davies (1941), pp. 40–3.
53. Langdon-Davies (1941), p. 44.
54. Osborne (2009), p. 70.
55. Home Guard Instruction No. 26, 1941; DADHG, 11 February 1941: TNA WO 199/3249.
56. Knights (1942), pp. 25, 28.
57. Wintringham (1941e), p. 20.
58. Fine (1944), p. 26.
59. Wiltsher (1946), p. 50.
60. Home Guard Inspectorate, 9 July 1940: TNA WO 165/92.
61. Home Guard, weapon and ammunition position, 7 October 1940: TNA WO 199/3249.
62. Home Guard monthly returns: TNA WO 199/3247.
63. 'Local Defence Volunteers', Notes of a Meeting on 5 June 1940: published in Graves (1943), pp. 70–5.
64. Home Guard returns, TNA WO 199/3247.
65. Langdon-Davies, *Sunday Pictorial*, 30 March 1941.
66. Quoted in Clarke (2016), p. 95.
67. Shore (1997), pp. 223–34. Shore was commissioned as a Weapon Training Officer with 2834 Anti-Aircraft Squadron, RAF Regiment, in 1942 and after the war transferred to the Manchester Regiment and briefly became an instructor in the BAOR Field Sniper School in Holland.
68. LDV Instruction No. 5, July 1940.
69. 'Local Defence Volunteers', Notes of a Meeting on 5 June 1940: published in Graves (1943), pp. 70–5; Ammunition Allotment No. 4, 21 January 1941: TNA WO 199/3249.
70. Shore (1997), p. 237.
71. Home Guard Instruction No. 27: Defence in Urban Areas, 1941, p. 1; Home Guard Instruction No. 51 Part II: Battle Drill (1943).
72. Banks (1940), p. 8.
73. Graves (1943), p. 32.
74. Allocation of American .300 rifles, 24 February 1941: TNA WO 199/3249.
75. Shore (1997), pp. 246, 248.
76. Shaw (1990), p. 233.
77. Memo of General Alan Brooke, C-in-C Home Forces, 19 December 1940: TNA WO 199/3249.
78. LDV returns, TNA WO 199/3247.
79. History of the 4th Worcestershire (Evesham) Battalion, Home Guard, p. 15.
80. Minutes of LDV Inspectorate, 2 July 1940: TNA WO 165/92.
81. Shore (1997), pp. 198–9, 233.
82. Harry 'Jimmy' Taylor, IWM SA 13714, quoted in Cullen (2011), p. 76.
83. Longmate (1974), p. 70.

84. TNA WO 199/3249.
85. Director of Ordnance Services, 5 August 1940: TNA WO 199/3249.
86. Anon (1944), p. 26.
87. Assistant Director of Ordnance Services, 18 January 1941: TNA WO 199/3249.
88. March 1942 correspondence between 30 Military Mission (Moscow) and War Office, March–April 1940: TNA WO 199/3249.
89. Minutes of Home Guard Inspectorate, 20 August 1940: TNA WO 165/92.
90. Fleming (1957), p. 200.
91. Minutes of Chiefs of Staff Committee, 6 June 1941: TNA CAB 80/28.
92. House of Commons debate, 11 March 1942: *Hansard*, vol. 378, cc.1129.
93. Lloyd to Regional Commands, July 1941: TNA WO 199/3249.
94. Lord Croft, House of Lords debate, 4 February 1942: *Hansard*, vol. 121, c.702.
95. Home Guard returns: TNA WO 199/3247.
96. Pile (1949), p. 220.
97. Quoted in Howard & Endicott (1941), p. 31.
98. Longmate (1974), p. 63.
99. War Office, 12 July and 25 September 1941: TNA WO 199/3249.
100. Home Guard monthly returns: TNA WO 199/ 3247.
101. LDV Instruction No. 9 Grenades; Capt. A. Southworth (1944), *Home Guard Pocket Manual*, p. 47. It is noteworthy that the 1940 edition of this manual made no mention of grenades.
102. Shaw (1990), pp. 208–9.
103. *Rochdale Observer*, 26 August 1942, p. 3.
104. Ironside Diaries for 28 May 1940: Macleod & Kelly (1962), pp. 343–4.
105. ACIGS to Eden, 11 June 1940: TNA WO 185/1.
106. *Molotoff Bombs: Instructions for Preparation and Use Against Tanks and Other Vehicles*, 1 June 1940: TNA WO 199/1891; Prendergast (1979), p. 139.
107. Southern Command to AA Command, 18 June 1940, and 4 Corps to Southern Command, 29 June 1940: TNA WO 199/1891.
108. CGS to Regional Commands, 22 June 1940: TNA WO 199/1891.
109. Southern Area to Southern Command, 31 July 1940: TNA WO 199/1891.
110. *Intelligence Report No. 3*: TNA CAB 63/167, f.129.
111. *Volunteer for Liberty*, No. 14, October 1941, p. 29.
112. Churchill to Ismay, 16 June 1940: TNA CAB 120/372.
113. Memo of 19 June 1940: TNA WO 185/1.
114. Ismay to Churchill, 29 June 1940: TNA CAB 120/372.
115. Ismay to Churchill, 26 June 1941: TNA CAB 120/372.
116. CGS to Regional Commands, 28 June 1940, and W.N. Stokes, Director of Ordnance Service, to Regional Commands, 13 July 1940: WO 199/1891.
117. ADOS to Ministry of Supply, 27 September 1947: TNA WO 185/23.
118. Ashworth (1998), pp. 42–3.
119. The shortages were not due to U-boat losses, which Tom Davis has shown amounted to only 4.6%: Davis (2014), p. 94.
120. Memo of General Alan Brooke, C-in-C Home Forces, 19 December 1940: TNA WO 199/3249.
121. Scales of issue, Thompson machine carbine, 24 May 1941: TNA WO 199/3249.
122. TNA WO 199/3247.
123. Longmate (1974), p. 75.
124. Radnor (1945), pp. 119–20.
125. Simak & Pye (2013), p. 118.
126. TNA CAB 123/204.
127. Shaw (1990), p. 57.
128. Langdon-Davies (1941), p. 41; Slater (1941), p. 60.
129. Rigden (2001), p. 267.
130. TNA FO 898/70.
131. Hopkinson (1982), p. 179.

132. GHQ to Regional Commands, 6 May 1941: TNA WO 199/360; Cambridge Operational Instruction No. 17, December 1941: TNA WO 166/1193.
133. From the report of the Worcestershire TAA meeting of 18 October 1940, quoted in Wilks (2014), pp. 210–11.
134. Noel Coward (1943).
135. Langdon-Davies (1941), p. 19.
136. 'Troops available in Great Britain', 8 June 1940: TNA CAB 106/1202.
137. 'Replacement of Bren guns', 6 and 29 January 1941: TNA WO 199/3249.
138. Home Guard returns: TNA WO 199/3247.
139. Minutes of LDV Inspectorate, 12 July 1940: TNA WO 165/92.
140. Easterly (1998), p. 302.
141. Minutes of the Home Guard Inspectorate, 26 July 1940: TNA WO 165/92.
142. Langdon-Davies (1942), p. 91.
143. Pers. Comms. by Bill Hay to Mick Wilks, quoted in Wilks (2014), p. 51.
144. Home Guard Monthly Returns, February 1941: TNA WO 199/3247.
145. Graves (1943), p. 284.
146. Wilks (2014), p. 237.
147. RAC Half-yearly Progress Report No. 5: TNA WO 165/131.
148. Home Guard monthly returns: TNA WO 199/3247.
149. Quoted in MacKenzie, S.P. (1995), p. 94.
150. Atkin (2017), pp. 42–3.
151. Northover to Churchill, 27 March 1942: TNA PREM 3/428/10.
152. Prof. Lindemann to Winston Churchill, 3 July, 1940: TNA PREM 3/428/10.
153. Report of demonstration of anti-tank devices, 28 July 1940: TNA PREM 3/428/10.
154. MacKenzie, S.P. (1995), p. 94.
155. Ministry of Supply to General Eldridge, 8 November 1948: TNA WO 185/23; Circular, 12 February 1941: TNA WO 199/3249.
156. Director of Artillery to Ministry of Supply, 9 October 1947: TNA WO 185/23.
157. Blacker to Holland, 14 August 1940: TNA HS 8/262.
158. C-in-C Home Forces to Under-Secretary of State for War, 3 May 1941: TNA WO 199/3249.
159. Mobility of Spigot Mortars, 12 May 1942: TNA WO 199/363.
160. MacKenzie, S.P. (1995), p. 135.
161. Chief of General Staff, Home Forces to Regional Commands, 23 September 1941: TNA WO 32/9757.
162. GHQ Home Forces to Regional Commands, 25 November 1943: TNA WO 199/3249.
163. Major A. Shelley-Creake in the Worcestershire Regiment magazine, *Firm*, January 1949.
164. Artillery equipments – Home Guard, 30 January 1944: TNA WO 199/3249.
165. Artillery equipments – Home Guard, 30 January 1944: TNA WO 199/3249.
166. MacKenzie, S.P. (1995), p. 135.
167. DGHG to ICIGS, 21 August 1941: TNA WO 199/3249.
168. Alan Brooke Diary for 10 August 1940: Danchev & Todman (2001), p. 98.
169. GOC Western Command to GHQ, 16 April 1942: TNA WO 199/363.
170. Extract from HG Directorate Meeting No. 76 in Minute 17/8/HG, 'Role of Home Guard', Eastern Command, 15 September 1942: TNA WO 199/2489.
171. HF 3010/28/Ops, 26 October 1942: TNA WO 199/2489.
172. Wilks (2014), p. 209.
173. John Brophy, *Sunday Graphic*, 8 June 1941.
174. Churchill to Margesson, 23 November 1941: TNA PREM 223/9.
175. Stanley Brand, IWM SA 27347.
176. Wilks (2014), p. 44.
177. *Bromsgrove, Droitwich, & Redditch Weekly Messenger*, 11 November 1944, quoted in Wilks (2014), p. 209.
178. Langdon-Davies (1942), p. 14.
179. Minutes of LDV Inspectorate, 23 July 1940: TNA WO 165/92.

180. Minutes of LDV Inspectorate, 30 July 1940: TNA WO 165/92.
181. Minutes of Home Guard Inspectorate, 2 August 1940: TNA WO 165/92.
182. Minutes of Home Guard Inspectorate, 10 September 1940: TNA WO 165/92.
183. Minutes of Home Guard Inspectorate, 20 August 1940: TNA WO 165/92.
184. Minutes of Home Guard Inspectorate, 30 July 1940: WO TNA WO165/92.
185. Minutes of Home Guard Inspectorate, 3 September 1940: WO TNA WO165/92.
186. Orwell Diary for 1 September 1940: Orwell & Angus (1968b), p. 370.
187. Mills & Carney (2001), p. 20; *see* Whittaker (1990) for a complete list of codes used on Home Guard county flashes.
188. Discussed in detail in Mills & Carney (2001), pp. 105–14.
189. Minutes of Home Guard Inspectorate, 2 August 1940: TNA WO 165/92.
190. Minutes of Home Guard Inspectorate, 6 August 1940: TNA WO 165/92.
191. House of Commons debate, 8 April 1941: *Hansard*, vol. 370, c.1402.
192. House of Commons debate, 22 May 1940: *Hansard*, vol. 361, c.240; Appendix 1.
193. Davison (2009), p. 273.
194. Minutes of Home Guard Inspectorate, 3 September 1940: TNA WO 165/92.
195. Minutes of Home Guard Inspectorate, 26 November 1940: TNA WO 165/92.
196. Minutes of Home Guard Inspectorate, 2 August 1940: TNA WO 165/92.

Chapter 6: Aid from the USA

1. Hall, H.D. (1955), p. 495.
2. Hall, H.D. (1955), p. 138.
3. 'We will not slow down or detour', an address by President Franklin D. Roosevelt at Charlottesville, Va., to graduating class, University of Virginia and broadcast over the radio, 10 June 1940.
4. Hall, H.D. (1955), pp. 143, 145.
5. War Office circular, 18 January 1941: WO 199/3249.
6. 'Two Million Resolute Men', Churchill broadcast from USA, 14 May 1943: published in the *Listener*, 20 May 1943, p. 589.
7. Hopkinson (1982), p. 179.
8. Wilkinson & Astley (1993), p. 73.
9. House of Commons debate, 7 May 1940: *Hansard*, vol. 360, c.1120.
10. *The Times*, 11 May 1940.
11. Memo of Anthony Eden, War Cabinet meeting, 8 July 1940: TNA CAB 67/7/108.
12. Ministry of Information, *Stay Where You Are*, July 1940.
13. Ministry of Information, *Beating the Invader*, May 1941.
14. The Convention was to lead to the acceptance by the Nuremburg War Crimes Tribunal in 1946 that the Nazis had the right to execute partisans, as long as it was preceded by a token legal process. See United Nations War Crimes Commission, *Law Reports of Trials of War Criminals*, Vol. VIII, 1949.
15. 'Politics and Propaganda', *American Rifleman*, September 1940, p. 4.
16. Wintringham (1940b), p. 78.
17. Wickham Steed to Macneil of Barra, 30 November 1940: TNA CAB 115/489.
18. Davis (2014), pp. 1–13.
19. Davis (2014), p. 108; discussion with Tom Davis in May 2018 confirmed his analysis that the forty Thompsons donated by the US Treasury Procurement were included in the ACDBH total.
20. Longmate (1974), p. 66.
21. House of Commons debate, 22 May 1940: *Hansard*, vol. 361, c.257.
22. Atkin (2017), pp. 47–8; the 1941 SIS scheme to acquire handguns is alluded to in TNA WO 199/3249.
23. The British Purchasing Commission was formed before the outbreak of war to arrange the production and purchase of armaments from North American manufacturers. Purvis became Director General of British purchasing in the United States in November 1939, and in the following January Chairman of the Anglo-French Purchasing Board. In February 1941 Purvis was appointed Chairman of the British Supply Council in North America and was a major

influence in shaping the Lend-Lease Act with President Roosevelt. He was killed in an air crash on 14 August 1941.

24. Purvis to Monnet, 1 July 1940: TNA CAB 115/489.
25. Quoted in draft Memorandum by the Chairman of the North American Supply Committee, 7 September 1940: TNA CAB 115/489.
26. Macneil of Barra to Sir Clive Baillieu (Director General, BPC), 27 May 1941: TNA AVIA 38/533.
27. M.B. to F.E. Evans (Foreign Office), 18 September 1941: TNA FO 371/26242.
28. Cotton to Beaverbrook, 27 August 1940: TNA AVIA 9/1.
29. E.G. Compton to Beaverbrook, 4 September 1940: TNA AVIA 9/1.
30. Consul General New York to Ministry of Supply, 3 September 1940: TNA AVIA 9/1.
31. Cotton to Beaverbrook, 6 September 1940: TNA AVIA 9/1.
32. Macneil of Barra to Ministry of Supply, 3 September 1940: TNA CAB 115/489.
33. Beaverbrook to Eden, 3 October 1940: TNA AVIA 9/1.
34. Laurence Carr (War Office) to J.E. Griffiths (Ministry of Aircraft Production), 13 September 1940: TNA AVIA 9/1.
35. Gorell-Barnes to Turner (Ministry of Supply), 6 September 1940: TNA CAB 115/489.
36. Foreign Office to H.M. Ambassador, Washington, and Salter to Purvis, 6 September 1940: TNA CAB 115/489; Summary note by Salter, Chairman of the North American Supply Committee, 7 September 1940: TNA CAB 115/489 and TNA FO 371/24263/4175.
37. Cotton to Beaverbrook, 6 September 1940: TNA AVIA 9/1.
38. Scudder's role is mysterious. On 15 June 1941 Macneil wrote to Henry Wickham Steed (Chairman of the CCPH) trying to establish who Scudder actually represented but a puzzled Wickham Steed replied saying he thought Scudder represented the ACDBH. An equally puzzled Cutting then wrote to Wickham Steed saying he believed Scudder was a member of the CCPH (correspondence in TNA CAB 115/489). In March 1941 he was lecturing in London on behalf of the William Allen White Committee. Scudder had served in a British ambulance unit in Italy during the First World War.
39. Gorell-Barnes (Cabinet Office) to Balfour (Foreign Office), 7 September 1940: TNA FO 371/24263/4175.
40. Summary note by Salter, Chairman of the Central Office for North American Supplies, 7 September 1940: TNA CAB 115/489 and TNA FO 371/24263/4175.
41. Summary note by Salter, Chairman of the Central Office for North American Supplies, 7 September 1940: TNA CAB 115/489 and TNA FO 371/24263/4175.
42. Gorell-Barnes to Salter, 9 September 1940: TNA CAB 115/489.
43. E.G. Compton to Beaverbrook, 24 September 1940: TNA AVIA 9/1.
44. Marquess of Lothian to Foreign Office, 13 September 1940: TNA FO 371/24263/4175 and CAB 115/489.
45. Defence (LDV) Regulations, 17 May 1940: TNA WO 199/3236; *see also* Appendix 1.1.
46. Note by W.J. Hasler appended to note of T.H. Brand (North America Supply Committee of Cabinet Office) to Hasler, 19 November 1940: TNA CAB 115/489.
47. *Victoria Advocate*, 12 November 1940, pp. 1–2.
48. T.H. Brand to G.W. Turner (Ministry of Supply), 19 November 1940: TNA CAB 115/489.
49. Mss note to minute of Turner to Mr Ronald, Foreign Office, 19 April 1941: TNA FO 371/26242.
50. Wickham Steed to The Macneil of Barra, 11 April 1941: TNA CAB 115/489.
51. Draft memo by Salter, undated (September 1940): TNA AVIA 9/1; Chairman, North American Supply Committee (Sir Arthur Salter), 7 September 1940: TNA FO 371/24263.
52. Note to Beaverbrook, 25 September 1940: TNA AVIA 9/1.
53. *Syracuse Herald-American*, 19 June 1941.
54. *Daily Telegraph*, 17 September 1940.
55. *Scarsdale Inquirer*, No. 44, 29 November 1940.
56. *Manassas Journal*, Virginia, 6 February 1941.
57. Wickham Steed to The Macneil of Barra, 13 December 1940: TNA CAB 115/489.
58. Quoted in Mace (2007b), p. 55.
59. *Press and Journal*, 5 May 1941.

60. *Times Herald* of Olean, New York, 11 November 1940.
61. 'Zero Hour', *American Rifleman*, December 1940, p. 4.
62. As *Lincolnshire Echo*, *Birmingham Gazette*, *Liverpool Daily Post*, *Belfast Newsletter*, *Western Morning News*, *Daily Herald*, *Courier and Advertiser* for 14 November 1940 and *Winnipeg Free Press*, 7 December 1940.
63. *New Yorker*, 2 November 1940.
64. *Daily Mail*, 2 November 1940.
65. Cotton to Beaverbrook, 12 December 1940: TNA AVIA 9/1.
66. *New York Times*, 24 February 1941.
67. Telegram from New York to Air Ministry, 12 October 1940: AVIA 9/1.
68. Eaton Griffith (Ministry of Aircraft Production) to Lawrence Carr (War Office), 14 September 1940: TNA AVIA 9/1.
69. Alan Brooke Diary for 17 August 1940: Danchev & Todman (2001), p. 100.
70. Eden to Beaverbrook, 2 October 1940: TNA AVIA 9/1.
71. Beaverbrook to Eden, 3 October 1940: TNA AVIA 9/1.
72. Wickham Steed to The Macneil of Barra, 15 January 1941: TNA CAB 115/489.
73. Quoted in Mace (2007a), pp. 50, 52.
74. Correspondence between Ministry of Supply and Foreign Office, April and May 1941: FO 371/26242.
75. The Macneil of Barra to Wickham Steed, 7 March 1941: TNA CAB 115/489.
76. The Macneil of Barra to Wickham Steed, 26 May 1941: TNA CAB 115/489; *Evening News*, 25 June 1941.
77. John Colville to Helen Parkins Gauntlett, 25 June 1941: TNA FO 371/26242.
78. *Dundee Courier and Advertiser*, 21 August 1941; *Scotsman*, 27 January 1942: with thanks to Alan David for the information.
79. Gulvin (1980), p. 71.
80. *Bronxville Review-Press*, 12 December 1940.
81. Hall-King (Ministry of Aircraft Production) pencilled note, 11 June 1941; Helen Parkins Gauntlett to John Balfour (Foreign Office), 10 June 1941: TNA FO 371/26242.
82. Macneil of Barra to Wickham Steed, 5 June 1941: TNA CAB 115/489 and FO 371/26242.
83. Wickham Steed to Macneil of Barra, 20 June 1941: TNA CAB 115/489.
84. Note of Evans (Foreign Office), 16 June 1941: TNA 371/26242.
85. TNA FO 371/26242.
86. Macneil of Barra to Wickham Steed, 2 June 1941: TNA CAB 115/489.
87. Ministry of Supply to BPC and Wickham Steed, 4 June 1941: TNA CAB 115/489.
88. Helen Parkins Gauntlett to Cutting, 10 June 1941; Cotton to Beaverbrook: TNA FO 371/26242.
89. Burns to Cotton, 11 July 1940: TNA FO 371/26242.
90. G.W. Turner to Hancock (BPC), 19 June 1941: TNA CAB 115/489.
91. Hall-King (Ministry of Aircraft Production) pencilled note, 11 June 1941: TNA FO 371/26242.
92. Note by Hall-King, 18 June 1941: TNA FO 371/26242.
93. Helen Parkins Gauntlett to Herbert Morrison, 17 June 1941: TNA FO 371/26242.
94. Minutes of inter-departmental meeting, 1 July 1941: TNA FO 371/26242.
95. Minute of a meeting of Balfour with Helen Parkins Gauntlett, 24 June 1941: TNA FO 371/26241.
96. Macneil of Barra to Ministry of Supply, 22 July 1941: TNA CAB 115/489.
97. J. Drew (Home Defence Executive) to F.E. Evans (Foreign Office), 20 August 1941: TNA FO 371/26242; Hasler (Cabinet Office) to Brand (Committee for North American Supplies), undated: TNA CAB 115/489.
98. Beaverbrook to Macneil, 31 July 1941: TNA CAB 115/489.
99. Helen Parkins Gauntlett to Commands and TAAs, 22 August 1941: TNA WO 199/3238.
100. Lord Halifax to Foreign Office, 3 August 1941: TNA FO 371/26242.
101. Hall-King, 21 August 1941: TNA FO 371/26242.
102. Foreign Office telegram, 27 August 1941: TNA FO 371/26242.

103. Macneil to Findlater Stewart, 27 August 1941, and Findlater Stewart to Macneil, 29 August 1941: TNA CAB 115/489.
104. Note by F.E. Evans (Foreign Office), 17 September 1941: TNA FO 371/26242.
105. Howard & Endicott (1941), pp. 14, 85.
106. Note by F.E. Evans (Foreign Office), 17 September 1941: TNA FO 371/26242.
107. Findlater Stewart to D. Elliot (Ministry of Supply), 11 November 1941: TNA T 161/1425/3.
108. Macneil to Wickham Steed, 16 January 1941: TNA CAB 115/489.
109. Macneil to Wickham Steed/Gauntlett, 15 June 1941: TNA CAB 115/489; Findlater-Stewart to Sir Gerald Campbell, 18 September 1941: TNA FO 371/26242.
110. Wickham Steed to Macneil, 20 June 1941: TNA CAB 115/489.
111. Cutting to Wickham Steed, 23 June 1941: TNA CAB 115/489.
112. Macneil to Findlater Stewart, 26 August 1941, and Findlater Stewart to Macneil, 10 September 1941: TNA CAB 115/489.
113. Findlater Stewart to Macneil, 10 September 1941: TNA CAB 115/489.
114. Findlater Stewart to D. Elliot (Ministry of Supply), 11 November 1941: TNA T 161/1425/3.
115. F.G. Lee (Treasury) to Mr Bromley, 21 November 1941: TNA T 161/1425/3.
116. Mace (2007a), p. 53.
117. *Evening Express*, 21 February 1941.
118. Mace (2007a), p. 53.
119. These are all illustrated on the Imperial War Museum website.
120. *New Yorker*, 2 November 1940, pp. 14–15.
121. *American Rifleman*, August 1941, p. 58.
122. Skennerton (1988), pp. 20–2.
123. Home Guard monthly returns, 1941: WO 199/3247; Davis (2014), pp. 87–8.
124. 'Arms for the Home Guard: the story of an idea', *Picture Post*, November 1940, p. 19.
125. *New Yorker*, 2 November 1940.
126. *Daily Press (Newport News)*, 7 March 1941.
127. Findlater Stewart to D. Elliot (Ministry of Supply), 11 November 1941: TNA T 161/1425/3.
128. Intercept of telegram from Wickham Steed to Cutting, 19 May 1941: TNA FO 371/26241.
129. Macneil to Ministry of Supply, 22 July 1941: TNA CAB 115/489.
130. Graves (1943), pp. 284–5.
131. Wilkinson & Astley (1993), p. 72; Davis (2014), p. 107.
132. *Albuquerque Journal*, 16 September 1940, *Bronxville Review*,12 December 1940.
133. *New Yorker*, 2 November 1940, pp. 14–15.
134. *Western Morning News*, 14 November 1940.
135. Cotton to Beaverbrook, 12 December 1940: TNA AVIA 9/1; Mace (2007b), p. 50.
136. Wickham Steed to Macneil, 11 April 1941: TNA CAB 115/489.
137. The rifle is in the National Sporting Arms Museum at Fairfax, Virginia.
138. Edwards (1959), p. 43.
139. Mace (2007b), p. 50.
140. Wickham Steed to Macneil, 28 June 1941: TNA CAB 115/489.
141. Cutting to War Office, 7 July 1948: TNA FO 371/68071.
142. Cutting to Vice Consul, New York, 27 May 1947: TNA FO 371/68071.
143. Cutting to War Office, 7 July 1948: TNA FO 371/68071.
144. Wickham Steed to C.J. Child, 2 August 1948: TNA FO 371/68071.
145. Letter from Consulate-General, New York to Foreign Office, 30 June 1948: TNA FO 371/68071.
146. Kieser (1997) p. 32.
147. Sweeny (1991), p. 106.
148. *Defiance Crescent News*, 23 July 1940; Billingham (1942), p. 59.
149. Sweeny (1991), p. 106.
150. *Evening Despatch*, 9 January 1941, p. 5.
151. Billingham (1942), pp. 59–61.
152. Stewart (2015), p. 84.

Chapter 7: Training the Home Guard

1. Hall, J.W. (1946), p. 298.
2. Orwell Diary for 23 August 1940: Orwell & Angus (1968b), p. 368.
3. Wintringham (1940e).
4. Bertram Willmore of Wood Norton: with thanks to Mick Wilks and his research at the Army Medals Office, Droitwich.
5. Wintringham (1940b), p. 63.
6. LDV Instruction No. 5, July 1940.
7. Brophy (1940b), p. 8.
8. Minutes of LDV, 27 June 1940: TNA 165/92.
9. Home Guard Inspectorate, 27 June 1940: TNA WO 165/92.
10. Lord Croft, House of Lords debate, 11 July 1940: *Hansard*, vol. 116, c.923.
11. Brophy (1940a), p. 12.
12. Home Guard Instruction No. 26, 1941.
13. Wintringham (1940b), p. 279.
14. John Langdon-Davies, *Sunday Pictorial*, 6 October 1940.
15. Hopkinson (1982), pp. 177–9.
16. Panter-Downes (1940), pp. 44–5.
17. Minutes of LDV Inspectorate, 16 July 1940: TNA WO 165/92.
18. Minutes of LDV Inspectorate, 19 July 1940: TNA WO 165/92.
19. Liddell Diary, 18 July 1940: TNA KV4/186, f.532.
20. Panter-Downes (1940), p. 36.
21. Home Guard Inspectorate, 12, 16, 19 July 1940: TNA WO 165/92.
22. Atkin (2017), pp. 89, 180–8.
23. Graves (1943), p. 79.
24. *Life*, 21 October 1940.
25. Panter-Downes (1940), p. 36.
26. Panter-Downes (1940), p. 36.
27. Panter-Downes (1940), p. 38.
28. Graves (1943), p. 79.
29. Panter-Downes (1940), p. 40.
30. Panter-Downes (1940), p. 44.
31. Panter-Downes (1940), p. 39.
32. Penrose (1941), p. 4.
33. Penrose (1941), p. 88.
34. Panter-Downes (1940), p. 43.
35. Minutes of the Home Guard Inspectorate, 10 September 1940: TNA WO 165/92.
36. Minutes of Home Guard Inspectorate, 10 September 1940: TNA WO 165/92.
37. *Daily Herald*, 10 December 1940, p. 3.
38. Home Guard School Administrative Instructions, 3 January 1941: TNA WO 199/3238.
39. Minutes of Home Guard Inspectorate, 5 November 1940: TNA WO 165/92.
40. Street (1942), pp. 95–8.
41. Davison (2000), p. 357; TNA HO 250/11/455.
42. Anon (1940), *Notes of Lectures given at the Home Guard Training School Hurlingham.*
43. 'My Country Right or Left: John Langdon-Davies and Catalonia' in Buchanan (2007), pp. 141–57.
44. Langdon-Davies (1941), p. 43.
45. Street (1942), pp. 92–5.
46. *Sunday Pictorial*, 27 July 1941, p. 14.
47. Langdon-Davies (1941), p. 68.
48. *Scotsman*, 18 June 1941, p. 4.
49. *Glasgow Herald*, 1 June 1942.
50. *Scotsman*, 10 June 1942.

51. *Birmingham Evening Dispatch*, 4 September 1942, p. 3.
52. Anon. (1943), p. 5.
53. Wilks (2014), p. 200.
54. Darwin (1946), pp. 199–200.
55. MacKenzie, S.P. (1995), p. 124.
56. Graves (1943), p. 224.

Chapter 8: A People's Army?

1. Priestley (1940a).
2. Sir Edward Grigg, House of Commons debate, 19 November 1940: *Hansard*, vol. 365, c.1887.
3. Mss note on Defence (Local Defence Volunteers) Regulations, 17 May 1940: TNA 199/3242; Churchill, A.W. (1946), p. 32.
4. Pile (1949), p. 257.
5. Council of the County Territorial Associations, 4 July 1940, quoted in Mills & Carney (2001), p. 15.
6. McCann (2001), p. 27; Bond (ed.) (1974), p. 6.
7. Wintringham (1940b), pp. 121–2.
8. Review of *Armies of Freemen* by Tom Wintringham, *Daily Worker*, 13 November 1940.
9. Orwell, 'As I Please', *Tribune*, 14 March 1944, republished in Davison (2015), p. 132; Orwell (1941b), p. 497.
10. *Tribune*, 20 December 1940.
11. *New Left News*, No. 55, January 1941. The SA (*Sturmabteilung*) or 'Storm Detachment' was the original paramilitary wing of the Nazi Party.
12. 'Don't let Colonel Blimp ruin the Home Guard', *Evening Standard*, 8 January 1941.
13. Orwell (1941a), p. 318.
14. Orwell, 'My Country Right or Left', p. 41.
15. Appendix to 'Seaborne and Airborne Attacks on the United Kingdom', 10 May 1940: TNA CAB 66/7/33.
16. *Daily Worker*, 7 October 1939.
17. *Daily Worker*, 29 May 1940.
18. *Labour Monthly*, June 1940, pp. 327–9.
19. *Volunteer for Liberty*, July 1940, p. 1.
20. Gollanz (1941), pp. 53, 61–3.
21. Wintringham (1941a), p. 102.
22. Alexander (1982), p. 246.
23. TNA CAB 93/5; Baxell (2012), p. 419.
24. Internal Security Instructions 1933 and 1937, January 1939: TNA KV 2/609.
25. Note of 22 May 1939: TNA KV 2/609.
26. Edwards MI5 file: TNA KV 2/609.
27. Edwards MI5 file: TNA KV 2/610.
28. Note by Roger Hollis, 10 December 1942: TNA KV 2/610.
29. *Daily Worker*, 5 May 1940.
30. Edwards MI5 file: TNA KV 2/610.
31. Baxell (2012), pp. 410–24.
32. *Daily Worker*, 18 July 1940.
33. Liddell Diary, 26 August 1940: TNA KV4/186, f.580.
34. *Tribune*, 20 December 1940.
35. He was no longer a member of the IBA by November 1941: List of IBA members, November 1941: TNA KV 5/46.
36. List of IBA members, November 1941: TNA KV 5/46; Home Guard Enrolment Form and Military ID Card, thanks to daughter, Helen Cadman.
37. Quoted in Purcell (2006), p. 18. André Marty, Political Commissar of the International Brigades during the Spanish Civil War, was a ruthless disciplinarian and admitted ordering the execution of around 500 members of the International Brigades.

38. Wintringham (1939), p. 55.
39. Liddell Diary, 5 September 1939: TNA KV 4/185, f.21.
40. Home Guard Instruction No. 26, 1941; Home Guard Instruction No. 38, 1941: TNA WO 199/3238.
41. Wintringham (1940b), p. 118.
42. Liddell Diary, 18 July 1940: TNA KV 4/186, f.532.
43. Note in Slater MI5 file: TNA KV 2/2325.
44. Piling, J. (1940), *Report on Osterley Park LDV Training School*, 5–6 August 1940: Wintringham papers, King's College London Archive.
45. TNA KV 2/992–996.
46. W.A. Alexander (MI5) to Major J.T. Avison (HQ Aldershot Command), 1 January 1941: TNA KV 2/2325.
47. Letter of CPGB, 7 January 1941, in Slater MI5 file: TNA KV 2/2325.
48. Slater (1941), p. 79.
49. Hollis, note of 17 July 1943, in Slater MI5 file: TNA KV 2/2326.
50. Hollis, note of 17 July 1943, in Slater MI5 file: TNA KV 2/2326.
51. Orwell (1941b), p. 497.
52. Home Guard Instruction No. 38, 1941: TNA WO 199/3238.
53. Wintringham, 'The Truth About Guerrilla Warfare', *Tribune*, 19 September 1941, p. 9.
54. Minutes of Committee on Communism, 17 November 1942: TNA CAB 93/5.

Chapter 9: Women and the Home Guard

1. In December 1941 conscription of women into full-time service within the ATS was introduced. Over 76,000 ATS went on to serve in Anti-Aircraft Command, undertaking a range of skilled technical tasks such as range-finding and operating the gun-laying radar, and although they did not pull the trigger of a 3.7-in anti-aircraft gun, their roles were fundamental to allowing that gun to hit its target. They also began to operate searchlight batteries. By the end of the war there were over 190,000 members of the ATS; 335 members were killed on duty.
2. Robertson to Miss B. Gooch, 2 October 1942: TNA WO 32/9423.
3. Defence (LDV) Regulations, 17 May 1940: TNA WO 199/3236.
4. BBC interview with Edna Selwyn, 1990: IWM SA 11228, quoted in Summerfield & Peniston-Bird (2007), p. 73.
5. Gough (1954), p. 242.
6. In 1939 only 45 out of 183 police forces employed policewomen, with a total number of policewomen in 1939 of only 246, usually limited to duties associated with women and children or support duties.
7. MacKenzie, S.P. (1995), p. 83.
8. House of Commons debate, 25 June 1940: *Hansard*, vol. 362, c.281.
9. House of Commons debate, 2 July 1940: *Hansard*, vol. 362, c.644.
10. War Office Instructions 27/Gen/2594 (A.G.1.A.).
11. Minutes of War Cabinet, 10 July 1940: TNA CAB 65/8/11 f.77.
12. Minutes of LDV Inspectorate, 19 July 1940: TNA WO 165/92.
13. Minutes of Defence Committee, 19 July 1940: TNA CAB 69/1/5; Memo of Home Secretary at War Cabinet Meeting on 24 July 1940: TNA CAB 67/7/9 f.154.
14. Minutes of the Home Guard Inspectorate, 9 August 1940: TNA WO 165/192.
15. Minutes of the Home Guard Inspectorate, 13 August 1940: TNA WO 165/92.
16. Minutes of the Home Guard Inspectorate, 20 August 1940: TNA WO 165/92.
17. Not to be confused with Percy James Grigg who was at this time Permanent Under-Secretary of State for War and who became Secretary of State for War in February 1942.
18. House of Commons debate, 6 November 1940: *Hansard*, vol. 365, c.1355.
19. House of Commons debate, 19 November 1940: *Hansard*, vol. 365, c.1897.
20. House of Commons debate, 19 November 1940: *Hansard*, vol. 365, cc.1928–9.
21. Mavis Tate chaired the Women's Power Committee of 1941 and the Equal Pay Campaign Committee of 1942. She committed suicide in 1947.

22. *The Times*, 22 January 1942.
23. Wintringham (1940c), pp. 9–24.
24. Wintringham (1940b), p. 73.
25. Panter-Downes (1940), p. 38.
26. Langdon-Davies (1941), p. 4.
27. Langdon-Davies (1941), p. 54. He was one of the signatories of a less controversial February 1942 petition organized by Helen Gywnne-Vaughan on behalf of the WHDC, calling for the admission of women to the Home Guard.
28. *Sunday Pictorial*, 24 November 1940; Langdon-Davies (1941), p. 128.
29. *Sunday Pictorial*, 24 November 1940; Langdon-Davies (1941), p. 131.
30. Tate to Eden, 10 December 1940: TNA WO 32/9423.
31. Eastwood, 'Employment of Women in the Home Guard', 27 December 1940: TNA WO 32/9423.
32. Minute of Bridgeman, 30 June 1941; Bridgeman to Lady Reading, 1 August 1941: TNA WO 32/9423.
33. H.P. Currey, 3 September 1941, GOC South Eastern Command, 24 September 1941: TNA WO 32/9423.
34. Major General Sir W.D. Brownrigg to Bridgeman, 29 September 1941: TNA WO 32/9423.
35. Bridgeman to Brownrigg, 1 October 1941: TNA WO 32/9423.
36. Verney to Whateley, 17 October 1941: TNA WO 32/9423.
37. Letter of Jones to Summerskill, copied to Churchill, 31 October 1941: TNA WO 32/9423.
38. Note by Churchill to War Office, 6 November 1941: TNA WO 32/9423.
39. *Daily Mail*, 29 October 1941: TNA WO 32/9423.
40. Bridgeman to GOC London District, 27 October 1941: TNA WO 32/9423.
41. J.C. Hendra to Captain Booth, Surrey Home Guard, 6 November 1941: TNA WO 32/9423.
42. Message to regional army commands, 29 October 1941: TNA WO 32/9423.
43. Summerskill to Margesson, 5 December 1941: TNA WO 32/9423.
44. Oswald Allen, Ministry of Home Security, to Bridgeman, 10 December 1941: TNA WO 32/9423.
45. Izzard (1969), p. 344.
46. Letter of Helen Gwynne-Vaughan to Under Secretary of State for War, 21 January 1942: TNA WO 32/9423.
47. Record of a meeting between Grigg and Summerskill, 27 February 1942: TNA WO 32/9423.
48. 'Women sign on for Home Defence', *Picture Post*, 14 February 1942, p. 7.
49. 'Women sign on for Home Defence', *Picture Post*, 14 February 1942, p. 7.
50. Summerskill (1967), p. 74.
51. Eric Speed (Principal Private Secretary, War Office) to Bridgeman, 27 February 1942: TNA WO 32/9423.
52. Bridgeman to CGS, Home Forces, 13 March 1942: TNA WO 32/9423.
53. Summerskill to Sir Percy James Grigg, 29 March 1942: TNA WO 32/9423.
54. Minute of Frederick Bovenschen (Permanent Under-Secretary of State for War), 22 April 1942: TNA WO 32/9423.
55. P.J. Grigg to E. Summerskill, 1 May 1942: TNA WO 32/9423.
56. Summerskill to Sir Percy James Grigg, 3 May 1942: TNA WO 32/9423.
57. Notes on meeting of the Inter-Parliamentary Home Guard Committee, 21 July 1942: TNA WO 32/9423.
58. Paget to Duncan Sandys, 5 September 1942: TNA WO 32/9423.
59. Paget to Sir James Grigg, 25 September 1942: TNA WO 32/9423.
60. Robertson to Bevin, 2 October 1942: TNA WO 32/9423.
61. Director General, Home Guard, 1 October 1942: TNA WO 32/9423.
62. TNA CAB 123/204.
63. Note of meeting between Bridgeman and Summerskill, 27 October 1943: TNA WO 32/9423.
64. Quoted in Summerfield & Peniston-Bird (2007), p. 78.
65. Bridgeman to Secretary of State, 30 January 1943: TNA WO 199/9423.

66. Note of meeting between Bridgeman and Summerskill, 27 October 1943: TNA WO 32/9423.
67. Morrison to Grigg, 6 January 1943: TNA WO 199/9423.
68. House of Commons debate, 8 December 1942: *Hansard*, vol. 385, c.1414.
69. James Grigg to Morrison, 22 December 1942: TNA WO 32/9423.
70. Bridgeman to Secretary of State, 30 January 1943: TNA WO 32/9423.
71. Urgent Memorandum from War Office to Army Commands, 15 April 1943: TNA WO 32/9423.
72. House of Commons debate, 20 April 1943: *Hansard*, vol. 388, cc.1532.
73. Note for Secretary of State, April 1943: TNA WO 32/9423.
74. Mills & Carney (2001), p. 119.
75. Home Guard monthly returns: TNA WO 199/3247.
76. Meeting of Lord President's Council, 1 February 1943: TNA CAB 123/204.
77. Summerfield & Peniston-Bird (2007), p. 78.
78. Graves (1943), pp. 342–3.
79. Carroll (2002), p. 88.
80. Lowry (2010), pp. 15–16.
81. Graves (1943), p. 325.
82. Graves (1943), p. 186.
83. Smith (1945), p. 122.
84. Smith (1945), p. 122.
85. Interview with Mary Warschauer, IWM SA 16762.
86. Pers. comm. Janet Hollington, 2013.
87. Summerfield & Peniston-Bird (2007), pp. 84, 141.
88. Ruddy (2007), p. 129.
89. House of Commons debate, 27 November 1951: *Hansard*, vol. 494, c.1129.

Chapter 10: The 1950s Home Guard

1. *Defence*, October 1944, 12(107):52.
2. *Chelmsford Chronicle*, 9 February 1945; *Gloucester Citizen*, 21 May 1945; *Bath Chronicle and Weekly Gazette*, 26 May 1945.
3. Executive Committee of the Army Council, P(45)108 and M(45)42 minute 227: TNA WO 163/98.
4. Memo from DTA&C to DCIGS, 5 May 1948: TNA WO 199/3236.
5. Standing Committee, Army Post-War Problems, P(48)41: TNA WO 32/13657; Home Guard and Civil Defence, 1948–50: TNA WO 199/3301.
6. Executive Committee of the Army Council, P(49)30: TNA WO 32/13657.
7. Wilks (2007), p. 224.
8. ECAC P(50)2: TNA WO 32/13658.
9. Minutes of an MOD Working Party, 11 September 1951: TNA WO 199/3302.
10. Home Office Minutes of 11, 18 and 22 September 1951: TNA HO 45/25009.
11. *The Times*, 19 June 1951.
12. Possibility of Airborne Attack on the United Kingdom, 10 April 1953: TNA PREM 11/372.
13. House of Commons debate, 22 November 1951: *Hansard*, vol. 494, c.577.
14. House of Commons debate, 13 September 1950: *Hansard*, vol. 478, c.1233.
15. House of Commons debate, 22 November 1951: *Hansard*, vol. 494, c.625.
16. *The Times*, 22 November 1951.
17. Home Office Minutes, December 1951 and January 1952: TNA HO 45/25009.
18. House of Commons debate, 27 November 1951: *Hansard*, vol. 494, c.1129.
19. TNA DEFE 7/598.
20. House of Commons debate, 8 April 1952: *Hansard*, vol. 498, c.2462; *The Times*, 9 April 1952.
21. *The Times*, 28 April 1952.
22. *Berrow's Journal*, 30 October 1954.
23. *Evening News*, 5 September 1952.
24. ECAC/M/(52)24, 26 September 1952: TNA WO 163/119.
25. House of Commons debate, 12 November 1952: *Hansard*, vol. 507, cc.945–50.

26. Allsop (1954), p. 13.
27. *The Times*, 13 December 1954.
28. Allsop (1954), p. 14.
29. Allsop (1954), p. 15.
30. Allsop (1954), p. 54.
31. Shaw (1990), p. 59.
32. Under the National Service Act 1948, healthy males aged 17 to 21 years old were expected to serve in the armed forces for 18 months, and remain on the reserve list for four years. Reserved occupations were limited to coal mining, farming and the merchant navy. In October 1950, in response to the British involvement in the Korean War, the service period was extended to two years. National Service only began to be phased out from 1957, with the last call-ups being on 31 December 1960.
33. Allsop (1954), p. 54.
34. *Daily Graphic*, 26 September 1952, quoted in Sainsbury (2008), p. 56; War Office correspondence: TNA PREM 11/255.
35. Cabinet Minutes, 29 October 1953: TNA WO 32/14945.
36. Macmillan to CSO, MOD, 9 December 1954, and reply of 13 December 1953: TNA DEFE 7/598.

Chapter 11: The Home Guard in Wartime Popular Culture

1. http://spartacus-educational.com/2WWcrime.htm.
2. 'Jimmy' Taylor, IWM SA 13714.
3. Southern Command to Area Commands, 31 May 1940: TNA WO 199/1886.
4. George Thomas for Chief Censor, 18 June 1940: TNA CAB 21/1473.
5. Collis & Dodd (1985), pp. 21–33.
6. Cecil Day-Lewis, *Watching Post*, June 1940. First published in the limited edition *Poems in Wartime* (1940), p. 10. Republished in *Word Over All* (1943), p. 27.
7. Sean Day-Lewis (1980), p. 131.
8. Cecil Day-Lewis, *The Stand-To*, first published in *Poems in Wartime* (1940), p. 13. Republished in *Word Over All* (1943), p. 28.
9. Priestley (1940b), pp. 9, 12.
10. Priestley (1940b), pp. 36–7.
11. Graham Greene in the *Spectator*, 13 December 1940.
12. House of Commons debate, 4 June 1940: *Hansard*, vol. 361, c.796.
13. Morton (1942), pp. 286–7.
14. Morton (1942), p. 288.
15. Bartholomew (2004), pp. 179, 184.
16. Wintringham (1940b), pp. 77–8.
17. Levy (1941), p. 14.
18. Greene (1940).
19. Boothroyd (1941), Preface.
20. Bairnsfather, B., 'Fragments from France' (*Bystander*), vols 1–8, 1916–19.
21. Thomas (1942), p. 2.
22. Uttley (1941), p. 62.
23. Shaw (1990), p. 157.
24. Greene (1940).
25. Harry Gifford/Fred Cliffe/George Formby, 1942.
26. Morgan (1961), pp. 141–2.
27. Anon (1944), p. 19.
28. MacKenzie, Compton (1943), p. v.
29. *County Express and Dudley Mercury*, 24 May 1941.
30. Watkins (1943), p. 21.
31. As Street (1942).
32. Churchill, A.W. (1946), p. 6.

33. Walter Kirke to Carden Roe, 18 June 1943: IWM Carden Roe Papers DD/77/165/1.
34. Graves (1943), pp. 79, 177.
35. Black (2011), p. 114.
36. *Manchester Guardian*, 11 September 1943, quoted in Black (2011), p. 120.
37. Brophy & Kennington (1945), p. 26.
38. Smith (1945), p. 11.
39. Smith (1945), p. 44.
40. Review of *Britain's Home Guard* by Hamilton Fyfe in *War Illustrated*, 29 March 1945, 8(203).
41. Editor, *Army Quarterly* to W. Carden Roe, 25 February 1946: IWM Carden Roe Papers DD/77/165/1.
42. 'Home Guard 1939–45', written in 1951: TNA WO 199/3243.
43. *Tribune*, 25 August 1949.

Chapter 12: The 'Dad's Army' Effect

1. Quoted in Summerfield & Peniston-Bird (2007), pp. 171–2.
2. Danny Buckland, *Sunday Express*, 23 November 2014.
3. Maurice 'Peter' Bradshaw, IWM SA 12958.
4. Perry (2002).
5. Street (1942), p. 123.
6. Summerfield & Peniston-Bird (2007), p. 289.
7. Graves (1943), p. 168.
8. Shaw (1990), p. 233.
9. Street (1942), p. 106.
10. Greene (1940), p. 24.
11. George Orwell (1938), *Homage to Catalonia*, ch. 3.
12. Fine (1944), p. 32.
13. Morgan-Russell (2004), pp. 41–2.
14. McCann (2001), p. 6.
15. McCann (2001), p. 177.
16. Foreword to Bairnsfather, Bruce (1916), *Fragments from France*, Bystander magazine, p. 3.
17. Longmate (1974), p. 126.
18. Longmate (1974), p. 85.
19. Longmate (1974), p. 125.
20. Howard & Endicott (1941).
21. Longmate (1974), p. 126.
22. Longmate (1974), p. 102.
23. Morgan-Russell (2004), p. 41.
24. *Notes for the Home Guard on Road Blocks and Check Points*, 1941, pp. 3–4.
25. *Tank Hunting and Destruction: Military Training Pamphlet No. 42*, August 1940; *Tanks and Tank Destruction: LDV Instruction Leaflet No. 8*, September 1940; Longmate (1974), p. 69.
26. Longmate (1974), p. 88.
27. Longmate (1974), p. 40; Ruddy (2007), p. 180.
28. *Daily Mail*, 4 February 2016.
29. Fleming (1957), p. 9.
30. Summerfield & Peniston-Bird (2007), p. 208.
31. *Bulletin of the Military Historical Society*, May 1996, 46(184).
32. MacKenzie (1995), p. 1.
33. 'Mainwaring, George' (2013), *The Walmington-on-Sea Home Guard Training Manual: As Used by Dad's Army*, Orion.
34. Cullen (2011), p. 201.
35. Scott (2011).
36. Scott (2011), p. xvii.
37. *Daily Mail*, 2 June 2011, recovered from http://www.dailymail.co.uk/news/article-1393380/Real-life-sitcom-Diary-reveals-Home-Guard-funnier-Dads-Army.html.

38. Scott (2011), pp. 39–40, 61, 95.
39. McCutcheon (2010), Introduction.
40. McCutcheon (2010).
41. Ruddy (2007), p. 11.
42. Gilles (2006), p. 57.
43. Bathhurst, Bella, 'Inside the real life Dad's Army training camp', *Telegraph*, 2 February 2016.
44. Revised edition as Purcell & Smith (2012).
45. Pers. comm. via Mick Wilks.

Conclusion

1. Watkins (1943), p. 21.
2. Poem by Sir A.P. Herbert upon the stand-down of the Home Guard in 1944. Reproduced in Jager (1945).

Bibliography

Addison, Paul & Crang, Jeremy (2011), *Listening to Britain* (Vintage, London).

Alexander, Bill (1982), *British Volunteers for Liberty* (Lawrence & Wishart, London).

Allingham, Marjory (1941), *The Oaken Heart* (Michael Joseph, London).

Allsop, Kenneth, 'Do we need a Home Guard?' (*Picture Post*, 2 October 1954, 13–15, 54).

Angell, Stewart (1996), *The Secret Sussex Resistance* (Middleton Press, Midhurst).

Anon (1940), *Notes of Lectures Given at The Home Guard Training School, Hurlingham* (published by Sir Hubert Gough, London).

Anon (1943), *History of the 4th Worcestershire (Evesham) Battalion, Home Guard* (Journal Press, Evesham).

Anon (1944), *We Also Served; the story of the Home Guard in Cambridgeshire and the Isle of Ely 1940–1943* (Cambridge).

Anon (1945a), *From Brassard to Battledress: the history of the 46th Battalion, County of Lancaster Home Guard* (Manchester).

Anon (1945b), *The Watch on the Braids: the records of an Edinburgh Home Guard company 1940–44* (William Blackwood & Sons Ltd, London).

Arnold, Ralph (1962), *A Very Quiet War* (Rupert Hart-Davis, London).

Ashworth, E.W. (1998), 'Dad's Army against the Panzers' (*Military Illustrated*, No. 120, May 1998).

Atkin, Malcolm (2015), *Fighting Nazi Occupation: British Resistance 1939–1945* (Pen & Sword, Barnsley).

Atkin, Malcolm (2016), *Myth and Reality: the Second World War Auxiliary Units* (online https://independent.academia.edu/MalcolmAtkin).

Atkin, Malcolm (2017), *Section D for Destruction: forerunner of SOE* (Pen & Sword, Barnsley).

Banks, A.G. (1940), *A.G.'s Book of the Rifle* (Jordon & Sons, London).

Bartholomew, Michael (2004), *In Search of H.V. Morton* (Methuen, London).

Baxell, Richard (2012), *Unlikely Warriors: the British in the Spanish Civil War and the struggle against fascism* (Aurum Press, London).

Billingham, Mrs Anthony (1942), *America's First Two Years* (Pilot Press, London).

Birdswood, The Lord (1952), *The Worcestershire Regiment, 1922–50* (Gale & Polden, London).

Black, Jonathan (2011), *The Face of Courage: Eric Kennington, Portraiture and the Second World War* (Philip Wilson, London).

Bond, B. (ed.) (1974), *Chief of Staff: the Diaries of Lieutenant-General Sir Henry Pownall, Vol. Two 1940–44* (Leo Cooper, London).

Boothby, The Lord (1978), *Boothby: Recollections of a rebel* (Hutchinson, London).

Boothroyd, Basil (1941), *Home Guard Goings-On* (George Allen & Unwin, London).

Bousfield, M. (ed.) (2014), *Dulwich LDV Log-Book 1940–1941* (Olympia, London).

Bridgeman, Viscount (1942), 'The Home Guard' (*Royal United Services Institute Journal*, vol. 87, no. 546, 140–51).

Broad, Lewis (1955), *Sir Anthony Eden: the chronicles of a career* (Hutchinson, London).

Brophy, John (1940a), *Home Guard – a handbook for the L.D.V.* (Hodder & Stoughton, London).

Brophy, John (1940b), *A Home Guard Drill Book and Field Service Manual* (Hodder & Stoughton, London).

Brophy, John & Kennington, Eric (1945), *Britain's Home Guard: a character study* (Harrap, London).

Buchanan, Tom (2007), *The Impact of the Spanish Civil War on Britain: War, Loss and Memory* (Sussex Academic Press).

Cairncross, Alec (1989), *The Robert Hall Diaries 1947–53* (Routledge, London).
Calder, Angus (1991), *The Myth of the Blitz* (Jonathan Cape, London).
Carroll, David (2002), *Dad's Army: the Home Guard 1940–44* (Sutton Publishing, Stroud).
Christie, Maurice Arthur (2004), *Mission Scapula* (M.A. Christie, London).
Churchill, A.W. (1946), *From 'Stand-To' to 'Stand-Down'* (Jakemans Press, Hereford).
Churchill, Winston (1954), *The Second World War: Volume Four: The Hinge of Fate* (Cassell, London).
Clarke, Dale (2016), *Britain's Final Defence: arming the Home Guard 1940–44* (History Press, Stroud).
Collier, Basil (1957), *The Defence of the United Kingdom* (HMSO, London).
Collis, Robert & Dodd, Philip (1985), 'Representing the Nation: British Documentary Film, 1930–1945' (*Screen*, vol. xxvi, no. 1, Jan–Feb 1985, 21–33).
Colville, John (1985), *The Fringes of Power: Downing Street Diaries 1939–1955* (Hodder & Stoughton, London).
Connelly, Mark & Willcox, David (2006), '"Are you tough enough?": the image of the Special Forces in popular culture, 1939–2004' (*Historical Journal of Film, Radio & Television*, 25:1, 1–25).
Cronk, J.G. (1943), *Explosives for the Home Guard* (Gale & Polden, Aldershot).
Cullen, Stephen (2011), *In Search of the Real Dad's Army* (Pen & Sword, Barnsley).
Danchev, Alan & Todman, Daniel (2001), *War Diaries of Field Marshal Lord Alanbrooke* (Weidenfeld & Nicolson, London).
Darwin, Bernard (1946), *War on the Line: the Southern Railway in Wartime* (Southern Railways, London).
Davis, Tom (2014), *Great Britain – The Tommy Gun Story* (USA).
Davison, Peter (ed.) (2000), *George Orwell: A Patriot After All, 1940–41* (Secker & Warburg, London).
Davison, Peter (ed.) (2009), *George Orwell Diaries* (Harvill Secker, London).
Davison, Peter (ed.) (2015), *George Orwell: I Have Tried to Tell the Truth, 1943–44*, vol. XVI, Collected Works (Secker & Warburg, London).
Day-Lewis, Cecil (1940), *Poems in Wartime* (Jonathan Cape, London).
Day-Lewis, Cecil (1943), *Word Over All* (Jonathan Cape, London).
Day-Lewis, Sean (1980), *C. Day-Lewis: An English Literary Life* (Weidenfeld & Nicolson, London).
Easterly, William (1998), *The Belgian Rattlesnake: The Lewis Automatic Machine Gun* (Collector Grade Publications, Ontario, Canada).
Edwards, William B. (1959), 'Guns in our Bundles for Britain' (*Guns*, December 1959, 32–3, 41–3).
Edwards, William B. (1988), 'The Disarmament of Great Britain' (*American Rifleman*, January 1988, 34–7, 68–70).
Featherstone, Simon (1986), 'The Nation as Pastoral in British Literature of the Second World War' (*Journal of European Studies*, 16, 155–68).
Fernbach, David (1982), 'Tom Wintringham and Socialist Defense Strategy' (*History Workshop Journal*, 14 (1), 63–92).
Fine, Simon (1944), *With the Home Guard* (Alliance Press, London).
Fisk, Robert (1983), *In Time of War* (Gill & Macmillan, 1983).
Fleming, Peter (1952), 'Bows and arrows' (*Spectator*, 4 April 1952, 13).
Fleming, Peter (1957), *Invasion 1940* (Rupert Hart-Davis, London).
Gilles, Midge (2006), *Waiting for Hitler* (Hodder & Stoughton, London).
Gollancz, Victor (1941), *The Betrayal of the Left* (The Left Book Club, London).
Gough, General Sir Hubert (1954), *Soldiering On* (Arthur Barker, London).
Graves, Charles (1943), *The Home Guard of Britain* (Hutchinson, London).
Greene, Graham (1940), 'The Lieutenant Died Last' (*Collier's Weekly*, 29 June 1940, 9–10, 24).
Gulvin, Keith (1980), *Kent Home Guard* (North Kent Books, Rochester).
Hall, H. Duncan (1955), *North American Supply* (HMSO, London).
Hall, Ian (2015), *Most Secret: Uncovering the story of Northumberland's Underground Resistance – the Auxiliary Units of WW2* (Wanney Books, Northumberland).
Hall, J.W. (1946), *The Trial of William Joyce* (William Hodge & Co., London).
Hart-Davis, Duff (1987), *Peter Fleming: A Biography (Oxford Lives)*, (Oxford Paperbacks; first publ. 1974).
HHT (1945), *Home Guard Humour* (Rylee Ltd, Birmingham).

Hoare, Adrian (2002), *Standing Up To Hitler: the story of Norfolk's Home Guard and 'Secret Army' 1940–44* (Countryside Books, Newbury).
Hopkinson, Tom (1982), *Of This Our Time: a journalist's story 1905–1950* (Hutchinson, London).
Howard, John K. & Endicott, H. Wendell (1941), *Summary Report: British Home Guard* (Massachusetts Committee on Public Safety, USA).
Hylton, Stuart (2004), *Kent and Sussex 1940* (Pen & Sword, Barnsley).
Izzard, Mollie (1969), *A Heroine in Her Time* (Macmillan, London).
Jager, Harold (1945), *The Rise and Ascent of No. 2 Platoon (Wirral Home Guard)* (Daily Post, Liverpool).
Johnstone, Monty (1997), 'The CPGB, the Comintern and the War, 1939–1941: Filling in the Blank Spots' (*Science & Society*, 61).
Kerr, Alfred (1940), *The Art of Guerrilla Fighting and Patrol* (Jarrolds, London).
Kieser, Egbert (1997), *Hitler on the Doorstep: Operation Sealion* (Arms & Armour Press/Weidenfeld & Nicolson, London).
Knights, Charles (1942), *What the HG Needs to know about Explosives* (Bernards, London).
Lampe, David (1968), *The Last Ditch* (Cassell, London).
Langdon-Davies, John (1940), *Home Guard Training Manual* (John Murray & Pilot Press, London).
Langdon-Davies, John (1941), *Home Guard Warfare* (Routledge, London).
Langdon-Davies, John (1942), *Home Guard Fieldcraft Manual* (John Murray & Pilot Press, London).
Levy, 'Yank' (1941), *Guerrilla Warfare* (Penguin Books, London).
Lidstone, G.H. (1945), *On Guard! 10th (Torbay) Battalion, Devonshire Home Guard* (Torbay Times, Torbay).
Lindsay, Donald (1987), *Forgotten General: A Life of Andrew Thorne* (Michael Russell Publishing, Salisbury).
Longmate, Norman (1974), *The Real Dad's Army: The Story of the Home Guard* (Arrow, London).
Lowry, Bernard (2010), *The Shropshire Home Guard* (Logaston Press, Hereford).
Lowry, Bernard & Wilks, Mick (2002), *The Mercian Maquis* (Logaston Press, Hereford).
McCann, Graham (2001), *Dad's Army* (Fourth Estate, London).
McCutcheon, Campbell (ed.) (2010), *Home Guard Humour* (Amberley, Stroud).
Mace, Martin (2007a), 'The Unofficial Lend-Lease: Part 1', *Britain at War Magazine* (November 2007).
Mace, Martin (2007b), 'The Unofficial Lend-Lease: Part 2', *Britain at War Magazine* (December 2007).
MacKenzie, Compton (1943), *Keep the Home Guard Turning* (Chatto & Windus, London).
MacKenzie, Compton (1947), *Whiskey Galore* (Chatto & Windus, London).
MacKenzie, S.P. (1995), *The Home Guard: a military and political history* (Oxford University Press).
Macleod, Roderick & Kelly, Denis (eds) (1962), *The Ironside Diaries 1937–40* (Constable, London).
Marks, Leo (2000), *Between Silk and Cynanide: A Codemaker's War 1941–1945* (HarperCollins, London).
Marshall-Cornwall, James (1984), *Wars and Rumours of War: a memoir* (Secker & Warburg, London).
Mercaldo, Luke (2011), *Allied Rifle Contracts in America* (Wet Dog Publications, Greensboro, USA).
Miksche, F.O. (1941), *Blitzkrieg* (Faber & Faber, London).
Millgate, Helen (1998), *Mr Brown's War: a Diary of the Second World War* (Sutton Publishing, Stroud).
Mills, Jon & Carney, Terry (2001), *In the Space of a Single Day* (Wardens Publishing, Kent).
Morgan, Frederick (1961), *Peace and War: a soldier's life* (Hodder & Stoughton, London).
Morgan-Russell, Simon (2004), *Jimmy Perry and David Croft* (Manchester University Press).
Morton, H.V. (1942), *I Saw Two Englands* (Methuen, London).
Muggeridge, Malcolm (1973), *Chronicles of Wasted Time: The Infernal Grove* (Collins, London).
Ogilvy-Dalgleish, J.W. (1955), *The Rutland Home Guard of 1940–44* (privately published, Oakham).
Orr, David (2008), *Duty without Glory: the story of Ulster's Home Guard* (Redcoat Publishing, Co. Down).
Orwell, George (1940), 'My Country Right or Left', *Folios of New Writing*, Autumn 1940 (Hogarth Press), pp. 36–41.
Orwell, George (1941a), 'London Letter' (*Partisan Review*, vol. 8, no. 4, July–August 1941, 315–23).
Orwell, George (1941b), 'London Letter' (*Partisan Review*, vol. 8, no. 6, Nov–Dec 1941, 491–8).
Orwell, Sonia & Angus, Ian (eds) (1968a), *George Orwell, The Collected Essays, Journalism and Letters of George Orwell. Volume I: An Age Like This 1920–40* (Secker & Warburg, London).

Orwell, Sonia & Angus, Ian (eds) (1968b), *The Collected Essays, Journalism and Letters of George Orwell. Volume II: My Country Right or Left 1940–1943* (Secker & Warburg, London).

Osborne, Brian (2009), *The People's Army: The Home Guard in Scotland 1940–1944* (Birlinn, Edinburgh).

Oxenden, Nigel (2012 reprint), *Auxiliary Units: History and Achievement 1940–1944* (typescript 1944; first publ. 1998) (BRO Museum, Parham).

Panter-Downes, Mollie (1940), 'A reporter at large – making it dirty for them' (*New Yorker*, 7 September 1940, 36–45).

Penrose, Roland (1941), *Home Guard Manual of Camouflage* (Routledge, London).

Perry, Jimmy (2002), *A Stupid Boy* (Century, London).

Pile, Sir Frederick (1949), *Ack-Ack: Britain's Defence against Air Attack during the Second World War* (Harrap, London).

Prendergast, John (1979), *Prender's Progress* (Cassell, London).

Priestley, J.B. (1940a), *Britain Speaks* (Harper, London).

Priestley, J.B. (1940b), *Postscripts* (Heinemann, London).

Pryce-Jones, David (1975), 'Britain's Secret Resistance Movement', in Cox, R. (1975), *Operation Sealion* (Thornton Cox Ltd), pp. 177–86.

Purcell, Hugh (ed.) (2006), *We're Going On: the collected poems of Tom Wintringham* (Smoke Stack Books, Middlesbrough).

Purcell, Hugh, with Phyll Smith (2012), *The Last English Revolutionary: Tom Wintringham, 1898–1949* (Sussex Academic Press (revised edn; first publ. 2004)).

Quayle, Anthony (1990), *A Time To Speak* (Barrie & Jenkins, London).

Radnor, John (1945), *It All Happened Before* (Harrap, London).

Ransted, Chris (2017), *Bomb Disposal in World War II* (Pen & Sword, Barnsley).

Rigden, Denis (2001), *SOE Syllabus: lessons in ungentlemanly warfare, World War II* (Public Record Office, London).

Robinson, Ernest (1940), *Rifle Training For War* (Cassell & Co., London).

Rowe, Mark (2010), *Don't Panic* (History Press, Stroud).

Ruddy, Austin (2007), *To The Last Round: the Leicestershire and Rutland Home Guard 1940–1945* (Breedon Books, Derby).

Scott, Ronnie (ed.) (2011), *The Real Dad's Army: The War Diaries of Col. Rodney Foster* (Viking, London).

Searle, Adrian (1989), *Isle of Wight at War 1939–45* (Dovecote Press, Wimborne).

Searle, Alarec (2009), 'Ideology and total war: military intellectuals and the analysis of the Spanish Civil War in Britain, 1936–1943' (*Militärgeschichtliche Zeitschrift (MGZ)*, vol. 68, issue 2, 321–44).

Shaw, Frank & Joan (1990), *We Remember the Home Guard* (Ebury Press, London).

Shore, Clifford (1997), *With British Snipers to the Reich* (Greenhill Books, London).

Sillitoe, Percy (1955), *Cloak without Dagger* (Cassell, London).

Simak, Evelyn & Pye, Adrian (2013), *Churchill's Secret Auxiliary Units in Norfolk and Suffolk* (self-published).

Skennerton, Ian (1988), *British Small Arms of World War Two* (Greenhill Books, London).

Slater, Hugh (1941), *Home Guard for Victory* (Gollancz, London).

Smith, H. (1945), *Bureaucrats in Battledress: a History of the Ministry of Food, Home Guard* (R.E. Jones & Bros, Conway).

Stewart, Andrew (2015), *The King's Private Army: protecting the British royal family during the Second World War* (Helion, Solihull).

Stichelbaut, Birger *et al.* (2009), *Images of Conflict: Military Aerial Photography & Archaeology* (Cambridge Scholars Publishing, Cambridge).

Street, A.G. (1942), *From Dusk Till Dawn* (Harrap, London).

Summerfield, Penny (2000), 'She wants a gun not a dishcloth: gender, service and citizenship in Britain in the Second World War', in DeGroot, D. & Peniston-Bird, C. (eds), *A Soldier and a Woman: sexual integration in the military* (Longman, London), pp. 119–34.

Summerfield, Penny & Peniston-Bird, Corinna (2000), 'Women in the firing line: the home guard and the defence of gender boundaries in Britain in the Second World War' (*Women's History Review*, 9(2):231–55).
Summerfield, Penny & Peniston-Bird, Corinna (2007), *Contesting Home Defence: Men, Women and the Home Guard in the Second World War* (Manchester University Press).
Summerskill, Edith (1967), *A Woman's World: Her Memoirs* (Heinemann, London).
Sweeny, Charles (1991), *Sweeny* (Wingham Press, Canterbury; 2nd edn; orig. publ. 1990, Harrap Press).
Thomas, S. Evelyn (1942), *Laughs with the Home Guard* (Harrap, London).
Thompson, Laurence (1966), *1940: Year of Legend, Year of History* (Collins, London).
Turner, Des (2011), *SOE's Secret Weapons Centre: Station XII* (History Press, Stroud).
Turner, E.S. (1961), *The Phoney War on the Home Front* (Michael Joseph, London).
Uttley, Alison (1941), *Hare Joins the Home Guard* (Collins, London).
Verlander, Harry (2010), *My War in SOE* (Independent Books, Bromley).
Ward, Arthur (1997), *Resisting the Nazi Invader* (Constable, London).
Ward, Arthur (2013), *Churchill's Secret Defence Army* (Pen & Sword, Barnsley).
Warwicker, John (2004), *With Britain in Mortal Danger: Britain's Most Secret Army of WWII* (Cerberus, Bristol).
Warwicker, John (2008), *Churchill's Underground Army* (Pen & Sword, Barnsley).
Watkins, A.H. (1943), *Home Guard Rhymes* (Practical Press, London).
Watts, C.N. (1916), *Notes on Street Fighting* (Forster Groom & Co. Ltd, London).
Weinbren, Daniel (1997), *Generating Socialism: Recollections of Life in the Labour Party* (Sutton Publishing, Stroud).
West, Nigel (2005), *The Guy Liddell Diaries, Volumes I and 2* (Routledge, London).
Whipp, Derek (1942), *Street and Guerrilla Fighting* (Nicholson & Watson, London).
Whittaker, L.B. (1990), *Stand Down* (Ray Westlake Military Books, Newport).
Wilkinson, Peter (2002), *Foreign Fields* (Tauris Publishers, London; first publ. 1997).
Wilkinson, Peter & Astley, Joan Bright (1993), *Gubbins and SOE* (Pen & Sword, London).
Wilks, Mick (2007), *The Defences of Worcestershire and the southern approaches to Birmingham in World War II* (Logaston Press, Herefordshire).
Wilks, Mick (2014), *Chronicles of the Worcestershire Home Guard* (Logaston Press, Herefordshire).
Wiltsher, H.J. (1946), *The History of the 1st (Loyal City of Exeter) Battalion, Devon Home Guard* (W. Chudley & Son, Exeter).
Wintringham, Tom (1939), *How to Reform The Army* (Fact, London).
Wintringham, Tom (1940a), *Deadlock War* (Faber & Faber, London).
Wintringham, Tom (1940b), *New Ways of War* (Penguin, London).
Wintringham, Tom (1940c), 'Against Invasion: the lessons of Spain' (*Picture Post*, 15 June 1940, 9–24).
Wintringham, Tom (1940d), 'Arm the Citizens' (*Picture Post*, 29 June 1940, 9–21).
Wintringham, Tom (1940e), 'The Home Guard Can Fight' (*Picture Post*, 21 September 1940, 9–17).
Wintringham, Tom (1941a), *The Politics of Victory* (Routledge, London).
Wintringham, Tom (1941b), *The Home Guard Can Fight* (HMSO, London).
Wintringham, Tom (1941c), 'Train the Home Guard for a Modern War' (*Picture Post*, 17 May 1940, 24–8).
Wintringham, Tom (1941d), 'Your job in an invasion' (*Picture Post*, 24 May 1941, 9–19).
Wintringham, Tom (1941e), 'We make our own mortar for 38/6d' (*Picture Post*, 26 July 1941, 18–20).
Wintringham, Tom (1942), *Peoples' War* (Penguin, London).
Wood, Derek (1976), *Attack Warning Red* (Macdonald & Jane's Publishing, London).
Wynn, Neil A. (2006), 'Race War: Black American GIs and West Indians in Britain during the Second World War' (*Immigrants & Minorities*, 24(3):324–46).
Yelton, David (2002), *Hitler's Volkssturm: The Nazi militia and the fall of Germany 1944–1945* (University of Kansas Press, USA).

Index